'Millions Like Us'?

For Anne:
a colleague and a friend

'Millions Like Us'?

British Culture in the Second World War

Edited by
Nick Hayes and Jeff Hill

LIVERPOOL UNIVERSITY PRESS

First published 1999 by
LIVERPOOL UNIVERSITY PRESS
Senate House, Abercromby Square
Liverpool, L69 3BX

British Library Cataloguing-in-Publication Data
A British Library CIP record is available

ISBN 0–85323–763–8 *cased*
0–85323–773–5 *paper*

Typeset in Sabon and Gill Sans by Carnegie Publishing,
Chatsworth Rd, Lancaster
Printed and bound in the European Union by
Redwood Books Ltd, Trowbridge, UK

Contents

List of Figures and Tables

Figures

Tables

Notes on Contributors

Johanna Alberti teaches for the Open University. She has published two books and several articles on inter-war women's history, and is currently working on a book on the impact of feminism and gender studies on the writing of history.

Norman Baker was originally a specialist in eighteenth-century political and economic history, being the author of *Government Contractors: The British Treasury and War Supplies, 1775–83*. More recently, he has pursued research in sport in Britain since the Second World War and has published in journals in the USA, Australia and the UK. He is on the faculty of the History Department at the State University of New York at Buffalo.

John Baxendale is Principal Lecturer in Social and Cultural History at Sheffield Hallam University. His research interests are in twentieth-century popular culture and identity, and he is the co-author (with Chris Pawling) of *Narrating the Thirties: A Decade in the Making* (1996). He is currently working on a study of J. B. Priestley, and co-writing a book on representations of 1960s Britain.

Michael Bromley is Lecturer in the School of Journalism, Media and Cultural Studies at the University of Wales, Cardiff. He is co-editor (with Tom O'Malley) of *A Journalism Reader* (1996) and (with Hugh Stephenson) of *Sex, Lies and Democracy: The Press and the Public* (1998). He has also published on the British newspaper industry and the press of Northern Ireland in the twentieth century.

James Chapman is Lecturer in Film and Television Studies at the Open University. His publications include *The British at War: Cinema, State and Propaganda, 1939–1945* (1998), and articles in *The Historical Journal of Film, Radio and Television* and the *Journal of*

Popular British Cinema. He is currently working on *Licence to Thrill: A Cultural History of the James Bond Films.*

Colin Griffin is Reader in Economic and Social History at Nottingham Trent University. He has written extensively on aspects of labour and industrial history, particularly on the coalmining industry. He is author of the three-volume history of *The Leicestershire Miners* (1982, 1988, 1989) and editor of the twentieth-century section of *The Centenary History of Nottingham* (1997).

Nick Hayes is Lecturer in Modern and Contemporary History at Nottingham Trent University. He has published in the areas of local political culture – *Consensus and Controversy* (1996) – and the arts, architecture and the press. He is currently working on a study of non-traditional forms of housing construction in the aftermath of war.

Jeff Hill teaches in the Department of International Studies at Nottingham Trent University. After carrying out research into the British labour movement, he turned his attention to popular culture and sport in the twentieth century, and has published various articles on these subjects. He is the author of *Nelson: Politics, Economy, Community* and co-editor (with Jack Williams) of *Sport and Identity in the North of England.* He is currently working on *Sport and Leisure in Twentieth-Century Britain.*

Robert Mackay is Senior Lecturer in Modern History at Nottingham Trent University. He is the author of *The Test of War: Inside Britain 1939–45* (1999) and is working on a book on music in Britain during the Second World War.

Siân Nicholas is Lecturer in History at the University of Wales, Aberystwyth. Her publications include *The Echo of War: Home Front Propaganda and the Wartime BBC 1939–45* (1996). She is currently carrying out research into the development of the British news media in the 1920s and 1930s, and writing a history of the mass media in twentieth-century Britain.

Acknowledgements

Dorothy L. Sayers's poem, *The English War*, first published in *The Times Literary Supplement*, is reprinted by permission of David Higham Associates. The cartoons on p. 14 are reproduced courtesy of *Punch*. Thanks are due to BFI Stills, Posters and Designs for providing the film illustrations: those from *The Demi-Paradise* (p. 49) and *Millions Like Us* (p. 55) appear courtesy of the Rank Organization, while that from *Fires Were Started* (p. 53) is Crown copyright. Other stills appear courtesy of the Hulton Getty Picture Library and the BBC Archive. Our thanks are also recorded to the British Newspaper Library and to the individual newspapers for permission to reproduce facsimiles from the *Daily Herald* and *Daily Mirror* and to the Hulton Getty for permission to reproduce from *Picture Post*. The editors are grateful to the Lilly Library, Indiana University, Bloomington, for its permission to quote from the letters of Ray Strachey to her mother, Mary Berenson. We would like also to thank the Coal Industry Social Welfare Organization for its help particularly in providing the illustration on p. 270, and the staff at the Modern Records Centre, University of Warwick, the Public Records Office, Kew and the BBC Written Archive, Caversham Park, Reading. Nottingham Trent University financially underwrote the day conference which allowed contributors to meet and compare views and notes. A particular vote of gratitude must be extended to Keith Laybourn, University of Huddersfield, and Tony Mason, then at the University of Warwick and now with De Montfort University, who agreed to act as external referees for the collection as a whole. Ian Inkster, Nottingham Trent University, also deserves our thanks for commenting on individual contributions, as does Janet Elkington for her general and administrative support. Norman Baker wishes a special a vote of thanks to be extended to his wife, Sheila, who tolerated her holiday schedule being determined by his research priorities. Such a sentiment, duly personalized, is no doubt one commonly extended by all the contributors to their long-suffering spouses, friends and colleagues. Finally, we thank Robin Bloxsidge and Frances Hackeson for their patience and support.

Footnote Abbreviations

MRC	Modern Records Centre, University of Warwick
PRO	Public Records Office, Kew
Hansard	*House of Commons Debates, 5th Series*

An 'English War', Wartime Culture and 'Millions Like Us' [1]

Nick Hayes

> Praise God, now, for an English War –
> The Grey Tide and the Sullen Coast,
> The menace of the urgent hour,
> The single island, like a tower,
> Ringed with an angry host … .
>
> When no allies are left, no help
> To count upon from alien hands,
> No waverers remain to woo,
> No more advice to listen to,
> And only England stands.
>
> This is a war we always knew … . [2]

Dorothy Sayers's opening words, published shortly after the fall of France and the symbolic resurrection of Dunkirk, typically capture that moment of splendid isolation – dichotomously tensioned by patriotic resolution, yet fearful uncertainty – of the summer of 1940 which, in turn and in so many ways, encapsulates the popular image of Britain in the Second World War then and now. In 1940 Britain stood alone in Europe, and, according to Sayers (and many others), curiously was resolutely glad of this ('Now we know where we are! No more bloody allies!', was apparently a common refrain); [3]

1. The phrase is taken from the Launder and Gilliat 1943 film of the same name, but here is used as being indicative of a supposed wartime inclusiveness, nationally and culturally, in terms of audience and authorship which cut across class and other social divides.
2. From D. L. Sayers, *The English War*, *Times Literary Supplement* (hereafter *TLS*), 7 September 1940.
3. Cited in A. Calder, *The People's War* (London, Jonathan Cape, 1969), p. 113.

an island defeated yet still unconquered, vigilant, historically defiant, and despite 'The flying death that swoops and stuns', with God's help ready to 'keep, by might and main,/ Inviolate seas, inviolate skies' and fight again. This *English War* (which in its retelling overtly by-passes Celtic sensibilities) was, when so simply put, a war of survival against tyranny; a war England had fought and won before (against Louis, Philip, 'the conquering Corsican') so that even foreigners – those 'men who love us not, yet look/ To us for liberty' – might too be free.[4] And it was a war Britain now had to win once more. Sayers's prayer instantly plays upon this historic conflation of certainty: conjuring a separate cultural lineage, a race apart – of Cinque ports, Plymouth Sound and 'tall adventurers' called home by the beat of Drake's drum – 'the noise which breaks our sleep'; it reminds its audience that those who fight in 1940 by sea and air 'Are the same men their fathers were'. Standing alone, the British were told – by government, by other agencies, by individuals like Sayers and by each other – *who* they were; so that, for example, the projected heroism of these early war years became a defining episode, which through repetition, was etched into our national consciousness where it remains today.[5]

Sayers is and was, of course, better known for her detective stories than her contribution to poetry – albeit that in 1940 *The English War* embraced a wider rhetoric of public defiance. Even so it is surprising – and indicative of the transient uncertainty and outward bravado of 1940 – to find the work immediately cited as evidence of a wartime 'poetic renaissance'. An accompanying, albeit portentous, *TLS* editorial entitled 'The Heroic Theme' contemporaneously roots that claim:

> The hour is propitious ... there is now sterner stuff in the leaven. A stirring thrills the air. This is the time for epic ... for the lifting of hearts as well as the shedding of tears over hopes foredone and the chaunting of anthems for doomed men ... . Poetry can draw its spiritual ecstasy from the evil that menaces, the forces that have sworn to overthrow our English heritage. This is the moment for songs of defiance, hymns of deliverance. We are privileged spectators of a miracle. Who dare speak of insouciant youth? But yesterday we

4. Sayers, *English War*.
5. For an extension of this theme, see **John Baxendale, '"You and I – All of Us Ordinary People": Renegotiating "Britishness" in Wartime'** and **Jeff Hill, 'Postscript: A War Imagined'**, in this volume.

bewailed the degeneracy of the time; today we are aware of something
spiritual alive and strong in a materialistic age.[6]

Clearly here cultural and societal regeneration – and perhaps even
spiritual rebirth – are intrinsically linked, located in the demands
and expressions of war. Indeed, typically much of what was written,
said, filmed and broadcast at the time (and which has been repeated,
refined and theorized about since) rested upon such an explicit
assumption: namely that clear disjunctures existed between societies
at war and peace.[7] Yet it is equally important to recognize that the
war existed contextually in different episodes. It passed through
different periods and moods: from the heady mysticism of 1940
captured above, to the extended period of aimlessness, tensions,
tedium and low morale which preceded the opening of a 'second
front'; just as it resided in 'the sheer diversity of wartime experience
of different individuals, different locations, different organisations
and different social groups'.[8]

This collection of research essays into key areas of cultural production and reception during the period 1939–45, therefore, accepts
as its starting point the relative 'totality' of the Second World War:
measured comparatively, for example, by the breadth of state involvement and direction, and levels of British social and industrial
mobilization and dislocation. It also accepts that how 'total' war
was presented, understood and remembered by contemporaries
differentiated it from other earlier conflicts, and that this carried
with it its own cultural and institutional imperatives.[9] This was

6. Editorial, *TLS*, 7 September 1940.
7. This disjuncture, for example, provides the nexus for linkages between total
   war and social change. The most concise and influential statement of such
   ideas remains A. Marwick, 'Introduction', in *Total War and Social Change*, ed.
   A. Marwick (Basingstoke, Macmillan, 1988), pp. x–xxi.
8. J. Harris, 'War and Social History: Britain and the Home Front during the
   Second World War', *Contemporary European History*, 1 (1992), pp. 32–3.
   For example, these episodic fluctuations found form in the type of music
   composed: see **Robert Mackay, 'Safe and Sound: New Music in Wartime
   Britain', in this volume.**
9. For a critical appraisal of the broader issues, see for example, I. Beckett,
   'Total War', in *Warfare in the Twentieth Century: Theory and Practice*, ed.
   C. MacInnes and G. D. Sheffield (London, Unwin Hyman, 1988), pp. 1–23.
   For a concise assessment of the impact of the Second World War on state
   functions and responsibilities, see J. Cronin, *The Politics of State Expansion:
   War, State and Society in Twentieth Century Britain* (London, Routledge,

particularly noticeable in the construction of ideas of inclusiveness and commonality, where 'the people' pulled together to win the war and secure a socially equitable peace. At the same time this collection also seeks to explore the diversity of experience and rationale at both the institutional and personal levels; and reflect on these against this backdrop of a projected 'Millions Like Us' homogeneousness. Whether or not the war did facilitate a coming-together of cultural ideals and objectives – both new and old – within a contemporary emphasis on inclusiveness remains a recurring thematic foundation of many of the essays.

The volume unusually brings together work on many different agencies of the period in operating areas largely neglected by past studies. Some of these agencies were war-specific: for example, the Council for the Encouragement of Music and the Arts (CEMA), formed shortly after war broke out, and which survived after 1945 as the Arts Council; or the Entertainments National Services Association (ENSA), which was quickly resurrected in 1938 after earlier service in the First World War, only to wither away rapidly once more with the war's end. Other agencies in the study were already major national institutions and industries in their own right. Each, however, had differing lineages in terms of establishment, structure and heritage: ranging from the recently formed BBC, with its public-service ethos and state-granted monopolistic controls over domestic broadcasting; to the culturally diverse and rapidly expanding national commercial press; or a British film industry, comprising producers (both commercial and non-commercial) and distributors, but where the former had been largely overshadowed, in terms of output and popularity, by their American counterpart.[10] Each, because of its objectives, and its relationship with its audience and government,

1991), pp. 131–52. For the social/intellectual legacy of how total war was viewed and represented, see J. Meuller, 'Changing Attitudes Towards War: The Impact of the First World War', *British Journal of Political Science*, **21** (1991), pp. 1–28; J. M. Winter, *Sites of Memory, Sites of Mourning* (Cambridge, Cambridge UP, 1995).

10. See **Siân Nicholas, 'The People's Radio: The BBC and its Audience, 1939–1945', in this volume** for further discussion of the relationship between the BBC (and commercial radio) and its audience. For an excellent reappraisal of domestic audience reactions to British and American films in the 1930s and 1940s, see R. McKibbin, *Classes and Cultures: England 1918–1951* (Oxford, Oxford UP, 1998), pp. 427–56.

reacted differently to the needs, circumstances and opportunities of the war as these developed from 1939. At the same time, diversity needs to be balanced against those commonly held objectives and shared perceptions which did exist: expressed, for example, through the positive projections of military and civilian prowess, and, notably for this collection, via the production of wartime images of inclusiveness which appear centrally in 'people's war' imagery.

Agencies, in the sense used here, include not just those institutions where cultural production was the primary objective, but also those where it was an adjunct to other key functions: there are essays, therefore, on how cultural provision was viewed and developed by the Labour movement (particularly significant, given the reputed leftward trend within wartime society), and within one significant division of that movement – the mining industry. The collection covers, too, an examination of how the war impacted on that most ubiquitous of cultures – sport and recreation – and on the myriad of largely voluntary agencies associated with its governance. Yet it also explores the role of the individual agent, with studies on established writers and composers, and how each related, personally, to the collective rationales and experiences of wartime. Social meaning, however, is not solely derived from an examination of the production side of this cultural equation, and several of the essays investigate how 'the people' reacted to the war-induced images, representations and performances with which they were presented. Frequently performance took the form of familiar transmissions, via already customary media, where it was the message itself which was overtly war-orientated. But occasionally, both the medium and the message were largely unfamiliar – as with taking 'good' culture directly to factory audiences. In fact, graduations between these two boundaries were relatively commonplace; so that, for example, mainstream wartime cinema deployed techniques which, before the war, had been more commonly associated with documentary film-making. Such trends underpinned claims for a new-found cultural classlessness during wartime: broadly speaking, that is, a 'people's culture' for a 'people's war'.

For many contemporaries the questions of a greater wartime eclecticism and of a commented upon improvement in the overall quality of cultural life were seen to walk together, hand in hand. For others it was less a matter of a greater diffusion than of the processes of the war interreacting to raise artistic achievement. Although all the essays, to a greater or lesser extent, confront this relationship between war and a qualitative improvement in cultural activity, what each author examines varies according to both the subject matter and point of view. For some – Robert Mackay and Johanna Alberti, for example – writing on the process of individual creativity and the conditions in which it occurs, there are aesthetic judgements to be made about the quality of what is produced. For other essayists, this aspect of cultural production is less important than the meanings communicated through cultural artefacts: their aesthetic worth is less the issue for discussion than the part played by cultural activity in the social order.

War, it has been said, 'quickens the pulse'.[11] There is, however, no unifying assumption within this volume that this was indeed the case: the essays offer a diversity of opinions here and on other themes. Nor implicitly is it assumed that specific cultural outcomes, where present, were necessarily positive and purposeful (they might equally be viewed as retrogressive or accidental), or universal and lasting.[12] Nevertheless, we need to be aware that, partly because of immediate wartime needs, contemporary actions were frequently presented through this positive filter: for example, that Britain was fighting *for* what was best in civilization, *against* Nazi philistinism and brutality, and that the best of British culture was, therefore, important and ought to be more widely shared – both domestically and overseas. At the same time depictions of Englishness – even wartime Englishness – still varied.[13] For example, just as Sayers offered a markedly insular and martial perspective, the novelist Sir Hugh Walpole – in an essay wrapped around *The English War* on the page – cautioned contemporaries against continuing to export a sentimentalized fiction of English life (as he looked forward to painting a post-war picture of an England free of past 'snobbery, cant, hypocrisy'). In its lead that day, however, the *TLS* was markedly less questioning: commending instead the intrinsic value of 'spreading the spirit of our literature abroad' in stressing British cultural achievement (the purpose of this special edition). Inside, essays listed the contribution of English thought and publications overseas to freedom, constitutionalism and civilization (and, in a more practical form, to

---

11. A. Marwick, *Culture in Britain since 1945* (Oxford, Blackwell, 1991), p. 14.
12. Marwick, *Total War*, p. xiv.
13. See particularly, **Baxendale**, ' "You and I".'

our export balances).[14] Even here within the one short publication, therefore, we find overt conformity juxtaposed with independence of mind and bombast.

The importance of exporting a 'favourable' image of Britain and Britishness was a cornerstone of wartime policy. It is axiomatic too that, even at a time of physical isolation and heightened national awareness, the Second World War further opened up British society to external forces: most notably with the wartime American GI presence pushing forward existing American influences on British popular culture.[15] Nevertheless, boundaries, however artificial, have to be drawn. The stress within this collection focuses squarely on the home-front relationship between domestic production and consumption, and thus it largely sets to one side external influences and service life generally. Equally, space, and the interests of the contributors, does not permit a detailed exploration of a separate Scottish, Welsh or Irish national experience; we leave these episodes to others, and treat Britain and the British (as opposed to Sayers's emphasis solely on England) as a predominantly urban-dwelling, albeit regionalized, whole. Against the trend in social history, we do not offer either a gender or class-specific analysis as a founding theme (again this did not suit the individual purpose of most contributors); we address such stratifications as they arise within the broader context, for example, of a 'Millions Like Us' wartime inclusiveness.[16] Ours is largely

14. H. Warpole, 'English Domestic Fiction: Its Influence Abroad'; B. I. Evans, 'England's Treasury of Literature: Missionaries of the Mind'; G. Faber, 'Britain's Ambassadors', *TLS*, 7 September 1940.

15. For the perceived importance of British image overseas, and especially in America, see A. Aldgate and J. Richards, *Britain Can Take It: British Cinema in the Second World War* (Edinburgh, Edinburgh UP, 2nd edn, 1994); A. Calder, *The Myth of the Blitz* (London, Jonathan Cape, 1991); N. Cull, *Selling War: The British Propaganda Campaign against American 'Neutrality' in World War Two* (Oxford, Oxford UP, 1995). For the American presence in Britain, see, for example, J. Gardiner, *'Over Here' – the GIs in Wartime Britain* (London, Collins & Brown, 1992); D. Reynolds, *Rich Relations: the American Occupation of Britain 1942–1945* (London, Harper Collins, 1995).

16. For an analysis of war and rural communities, see A. Howkins, 'A Country at War: Mass-Observation and Rural England', *Rural History*, 9 (1998), pp. 75–97. Recent work on gender, culture and the Second World War includes *Nationalising Femininity: Culture, Sexuality and British Cinema in the Second World War*, eds C. Gledhill and G. Swanson (Manchester, Manchester UP, 1996); G. Dawson, *Soldier Heroes: British Adventure, Empire and the Imagining of Masculinities* (London, Routledge, 1994).

a view from 'above' of cultural life. But by this we do not mean a ruling-class view 'from above', although many of the players considered did belong to an intellectual and/or administrative elite. Instead we take a largely institutional 'view' of cultural production (be it public, commercial, voluntary or socially based), and juxtapose with this the contributions and motivations of key notables, and that of audience reactions to what was offered, under the unusual circumstances of war. As one of many historians has noted only recently: 'There was general agreement that this was a "good war"'; one fought in a just cause, devoid of warmongering complicity; one which promoted social amelioration and unity; and which (for the British at least) lacked the futility and sordid traumas of trench warfare of 1914–18.[17] Whether or not it was a 'good war' for British culture overall, and for the individuals, agencies, institutions and public associated with its production, dissemination and consumption remains to be tested.

I

Opinions vary significantly as to the success or otherwise of the domestic marriage between cultural production and consumption. Fussell's assessment, for example, of British and American popular cultural outlets during the Second World War is singularly negative: providers, he argues, behaved as if they were 'the creatures of government'; they 'spoke with one voice', conveying 'the same sanguine war message', frequently in whitewashing terms, within the overall parameters of an 'Allied ideological vacuum'. To be sure, there were exceptions amongst both providers and audiences within this rendition: 'extremely intelligent discourse' on the BBC (albeit within a masking staple diet of 'one popular song after another') or an apparent preference for serious music amongst the troops. Nevertheless, by and large, wartime culture was homogenous, but also shallow and boring; and the analytical tools of scepticism, irony and doubt were early war casualties.[18]

17. P. Clarke, *Hope and Glory: Britain 1900–1990* (Harmondsworth, Penguin, 1997 edn), p. 207.
18. P. Fussell, *Wartime: Understanding and Behaviour in the Second World War* (Oxford, Oxford UP, 1989), pp. 180–95. For a similarly pessimistic assessment of artistic life, see R. Hewison, *Under Siege: Literary Life in London 1939–1945* (London, Weidenfeld & Nicolson, 1977).

Yet Fussell also suggests that the war 'forced everyone back onto traditional cultural possessions and responses and forced people to consider which things were valuable enough to be preserved and enjoyed over and over again'.[19] Indeed, judging by the recent historiography, when Churchill famously predicted that the ensuing war would be Britain's 'finest hour', he could well have been addressing his remarks directly to the nation's cultural producers in ways which went beyond simply praising the patriotic and rousingly 'heroic' lionizing of initial offerings. Marwick, for example, has drawn attention to contemporary expression suggestive of a cultural renaissance within the arts in wartime Britain. Nor, apparently, was this an isolated or narrowly based occurrence. Aldgate characterizes the war period as an era of 'unprecedented popularity' for British film when critics remarked on the 'great improvement in quality'; likewise Richards notes it to be 'the golden age' of British film music – a measure of the new-found artistic and intellectual commitment by individuals to the national effort in the struggle against fascism.[20] The list continues. After an unsteady beginning, theatregoing became increasingly popular; moreover, we are told, the urge to promote and accept new ideas became as apparent under the proscenium arch as outside. Much remarked upon, too, as the war progressed, was the qualitative improvement in light entertainment and comedy production, again attracting new social audiences. Basil Dean, the theatrical producer and Director of ENSA, for example, paid warm tribute to BBC wartime broadcasting, not least its 'brilliant comedy broadcasts of a standard unknown before the war'.[21]

As it is with historians, so divisions occurred within contemporary opinion. The influential wartime arts journal *Horizon* was hardly less complimentary than Fussell in its overall assessment. Writing in 1944, Cyril Connolly, its editor, pointed to a five-year 'decline in all the arts, ... Books are becoming as bad as they are ugly; newspapers continue to be as dull with four pages as they were with once with forty; reviewing has sunk to polite blurb-quoting; ... the B.B.C.

19. Fussell, *Wartime*, pp. 228–51, esp. p. 245.
20. Marwick, *Culture*, p. 14; Aldgate and Richards, *Britain Can Take It*, pp. 2, 17; J. Richards, *Films and British National Identity* (Manchester, Manchester UP, 1997), p. 283.
21. W. Harrington and P. Young, *The 1945 Revolution* (London, Davis Poynter, 1978), pp. 46–7; D. Dean, *Theatre at War* (London, Harrap, 1956), pp. 177, 269–70; S. Nicholas, *The Echo of War: Home Front Propaganda and the Wartime BBC, 1939–45* (Manchester, Manchester UP, 1996), ch. 4.

pumps religion and patriotism into all its programmes; mediocrity triumphs.' Commenting on the Forces exhibition at the National Portrait Gallery – that 'uncensored representation of popular taste' – the art critic Herbert Read likewise exclaimed that 'even a worm could lift its head above this level. What stretches before us is the sordid scum left behind by a receding civilization. Aesthetic criticism has no function here: it is an affair for the social pathologist.' Nor was his critical venom directed solely against this particular example of the 'people's art'. He continued: the 'art of pure intuition' is similarly 'left high and very dry by the same receding tide ... the [social] environment is changing very rapidly: war is dissolving it'. The bonds between art and society had been broken. Contemporary art had lost its prophetic function, its organic vitality.[22]

Yet not all contemporaries shared this pessimistic overview. Instead, public discourse laid significant emphasis, not just on social *rapprochement*, a greater egalitarianism and a common heritage, but, within this, on an accompanying, broadly based and unifying cultural eclecticism in wartime society. Particular attention was drawn to the increasing popularity of what was generally deemed 'good culture'.[23] Certainly, Dean placed great stress on what he saw as a steadily improving popular wartime taste. Interestingly, he saw ENSA's own 'outstanding achievement', not in terms of its day-to-day variety provision, for which it remained best known, but in its later symphony activity in 'taking the finest music to millions of men and women in the forces and factories'.[24] Likewise, Cecil Day Lewis, writing in the popularist *Picture Post*, noted that:

22. C. Connolly, 'Comment', *Horizon*, **10**:60 (December 1944), p. 367, cited also in Hewison, *Under Siege*, p. 172 and Fussell, *Wartime*, p. 219; H. Read, 'Vulgarity and Impotence: Speculation on the Present State of the Arts', *Horizon*, **5**:28 (April 1942), pp. 268–70. Read, however, was generally supportive of the concept of worker-created art: see H. Read, *To Hell with Culture* (London, Kegan Paul, 1941).

23. See Nick Hayes, 'More Than "Music-While-You-Eat"? Factory and Hostel Concerts, "Good Culture" and the Workers' and Colin Griffin, 'Not Just a Case of Baths, Canteens and Rehabilitation Centres: The Second World War and the Recreational Provision of the Miners' Welfare Commission in Coal-mining Communities', in this volume.

24. Dean, *Theatre at War*, pp. 213–14. For a similar missionary emphasis, see F. Leventhal, '"The Best for the Most": CEMA and State Sponsorship of the Arts in Wartime, 1939–1945', *Twentieth Century British History*, **1** (1990), pp. 289–317.

The war had created certain spiritual conditions, favourable to literature and the other arts; it throws into high relief spiritual and emotional problems which, in peacetime, many of us pass over lightly. We take ourselves on the whole more seriously; we ask ourselves more difficult questions – Is all this killing worthwhile? What is to happen to us after the war? – and, by asking these questions, we enter into the region of values, a region where literature has always been in demand as a guide.[25]

At face value the accompanying text hardly validated his broader claims: here we are told that apart from government illustrated texts – *Battle of Britain*, *Bomber Command*, *Front-Line* – the books people were buying increasingly were technical texts on engineering, patching old clothes and making the most of rations – all of which helped them practically to adapt to war conditions. Nevertheless, within a wartime climate of cultural optimism which publicly eschewed negativity in favour of positive reinforcement, Day Lewis and others likewise construed this focus on factual 'serious reading' positively: as a rejection of the 'sentimentality and sugar fantasy' of 'trash' fiction and a solid foundation for the future reading of imaginative literature.[26] Yet the actualities of popular reading tastes have subsequently been recorded and interpreted differently: a strong preference for the 'escapist' lowbrow literature of love stories, adventure novels and thrillers (for example, the wartime best-seller – James Hadley Chases's *No Orchids for Miss Blandish*), where wartime realities, if anything, made the selection of escapist literature something of which to be less ashamed amongst readers of all classes. Notably, it was exactly this 'escapist' rationale which radical and conservative cultural improvers alike, in commonly identifying a commercially orientated popular 'leisure problem', strongly opposed and sought to change.[27]

25. C. Day Lewis, 'Do We Read Better Books In Wartime?', *Picture Post*, 25 March 1944. Day Lewis was also a prolific detective-story writer, under the pseudonym 'Nicholas Blake'.
26. Ibid.; Calder, *People's War*, pp. 511–13.
27. J. McAleer, *Popular Reading and Publishing in Britain 1914–1950* (Oxford, Oxford UP, 1992), pp. 71–99; S. Chibnall, 'Pulp Versus Penguins: Paperbacks Go To War', in *War Culture: Social Change and Changing Experience in World War Two*, eds P. Kirkham and D. Thoms (London, Lawrence & Wishart, 1995), pp. 131–49; S. Fielding, P. Thompson and N. Tiratsoo, *'England Arise!': The Labour Party and Popular Politics in 1940s Britain* (Manchester, Manchester UP, 1995), pp. 135 ff.

Other unexpected benefits, opportunities and oddities also apparently arose from wartime life. Arts enthusiasts quickly realized that the Blitz provided 'a great opening for encouraging the appreciation of serious music in the most unlikely surroundings'. The first Emergency Shelter Concerts in working-class areas consisted mostly of popular songs and community singing, but CEMA reported: 'soon the introduction of better music began to be appreciated and the demand for it increased considerably'. Lecture recitals followed, with apparently 'conspicuous success'. More surprisingly still, perhaps, in marked contrast to the 'rough type of audiences' in the docklands, when emergency concerts were requested and given in London's West End 'they were found to be entirely superfluous ... the majority [of shelterers being] not really prepared to listen or keep quiet and let anyone else listen'.[28] Such testimony seemingly strikes at the core of the debate over war-induced cultural change; read one way it is suggestive, not merely of a cultural amelioration and mixing of tastes, but perhaps even of an inversion of traditional class-based attitudes. Providers, not surprisingly when assessing their own contribution to Britain's victory and wartime inner coherence, tended to reflect and adhere to such optimistic interpretations of a broad conformity to a positive wartime ideal of higher values. Yet contextually, problems remain. One reason, for example, why West Enders were less than attentive to CEMA's offerings was that 'the people in these shelters seemed to be thoroughly comfortable already with canteens, dancing, etc.' For East Enders, as one local clergyman commented, 'the mere enlivenment of shelter life by any kind of entertainment is good', although he later added, 'we feel a responsibility for the introduction, as judiciously as possible, of a better type of programme'.[29]

It was not simply that wartime encouragement brought Shakespeare, classical music and other examples of 'good' culture to the workers; wartime public subsidies, through ENSA, also extended to 'popular' performance, thus physically and regularly taking '"Max Miller" [and other popular entertainers] to the middle classes' directly at their place of work and further moving the boundaries of cultural

28. PRO EL1/13, CEMA Paper 85, Emergency Concerts, c. February 1941; CEMA Paper 74, Rest Centre and Shelter Concerts, 3 January 1941.
29. Ibid.

diffusion.[30] How successful this policy of parallel diffusion was remains a matter for conjecture, where the actualities of audience
reaction at times sit uneasily with contemporary published accounts.
Indeed, not everyone openly approved of the movement towards a
greater eclecticism, which from above was frequently decoded more
in terms of a move to homogeneous mediocrity and levelling-down.
As *Punch* sardonically prophesied in 1944, audiences were soon
likely to see Sir Henry Wood conducting his 'Boogie Woogie Rag-
timers' at the Palais de Danse and 'Buddy Wully' conducting the
Philharmonic at the Guildhall![31]

This is not to understate the ubiquitous and flourishing – if
frequently derided – presence of 'middlebrow' tastes before 1939;
nor is it to suggest that in certain areas – in music, for example, as
opposed to literary consumption – no common culture within Britain
existed across the class, gender and age divides. As McKibbin notes,
'popular commercial music was genuinely popular ... a common
musical culture existed, even if some were reluctant members of it
[because] it was very difficult to escape popular music and
dance'.[32] At the same time inter-war public-service broadcasting, it
is argued, heightened rather than assuaged the social antagonisms
of musical tastes, so that the 'common musical culture' sought by
the Reithian BBC foundered on 'the depth of [mutual] hostility felt
by highbrow and lowbrow alike'. Yet in wartime, radio came to
align itself with 'the people' – and thus socially the war effort – in
ways only tentatively present previously. The increase in variety and
popular music (intended to be non-excluding and thus boost morale)
made radio more attractive and relevant to working-class tastes and

30. R. Shaw, *The Arts and the People* (London, Jonathan Cape, 1987), p. 138.
    Because of contractual disagreements, many leading variety entertainers –
    including Miller – boycotted the BBC during the 1930s. Their services were
    restored during wartime: P. Scannell and D. Cardiff, *A Social History of Broad-
    casting. Volume One 1922–1939. Serving the Nation* (Oxford, Blackwell,
    1991), pp. 226–9.
31. **Hayes, 'More Than "Music-While-You-Eat"?';** *Punch*, 7 June 1944. For
    similar themes see *Punch*, 29 January 1941, 1 April 1942. See also, for example,
    the attitudes of Naomi Mitchison and Virginia Woolf, **Johanna Alberti, 'A
    Time for Hard Writers: The Impact of War on Women Writers', in this
    volume.** For a vivid celebration of cultural eclecticism and people's war
    imagery, see H. Jennings's film *Listen to Britain* (1941).
32. McKibbin, *Classes and Cultures*, p. 390, passim.

Figure 1   Wartime cultural eclecticism? On the Home Front, *Punch*, 7 June 1944.

Figure 2   And in the Services, *Punch*, 1 April 1942.

beyond, while comedy and talks broadcasts acquired a classless quality in their appeal.[33]

Contemporaries, and subsequently historians, have focused strongly on wartime transitions, and in particular, on the wartime growth of what might be labelled a classless 'people's culture' – one which was supportive of the ideals and not just the productive practicalities of a 'people's war'. This in turn has spawned its own polemically based variant on the familiar theme of what went wrong, here culturally, after 1945. For improvers, this 'people's culture' meant arts for all.[34] Yet in the post-war period British culture once again resonated within class boundaries in many, if not all, areas of activity and control, being traditional in values and largely conservative in emphasis.[35] Broadly, the underpinning explanations put forward to explain this peacetime regression fall within three overlapping themes: Labour's failure before and after its landslide victory in 1945 to provide a socialist agenda, so that instead conservative forces reaffirmed their cultural hegemony; that the arts particularly, and culture generally, were too narrowly defined and educational opportunities were ignored; that attention focused on metropolitan excellence and so the chance for a broader, diffused culture was lost.[36] Yet at the same time, within the freedom afforded through market choice, traditional working-class entertainments flourished after 1945. As Addison notes, '[n]ever before in British history had

33. Scannell and Cardiff, *Social History of Broadcasting*, p. 221; D. Cardiff and P. Scannell, '"Good luck war workers!" Class, politics and entertainment in wartime broadcasting', in *Popular Culture and Social Relations*, eds T. Bennett, C. Mercer and J. Woolacott (Milton Keynes, Open UP, 1986), p. 98; Nicholas, *Echo of War*, pp. 51–3, 259. See Nicholas, 'The People's Radio' for further discussion.

34. For example, J. Fryth, 'Days of Hope: The Meaning of 1945', and A. Croft, 'Betrayed Spring; The Labour Government and British Literary Culture', in *Labour's Promised Land?: Culture and Society in Labour Britain 1945–51*, ed. J. Fryth (London, Lawrence & Wishart, 1995), pp. 7–8, 197–223; D. Watson, 'Where do we go from here?: Education, theatre and politics in the British Army, 1942–1945', *Labour History Review*, 59 (1994), pp. 57–67.

35. K. O. Morgan, *Labour in Power 1945–1951* (Oxford, Oxford UP, 1984), pp. 318–26; see also Norman Baker, 'A More Even Playing Field? Sport During and After the War', in this volume.

36. Fryth, *Labour's Promised Land*, passim; R. Hewison, *Culture and Consensus: England, Art and Politics Since 1940* (London, Methuen, 1995); R. Hutchison, *The Politics of the Arts Council* (London, Sinclair Brown, 1982); A. Sinfield, *Literature, Politics and Culture in Postwar Britain* (London, Basil Blackwell, 1989).

so much been enjoyed by so many'.[37] Such contrasting realities usefully remind us of the need to reassess, not just Labour's contemporary cultural creed, but reconstruction objectives generally. Setting an agenda for peace was integral to the concept of a 'people's war', in which construction cultural providers played an active and positive role.[38] It also highlights the difficulty in identifying directly, rather than through published mediated accounts, what it was that 'the people', however broadly defined, actually did want.[39]

II

The wartime motif of cultural inclusiveness, in that it remained central to wartime discourse, remains central, too, to this collection. Yet the question remains: how appropriate is it to talk of a vital war-specific cultural commonality generally? 'War', Richards suggests, 'always brings the concept of national identity into sharp focus for identity is at the heart of the national propaganda effort.' Refashioning Britishness meant, not only a focus on past cultural achievement within a wartime strategy of a broader unifying diffusion of a 'people's culture', but also on contemporary constructions of future social amelioration.[40] Certainly the directed idea of a 'people's war' (one fought for a better tomorrow by a nation brought together through shared experiences, sacrifices and dangers which overrode previous social divisions) was widely promoted by government and the media so that it quickly acquired a common currency. Indeed,

37. Morgan, *Labour in Power*, p. 312; P. Addison, *Now the War is Over* (London, Pimlico, 1995 edn), p. 113. For the interplay between cultural reformers and popular leisure post-war, see Fielding *et al.*, *'England Arise!'*, pp. 135–68.
38. James Chapman, 'British Cinema and "the People's War"' and Jeff Hill, '"When Work is Over": Labour, Leisure and Culture in Wartime Britain', in this volume.
39. See, for example, Michael Bromley, '"Was it the *Mirror* Wot Won it?" The Development of the Tabloid Press During the Second World War' and Hayes, 'More Than "Music-While-You Eat"?', in this volume.
40. Richards, *Films and British National Identity*, p. 85; R. Weight, 'State, Intelligentsia and the Promotion of National Culture in Britain, 1939–45', *Historical Research*, 69 (1996), pp. 83–101. Unusually, Weight argues that the British intelligentsia actively embraced the patriotic celebration of British cultural tradition, but was largely absent from discourses promoting social change and reconstruction.

where government-led propaganda carried a message popularly interpreted as antithetical to this design it was heavily criticized.[41] Yet Calder also points out that, while the phrase was widely accepted, the inclusive pronoun 'us' meant different things to different people: for 'the miners it meant the miners; for the working class it meant the working class; for those sections of the middle class who now deserted the "Old Gang", it meant managers and workers, bosses and clerks rowing together towards the Happy Island, lending each other a hand to build the New Jerusalem'.[42]

Contemporaries, too, drew attention to continuing inequalities and social divisions. What most irritated J. B. Priestley (identified by Calder as one of the people's 'prophets') when visiting 'escapist' Bournemouth in 1941 was that very inequality of sacrifice: that its 'cocktail bars, salmon and lobster', 'good air and sunlit gardens', 'orchestras and entertainments' were available only to the 'leisurely and well-to-do' residents and wartime escapees, and not offered instead 'to the people who need a change and rest and holiday the most' – the 'exhausted folk from *blitzed* Plymouth – and not only the homeless, but also the doctors and wardens and the like who ... were dropping with fatigue and strain'.[43] Selfishness, and a strong, if perhaps decreasing, resistance to social change equally formed part of the home-front experience; indeed, Marwick suggests that its presence makes the potency of a 'people's war' dynamic for

41. I. McLaine, *Ministry of Morale: Home Front Morale and the Ministry of Information in World War Two* (London, George Allen & Unwin, 1979), pp. 27–33.
42. Calder, *People's War*, p. 138. For a recent interpretation stressing similar views of national and sectional unity within a broader disunity and cultural conservatism, see S. Fielding, 'The Good War: 1939–1945', in *From Blitz to Blair*, ed. N. Tiratsoo (London, Weidenfeld & Nicolson, 1997), pp. 25–52. Calder also draws attention to other significant sectors of wartime society – in shorthand form his 'Celts, Reds and Conchies' – which also lay outside any conventional national construction of an all-embracing unity, Calder, *Myth of the Blitz*, ch. 4. See also **Baxendale, '"You and I"'.**
43. J. B. Priestley, 'I Look at Bournemouth', *Picture Post*, 21 June 1941. For similar themes on the need for, and lack of, equality of sacrifice, see his *Postscripts* (London, Heinemann, 1940), pp. 86–90, 6 October 1940. For air-raid shelters, for example, see Calder, *Myth of the Blitz*; T. Harrisson, *Living through the Blitz* (Harmondsworth, Penguin, 1978). For strikes and industrial relations see, C. Wrigley, 'The Second World War and state intervention in industrial relations, 1939–45', in *A History of British Industrial Relations, 1939–1979*, ed. C. Wrigley (Cheltenham, Edward Elgar, 1996), pp. 12–43.

change only the more notable when measured by the subsequent gains accrued.[44]

For British civilians, the Second World War marked a turning point where vulnerability to direct attack, exposed psychologically in the preceding decades, became at times an everyday reality for many urban dwellers; no longer were civilians culturally separated from soldiers by the unbridgeable existential gap that existed in 1914–18.[45] Writing at the same time as Priestley, the American journalist, Ralph Ingersoll, although reportedly searching for evidence of social division and a resilient snobbery, found instead a 'bomb-inspired social revolution in England', a new commonality – that is a new *'us'* – constituted around the

> breaking down of its hard class consciousness into classlessness ... .
> A nation cannot sleep wherever it finds itself at night and with whomever happens to lie down next to it and not have things happen to its class distinctions. A nation cannot be in such desperate need of skill and so deeply indebted to whoever has it regardless of class without things happening to it.[46]

Such ubiquitously projected 'heroic' imagery – with its associated ideas of social bonding and new commonality – carried, as it still does today, a politically powerful message.[47] Tom Harrisson, in reviewing the text, thought it had an 'interesting clarity ... which made it the most worth reading of these Home Front Books so far'. Yet he also adds a strongly worded codicil in pointing to the 'usual superficially extravagant accounts of British morale' contained within it and to many other 'inaccuracies'. 'It is sad to think', he concludes, 'that historians may go to the volumes of these journalists, after the war, to reconstruct the picture of what really happened.' Yet, at the same time, perhaps Harrisson ignores the importance of the specific moment: that brief period in 1940, Harris suggests, when

44. A. Marwick, 'People's War and Top People's Peace? British Society and the Second World War', in *Crisis and Controversy: Essays in Honour of A. J. P. Taylor*, eds A. Sked and C. Cook (Basingstoke, Macmillan, 1976), pp. 148–63.

45. S. Hynes, *A War Imagined: the First World War and English Culture* (London, Bodley Head, 1991). See **Alberti, 'A Time for Hard Writers'**.

46. R. Ingersoll, *Report on England* (London, Bodley Head, 1941), pp. 231–2. For a recent, if qualified, text with a similar emphasis, see P. Zeigler, *London at War 1939–1945* (London, Sinclair Stevens, 1995).

47. Fielding, 'The Good War'.

'fear, excitement, desperation and the random immediacy of death induced in many people an almost ecstatic sense of transcendence of self and immersion into a mystic whole'.[48]

In the more openly fictional 1943 film *Millions Like Us*, which provides the title for this collection, the *'us'* was constructed principally through the sampled lives of young British women of differing national/regional and class backgrounds and temperaments (in noticeable contrast to Sayers's *English War*), conscripted to work and live together in a munitions factory and hostel.[49] With its stress on home-front comradeship, endurance without heroics, and matter-of-factness (it resonates, for example, with everyday images of popular culture), *Millions Like Us* – typically of British films of the later war period – is about 'ordinary people' in a realistic contemporary setting.[50] So it is, as the initially diffident Celia Crowson (the principal character) quickly finds a personally transforming niche through war work (although naturally she retains her quintessential feminine demureness). She also marries an equally reserved Scottish sergeant air-gunner, soon to be killed over Germany. Celia, of course, continues her war work. During a canteen concert finale, a tearful Celia is drawn into singing 'There was I Waiting at the Church' – an ironic metaphor for the couple's dashed optimism – as the nation's bombers roar over head. As Christine Gledhill comments:

> In the communal ritual of the canteen singsong, the choreographed documentary camera movement ... invites us not simply to join a public gaze, but to become a part of what we gaze at .... The closure of the film in community singing speaks in a self-reflexive way to the social role of cinema in wartime as itself a communal home.[51]

48. T. Harrisson, Mass-Observation Report 732, Review of 'Report on England', 11 June 1941. See also D. R. Costello, '*Searchlight Books* and the Quest for a People's War, 1941–42', *Journal of Contemporary History*, **24** (1989), pp. 257–76. Harris, 'War and Social History', pp. 32–3; see **Alberti, 'A Time for Hard Writers'**. Addison, *Now the War is Over*, p. 3, argues that political and economic necessity, rather than wartime psychological exhilaration (caught in the 'heroic imagery' of social solidarity), provided the 'mainspring' for social change.
49. See **Chapman, 'British Cinema'**.
50. Richards and Aldgate, *Britain Can Take It*, pp. 326–7; **Chapman, 'British Cinema'**.
51. C. Gledhill, 'An abundance of understatement: documentary, melodrama and romance', in Gledhill and Swanson, *Nationalising Femininity*, p. 221. Celia's marriage is viewed in similar publicly communal terms. See also T. Pulleine, 'Millions Like Us', *Monthly Film Bulletin*, **49**:581 (June 1982).

As in other classic Second World War representations, individual desires and ambitions are subordinated to collective need: the 'audience's pleasure comes from seeing the maintenance of group effort ... the individual's choking back of grief over the death of a loved one and the resumption of teamwork towards victory'.[52] In one further example of time-specific disjuncture, while war films as a genre remained extremely popular through the 1950s, those made after 1945 quickly abandoned this key motif of cross-class/regional unity.[53]

Recent histories have viewed sceptically claims that the war caused lasting change. They have also identified a widespread cynicism towards the promises made by political elites and questioned particularly the impact that reformist political discourse had 'on the ground', demanding not just a generalized approbation but a wider detailed appreciation of reconstruction proposals as evidence for the public's approval.[54] Such an understanding then, as today, was always unlikely. At the same time popular understanding, precisely because the war years were to varying degrees extraordinary and collectivist in public focus, depended more heavily on formally and informally transmitted public messages, stories and appreciations to take it beyond any one individual's limiting experience. News remained at

52. Charles Barr, cited by Calder, *Myth of the Blitz*, p. 237.
53. Instead, war films reverted to the stock officer as hero, other ranks as comic figures, characteristics of the 1930s. Women, if present, were predominantly depicted as wives, mothers and sweethearts: J. Ramsden, 'Refocusing "The People's War": British War Films in the 1950s', *Journal of Contemporary History*, 33 (1998), pp. 56–7. By contrast, the Gainsborough melodrama, popular at the war's end, portrayed a violent intensity of gender and class conflict which offered contemporary reassurances in a 1940s of social upheaval: Gledhill, 'An abundance of understatement', pp. 223–4. For the inter-war portrayal of a conservative Englishness (patriotic, unemotional, unintellectual, masculine) through the officer-class experiences of 1914–18, see J. M. Winter, 'British national identity and the First World War', in *The Boundaries of the State in Modern Britain*, eds S. J. D. Green and R. C. Whiting (Cambridge, Cambridge UP, 1996), pp. 261–77. This theme of the gallant, martial Englishman found form, also, in some wartime productions: for example, *The Lion Has Wings* (1939) and *In Which We Serve* (1942).
54. See, for example, Fielding *et al.*, *'England Arise!'*; T. Mason and P. Thompson, '"Reflections on a Revolution"? The political mood in wartime Britain', in *The Attlee Years*, ed. N. Tiratsoo (London, Pinter, 1991), pp. 54–70. The seminal study opposing this view remains P. Addison, *The Road to 1945: British Politics and the Second World War* (London, Jonathan Cape, 1975); and more recently, J. Hinton, '1945 and the Apathy School', *History Workshop Journal*, 43 (1997), pp. 266–73.

a premium because the costs and disruptions of war were high.[55] Within these narratives, the conception and transmission of images of enhanced, albeit idealized, behavioural conformity – reinforced by examples of negligent nonconformity, as in Bournemouth – remained prominent. What we (as the nation) were fighting for and against, the sacrifices made, the victories achieved, has traditionally been recorded as having a powerful communal as well as a private resonance.[56] Moreover, an abundance of survey and private data exists which testifies, at one level of personal consciousness, to the 'extraordinary degree of unanimous and single-minded commitment to unqualified resistance to Hitler', and the little support that existed for the view that the war was not worth fighting.[57] Public morale responded directly to whether the war news was good or bad, and, as importantly, the manner in which it was communicated: that is, positively when delivered in a humanized or dramatic form, or immediately after the event; and negatively, if it was thought evasive in character. In all these senses, winning the war had a strong immediate and communal priority, which found expression in a myriad of contingent group activities and collective cultures (from joining voluntary organizations such as the Home Guard and the Women's Voluntary Service to listening punctiliously to the BBC news). Moreover this was, to degrees, a closed loop, in which collective participation – and by extension the representations thereof and the ideals attached – carried an enhanced potential to modify private thoughts and actions. Central to Calder's work on the Blitz is the conception that, however flawed was the official image of British civilians pulling together, it nevertheless provided a standard against which people set and measured their own behaviour patterns. For Addison, 'egalitarianism and community feeling became, to a great extent, the pervasive ideals of social life: whether or not people lived up to them, they knew that they *ought* to'.[58]

Yet if individual priorities were modified by a broader, societal

55. Sinfield, *Literature*, p. 23; Calder, *People's War*, p. 504; S. Nicholas, *Echo of War*, passim. See **Bromley, '"Was it the *Mirror* Wot Won it?"'**.
56. For a sceptical examination of the unity of public discourse, see **Baxendale, '"You and I"'**. For personal reflections on the linkages between the individual writer and wartime community, see **Alberti, 'A Time for Hard Writers'**.
57. Harris, 'War and Social History', pp. 27–8.
58. Nicholas, *Echo of War*, pp. 190 ff.; Calder, *Myth of the Blitz*; Addison, *Road to 1945*, pp. 18–19 (original italics).

dynamic representing enhanced wartime communal ideals and objectives, circumstance and perception within the personalized specifics of everyday home-front life still took a high, and frequently conflicting, precedence. Take the collective war-specific themes of factory and hostel *esprit de corps* depicted within *Millions Like Us* as typical of the publicly transmitted dialectic between competing individual and community interests. The film was made to alleviate acknowledged female anxieties about factory life; it sought to ac-centuate inclusive workplace camaraderie within a war environment of common purpose and identity.[59] Yet contemporary published sources set clear limits to the authority of collective appeals in influencing young women's attitudes to compulsory labour. Mass-Observation's factory study (published in October 1943) accepted that 'the majority of them are so little interested in the war that they do not care whether their work is important or not'. Within the machine shop 'never was there any shadow of public opinion directed against slacking or dodging of any kind. Expert dodgers are merely envied for their ability to get away with it.' It concluded:

> It is a well known fact that the average working-class woman's interest in the war is kept alive, not so much by the large-scale tragedies, like the loss of this, that or the other bit of territory, but by the personal inconveniences: rationing, blackout, shortages and so on. And from these inconveniences someone who works in a war factory, with an adequate canteen, for twelve hours a day, is automatically excluded. ... [this being] the main reason for the almost complete lack of war feeling which characterises the machine shop.[60]

The self-evidence of Mass-Observation's truths requires qualification: contextually they are the product of a social movement with its own quasi-political objectives – which in wartime were directed particu-larly towards securing greater governmental and industrial efficiency

59. For differing assessments of *Millions Like Us* as a normative narrative on contemporary opinion, see, for example, Gledhill and Swanson, *Nationalising Femininity*, pp. 203, 221, 242–4, 252. For positive contemporary responses as to its true-to-life qualities, see J. Richards and D. Sheridan, *Mass-Observation at the Movies* (London, Routledge & Kegan Paul, 1987), pp. 238, 263, 277–8.
60. Mass-Observation, *War Factory* (London, Gollancz, 1943), pp. 45, 47–8; see also Mass-Observation, *People in Production: An Inquiry into British War Production* (London, John Murray, 1942). For interest in, and practical treat-ment of, basic inconveniences such as rationing, see Nicholas, *Echo of War*, pp. 70–85.

– and *a priori* assumptions covering working-class behaviour patterns.[61] Nevertheless, this study (commissioned by the factory management to enquire into poor female productivity) offers little evidence that war forged a melding of vital personal and collective priorities; indeed, the process of war perhaps atomized, rather than unified. War alienation was attributed to the all-found nature of these young women's immediate lifestyle. 'Is it surprising', it asked, that 'a girl should begin to feel isolated from the outside world and lose her sense of responsibility towards it ... [when] by the nature of her work and its long hours ... she [was] cut off from the daily life of her community [and] sheltered from its day to day difficulties'? Total inclusivity within this particular war culture was viewed, therefore, in wholly negative terms.[62]

According to Mass-Observation, this was only part of a broader societal malaise of collective 'aimlessness, irresponsibility and boredom'. Taken in conjunction with the results from other fieldwork, Harrisson concluded, these 'factory girls' exemplified

> the dangerous decline in positive citizenship, especially among the young .... Wherever we turn today we find evidence of this cultural passivity. The *laissez faire* of leisure, and its dangerous separation from work, is immediately and primarily responsible .... Even now, when Britain is a-hum with plans, these basic social and 'spiritual' matters are practically ignored.[63]

61. *War Factory* – based on the reports of a full-time investigator working incognito on the factory floor – is variously described as providing 'a superb picture of the responses of a group of women, mainly unaccustomed to industrial work', and as a personal study which is 'highly subjective', yet offers a 'useful corrective'. See P. Summerfield, 'Mass-Observation: Social Research or Social Movement?', *Journal of Contemporary History*, 20 (1985), pp. 439–52; D. Sheridan, 'Introduction', in Mass-Observation, *War Factory* (London, Hutchinson edn, 1987). For an exploration of the class and gender assumptions underwriting Mass-Observation enquiries, see P. Gurney, '"Inter-Sex" and "Dirty Girls": Mass-Observation and Working-Class Sexuality in England in the 1930s', *Journal of the History of Sexuality*, 8 (1997), pp. 256–90.

62. Mass-Observation, *War Factory* (1943), pp. 42–3, 47, 49–50. For a brief assessment of a corresponding apathy within the armed forces to current affairs, see Fielding *et al.*, *'England Arise!'*, pp. 28–30, 64–5; J. A. Craig, 'Politics on Parade: Army Education and the 1945 General Election', *History*, 81 (1996), pp. 215–27.

63. T. Harrisson, 'Industrial Survey', in Mass-Observation, *War Factory*, p. 9. For an exploration of enhanced wartime public anxiety regarding teenage girls and young women, see S. Rose, 'Girls and GIs: Sex and Diplomacy in Second World War Britain', *International History Review*, 19 (1997), pp. 146–60.

Such concerns had strong pre-war antecedents, especially but not exclusively in left-of-centre and progressive discourse.[64] The 'movement to raise the moral and cultural standards of the general public', Addison suggests to be a key but neglected theme of 1940s history, where the imperative of citizenly 'service' was constantly invoked by social reformers like Bevan, Beveridge and Keynes over and above the material motivations of welfare. The community, in return, was charged with enriching the lives of its citizenry. Operating within this was an expanding 'war-born' definition of the social attributes of universal democratic citizenship – linked to ideas of full employment, conscription and mass mobilization. Beveridge, for example, had previously viewed social insurance, not only as a means of meeting need, but as an agency for promoting group solidarity, and bringing individuals and institutions into partnership with the state. This emphasis on 'social cohesion was still powerfully present in the Beveridge Report, but now it was [offered as] a cohesion that was ethical as well as merely organizational', where citizenship delineated a common freedom from, and the 'common condemnation' of, 'the scandal of physical want'.[65]

Indeed many contemporaries drew optimistic conclusions from the changing borders of wartime lifestyle, within which they projected an expanding cultural function for government. Summarizing factory hostel practice, *The Architectural Review*, with a weather eye to promoting new socio-architectural forms after the war, reported:

> Here people of practically all ages and of both sexes have built up a
> new life for themselves, away from their normal background and
> friends. They had to rely not only for work, board and lodging, but

64. See **Hill, '"When Work is Over"'**, Baker, 'A More Even Playing Field?', and **Griffin, 'Not Just A Case of Baths'**.

65. Ibid.; Addison, *Now the War is Over*, p. 134; J. Harris, *William Beveridge: A Biography* (Oxford, Clarendon, 1997 edn), pp. 411–12. The classical wartime statement on future cultural provision is, of course, J. B. Priestley, 'When Work is Over', *Picture Post*, 4 January 1941 (see **Hill, '"When Work is Over"'**, for further discussion of this text). For a succinct overview of the interplay between planning and idealism, see M. Daunton, 'Payment and Participation: Welfare and State-Formation in Britain 1900–1951', *Past and Present*, **156** (1996), esp. pp. 207–12. For Labour's support of ethical socialism, see M. Francis, 'Economics and Ethics: The Nature of Labour's Socialism', *Twentieth Century British History*, **6** (1995), pp. 220–43.

also for educational and recreational facilities on communal services
provided by the State ... . Not a grey and dull existence regulated
by the State machine, but a vigorous one, in which many have found
potentialities of mastering and enjoying life, that had been latent but
undeveloped in the sheltered life of the pre-war period ... . The
people have experimented in a sort of life which, if not exactly to
be copied in peacetime, will form part of the post-war existence.[66]

Such positive constructions of wartime life, frequently set against a
backdrop of 1930s waste, were an important commonplace through
which a better 'planned' tomorrow celebrated the benefits of socially
mixed, communally orientated living, and greater community
provision and responsibility.[67] Such preoccupations found a matching
resonance in Labour's post-war social policy. It met with only
limited degrees of success.[68] Indeed, the wartime hostels praised by
reformers remained essentially unpopular: 'many [workers] chose
even over-crowded billets or long journeys to work' in preference.
(Remember in *Millions Like Us* the taxi driver's disparaging
comments on hostel life and the emphasis within the film to alter
that view.) Recreationally, residents opted for the cinema shows
and dances of popular acquaintance, rather than the educational and other leisure facilities provided by numerous voluntary

66. H. Robertson, 'An Experimental Wartime Community', *The Architectural
    Review*, March 1945, p. 84.
67. Ibid.; for the impact of the planning debate and movement, see S. Brooke,
    Labour's War: The Labour Party during the Second World War (Oxford, Oxford
    UP, 1992); J. Stevenson, 'Planners' Moon? The Second World War and the
    planning movement', in *War and Social Change: British Society in the Second
    World War*, ed. H. Smith (Manchester, Manchester UP, 1986), pp. 58–77;
    J. Tomlinson, 'Planning: Debate and Policy in the 1940s', *Twentieth Century
    British History*, 3 (1992), pp. 154–74. For the cultural interplay between the
    1930s and 'people's war' rhetoric, see J. Baxendale and C. Pawling, *Narrating
    the Thirties. A Decade in the Making: 1930 to the Present* (Houndmills,
    Macmillan, 1996), pp. 116–39. For the importance of negative views of the
    1930s to Labour's 1945 victory, see S. Fielding, 'What did "The People"
    Want?: The Meaning of the 1945 General Election', *Historical Journal*, 35
    (1992), pp. 623–39.
68. Central Housing Advisory Committee, *Design of Dwelling* (Dudley Committee)
    (London, HMSO, 1944); Addison, *Now the War is Over*, pp. 70–9; Fielding
    et al., *'England Arise!'*, pp. 102–34. For a generally positive assessment of the
    importance of community on post-war new estates, see M. Clapson, *Invincible
    Green Suburbs, Brave New Towns. Social Change and Urban Dispersal in
    Post-war England* (Manchester, Manchester UP, 1998).

societies.[69] On either count, therefore, 'the people' apparently opted for the familiar and personal, rather than the communal and new. Popular humour and popular culture throughout the war, Harris argues, was 'not collectivist but anarchic, celebrating not the unity of mankind but its absurdity ... and the fallibility of all in authority'. If this so obviously ignores the communal emphasis, for example, within 'people's war' films like *Millions Like Us*, it also points succinctly to the continuing importance, emergencies aside, of pre-war attitudes to the basics of privacy and individualism at home, and industrial divisions at work, amongst all but the few who were 'ideologically committed to a more thorough-going, principled collectivism'.[70]

III

The pivotal role of the state in wartime is arguably central in explaining cultural disjunctures and reconstructional form overall (although, equally, governing ideologies in certain key areas such as sport remained largely untouched).[71] 'The requirements of wartime morale', Sinfield notes, 'transformed the relationship between the state and cultural production.'[72] Within its monopolistic control over information and event management, government also initiated a new intellectual patronage system through organizations like CEMA and the Army Bureau of Current Affairs (ABCA). Notwithstanding this, the willingness with which the intelligentsia and artistic community entered state-directed employment remains keenly debated. Hewison sees the intellectual as 'driven into National Service', denied 'fulfilment' and isolated, 'unable to find a proper role in wartime society'.

69. P. Inman, *Labour in the Munitions Industries* (London, HMSO, 1957), pp. 246–57; H. M. D. Parker, *Manpower: A Study of Wartime Policy and Administration* (London, HMSO, 1957), pp. 401–2. For hostel entertainments, see **Hayes, 'More Than "Music-While-You-Eat"?'**.
70. Harris, 'War and Social Change', p. 32. For the importance of privacy and disinterest in the neighbourhood, see Mass-Observation, *An Enquiry into People's Homes* (London, John Murray, 1943), pp. 160–213.
71. Beckett, 'Total War'; P. Addison, 'The Road from 1945', in *Ruling Performance: British Governments from Attlee to Thatcher*, eds P. Hennessey and A. Seldon (Oxford, Blackwell, 1987), pp. 5–27. For Labour thinking on the role of the state, see **Hill, 'When Work is Over'**; for the state's key role in media production, see **Chapman, 'British Cinema'**; for its limited impact in sport, see **Baker, 'A More Even Playing Field?'**.
72. Sinfield, *Literature*, pp. 47–8.

Weight, by contrast, argues that far from being 'virulently censored' state 'victims', an already politically disillusioned left/liberal intelligentsia readily embraced a 'Churchillian vision of Britain' in which a heroic people lived out its historic destiny defending 'the traditions and achievements of the nation'.[73] (It was, after all, those traditions which protected artistic and critical freedom.) Indeed, the relationship between the individual and the state (and its wartime objectives) perhaps inevitably remained problematic even when both parties nominally favoured *rapprochement*. For example, while accepting that this was 'a war for survival', writers nevertheless observed that state policy actively hindered literary conscription: authors were called up or, unable to use their 'special talents' in the country's interest, volunteered; or they could not 'get leave' from their units to write, or alternatively, 'get the passes from the M.O.I. to collect the material'. Yet creative writers, it was argued, *should be used to interpret the war world so that cultural unity is re-established and* [the] *war effort emotionally co-ordinated'.*[74]

After 1945, too, the social relationship between individual autonomy and state direction remained central to general philosophical debate, encouraged by the continuing rhetoric afforded to centralized planning. Setting the parameters of state control also found its place in the field of cultural provision and production.[75] The Arts Council, for example, took great pride, when writing its own post-war history, in proclaiming that it was 'not a Government Department, and bears little resemblance to those Ministries of Fine Arts which exist in many other countries'. Instead, with bipartisan political support, the Council operated according to the supposed 'arm's length principle' of political detachment.[76] Nevertheless, Minihan's assessment is that in a 'very

73. Hewison, *Under Siege*, pp. 67–9, passim; Weight, 'State, Intelligentsia', pp. 83–4. For individual motivations, see **Alberti, 'A Time for Hard Writers'** and **Mackay, 'Safe and Sound'**. For elite discourse, see **Baxendale, '"You and I"'**.
74. A. Calder-Marshall, C. Connolly, B. Dobrée, T. Harrisson, A. Koestler, A. Lewis, G. Orwell and S. Spender, 'Why not War Writers? A Manifesto', *Horizon*, 4 (October 1941), pp. 236–8 (original emphasis).
75. See, for example, Tomlinson, 'Planning'; D. Morgan and M. Evans, 'The Road to Nineteen Eighty-Four: Orwell and the post-war reconstruction of citizenship', in *What Difference Did the War Make*, eds B. Bravati and H. Jones (Leicester, Leicester UP, 1993), pp. 48–62.
76. *The First Ten Years: The Eleventh Annual Report of the Arts Council of Great Britain* (London, 1956), p. 15. For the wartime debate on a Ministry of Arts, see Weight, 'State, Intelligentsia', pp. 97–8.

direct sense', war made possible significant progress towards a national arts policy during the 1940s to the degree that the incoming Labour government effectively 'nationalized culture'.[77] Cultural critics have long argued that government control was more 'wrist's length' than 'arm's' within a continuity of hegemonic domination, and that the Arts Council, in rejecting the people's culture of wartime practice, instead became a force for cultural conservatism and privilege perpetuated.[78] Certainly a 'nationalized' culture meant, in parliamentary terms, consensually supported state subsidies and several pieces of legislation, 1945–51, which sought to provide public entertainment, recreation and education through the arts (for example, the ill-fated National Theatre Act 1949, limited financial support to the British film industry and the widely ignored authority granted to local councils to subsidize entertainments and arts provision).[79] Practically, however, only in Arts Council funding was a significant step forward taken.

Yet, as Pick has commented, given its economic circumstances, 'it was an astonishing time for Britain to begin wholesale financial support of the arts'.[80] Why did this occur? A belief certainly existed among cultural elites that Britain was fighting for what was 'best' in European civilization and that this product should be widely diffused. But for Weight and Minihan, the projected nationalization of 'culture' encompassed more: a hope within the establishment that

> a popular knowledge of, and participation in, the arts would nurture good citizens by refining the sensibilities of the British people, and so making them more able to appreciate what, in 1940, the Board of Education had called 'the value and reality of cultural roots' ... which, they believed, would be a foundation stone on which post-war reconstruction could be built.[81]

77. J. Minihan, *The Nationalization of Culture: The Development of State Subsidies to the Arts in Great Britain* (London, Hamish Hamilton, 1977), pp. 216, 235.
78. R. Williams, 'The Arts Council', *Political Quarterly*, 50 (1979), p. 159; Hewison, *Culture and Consensus*, p. 48; Sinfield, *Literature*, pp. 50–8. For an opposing view on political independence, see Hutchison, *Politics*, pp. 15–44.
79. Minihan, *Nationalization of Culture*, pp. 235–43; Institute of Municipal Entertainment, *A Survey of Municipal Entertainment in England and Wales for the two years 1947/8 and 1961/2* (IME, 1964).
80. J. Pick, 'The Best for the Most', in *The State and the Arts*, ed. J. Pick (Eastbourne, Offord, 1980), p. 9.
81. Weight, 'State, Intelligentsia', p. 98; Minihan, *Nationalization of Culture*, p. 235. Hutchison, *Politics*, p. 15, in ignoring this element, describes any claim of 'nationalization' as an 'absurd' misrepresentation.

This, too, was not a new sentiment: it found form through earlier Reithian policy at the BBC (which linked cultural provision to nationalism and education), and in, for example, the 'arts for the people' tours during the 1930s.[82] Yet, according to Weight, active participation in the Second World War increased the status of writers, artists and critics, who – having found their patriotic voice and rejected 1930s radicalism – were given a 'place at the heart of the State and the media to an unprecedented degree by an Establishment which fully realized how useful the arts could be'. Social reintegration, he asserts, saw the birth of a new cultural establishment 'as powerful as that which was to govern other areas of national life over the next thirty years'.[83] Within this paradigm, if Marwick is right in asserting that the 'vital question at any time is – how are the arts financed?', in terms of how culture is 'valued' and patronized by 'society' – then it is equally significant that state support for the wartime providers of popular culture and popular education, ENSA and ABCA, was allowed to lapse.[84] In this sense the strong division between cultures – with 'good' culture being supported and validated through subsidy, while popular culture followed the dictates and uncertainties of commercial viability – was not only maintained but reinforced. Only in the extensive field of voluntary activity did the arts and popular cultures retain a rough parity, albeit negatively in terms of their lack of central government subsidy.

IV

Where, therefore, do we finally stand? In premising that distinctive wartime social disjunctures can indeed be identified, two broader chains of thought seem central to any analysis of British wartime cultures. The first is the extent to which cultural activity, in areas as diverse as the arts and sport, was affected by the more obviously apparent structural changes within wartime society. This raises the very literal problems of material shortfalls in resources, or of new

82. Scannell and Cardiff, *Social History of Broadcasting*, pp. 7–14; Minihan, *Nationalization of Culture*, pp. 183–4.
83. Weight, 'State, Intelligentsia', pp. 98–9.
84. A. Marwick, 'The arts, books, media and entertainments in Britain since 1945', in *Understanding Post-War British Society*, eds J. Obelkevich and P. Catterell (London, Routledge, 1994), p. 180.

or lost audiences because of geographic dislocation or enemy hostilities. More interestingly, perhaps, it calls into question the ways
in which the war provided new or extended remits for each area of
activity: for example, linking cultural provision integrally to, or
making it the underpinning foundation of, war or post-war objectives
(notably in seeking to redefine and bolster senses of identity and
belonging, or ideas of what Britain was fighting for). This process
might, additionally, enhance the cultural medium through which such
policies were actively pursued. Accentuating the positive, to borrow
Fussell's turn of phrase, extended beyond the reporting of 'good
news', into the realms, for example, of providing culturally improving
activities and images to sit beside the wider diffusion of morale-
boosting and more popular forms of entertainment. In total, we
might say, this represented a 'people's culture': that which might
loosely be labelled as part of the cultural apparatus of the economic
and social politics of the 'people's war'. But important, too, when
considering the question of disjuncture is the episodic nature of the
war, where individual and collective experiences varied considerably
according to location, occupation and chronology. Set against these
internal discontinuities and contradictions, the 'people's culture'
offered 'approved' images and representations which formed a public
bedrock of continuity and certainty.

Second, and building from this, we can identify a need to explore
how and if wartime responses (whether producer, audience or state
led) interreacted through cultural provision to produce fresh
dynamics rooted in the immediate opportunities which war provided,
but which generated a life-force of their own. This, as we have seen,
might manifest itself in a number of forms: a new-found productional
excellence or a classless motif; or perhaps a hitherto unrecognized
market for inspirational activities linked 'spiritually' to the community-based organics of the war itself. The wartime movement, for
example, promoting cultural eclecticism, arguably had strong roots
in all three productional, institutional and audience-based compo-
nents. Yet motive forces might equally be registered negatively, in
terms of disenchantment, or through a strong affirmation for the
reassuringly familiar. It might also be largely illusory, accidental or
self-affirming. Central to determining this force and direction, perhaps, was how individuals, or individual groups and agencies,
interlocked with, and reacted to, the predominant objectives and
projected ideologies of wartime Britain (an agenda set by an increas-

ingly powerful state but which also contained strongly personalized, innate values linked to wartime disruptions and costs). Certainly public imagery and rhetoric focused squarely on notions of commonality and community, enhanced ideals of which were to outlive the duration of the war itself. But the inception of wartime actions, or the reception of reforms and plans for reconstruction, might equally depend on the less tangible and defined: a conformity to what Sayers, for example, prayed for in 1940 as an adjunct to war – an English peace whose nebulous values included 'Some sense, some decency, perhaps/ Some justice, too, if we are able'.[85]

Indeed, whether or not clear directional processes between policy and outcomes existed, in terms of conforming to broader wartime constructs, is in itself controversial. Siân Nicholas will argue, for example, that the wartime BBC's successes were less planned than accidental, that when it self-consciously set out to preserve a national unity and culture it rarely succeeded, and that its real achievement lay in catering successfully for a diversity of tastes. Michael Bromley, in examining the specifics of information transmission through the wartime press, argues that it was more form than political content which determined the effectiveness of the reconstruction message. John Baxendale will question the very concept of a broadly understood meaning of common identity and purpose beyond that of a somewhat basic war-enhanced banal nationalism. Indeed, as Johanna Alberti argues, for many writers, the war broke the organic links between individual and societal values, while at the same time creating an inclusiveness and sense of belonging which set aside previous distinctions. In examining musical composition, Robert Mackay identifies the ubiquitous presence of an enhanced 'English' identity: inwardly conservative, musically backward-looking (and overtly patriotic where official influences predominated); yet organically expressive of those core 'civilized' values under threat. It proved to be a temporary influence only, however, in terms of longer-range trends.

Other essays in this collection offer similar insights into the relationship between cultural producers, audiences and other key agencies, and contemporary preoccupations and priorities. Jeff Hill, in commenting on the Labour movement's approach to cultural policy, notes its generally statist rationale, but one severely limited

---

85. Sayers, *English War*.

in content and approach, which ignored earlier traditional responses of developing an alternative culture. An optimistic belief in wartime cultural improvement underpinned this lack of urgency, but whether or not this was justified remains keenly contested (highlighting the problems of measuring popular taste directly). Colin Griffin, in examining working-class cultural preferences within the mining industry, suggests that tastes and commitment to non-commercial leisure provision varied widely, but that, after the war, an enhanced ideal of cultural provision, community-oriented and broadly-based, presided; while Nick Hayes, in examining factory concerts for workers, argues that the idea of a war-enhanced cultural eclecticism, including a new audience for 'good' culture, was, and continues to be, widely exaggerated. Similarly, James Chapman's essay on British wartime cinema suggests that an important gap existed between those films which historians and contemporary critics deemed signifi-cant, aesthetically and in terms of social comment, and which apparently audiences grew to appreciate, and the films which cinema-goers actually preferred to watch. Certainly, as Norman Baker suggests, in the most widely diffused of popular cultures – sport and leisure – war did little to change governing attitudes, and it was left to broader, already established pressures like commercialization and the desire for competitive success to effect lasting change. Perhaps Marwick is right when he suggests that the 'cultural effects of war are more pervasive than proponents of continuity wish to recog-nize, but less decisive than proponents of discontinuity like to believe'.[86] This collection seeks to tease out further such nuances, in the arts and in other areas of cultural provision, by exploring some of the richness and diversity of that which constituted Britain's war experiences.

---

86. A. Marwick, 'War and the Arts – Is There a Connection?: The Case of the Two Total Wars', *War in History*, 2 (1995), p. 86.

British Cinema and 'The People's War'

James Chapman

The war film discovered the common
denominator of the British people.

Roger Manvell.[1]

The British cinema of the Second World War has typically been
characterized in terms of its representation of 'the people's war'.
The films which have attracted most critical attention are those
which presented a picture of the British people at war, united despite
class differences, and where the stories of individuals, heroic though
they may be, were sublimated into the greater story of the whole
nation pulling together at a time of national crisis. Commentators
have identified, for the first time in British feature films, an authentic, true-to-life representation of ordinary men and women. Roger
Manvell considered that films such as *Millions Like Us*, *San Demetrio,
London*, *Nine Men*, *The Way Ahead*, *Waterloo Road* and *The Way
to the Stars* 'showed people in whom we could believe and whose
experience was as genuine as our own'.[2] The reason for this new-
found realism is usually explained through the influence of the
documentary movement, the progressive left-wing sector of the British film industry, on the mainstream feature film producers. During
the 1930s documentary had been, at best, a marginal mode of film
practice which appealed to the intelligentsia and a small critical elite,
but which never won the approval of the majority of the cinema-going
audience, who preferred the escapist fantasies offered to them by

1. R. Manvell, 'The British Feature Film from 1925 to 1945', in *Twenty Years of
British Film 1925–1945*, eds M. Balcon, E. Lindgren, F. Hardy and R. Manvell
(London, The Falcon Press, 1947), p. 85.
2. Ibid.

both American and British feature films.[3] During the war, however, documentary entered the mainstream in that a number of British feature films were seen to exhibit certain aspects of the documentary style and technique. Critics identified a 'wartime wedding' between the documentary and the feature film.[4] The marriage of the fictional feature film with the documentary movement's concern for the authentic representation of everyday life contributed to the trend towards realism in British cinema which so met with the approval of the orthodox critical discourse of the time. The result was, according to this discourse, that a genuinely British national cinema could be seen to have emerged which rivalled Hollywood in both critical and popular acclaim. This view was expressed, for example, in a post-war survey by the Arts Enquiry, entitled *The Factual Film* (1947), whose authors included a number of leading documentarists such as Paul Rotha and Basil Wright. Rather than trying to emulate Hollywood films, the authors argued instead that 'the success of films such as *Millions Like Us*, *The Way Ahead*, *Waterloo Road* and *Way to the Stars* [sic] during the war, has shown that there is another way of overcoming Hollywood domination by producing films which reflect the British scene realistically in a way that would be impossible for Hollywood'.[5]

3. For an account of British cinema during the 1930s, including the preferences of British audiences, see R. Low, *The History of the British Film 1929–1939: Film Making in 1930s Britain* (London, George Allen & Unwin, 1985); J. Richards, *The Age of the Dream Palace: Cinema and Society in Britain 1930–1939* (London, Routledge & Kegan Paul, 1984) and J. Richards (ed.), *The Unknown 1930s: An Alternative History of the British Cinema, 1929–1939* (London, I. B. Tauris, 1998). There is an extensive literature on the history and achievements of the documentary movement, amongst which I. Aitken, *Film and Reform: John Grierson and the Documentary Film Movement* (London, Routledge, 1990) and P. Swann, *The British Documentary Film Movement, 1926–1946* (Cambridge, Cambridge UP, 1989) stand out as the most scholarly. More personal and anecdotal accounts are to be found in, for example, P. Rotha, *Documentary Diary: An Informal History of the British Documentary Film* (London, Secker & Warburg, 1973) and E. Sussex, *The Rise and Fall of British Documentary* (Berkeley, University of California Press, 1975).
4. The phrase appears to have originated with John Shearman, himself a documentary-film maker, in an article entitled 'Wartime Wedding' for *Documentary News Letter*, 6:54 (November/December 1946), p. 53.
5. The Arts Enquiry, *The Factual Film: A Survey Sponsored by the Dartington Hall Trustees* (London, Geoffrey Cumberlege and Oxford UP, 1947), p. 201.

The aim of this essay is to explore the role and nature of the British cinema during the Second World War. It will show how the cinema performed the dual roles of both a medium of entertainment and a vehicle of propaganda, and the extent to which these were compatible. And it will discuss the nature of British films themselves, explaining how and why the trend towards realism identified by contemporaries came about. Closely related to both these themes is the relationship between the film industry and official agencies, in particular the Ministry of Information (MoI), which was responsible for propaganda policy. The MoI has frequently been dismissed by commentators, its reputation forever tarnished as the 'Ministry of Dis-Information', a label which stuck long after it had ceased to be appropriate. The popular image of the MoI, enshrined in Evelyn Waugh's satire *Put Out More Flags* (1942), is one of muddle-headed amateurism and bureaucratic incompetence. In passing judgement on the MoI's Films Division in June 1940, for example, Basil Wright was dismissive in the extreme: 'A few sporadic and often ill-chosen films, a great deal of muddle and inefficiency, and a total lack of imagination have been its own contribution to the war effort.'[6] Latterly, however, the reputation of the MoI has been subject to a long-overdue rehabilitation. Indeed, the feature film director Michael Powell was even prompted to remark in his memoirs that 'The Ministry of Information was a great success, and its Films Division was one of its triumphs'.[7] The work of historians such as Ian McLaine

(*note 5 continued*) The Arts Enquiry had been set up in 1941, staffed initially by the Arts Department at Dartington Hall, and was linked with both the Nuffield College Social Reconstruction Survey and Political and Economic Planning (PEP), with which it shared offices in London. Four reports were sponsored, on the visual arts, the factual film, music and theatre, in order

> to give some account of the place of these arts in our national life, their economic and administrative background, their social importance and their value in general education. Many aspects of English life came under review during the war, and the Trustees felt it to be important that these arts should be considered as having a recognised place in national life.

The Factual Film was the work of a number of prominent documentarists, and thus reflected their views on realism and the importance of the documentary school of film-making.

6. *Spectator*, 21 June 1940, p. 837.
7. M. Powell, *A Life in Movies: An Autobiography* (London, Methuen edn, 1987), p. 383.

on the MoI, and of Anthony Aldgate and Jeffrey Richards on its relationship with the cinema, has also suggested that the Ministry was very far from being the lame duck that has so often been supposed.[8] The MoI not only guided the film industry on matters of propaganda, but, as this essay will show, was to be instrumental in facilitating the 'wartime wedding' between feature films and documentary.

I

For all that the Second World War has been seen as a 'golden age' for British films, the outbreak of war on 3 September 1939 did not augur well for the cinema. One of the first acts of the government was to close all places of public entertainment, including music halls and theatres as well as cinemas, fearing that they were potential death traps in the event of the air raid, which were widely expected upon the outbreak of war. The carnage which air raids might cause had been vividly brought to the screen in 1936 by Alexander Korda's film *Things to Come*, which had included a sequence where the city centre of 'Everytown' (bearing a marked resemblance to Piccadilly Circus) was destroyed by aerial bombardment – in one shot a cinema sustains a direct hit.

The closure of cinemas was a sensible precautionary move until the danger posed by air raids could be gauged. When those raids failed to materialize immediately, however, discontent at the closure soon became rife within the film industry. The cinema exhibitors, who were those immediately affected, were soon lobbying vociferously for the reopening of the cinemas. The trade paper *Kinematograph Weekly* took up the cause in its first wartime editorial, which put forward two arguments why the cinemas should be reopened at once. The first argument (and the less convincing of the two) was that the closure of public places of entertainment meant the only communal places left for people to gather were the pubs, which would be detrimental to public order and sobriety:

8. I. McLaine, *Ministry of Morale: Home Front Morale and the Ministry of Information in World War II* (London, George Allen & Unwin, 1979); A. Aldgate and J. Richards, *Britain Can Take It: The British Cinema in the Second World War* (Edinburgh, Edinburgh UP, 1994, 2nd edn).

If intoxication is becoming a public scandal, if public-houses have sold out of beer by 8 p.m. just because the people will insist upon being with a crowd of their fellows and there is nowhere else to go, then the time for re-opening the kinemas – and the theatres, and the music-halls – has become an urgent public necessity,

The second argument which it advanced was based on the principle that the cinema was a valuable provider of entertainment. With the outbreak of war, people's need for escapism would be greater than ever, and the trade's duty, therefore, was 'to present in pleasant, harmless form a relief from the very ugly world in which we are living today. Can one think of a safer anodyne to the disturbed public mind than the screen play?' In putting forward this argument, it must be remembered that the exhibitors had their own commercial interests to consider insofar as their immediate livelihood depended on the cinemas being reopened. The editorial, however, argued that the foremost concern of the exhibitors was not their own businesses, but, rather self-importantly, that 'we seriously appreciate our position as public servants', and, furthermore, that 'to help maintaining the mental balance of the community is no unworthy job of work'.[9] In this respect, the editorial was the first statement of what was to become a familiar argument from the cinema trade during the war, namely that it had a vital role to play as a provider of entertainment for the public.

The closure of the cinemas has bred a plethora of myths and misconceptions about the history of wartime cinema. The testimony of film-makers such as Thorold Dickinson suggested that the government intended to shut down the film industry. 'I went to the Ministry of Information,' Dickinson later recalled, 'and saw Sir Joseph Ball who was in charge of the Films division and discussed the position of the film industry with him. "You have nothing to worry about at all," he said, "because we are closing down all cinemas and so there will be no film industry".' [10] Such testimony must be treated with caution. While the film industry did send numerous delegations to lobby for the reopening of the cinemas, it is highly unlikely that they would have found Sir Joseph Ball, the first Director of the MoI's Films Division, unsympathetic to their cause. Ball, the former Director of the Conservative Party Research Department and Deputy

9. 'Reopen the Kinemas', *Kinematograph Weekly*, 7 September 1939, p. 2.
10. Quoted in R. J. Minney, *Puffin Asquith* (London, Leslie Frewin, 1973).

Director of the National Publicity Bureau, had been chosen to head
the Films Division because during the 1930s he had established good
relations with the 'leaders' of the British film industry, by which he
meant the commercial feature-film producers and the newsreel companies.[11] According to official documentation, Ball had hosted a
luncheon for a number of key trade figures shortly before the outbreak
of war, at which he 'informed all present that it was my desire and
intention to utilise to the full the enormous resources of the industry
itself, [and] to devote myself to securing the widest possible publicity
for our case on the screens throughout the world'. The result of the
meeting was the setting-up of a Trade Advisory Committee, which
Ball met once more after the outbreak of war 'for the purpose of
helping them to formulate and present their case for the re-opening
of the cinemas'.[12] Far from Dickinson's assertion that Ball had informed him the film industry would be closed down, it is clear that
Ball was very much in favour of using the screen to project images
of Britain, and, moreover, that he was on the side of the trade in
wanting to see the cinemas reopened as quickly as possible. The
MoI, in fact, contrary to the opinions of many commentators, was
aware from the outset of the value of film as a medium of both
entertainment and propaganda. A policy statement of November
1939, for example, declared:

> The Ministry is fully alive to [the] importance of films, both from
> [the] point of view of providing a valuable and popular form of
> entertainment and diversion, and as a medium for presenting our
> national case, not only at home, but throughout the world in a form
> to which the peoples of all countries are thoroughly accoustomed.
>
> Minister [is] therefore of opinion that the Films Division of the Min-
> istry has an important contribution to make to our national war effort.
>
> Plans for carrying out this function have already been made, and
> much preliminary work has already been done in connection with
> them; and he is satisfied that the plans themselves have been well
> conceived, and that the steps already taken have been in the right
> direction.[13]

11. See T. J. Hollins, 'The conservative party and film propaganda between the
    wars', *English Historical Review*, 96:379 (1981), pp. 359–69.
12. PRO INF 1/194, memo from Sir Joseph Ball to Lord Macmillan, 10 October
    1939.
13. Ibid., memo entitled 'Note on Policy of Ministry of Information With Regard
    to Films', 3 October 1939.

The MoI clearly intended that it would make use of film in some official capacity, even if its role was as yet only quite vaguely defined.

It has generally been held that it was due to Ball that the documentary film-makers were at first excluded from the official propaganda machinery. 'The documentary people, all of us, were left in the wilderness,' Edgar Anstey recalled. 'We weren't used because the Chamberlain government was very much opposed to everything we stood for, and they had their own film people, who moved into the Ministry of Information and were powerful in other quarters.'[14] The view of a deliberate policy of exclusion was endorsed by the Arts Enquiry: 'During this early period little use was made of the documentary group, even though the Government had its own Film Unit, the GPO Unit; the pre-war part played by the documentary film in the public service was completely ignored.'[15] In fact, as official documentation once again proves, Ball was well aware of the documentary movement and what it might offer. 'We can, in addition, finance or help to finance some of the best British documentary film producers for the production of short documentary films approved by us,' he said, only three weeks after the outbreak of war.[16] The reservations which the Chamberlain government had about making use of documentary were not wholly political, as the documentarists themselves believed, but also practical. Documentary, it was believed, was less useful for propaganda purposes than the feature film. This view was argued forcefully by no less a figure than the Foreign Secretary Lord Halifax:

> Documentaries are all very well in their own way, but they appeal at best to a public that can be counted in tens of thousands. But a big film is a dead loss unless it is seen by a rock bottom minimum of sixty million people, and success consists of being seen by a minimum of something nearer two hundred million people. Moreover, the real effect of films only comes by getting at the emotions. Documentaries of course can never do that.[17]

Halifax's comments provide further evidence of an awareness of film within the government, showing that some ministers at

14. Quoted in Sussex, *The Rise and Fall of British Documentary*, p. 119.
15. *The Factual Film*, pp. 63–4.
16. PRO INF 1/194, memo entitled 'Ministry of Information – Films Division: General Plan of Operations', 25 September 1939.
17. PRO FO 371/22839, memo by Lord Halifax, 21 October 1939.

least were alive to the potential of the medium as an instrument of propaganda.

In the event, the fears of the film trade that the government intended to keep the cinemas closed permanently were quickly shown to be misplaced. Cinemas in 'neutral and reception areas' were open again within a week of the outbreak of war, those in provincial towns and cities followed a week later, and by the beginning of October the West End of London had also followed suit. They were to remain open for the rest of the war, even at the height of the Blitz. There is even some anecdotal evidence to suggest that cinema-goers were none too worried about the dangers posed by air raids. 'Rather stupidly,' recalled Leslie Halliwell, then a young film fan growing up in Bolton, 'its audiences instinctively believed in the absolute impregnability of the Odeon, and in any case it was unthinkable to exchange the delights of Deanna Durbin or Donald Duck for the miseries of a communal shelter'.[18]

Cinema attendances during the war confirm the trade press's opinion that people would want more than ever to go to the cinema. Already, during the inter-war years, 'going to the pictures' had established itself as, in A. J. P. Taylor's phrase, 'the essential social habit of the age'.[19] Average weekly cinema attendance increased during the war, from an estimated 19 million in 1939 to a peak of 30 million in 1945. Moreover, this increase took place despite a rise in seat prices due to the new Entertainment Tax. Mass-Observation, which conducted an audience questionnaire in August 1940, two months before the first rise came into effect, found that 69 per cent of London cinema-goers thought their cinema-going routine would not be affected. It concluded that 'the cinema habit is deep rooted and is not easily affected'.[20] It should be considered, of course, that wartime austerity and rationing meant that there was a scarcity of consumer goods on which people could spend their disposable income, and so the cinema benefited to some extent from the absence of many other easily available forms of leisure. Nevertheless, there

18. L. Halliwell, *Seats in All Parts: Half A Lifetime at the Movies* (London, Granada, 1985), p. 86.
19. A. J. P. Taylor, *English History 1914–1945* (Oxford, Clarendon Press, 1965), p. 313.
20. M-O File Report 445, 'Film Questionnaire', by Len England, 8 October 1940, *The Tom Harrisson-Mass Observation Archive* (London, Harvester Press micro-fiche, 1983).

is no question that the cinema did provide an outlet for escapism
and relief from the everyday tensions of war. Exhibitors remarked
time and again that what their patrons wanted were light entertainment films, especially comedies. 'People want something that will
take them out of themselves and help them to overcome the depression of the black-out,' observed one Councillor H. F. Wren, a
delegate of the Bristol and West England branch of the Cinemato-
graph Exhibitors' Association. 'They do not want heavy drama –
they have all the drama they need in the news these days.'[21]

The most comprehensive investigation of wartime cinema audiences was conducted by the Wartime Social Survey in 1943. In brief,
it found that 70 per cent of adults said they sometimes went to the
cinema and that 32 per cent of the population as a whole went at
least once a week. This is a remarkably high figure which deserves
emphasis: the fact that a third of the population visited the cinema
on a regular basis is eloquent testimony to its popular appeal. When
demographically broken down, it was found that young adults and
children went to the cinema more than older people, that the working
classes went more than the middle classes, that people in urban areas
went more than those in rural areas, and that people in the Midlands,
North of England and Scotland went more than people in the South.
The overall social composition of the cinema audience was more or
less the same as it had been in the 1930s, suggesting a large degree
of continuity in who went to the pictures from before the war. It
would seem, therefore, that the wartime increase in cinema attendances was due not to more people going to the cinema than before,
but to the same people going more often. Furthermore, the Wartime
Social Survey also found that cinema-going was a more ingrained
habit for a wide section of the population, and that a significant
number of people, particularly among the working classes, relied on
the cinema newsreels for their diet of news and information. The
survey concluded that 'the larger groups of the population are relatively better represented in the cinema audience than they are in
the publics reached by other visual publicity media such as newspapers
and books'.[22] Thus it was that the cinema had an essential role to
perform in providing both entertainment and information for the
British public.

21. 'Open Forum', *Daily Film Renter*, 1 January 1940.
22. Quoted in J. P. Mayer, *British Cinemas and their Audiences* (London, Dennis
    Dobson, 1948), p. 275.

II

Within the British film industry there were two very different points of view on how the cinema could best fulfil its propagandist role. On the one hand the commercial trade interests saw propaganda as, at best, an adjunct to the entertainment value of films, which had to be preserved if audiences were to be satisfied. The trade's position was outlined by one journalist as early as September 1939:

> Which brings me to that difficult and much-abused word 'propaganda'. We must be preserved from the bland jingoism that still prevails in some official circles, but which does not correspond to to-day's national temper in the least. Nor do we want dreary documentaries of what the Ministry of Information sees fit to allow about the fighting Services.
>
> If the history of screen propaganda tells us anything at all, it tells us that the less blatant it is, the more effective the result. The one guide, of course, is that of genuine entertainment, in which almost anything can be put over.[23]

This position was to be held by the trade throughout the war. For example, the naval melodrama *Convoy* – the most successful British film of 1940 – was the sort of film which the trade press cited as fulfilling the dual criteria of entertainment and propaganda. 'The film is a worthy tribute to the Senior Service and, at the same time, grand popular entertainment,' declared *Kinematograph Weekly*. 'Put another way, patriotism with colossal box-office punch.'[24]

This view was not shared by the journal *Documentary News Letter*, organ of the documentary movement. It argued that the distinction between entertainment and propaganda value made by the trade press was artificial, and it criticized the nature of many feature films in which an over-obvious propaganda message had been tagged on virtually as an afterthought to a conventional narrative:

> To begin with there still exists a tendency to believe that entertainment value and propaganda value must be two separate considerations. Without entertainment value a film will be a commercial failure and therefore the mistake has often been made of arranging for the

23. P. L. Mannock, 'Our Production in War Time', *Kinematograph Weekly*, 28 September 1939, p. 19.
24. *Kinematograph Weekly*, 13 June 1940, p. 2.

entertainment value first and then trying to add such propaganda emphases as will not impair the entertainment. On this line of reasoning we generally end up with an old-fashioned thriller incorporating odd irrelevant lines of dialogue about freedom, persecution, fascism; or one of the characters will hold up the action while he makes a wordy and self-conscious speech about democracy ... .

The obvious weakness of this type of film is the clear division between what is regarded by its producers as entertainment and what has been added as propaganda. The audience is over-aware of the distinction. They see a conventional film made according to a familiar story-formula and either they immediately recognise the propaganda for what it is or they are suspicious of the pill which has been so imperfectly sugared.[25]

Films such as Ealing's Fleet Air Arm melodrama *Ships With Wings* (1941) and Leslie Howard's updated reworking of the 'Scarlet Pimpernel' story in *Pimpernel Smith* (1941) were dismissed because 'the war background of realism and fact is subsidiary to a personal story of romantic adventure'.

Quite clearly, then, the commercial trade and the documentary movement held very different views about propaganda. Given their opposing views, the notion of a 'wartime wedding' seems, on the face of it at least, rather unlikely. Yet the wedding did take place, and on several levels. In the first instance there was a crossover of personnel between the feature and documentary sectors. For example, Alberto Cavalcanti, the Brazilian who had been Supervising Producer of the GPO Film Unit since 1938, left to join Ealing Studios in 1940, and was followed later in the war by documentary director Harry Watt.[26] Some feature film makers, such as the twin brothers John and Roy Boulting, went the other way by joining the film units of the armed services, where they contributed to some of the celebrated official documentaries of the war. John joined the RAF Film Production Unit, for which he directed the training film *Journey Together* (1944) – one of the key films cited by John Shearman when he coined the phrase 'wartime wedding' – while Roy joined the Army Film and Photographic Unit, where he worked on actuality documentaries such as *Desert Victory* (1943) and *Burma Victory* (1945).

25. 'Feature Film Propaganda', *Documentary News Letter*, 3:5 (May 1942), p. 67.
26. See C. Barr, *Ealing Studios* (London, Studio Vista, 1993, 2nd edn) for a useful interpretative history of Ealing's wartime films, and the contribution made thereto by Cavalcanti and Watt.

The most significant manifestation of the 'wartime wedding', how-ever, occurred in the terms of official MoI policy. This was first evident in a Programme for Film Propaganda drawn up in January 1940 by Sir Kenneth Clark, Ball's successor as Director of the Films Division. The appointment of Clark, formerly the Director of the National Gallery, had been welcomed by *Documentary News Letter*, which believed that 'he will take immediate steps to end the inertia which has till now more or less immobilised the personnel of (among other branches of cinema) documentary'.[27] His Programme for Film Propaganda marked the first attempt to define schematically the place of both feature films and documentaries in official propaganda. It adopted the three main themes of British propaganda suggested by the first minister, Lord Macmillan – 'What Britain is fighting for', 'How Britain fights' and 'The need for sacrifices if the fight is to be won' – and suggested how these general principles could be adapted 'to the concrete, dramatic and popular medium of the films'.[28] The Programme suggested that the different modes of film practice could be matched to different propaganda objectives. Feature films were particularly well suited to the dramatization of 'What Britain is fighting for':

> *British ideas and institutions.* Ideals such as freedom, and institutions such as parliamentary government can be made the main subject of a drama or treated historically. It might be possible to do a great film on the history of British Liberty and its repercussions in the world (Holland in the 17th, France in the 18th centuries).

The suggested use of historical parallels to dramatize Britain's demo-cratic heritage prefigured a number of major feature films, including Carol Reed's *The Young Mr Pitt* (1942) and Laurence Olivier's *Henry V* (1944), both made with considerable official support. Documentary, by contrast, was better suited to the presentation of 'How Britain fights':

> *Documentaries.* A long series should be taken to show this country, France and the neutrals the extent of our war effort. There should be, in the first place, full and carefully worked out films of each of the fighting services; then shorter films of all the immediately sub-sidiary services, i.e. merchant navy, munitions, shipbuilding, coastal

27. *Documentary News Letter*, **1** (January 1940), p. 4.
28. PRO INF 1/867, Co-Ordinating Committee Paper No. 1, 'Programme for Film Propaganda', 29 January 1940.

command, fishermen, etc. Most of these subjects are susceptible of detailed treatment from different angles, e.g. one-reel films on the Bren Gun, the training of an anti-aircraft gunner, etc. The change from peace to war time conditions should be shown in a whole series drawn from every department of State.

Again, the Programme anticipated the wide range of documentaries made about all aspects of the British war effort. The Crown Film Unit (as the GPO Film Unit became at the end of 1940) came to specialize in feature-length narrative documentaries about different branches of the services, such as *Target for Tonight* (1941), *Coastal Command* (1942), *Close Quarters* (1943) and *Western Approaches* (1944). The smaller, independent documentary companies, for their part, tended to make short films about the home front, many of them specialized educational films distributed through the MoI's non-theatrical scheme.

In the event Sir Kenneth Clark, like his predecessor, stayed only a few months at the Films Division, but the general principles of his Programme for Film Propaganda were to provide the basis of much official film policy. The third and final Director of the Films Division was Jack Beddington, formerly the Assistant General Manager and Director of Publicity for the petroleum company Shell Mex. Significantly, Beddington was acquainted with the documentary movement through the work of the Shell Film Unit, which had acquired a favourable reputation during the 1930s for its educational films. In the histories of wartime cinema written by former documentarists, Beddington is credited with having ended the exclusion of documentary from the official propaganda machinery. 'Jack Beddington, that admirable man, when he was the director of the films division of the Ministry of Information, had the idea of bringing together what he called the ideas committee,' Paul Rotha said. 'This consisted of a number of writers and directors from feature films and a number of directors and others from documentary, who met round a table over beer and rather lousy sandwiches, once every fortnight.'[29] The Ideas Committee, set up at the end of 1941, became, in the words of film historians Porter and Litewski, 'the fount of feature film production ideology'.[30] Beddington not only demon-

---

29. Quoted in Sussex, *The Rise and Fall of British Documentary*, p. 140.
30. V. Porter and C. Litewski, 'The Way Ahead: Case History of a Propaganda Film', *Sight and Sound*, 50:2 (Spring 1981), p. 110.

strated his willingness to work with both the commercial trade and the documentarists, but he also actively encouraged the cross-fertilization between the two. To quote Rotha once again: 'The Ministry of Information Films Division, under Mr Jack Beddington, must be given credit for intermixing the documentary and studio film techniques, as well as interchanging their respective exponents.'[31]

In particular, Beddington used his influence to persuade commercial producers to move away from the overtly patriotic and melodramatic type of war films which typified the early years of the war and to concentrate instead on less sensational and more realistic stories. In March 1943 he issued a policy statement to the trade through the channel of the British Film Producers' Association, declaring that what the MoI wanted were 'first class war subjects realistically treated; realistic films of everyday life; high quality entertainment films', while what it did not want were 'war subjects exploited for mere cheap sensationalism; the morbid and the maudlin; entertainment stories which are stereotyped or hackneyed and unlikely because of their theme or general character to reflect well upon this country at home and abroad'.[32] In this respect official policy reflected a trend which was already evident across British cinema as a whole, a trend which is best exemplified by the production policy of Ealing Studios, which abandoned the melodramatic heroics of *Ships With Wings* for the sober realism of films like *The Foreman Went to France* (1942), *Nine Men* (1943) and *San Demetrio, London* (1943).

Ealing's production policy, according to studio head Michael Balcon, was 'first and foremost, to make a good film, a film that people would want to see, and at the same time to carry a message, or an example, which would be good propaganda for morale and the war effort'.[33] Balcon believed that there was a balance to be struck between the fictional and documentary elements of war films. He explained his outlook in a lecture which he gave to the Workers' Film Association at Brighton in 1943:

31. P. Rotha, with R. Griffith, *The Film Till Now: A Survey of World Cinema* (London, Vision Press, 1949 edn), p. 314.
32. 'Feature Films – MOI Policy', minutes of the British Film Producers' Association, 23 March 1943.
33. M. Balcon, *Michael Balcon Presents ... A Lifetime of Films* (London, Hutchinson, 1969), p. 148.

The balance between the strictly documentary and the story elements in this new type of film is still the most difficult thing to achieve. In our studios the first effort in that direction was [Pen] Tennyson's last film, *Convoy*. The subject was, as the title implies, a documentary one. Cameramen were sent out with convoys and much authentic material was obtained and, what is more strange, actually used in the film. I was very happy about *Convoy* at the time, as indeed I had every reason to be. It had a great success, both as regards prestige and returns, and was even referred to in the House of Commons as fine propaganda for the Navy. Looking back at it in the light of further experience in this new type of film I should say that the balance went a little too much in favour of the story at the expense of realism. I was very much happier with the result obtained in more recent of our films, such as *The Foreman Went to France*, *Next of Kin* and *Nine Men*. It is not difficult to see why, in two of these films, *The Foreman Went to France* and *Nine Men*, we struck a more satisfactory balance. By this time two of the leading makers of documentary films, Cavalcanti and Harry Watt, had joined us at Ealing Studios, and both these films make an admirable illustration of the alliance between the two schools.[34]

Balcon therefore attributed the new-found realism of Ealing's feature films to the influence of documentary personnel (Cavalcanti was associate producer of *The Foreman Went to France*; Watt directed *Nine Men*). The film which, in Balcon's view, best exemplified the new maturity and realism of the feature film was *San Demetrio, London*, based on the true story of the petrol tanker set on fire by a German pocket battleship in the middle of the Atlantic but successfully brought into port by some of her crew. *San Demetrio, London* is now generally regarded as the quintessential Ealing war film – Charles Barr, for example, describes it as 'the culmination of Ealing's war programme, the ideal fulfilment of Balcon's policy'[35] – but although it was very well received by the critics it was less successful at the box-office than the earlier, more flamboyantly heroic naval dramas such as *Convoy* and *Ships With Wings*. By the time it was released, at the very end of 1943, the public's appetite for films directly about the war was on the wane.

34. M. Balcon, *Realism or Tinsel* (Brighton, Workers' Film Association, 1944), pp. 10–11.
35. Barr, *Ealing Studios*, p. 35.

III

By the middle of the war the cross-fertilization between feature films and documentary had become evident. Roger Manvell later identified 1942 as the year when 'the "war story" with a patriotic slant began to give way to the "war documentary", which derived the action and to a greater extent the characterization from real events and real people'.[36] This trend was also noticed by critics at the time. In reviewing *We Dive at Dawn* (1943), for example, *The Times* opined that 'the best British films have been those which have not concerned themselves with the Gestapo and improbable adventures in occupied countries but have blended the discipline of the documentary with a minimum amount of the story-teller's licence and have gone about the work of showing how normal men react to the normal strains and stresses of war'.[37]

By 1943 another trend can be identified in the subjects of British films. There was a marked shift away from films about the armed services and a greater emphasis instead on the home front. Few films in the early years of the war had focused exclusively on the home front, and those which did tended to be comedies. Some war films, such as Noël Coward's naval drama *In Which We Serve* (1942), had included scenes featuring the domestic lives of its leading characters, but the narrative emphasis was still very much on men at war. By 1943, however, there were signs that the popularity of war films was in decline, and of interest shifting to the home front, where the effects of social change brought about by the war had started to become apparent. The cinema played its part in reflecting and negotiating this process of change in British society. The remainder of this essay will focus on three films released in 1943 – *The Demi-Paradise, Fires Were Started* and *Millions Like Us* – which all illustrated, albeit in different ways, the effects of 'the people's war' on British society. Furthermore, these three particular films all received some degree of official support, thus illustrating how their propaganda themes accorded with official policy.

The Demi-Paradise was produced by the Russian-born émigré Anatole de Grunwald and directed by Anthony Asquith. According to

36. R. Manvell, *Films and the Second World War* (London, J. M. Dent & Sons, 1974), p. 101.
37. *The Times*, 20 May 1943, p. 6.

Figure 3 *The Demi-Paradise* (BFI Stills, Posters and Designs/the Rank
Organisation)

its star Laurence Olivier, the film was instigated by Jack Beddington,
who

> asked me to undertake two pictures intended to enhance the British
> cause. One was *The Demi-Paradise*, whose object was to win the
> British public over to the idea of liking the Russians; hardly an
> insurmountable task, you would have thought, since Russia had now
> come into the war on our side.[38]

The other film, of course, was to be *Henry V*. The fact that Olivier
was released from his wartime service in the Fleet Air Arm to star
in *The Demi-Paradise* is indication of official support for the project,
as, earlier, his release to star in another film, *The Life and Death of
Colonel Blimp* (1943), had been refused because it was a project of
which the MoI disapproved.[39]

38. L. Olivier, *Confessions of an Actor* (London, Sceptre edn, 1987), p. 130.
39. See J. Chapman, 'The Life and Death of Colonel Blimp (1943) Reconsidered',
    Historical Journal of Film, Radio and Television, **15**:1 (March 1995), pp. 19–54.

In *The Demi-Paradise* Olivier plays Ivan Kutznetsoff, a Russian engineer who visits the English town of 'Barchester' before the outbreak of war, to negotiate the building of an icebreaker for which he has designed a new type of propeller. To the bemused Ivan, the English seem distant, old-fashioned and eccentric, more concerned with the cricket scores than with news of the worsening international situation. Although he secures the contract for the ship to be built, he returns home disillusioned after a failed romance with Ann Tisdall (Penelope Dudley Ward), granddaughter of the shipyard owner. Ivan returns to England during the Blitz in 1940 and is surprised to find that, far from being on the point of collapse as he had assumed, the English are carrying on in their own way. Then, when Hitler invades the Soviet Union, Ivan is astonished at the sympathy which is extended towards him, with the town using its annual pageant to raise money for his home town in Russia. The shipyard workers demonstrate their solidarity with their Russian ally by working around the clock to complete the icebreaker on schedule, despite the yard having been blitzed. The ship is launched as *Drushka* ('Friendship'), and Ivan realizes that he has come to regard the English as 'a grand, a great people'.

As Jeffrey Richards observes, *The Demi-Paradise* 'emerges far more as a celebration of England and Englishness than it is of Russia'.[40] The film cannot in any sense be described as 'realist': in the later tradition of Ealing comedy, it is quaint, whimsical and absurd. The fictional town of Barchester, which symbolizes England (not Britain), is populated by caricatures and eccentrics, such as the millionaire shipbuilder Tisdall (Felix Aylmer), whose hobby is quoting Bradshaw's railway timetable, and the spinsterish Miss Rowena Ventnor (Margaret Rutherford), who presides imperiously over the annual pageant. The narrative focus is very much on the upper middle classes: the Tisdalls, for all their democratic nature, are clearly very privileged, living in a large house with servants, their main concession to social change being to provide a home for evacuees. Moreover, the film presents an idealized image of class relations: as an employer Tisdall is generous and considerate, while the shipyard workers are hard-working and properly deferent. There is no suggestion of the

---

40. J. Richards, 'National Identity in British Wartime Films', in *Britain and the Cinema in the Second World War*, ed. P. M. Taylor (London, Macmillan, 1988), p. 50.

bitter resentment which many shipyard workers felt towards the government due to their unemployment in the 1930s and the fear which they had for their jobs after the war was over – a mood expressed in documentaries such as *Tyneside Story* (1944) and in John Baxter's feature *The Shipbuilders* (1943), but absent from the more romantic and sentimental world of *The Demi-Paradise*.

The critics were divided. Richard Winnington of the *News Chronicle* complained that 'it is really a backhanded way of showing us poor juvenile-minded cinemagoers that the England of Mrs Miniver and Mr Punch lives forever'.[41] But William Whitebait of *The New Statesman* clearly admired its whimsy, describing it as 'the nearest thing yet to [an] English René Clair' and 'amusing enough to beguile all but the very pious'.[42] For all the film's rose-tinted and unrealistic picture of English society, it does nevertheless stress those characteristics of tolerance, humour, tradition and sense of duty which many commentators have seen as defining national identity. There is a marked similarity between the England of *The Demi-Paradise* and the England described by George Orwell:

> England is the most class-ridden country under the sun. It is a land of snobbery and privilege, ruled largely by the old and silly. But in any calculation about it one has got to take into account its emotional unity, the tendency of nearly all its inhabitants to feel alike and act together in moments of supreme crisis ... .
>
> England is not the jewelled isle of Shakespeare's much-quoted message, nor is it the inferno depicted by Dr Goebbels. More than either it resembles a family, a rather stuffy Victorian family, with not many black sheep in it but with all its cupboards bursting with skeletons. It has rich relations who have to be kow-towed to and poor relations who are horribly sat upon, and there is a deep con-spiracy of silence about the source of the family income ... . Still, it is a family. It has its private language and its common memories, and at the approach of an enemy it closes its ranks.[43]

41. R. Winnington, *Drawn and Quartered: A Selection of Weekly Film Reviews and Drawings* (London, The Saturn Press, 1948), p. 14. The review originally appeared in the *News Chronicle*, 20 November 1943.
42. *The New Statesman and Nation*, 27 November 1943. (This review, and others which follow, are taken from the newspaper clippings on microfiche collections on individual films held by the British Film Institute Library; these do not usually provide page numbers.)
43. G. Orwell, *The Lion and the Unicorn: Socialism and the English Genius* (1941; Harmondsworth, Penguin edn, 1981), pp. 53–4.

In *The Demi-Paradise* (the title is a reference to Shakespeare's *Richard II*) the town of Barchester is akin to the family which Orwell describes. It, too, is rather stuffy, and the millionaire Tisdall is almost apologetic about his wealth, but when the war comes the people close ranks. For all the differences in wealth and social status, the film suggests that there is an overriding sense of national unity based on a common heritage.

Fires Were Started, by contrast, is very different in style and content. It was an official documentary film, produced for the MoI by the Crown Film Unit, which dramatized a day and night in the work of the Auxiliary Fire Service in the East End of London during the Blitz. It was one of the series of feature-length narrative documentaries made by Crown, which were themselves yet another manifestation of the 'wartime wedding' in that they were reconstructed in a film studio using scripted dialogue but were enacted by 'real' people rather than by professional actors. The Crown features all shared certain characteristics: their narratives were spare to the point of austerity, and, true to their documentary roots, they eschewed romantic subplots and focused instead on servicemen performing their day-to-day jobs. *Fires Were Started*, however, was the only one of the Crown features to focus on the home front. It was directed by Humphrey Jennings, the intellectual socialist aesthete once described by Lindsay Anderson as 'the only real poet the British cinema has yet produced'.[44] Jennings had made a number of short documentaries for the MoI, including *Heart of Britain* (1941), *Words for Battle* (1941) and *Listen to Britain* (1942), but *Fires Were Started* was to be his only feature-length film. Jennings's interests and sympathies lay with the working classes, and it is evident that he was concerned with portraying ordinary people in an authentic and unpatronizing light. 'It has now become 14 hours a day – living in Stepney the whole time – really have never worked so hard at anything or I think thrown myself into anything so completely,' he wrote to his wife during the shooting of the film. 'Whatever the results it is definitely an advance in film-making for me – really beginning to understand people and making friends with them and

---

44. L. Anderson, 'Only Connect: Some Aspects of the Work of Humphrey Jennings', in *Humphrey Jennings: Film-Maker, Painter, Poet*, ed. M. L. Jennings (London, British Film Institute, 1982), p. 53. Anderson's essay originally appeared in *Sight and Sound* in 1954.

Figure 4   *Fires Were Started* (BFI Stills, Posters and Designs/Crown copyright)

not just looking at them and lecturing or pitying them. Another general effect of the war.' [45]

The narrative of *Fires Were Started* focuses on the working classes. Apart from a new middle-class recruit, Barrett, the men are all working-class, and the first half of the film locates them in their social context, drinking beer and playing darts. The key scene is the celebrated 'One Man Went to Mow' sequence as the men, having changed into their uniforms, gather around the piano. Not only is this the means by which the new recruit is assimilated into the group (Barrett, playing the piano, is placed in the centre of the frame), but it establishes both the idea of the firemen as a team (they are all singing the same song) while at the same time asserting their individuality (for each member of the team there is a slightly different variation of the tune). After the leisurely first half-hour, the tempo of the film increases as the men are sent to fight a fire in the London docks. An ammunition ship is threatened by the fire, and, although

45. Quoted in Jennings, *Humphrey Jennings*, p. 31.

it is saved, one of the firemen, Jacko, dies while helping one of his colleagues to safety. In this respect the film played thorough one of the key themes of British propaganda, namely the recognition that sacrifices would have to be made if the war was to be won. The film ends with a sequence in which Jacko's funeral is intercut with shots of the ship sailing up the Thames, a bravura example of associative montage which clearly implies that Jacko's sacrifice has not been in vain.

Remarkably for a film which now seems so perfectly measured in pace and poetic in treatment, the production history of *Fires Were Started* was not without problems. The film was completed by October 1942, but its release was delayed because it met with resistance from distributors who 'criticised the picture severely as entertainment and as propaganda'.[46] The main complaint was that it was too slow and took too long to build up to the dramatic climax of the fire itself. Beddington agreed with this verdict, informing producer Ian Dalrymple that in his view 'the film can be very much improved from both a propaganda and an entertainment point of view'.[47] The Crown Film Unit, for its part, was stung by these criticisms, and in support of the film enlisted the influential critic C. A. Lejeune, who was shown a rough cut and, in a private letter to Beddington, declared:

> In my opinion, this is a film on which a stand should be made. It should be shown quickly, it should be shown widely, and it should be shown in its present form. ... I think it is one of the finest documentaries we have ever made. I am quite sure it will bring prestige to the unit and to British films generally. I can guarantee that what I call 'my' public will like it, and I have enough faith in the good heart of the wider public to believe that they will like it too. I have never yet known a film as honest and human as this one fail to get its message through. If it were my film, I should be very proud of it.[48]

In the event, a compromise was reached whereby the film was cut, though not to the extent originally demanded by the distributors. The original, longer version of the film was shown through the MoI's non-theatrical programme, under the title *I Was A Fireman*.

---

46. PRO INF 1/212, memo from Colonel A. C. Bromhead to Jack Beddington, 27 November 1942.
47. PRO INF 1/212, letter from Jack Beddington to Ian Dalrymple, 26 November 1942.
48. PRO INF 6/985, letter from C. A. Lejeune to Jack Beddington, n.d.

Figure 5 *Millions Like Us* (BFI Stills, Posters and Designs/the Rank
Organisation)

The critical reception of *Fires Were Started* for the most part bore
out Lejeune's verdict. *Documentary News Letter*, for example,
admired its human qualities, opining that it was 'the best handling
of people on and off the job that we've seen in any British
film'.[49] The view of the critics that the film gave a realistic picture
of the Blitz was echoed by several of the respondents to a Mass-
Observation survey of favourite films. 'Having lived through the
London blitz we naturally enjoyed this film', one man remarked.
'We were impressed with the way things were done and with the
lack of heroics.'[50] For some, therefore, the film was seen as much
as a record or document than as a propaganda film.

While *The Demi-Paradise* focused on the privileged world of the
upper-middle classes, and while *Fires Were Started* eulogized the

49. *Documentary News Letter*, 4:4 (April 1943), p. 200.
50. '1943 Directive Replies on Favourite Films', in *Mass-Observation at the Movies*,
    eds J. Richards and D. Sheridan (London, Routledge & Kegan Paul, 1987),
    p. 249.

heroism of the working classes, *Millions Like Us* was the film which gave the most complete picture of British society during the war in that it attempted to bring these two different worlds together. A commercial feature film, written and directed by Frank Launder and Sidney Gilliat for Gainsborough Pictures, *Millions Like Us* is widely regarded as one of the 'classics' of the war which can be placed within the 'wartime wedding' of feature and documentary. The project had, in fact, started out as a documentary. According to Launder, the MoI had suggested to them a film covering the entire war effort on the home front:

> With this object we toured the country, visiting docks, farms and coastal areas, and went to war factories and works all over Britain. We came to the conclusion that the best way to attract a wide public to a subject of this nature, which was what the Ministry wanted, was to cloak it in a simple fictional story.[51]

Gilliat took up the story thus:

> We were greatly impressed with the fate – if you like to call it that – of the conscripted woman, the mobile woman. And that's what we would have liked to call the thing if it hadn't been such a silly title! The MOI said they greatly liked the script, but it wasn't the extensive documentary they'd been wanting. However, they strongly recommended Gainsborough to make it with their blessing and co-operation. Ted Black [the producer] was happy to take it on.[52]

Gilliat's account of events is corroborated by official records, which show that the script for *Millions Like Us* 'was first commissioned by the Films Division and then sold at cost price to a feature production company'.[53] The film was therefore made as a commercial venture, but with the support of the MoI, which provided practical assistance, for example in facilitating location shooting at the Castle Bromwich aircraft factory near Birmingham.

Millions Like Us is an episodic narrative which follows, for the most part, the story of a young woman who is called up to work in an aircraft factory. Film historian Sue Harper has shown that it was made at a time when 'there was intense anxiety among women

---

51. Quoted in G. Brown, *Launder and Gilliat* (London, British Film Institute, 1977), p. 108.
52. Ibid.
53. PRO INF 1/947, report entitled 'Government Film Production and Distribution', 1946.

about conscripted labour'.[54] The main propaganda theme of the film is to address these anxieties, which it does by personalizing the general experience of millions of women workers into the story of Celia Crowson (Patricia Roc). When she is called for her interview at the Ministry of Labour and National Service, Celia has fantasies of a glamorous life in one of the women's services. She is horrified and near-hysterical at the thought of going to work in a factory. However, the interviewer tells her:

> There's nothing to be afraid of in a factory. Mr Bevin needs another million women, and I don't think we should disappoint him at a time like this. The men at the front need tanks, guns and planes. You can help your country just as much in an overall as you can in uniform these days.

Herein lies the main propaganda message of the film, incorporated into a fictional narrative and presented on a personal level. Celia is sent to a government hostel, where she meets women from a diverse range of social backgrounds: Gwen Price (Megs Jenkins), a working-class graduate of the University of Wales; Annie Earnshaw (Terry Randall), an eminently practical Lancashire girl; and Jennifer Knowles (Anne Crawford), a snobbish society girl. Upon completing their training, the women go to work in a factory making aircraft parts under the supervision of Charlie Forbes (Eric Portman), a bluff, no-nonsense Yorkshireman. The factory and hostel effectively become a surrogate family to Celia, who has left her own family home for the first time. Celia quickly takes to factory work, which she finds does not hold the terrors she had feared, but Jennifer's work is unsatisfactory and there is antagonism between her and Charlie. Gradually, however, the antagonism mellows into affection and a tentative romance. Celia also enjoys a romance with Fred Blake (Gordon Jackson), an air-gunner in the RAF. They get married, but Fred is killed shortly afterwards in a raid over Germany. The film ends with a scene in the factory canteen where the entertainer Bertha Wilmott leads the women in a communal song.

While the main theme of *Millions Like Us* was to allay women's fears about factory labour, there is also much in the film which illustrates in general terms the effects of war on British society. Evacuation, familial dislocation, the effects of rationing and austerity,

54. S. Harper, 'The Representation of Women in British Feature Films, 1939–45', in Taylor, *Britain and the Cinema in the Second World War*, p. 172.

and above all the suggestion of social levelling, are alluded to throughout. There are many incidental touches of humour, much of it provided by the characters of Charters and Caldicott (Basil Radford and Naunton Wayne), who appear in several brief asides unrelated to the main story. Charters and Caldicott, caricatures of English gentlemen, had been created by Launder and Gilliat for Alfred Hitchcock's *The Lady Vanishes* (1938), but had subsequently assumed a life of their own on both film and radio. They appear in *Millions Like Us* as officers in the Royal Engineers, and their scenes allude to the process of class levelling perceived to be under way, for example in finding their first-class train compartment overrun by evacuees. The metaphor is obvious but irresistible: the children (mostly scruffy urchins) enter the space previously designated 'first class', now an irrelevant distinction.

In other respects, however, the film addresses rather more fundamental questions about the nature of social change. It does this primarily through the romance which develops between Charlie and Jennifer. On one level their relationship represents the new social cohesion of wartime Britain, marking as it does the coming-together of working class and upper class, and of North and South. On another level, however, the film suggests that this might only be temporary, that the new-found unity might disintegrate once the war is over. This is illustrated through Charlie's reluctance to commit himself to marriage, telling Jennifer that:

> The world's roughly made up of two kinds of people. You're one sort and I'm the other. Oh, we're together now there's a war on, we need to be. But what's going to happen when it's all over? Shall we go on like this or are we going to slide back? That's what I want to know. I'm not marrying you, Jenny, till I'm sure.

Charlie therefore suggests that Britain was really two nations: on the one hand, the privileged classes represented by Jennifer, on the other hand, the working classes of which he is part. The war has brought them closer together, but Charlie voices a concern that when the war is over the need for social unity will be gone and the country will 'slide back' – by implication to the conditions of the 1930s, widely perceived during the war as a decade of bitter class division due to the depression and mass unemployment. In raising this question, the film exemplifies one of the most urgent concerns of the British people at the time: the nature of post-war society. People wanted some form of reassurance that the suffering and hardships endured during the war were going to be rewarded with a more just and egalitarian society when it was over. The film poses the question of what will happen after the war, but of course cannot answer it, so that Charlie and Jennifer's future together – and thus, by implication, the future of a more egalitarian Britain – is left hanging.[55]

Released towards the end of 1943, *Millions Like Us* was accorded a warm critical reception. The *Manchester Guardian*, for example, liked the realistic characterizations of the working classes, who were no longer merely the comic relief of pre-war films:

> Nothing more clearly marks the coming-of-age of the British cinema than its treatment of ordinary working people, especially as minor characters or in the mass. The clowns of ten years ago first became lay figures of sociological drama and then, with the war, patriotic heroes. In *Millions Like Us* they are real human beings, and the British film has reached adult maturity.[56]

And the *Monthly Film Bulletin* remarked favourably upon the 'realist atmosphere and a documentary touch to life in an aircraft factory'.[57] It was not only the critics who were moved by its realism, for the remarks of Mass-Observation's respondents suggest that audiences responded in the same way. '*Millions Like Us* I enjoyed because it was true to its title,' one woman remarked. 'These were real people, people one knew and liked, not film actors and actresses'.[58] And another respondent, a 25-year-old bombardier, said simply: 'Presents Britain and life as it is – we must have truth and integrity in our films.'[59]

55. Interestingly, the synopsis of the film given in Gainsborough's publicity material suggested that they will overcome their problems eventually: 'Charlie and Jennifer decide to postpone their wedding until they can adjust to the small differences that might, without care, smash their romance, but they both know that time will make such adjustments possible' (BFI microfiche for *Millions Like Us*). This is hardly the impression given by the film itself: the differences are far from small, and they do not know with any certainty what the future holds, as Charlie's words make clear.
56. *Manchester Guardian*, 28 December 1943.
57. *Monthly Film Bulletin*, **10**:120 (31 December 1943).
58. Richards and Sheridan, *Mass-Observation at the Movies*, p. 227.
59. Ibid., p. 238.

IV

What conclusions, therefore, can be drawn about the role and nature of the British cinema during the war? 'No doubt about it,' writes Leslie Halliwell, 'the cinema was providing a great morale booster as well as the nation's most effective weapon of propaganda.'[60] Moreover, it is evident that the value of the cinema for these purposes was recognized and actively supported by the government, principally through the agency of the MoI. Evidence of the rehabilitation of the MoI's Films Division in the eyes of its critics is provided by *Documentary News Letter*, which at the end of the war declared that 'the Films Division has become a great instrument of Government. We hope that it will not only be preserved but will flourish whatever the fate of the Ministry of Information.'[61] The post-war Labour government did maintain an interest in documentary through the Central Office of Information, though the Crown Film Unit was not to survive the return of the Conservatives in 1951.

The most celebrated films of the war are undoubtedly those which gave a sober, realistic portrait of ordinary people. Social historians have seen in films such as *Millions Like Us* evidence that British audiences had developed a taste for realism and had rejected the fictional fancies of Hollywood. Angus Calder, for example, writes:

> Audiences preferred home-made products which reconstructed the boredom and banality, as well as the heroism, of the People's War, to uncomprehendingly romantic American films about life in Britain, Calif. (The infamous *Mrs Miniver*, the saga of middle-class courage set in an olde worlde utopia, provoked very mixed reactions from British audiences).[62]

This verdict, however, requires some qualification. While it is true that British films enjoyed a new-found popularity with audiences, it was still the case that American films were the most successful at the box office. Although derided by many commentators for its rose-tinted and unrealistic image of England at war, Hollywood's *Mrs*

60. Halliwell, *Seats in All Parts*, p. 86.
61. 'The First Six Years', *Documentary News Letter*, 49 (1945), p. 87.
62. A. Calder, *The People's War: Britain 1939–1945* (London, Jonathan Cape, 1969), p. 369.

Miniver was nevertheless the most successful film of 1942.[63] Moreover, the testimony of Mass-Observation respondents suggests that it was well received by audiences: 'I like Greer Garson [Mrs Miniver] and find her a tonic as well as restful,' one Lancashire housewife remarked.[64] The greatest box-office success of the entire war was the Technicolor epic *Gone With The Wind*, which opened in the West End in April 1940 and was still playing on D-Day. And, while films such as *The Demi-Paradise* and *Millions Like Us* performed reasonably well, the most significant British film of 1943 in terms of popular taste was Gainsborough's *The Man in Grey*, which was so successful that the studio embarked on a cycle of costume melodramas which were to be the outstanding popular favourites of the mid-1940s, albeit that they were despised by the critics. Films such as *The Wicked Lady* (1945) were unashamedly escapist, and came as a tonic to increasingly war-weary audiences. There is, therefore, a difference between the films deemed significant by historians and those which were most popular at the time. Ironically, perhaps, just as British feature films won critical success in the middle of the war due to their realism, audience tastes were already turning in favour of costume, melodrama and fantasy.

63. Precise statistics regarding box-office returns are few and far between for this period. The annual 'book of form' compiled by R. H. 'Josh' Billings for *Kinematograph Weekly* provides the most useful indication of which films performed well at the box office, albeit that they are, inevitably, rather impressionistic.
64. Richards and Sheridan, *Mass-Observation at the Movies*, p. 261.

The People's Radio: The BBC and its Audience, 1939–1945

Siân Nicholas

The story of the British Broadcasting Corporation (BBC) during the Second World War provides one of the great mythologies of wartime Britain, embodied in the image of a nation of 'families clustered around their sets listening with reverence to speeches by Churchill, the news, or J. B. Priestley's Sunday night talks'.[1] This image of the BBC uniting the nation around the wireless, providing the news, information and entertainment which kept the nation's morale high through bad times and good, became one of the most enduring of the war, presented at the time in newspapers, films and over the airwaves themselves, and perpetuated long after.[2]

In many respects, of course, the evidence is compelling. The BBC nine o'clock news was heard by around 17 million people nightly throughout the war. Churchill's speeches regularly attracted 21 million listeners, Priestley's celebrated *Postscripts* of 1940 and 1941 10 million and *ITMA* 14 million. The highest percentage audience recorded during the war (and at any time by the BBC since) was 80 per cent of the adult listening audience (some 28 million), for a statement by the King on the night of D-Day. Yet, too often for historians of the war, mention of the BBC's wartime role extends little further than token references to Churchill, Priestley and *ITMA*. The propensity of people who lived through the war to claim they were 'too busy to listen to the radio' (even when closer

---

1. J. Seaton, 'Broadcasting and the Blitz', in J. Curran and J. Seaton, *Power Without Responsibility: The Press and Broadcasting in Britain* (London, Routledge, 1994 edn), p. 163.
2. Notably by the BBC itself: see, e.g., T. Hickman, *What Did You Do In The War, Auntie?* (London, BBC Books, 1995).

questioning shows a quite different picture) confirms the paradox of a medium too ubiquitous to recall.

Every day throughout almost the entire war, the BBC broadcast over 30 hours of programmes of every description over two domestic services. Some programmes regularly attracted audiences of 8–10 million weekly, others barely a tenth of this. Some were simultaneously broadcast on both services, some broadcast on one and repeated on the other, but most clearly belonged on either one or the other. The conventional view of the wartime BBC is of cumulative 'democratization' as the BBC became more obviously responsive to listeners' tastes. But even proponents of this view have underlined how contrived, patronizing and out of touch many of the BBC's 'people's' programmes were, how heavy-handed was much of the BBC's wartime propaganda, how resistant audiences were to much of the BBC's output, and how the appearance of probity in the news masked a reality of confusion, evasion and misinformation.[3]

This essay assesses the mythology of the wartime BBC by taking a new look at its relationship with its audience – or, more properly, its audiences. During the war, the function of radio itself changed, from a provider of private or familial enjoyment and self-improvement to a vital instrument of public information and entertainment. Its role extended beyond the home into both the workplace and public space. As the public role of radio changed, so too did its cultural function. The Corporation's pre-war 'cultural elitism' modified into an uneasy kind of 'elevated classlessness' that broke new ground in British broadcasting while clinging on to many of its established traditions.

I

During the 1930s radio became an integral part of everyday life in Britain. By 1939, 73 per cent of households nationwide owned a radio licence, suggesting a total potential audience of perhaps 35

3. See A. Briggs, *The War of Words* (London, Oxford UP, 1969); D. Cardiff and P. Scannell, '"Good Luck War Workers!" Class, Politics and Entertainment in Wartime Broadcasting', in *Popular Culture and Social Relations*, eds T. Bennett, C. Mercer and J. Woolacott (Milton Keynes, Open UP, 1986), pp. 93–116; S. Nicholas, *The Echo of War: Home Front Propaganda and the Wartime BBC, 1939–45* (Manchester, Manchester UP, 1996).

million out of a national population of 48 million.[4] This represented an astonishing growth in listening since the BBC's first broadcasts in 1922. By 1935, 98 per cent of the population could listen to at least one of the two BBC services – the National and the Regional – and the relative cheapness of simple radio sets (and the even cheaper alternative of subscribing to a 'relay' station) meant that, as George Orwell affirmed in 1937, 'Twenty million people are underfed, but literally everyone in England has access to a radio.'[5]

In these years, the BBC established itself as an unique broadcasting institution. Its two services broadcast a 'mixed' output of drama, talks, variety, music and evening news bulletins that aimed to provide, in the words of its first, and most celebrated, Director-General (Sir) John Reith, 'everything that is best in every human department of knowledge, endeavour and achievement'.[6] The BBC's broadcasting philosophy was synonymous with Reith: public service, high cultural standards, the educative function of broadcasting. This philosophy was inseparable from the BBC's perception of its audience as, in essence, the English suburban lower-middle to 'middle-middle'-class family.[7] 'Listening in' was part of private rather than public life, the

4. See M. Pegg, *Broadcasting and Society 1918–1939* (London, Croom Helm, 1983), pp. 7–9, 44; A. Briggs, *The Golden Age of Wireless* (London, Oxford UP, 1965), pp. 253–5. Throughout the period under consideration, the BBC's Listener Research Department worked on the conservative estimate that every 1 per cent of the audience represented 330,000 adult (i.e., over the age of 14) listeners. LR's pre-war and wartime methodology is detailed in Silvey, 'Methods of Listener Research', n.d. (1944), BBC Written Archive Centre, Caversham (hereafter BBC WAC) File R9/15/1, and summarized in Nicholas, *Echo of War*, p. 66 n. 22.

5. G. Orwell, *The Road to Wigan Pier* (London, Penguin, [1937] 1989), pp. 82–3. Relay (or rediffusion) stations relayed by wire a radio service to loudspeakers in subscribers' homes, that featured a selection of both BBC and continental broadcasts. It provided a cheaper service than owning a licensed set and was especially popular among poorer listeners and in blocks of flats. By the end of 1935 there were an estimated quarter of a million relay subscribers in Britain, representing a total audience of over a million. See Briggs, *Golden Age*, pp. 356–60, D. L. LeMahieu, *A Culture for Democracy: Mass Communication and the Cultivated Mind in Britain Between the Wars* (Oxford, Clarendon Press, 1988), p. 277.

6. J. C. W. Reith, *Broadcast Over Britain* (1924), quoted in P. Scannell and D. Cardiff, 'Serving the Nation: Public Service Broadcasting Before the War', in *Popular Culture: Past and Present*, eds B. Waites, T. Bennett and G. Martin (London, Croom Helm in association with the Open UP, 1982), p. 163.

7. Scannell and Cardiff, 'Serving the Nation', p. 168.

wireless set both literally and figuratively 'part of the furniture' of the home. The BBC addressed its audience not as a mass audience, 'but a constellation of individuals positioned in families'. The listener himself had an obligation 'to choose intelligently from the programmes offered to him'.[8] 'Tap listening', the undiscriminating use of radio as 'background noise', was considered worse than not listening at all; *Radio Times* exhorted listeners to turn their wirelesses off instead. To encourage discrimination in listening, regular scheduling of programmes was initially discouraged, 'continuity' was rejected, and five-minute interludes between programmes were not uncommon.

Against accusations that the BBC set out to give listeners what they 'needed' rather than what they wanted, Reith defended himself robustly: 'There is often no difference ... . Better to overestimate the mentality of the public than to underestimate it.'[9] Thus classical music occupied the most prominent position in BBC schedules. One of the first BBC household names was Sir Walford Davies, whose *Music and the Ordinary Listener* appears genuinely to have brought a new enjoyment of serious music into British households. The BBC's financial rescue and subsequent annual patronage of the Sir Henry Wood Promenade Concerts exemplified its role in elevating the cultural profile of serious music; the BBC also took pride in championing experimental music. In contrast, light music and dance music were initially ghettoized to late-night slots (when most of its potential audience was asleep), though responsibility for dance music was soon transferred to the Variety Department. Features (a largely untried radio form) and Drama (which aimed to be a 'national theatre of the air') maintained a high profile but probably relatively small audiences.[10] Talks played a significant part in schedules, but were generally considered among the least popular of broadcast items, often struggling for the appropriate tone in which to address their audience.[11]

The BBC's disdain for light entertainment was reciprocated by the variety industry. The culture of the music hall still dominated

8. *BBC Yearbook 1930* (London, BBC), p. 60.
9. Scannell and Cardiff, 'Serving the Nation', p. 163.
10. J. Drakakis, 'Introduction', in *British Radio Drama*, ed. J. Drakakis (Cambridge, Cambridge UP, 1981), p. 7; LeMahieu, *Culture for Democracy*, pp. 185, 188.
11. See D. Cardiff, 'The Serious and the Popular: Aspects of the Evolution of Style in the Radio Talk, 1928–1939', *Media, Culture and Society*, 2 (1980), pp. 29–47.

variety in Britain, and artistes and promoters alike were reluctant to trade a steady income around the halls for fleeting (and relatively poorly paid) moments of national radio fame. However, the creation of a BBC Variety Department in 1933, under the direction of Eric Maschwitz, began a process by which light entertainment became the most popular – if least regarded – part of the BBC's output. Meanwhile, Reith's original aim to make the BBC a forum for the informed citizen was progressively abandoned as the political parties maintained a stranglehold on political and topical broadcasts, and the news agencies a veto on wireless news broadcasts before 6 p.m. What the BBC News Department (created in 1934) did retain was an image of unsensational probity that clearly differentiated it from newspaper news. Above all, however, the public image of the BBC was exemplified in the so-called 'Reithian Sunday', a neo-Sabbatarian schedule that eschewed any light content in favour of religious services and serious music.

The BBC was not, of course, the only wireless service available to the British people, and the extent of alternative listening in this period is striking. The popularity of short-wave radio sets that could pick up European and even American stations, and above all the listening figures for the two continental English-language stations, Radios Luxembourg and Normandie, demonstrated both the BBC's limitations and the public's readiness to seek alternative wireless entertainment. For much of the day, most of the week, the BBC was clearly pre-eminent. But 11 per cent of listeners tuned to Luxembourg's light music and variety programmes regularly on weekdays in preference to the BBC, and in the early mornings (when the BBC did not broadcast at all) and on Sundays, the commercial stations dominated, with up to half the available audience listening in to Luxembourg alone.[12] This was proof, if it were needed, that for a substantial section of the British listening public, radio was seen above all as a source of light background listening.

The extent of alternative listening left the BBC (and the licence system which funded it) open to perennial attack, especially by the popular press which, having failed to recognize the potential of broadcasting in the early 1920s, now periodically vented its frustration against the BBC's 'cultural elitism'. In reply, the BBC tentatively sought to lighten its own output. In 1936, the BBC established a Listener Research Department to investigate audience attitudes

12. Briggs, *Golden Age*, pp. 362–5.

through an impressionistic research methodology comprising specialist 'listening panels' and local correspondents' reports.[13] Reith's
departure in 1938 made easier such obvious steps as the gradual
lightening of Sunday broadcasts, the establishment of regular programme schedules, and the moving of light and dance music
broadcasts to more popular and appropriate times. Parlour-game
shows, audience-participation shows and new comedy series such as
Band Waggon heralded a more vigorous mood in BBC Variety.[14] The
BBC's autumn plans for 1939 were 'the brightest ever', *Radio Times*
of 25 August 1939 promising more drama and light entertainment
than ever before, a brighter Sunday and 'plenty of controversy'.
There was even talk of introducing female announcers. Six days later
war broke out and the autumn plans were abandoned.

By the end of the 1930s the BBC held a unique place in British
life. But this was less by virtue of its monopoly status – for the
regularity with which relay stations took up commercial as opposed
to BBC programmes demonstrates the former's vigour in British
broadcasting culture – than by its success in seeming to embody the
nation itself in its values, ideals and broadcasts. Broadcasting in
Britain was defined by the BBC. When Hilda Jennings and Winifred
Gill, writing in 1939, affirmed that broadcasting was 'an equalising
and unifying factor in national life' (and that 'no innovation since
the coming of compulsory education has affected so large a proportion of the working population as the coming of broadcasting'), they
did not have Radio Luxembourg in mind.[15] Only in the celebrated
North Region operating out of Manchester did BBC programmes
truly seek to represent working-class life; meanwhile, intellectuals
periodically mocked the 'radio-ridden villas' of middle England.[16]

13. For many within the Corporation it was a fatal concession. See, e.g., Lionel
    Fielden's indictment of 'the hellish department which is called Listener
    Research' in his *The Natural Bent* (London, André Deutsch, 1960), p. 109.
14. See P. Scannell and D. Cardiff, *A Social History of British Broadcasting, Vol.
    I: Serving the Nation* (London, Basil Blackwell, 1991), ch. 12.
15. H. Jennings and W. Gill, *Broadcasting in Everyday Life* (London, BBC, 1939),
    p. 40. See also P. Scannell and D. Cardiff, 'The BBC and National Unity', in
    Impacts and Influences: Essays on Media Power in the Twentieth Century, eds
    J. Curran, A. Smith and P. Wingate (London, Methuen, 1987), pp. 157–73.
16. Evelyn Waugh, quoted in H. Carpenter, *The Envy of the World: Fifty Years
    of the BBC Third Programme and Radio 3* (London, Weidenfeld & Nicolson,
    1996), p. 5. For the North Region, see Scannell and Cardiff, *Serving the Nation*,
    ch. 15.

But Reith succeeded in co-opting a broadly middle-class consensus that legitimized both the medium of radio in British life and the BBC's own monopoly.[17] For most of the British people the Second World War itself began with a BBC radio broadcast: Chamberlain's statement to the nation on the morning of Sunday 3 September that Hitler had failed to respond to Britain's ultimatum 'and that consequently we are at war with Germany'. In a dangerous world listeners turned to the BBC, its most famous public corporation and newest national institution, as a source of stability and continuity.

II

The unifying role of the BBC during the war is taken so much for granted that few historians of wartime Britain do more than simply affirm the fact.[18] Yet the conditions of war fundamentally altered the relationship between the BBC and its listeners. As lives were disrupted and patterns of work and leisure changed, the BBC found itself with a discontented and demanding listening public all too ready to look elsewhere for wireless entertainment and information. The BBC was forced to change its conception of its audience as it found itself facing conditions that compromised many of its basic assumptions.

On the evening of 1 September 1939, two days before war broke out, the National and the Regional Programmes closed down and a single BBC 'Home Service' started broadcasting.[19] During the devastating air war that most believed would be Hitler's first move against Britain, the BBC saw its role as providing essential information and 'entertainment to keep people in good heart throughout the difficult days ahead'.[20] A service of light music, inspiring talks, and hourly bulletins of news and government announcements was

17. See LeMahieu, *Culture for Democracy*, pp. 182, 188 and passim for an interesting, if occasionally laboured, exposition of this thesis.
18. A. Calder, *The People's War: Britain 1939–1945* (London, Jonathan Cape, 1969) is an honourable exception. See pp. 357–66 and passim.
19. The government had decided that radio should continue in wartime as the single most convenient means of passing on information to the nation, but the Air Ministry had insisted on a single service, to reduce the threat of German planes navigating via BBC transmissions. See Broadcasting in Wartime Committee minutes, no. 47, 28 March 1938, BBC WAC R34/267.
20. *Birmingham Post*, 6 September 1939.

provided, to be augmented as soon as conditions allowed by 'ordinary broadcast programmes'.[21]

As it turned out, the BBC was thrown, like most of the population, by the refusal of the war to follow the anticipated pattern. Within weeks of the outbreak of war, Mass-Observation found that over half the population was 'fed up with the BBC' – though less at the paucity of useful information and the tedium of much of the 'light entertainment' on offer than at the BBC's apparent loss of independence and objectivity.[22] The press leaped in to criticize the broadcasters and reaffirm that radio would never take the place of newspapers. Parliament debated the 'very grave' public dissatisfaction with the BBC.[23] With people confined to the home by the blackout, with theatres, cinemas and other public entertainments closed and Radios Luxembourg and Normandie now off the air, many listeners turned instead to German English-language services, most notoriously Radio Hamburg, where William Joyce ('Lord Haw-Haw') was soon attracting an estimated third of British listeners to his Sunday night 'news' broadcasts.[24] For the first time the BBC found itself in the position of *needing* to attract audiences, for reasons (it appeared) of both national security and national morale.

The first significant development in the BBC's wartime outlook was the expanded role assigned to Listener Research (LR). The value of such research was first demonstrated in October 1939 when, amid public controversy about the timing of the BBC's new 12 noon lunchtime news bulletin, an LR investigation conclusively demonstrated (against a tide of anecdotal evidence from officials regarding working-class dining habits) that 1 p.m. was a better time for listeners. From December 1939, first the British Institute of Public Opinion, then (from 1943) the BBC itself, compiled a 'daily listening barometer', comprising both audience figures and a 'listener satisfaction index'. From the end of 1940, 'barometer and other evidence' had become a regular item on the Home Board's agenda, *not*, it was stressed, to influence day-to-day programme production (this would be to bow too crudely to popular

21. *Radio Times*, 5 September 1939.
22. Tom Harrisson Mass-Observation Archive, University of Sussex (hereafter M-O) File Report 90, 14 April 1940.
23. *Hansard*, Vol. 351, cols 1491–2, 28 September 1939.
24. LR/98, 8 March 1940, BBC WAC R9/14; see also PRO INF1/265 Files I and II.

tastes),[25] but to provide an informed context for policy and planning. In fact, the Listener Research Department played a vital role within the wartime BBC, providing a succession of detailed reports on programmes, listening conditions, listener opinions and wider public attitudes that complement in both methodology and findings the more well-known wartime surveys conducted by Mass-Observation and the Ministry of Information's Home Intelligence division. Although no formal attempt was ever made to use listener research to guide or shape BBC policy (indeed, almost all its enquiries were initiated by LR itself), the Listener Research Department provided the information by which producers could judge their output – and by which BBC departments could counter the demands of government ministers, service chiefs, or their own Board of Governors.

The second breakthrough development in the wartime BBC was the creation of an alternative service, the Forces Programme. For the first time, the BBC acknowledged that some sections of the wartime audience (in this case the vast numbers of men newly enlisted in the Forces) were listening in communal conditions where close attention to the wireless was either impossible or determined by the group. Current BBC provision was inadequate: soldiers of the British Expeditionary Force (BEF) encamped in France habitually tuned instead to the local Radio Fécamp. The prospect of a long siege winter led the War Office to propose a Forces radio programme as a means of securing troops' morale, and the BBC abruptly complied. 'For the Forces' took to the air virtually unannounced on 7 January 1940, broadcasting from 6 p.m. a service of programmes designed for the BEF in the conditions in which they listened, with variety, sport and especially popular music dominating, for, as Patrick Ryan, Ministry of Information liaison with the BBC and one of the Forces Programme's greatest advocates, pointed out, 'if we give them serious music, long plays, or peacetime programme talks, they will not listen.'[26] From June 1940, with the BEF back in Britain, the Forces Programme broadcast from 6.15 a.m. to 11 p.m.[27]

25. Neither, insisted Sir Stephen Tallents, should it be used to make 'disagreeable comparisons' concerning the respective popularity of goverment ministers. See Nicholas, *Echo of War*, p. 49.
26. Ryan to Tallents, 10 February 1940, quoted in Briggs, *War of Words*, p. 133.
27. There had been rumours of an additional programme during the last months of 1939. Collie Knox, radio critic of the *Daily Mail*, hoped that the two services would be 'divided into a North and South grouping ... so that the

The implications of the establishment of the Forces Programme were far-reaching, though few within the BBC were prepared to admit as much. Defended by BBC chiefs as a temporary venture, it marked the most decisive break yet with the BBC's Reithian past. The Reithian Sunday was effectively doomed, as the Board of Governors conceded the principle that variety was a fit genre 'for the moment' for Sunday nights (with the proviso that all Sunday programmes should be 'of the best quality', 'fortifying to the individual and a strengthening to the home').[28] More than that, the Forces Programme represented the BBC's acknowledgement that one of the functions of radio was to provide light background entertainment for the casual listener: servicemen in the first instance (with whom the Forces Programme was immediately popular), but also among the ordinary listening population (notably working-class housewives, whose existence as a significant component of the daily audience was one of the BBC's more striking wartime discoveries). By 1941 some 60 per cent of the civilian public was regularly tuning to the Forces Programme in preference to the Home Service; by 1942 among listeners aged 16–20 the figure was closer to 90 per cent. The Home Service continued to broadcast its share of light entertainment, and indeed gained ground when, in the approach to D-Day, the Forces Programme was 're-militarized' as the General Forces Programme and some of its most popular general-interest programmes transferred to the Home Service. But the Forces Programme's success in providing 'a sort of tap listening, available all day as a mental background and relief' led commentators to suggest that the experiment of listening 'light on one wavelength, heavy on the other' might be extended. Within two years, internal BBC proposals for post-war broadcasting had abandoned 'mixed' programming altogether, envisaging five culturally streamed stations, from a 'light programme' ('if not, the commercial stations will be waiting') to a service dedicated wholly to 'culture'.[29]

With the population in the throes of family disruption, job

(*note 27 continued*) whole country has more chance of getting ... the artists, and the entertainment which it appreciates and understands' (*Daily Mail*, 14 October 1939).

28. Board of Governors Minutes, no. 275, 6 December 1939, BBC WAC R1/1/7; *Melody Maker*, 6 January 1940.
29. See LR/433, 2 December 1941, BBC WAC R9/9/5; LR/556, 13 January 1942, R9/9/6; M-O File Report 1315, 'TH Radio column for *Observer*', 15 May 1942; LR/2459, 15 March 1944, R9/1/5; Carpenter, *Envy of the World*, p. 6.

relocation, evacuation and worse, war was inevitably a disrupter of listening. War work took people out of the home during the evenings and nights. During the height of the Blitz, the BBC estimated that its potential listening public fell by half after 8 p.m. as listeners headed for the shelters.[30] Meanwhile, radio sets were fragile and susceptible to bomb and blast damage. To repair a radio set, even for the most unexceptionable fault, became increasingly difficult. 'Wet' batteries were difficult to recharge, 'dry' batteries were increasingly hard to find. As war needs took precedence, replacement valves for radio sets became almost unavailable. By the end of 1942, the *Cambridge Daily News* reported, many people were reinstalling old one- or two-valve radios, or even rebuilding crystal sets. Among the most eagerly anticipated Lend-Lease imports were radio valves.[31] However, as home listening became more difficult, public listening increased. Just as wartime life was of necessity an increasingly communal experience, so radio listening broadened out from the family unit to the workplace, to pubs and restaurants, to canteens, air-raid shelters and public places. It was all but impossible to avoid the sound of a radio at some point in the day.[32] In response, the BBC found itself having to reorganize its output, rearrange its schedule and redefine its entire philosophy of broadcasting, to become less exhortative and patronizing, and more flexible, responsive and popular.

A policy document which LR circulated in August 1940 illuminated the BBC's changing perceptions of its audience. It began with a remarkable portrait of the 'average listener': provincial rather than suburban, blue- rather than white-collar, elementary-school educated, a reader of the Sunday papers but not much else, resigned to periods of unemployment, likely to be conscripted but unlikely to contemplate a commission, morale 'all right, he has no doubts about the necessity of beating Hitler, but he hasn't much faith in politicians and prefers not to think about the future'. Indeed, he was more often than not a she: a housewife who 'lost her looks when she was twenty-five', who went to the pictures at least once a week and 'uses the "wireless" even more than [her husband] does'. The report went on to acknowledge the importance to listeners of information

30. *Daily Express*, 30 September 1940.
31. Hickman, *What Did You Do*, p. 82; *Cambridge Daily News*, 5 November 1942; *Glasgow Evening News*, 14 October 1942.
32. It was during these years that the impersonal term 'listening' appears to have replaced the more intimate phrase 'listening in'.

and of a sense of national unity and common purpose, but also stressed the importance of familiar programmes, 'so-called background programmes', request shows ('it is probably difficult for us within the Corporation to realise what it means to average men to hear their own request broadcast'), discussion programmes ('not so much because [audiences] ought to think, but because they need to have something to think about') – and at least one weekly variety programme that would 'be common currency in the street and in the air raid shelter, in camps, in billets, or on leave, in the pub and in the senior common room ... [helping to] bind the nation together as a community'.[33] This proved the most prescient set of recommendations for wartime radio yet produced; just how to bind the nation as a community became the wartime BBC's key objective.

III

The pre-war BBC had demonstrated its unrivalled capacity to provide a sense of national unity. After a nervous start, the wartime BBC proved it could maintain this role with distinction. Yet the success with which the principal departments of the BBC adapted to the war was qualified by the persistent tension between the BBC's traditional aims and new imperatives. The war provided new opportunities to modify the more elitist definitions of national culture, but it was impossible entirely to cast off Reithian attitudes.

In wartime, the BBC's role as medium and arbiter of events of national moment took on a new prominence. BBC news, for instance, made remarkable advances in style, substance and reputation. Three-quarters of the nation listened to at least one bulletin a day, and the belief that 'if it's on the BBC it must be true' took on mythic (and often scarcely deserved) proportions. The position of the nine o'clock bulletin as the central focus of the listening day was underlined when, after a vigorous public campaign, the full minute it took for Big Ben to strike the hour before the nine o'clock news was adopted as a moment of daily national reflection.[34] It was also through the BBC that national figures spoke to the country. As First Lord of the Admiralty in the early part of the war Churchill built

33. 'Broadcasting Policy', LRD, 27 August 1940, BBC WAC R9/15/1.
34. See Nicholas, *Echo of War*, pp. 128, 205–6 and ch. 7 passim.

Figure 6 'Listening to Churchill', *Picture Post*, 2 August 1941 (© Hulton Getty)

up a powerful radio following, and once Prime Minister his broadcasts, though infrequent, created their own mythology (though a persistent recent myth, that he was impersonated on air *in absentia* by a BBC actor, is wholly without foundation). Audiences of on average around 60 per cent listened to his broadcast orations (as an adulatory feature in *Picture Post* detailed) in homes, pubs, restaurants and high streets across Britain.[35] A less predictable national figure, but equally part of the mythology of wartime broadcasting, was J. B. Priestley, whose phenomenally popular but controversial *Postscripts* (1940–41) were allegedly cancelled because of their left-wing

35. *Picture Post*, 2 August 1941, pp. 9–13. For details of Churchill's broadcasts, see D. J. Wenden, 'Churchill, radio and cinema', in *Churchill*, eds R. Blake and W. R. Louis (Oxford, Oxford UP, 1992), pp. 220–5. The most recent restatement of the Churchill impersonation myth is in P. Ziegler, *London at War* (London, Sinclair-Stevenson, 1995), pp. 81–2.

bias.[36] Ministers, service chiefs, literary, musical, even sporting celeb-rities, as well as the King, Queen and the royal princesses, addressed the nation over the air. The BBC celebrated the national days of not only the UK but also her allies (up to and including Red Army Day), as well as an annual National Day of Prayer. Cecil McGivern's celebrated Christmas Day features took their own place in the calen-dar of national broadcasting events, attracting higher audiences in each successive year of the war (peaking at 55.9 per cent for *The Journey Home*, broadcast on Christmas Day 1944).

To maintain national pride through patriotic identification with the nation's history, culture and people was considered one of the BBC's most important wartime tasks. Ostensibly an uncontroversial patriotic gesture, this 'deploying the poets' in such programmes as *For Ever England* or *The Land We Defend* became a highly contested feature of BBC output in the early years of war, accused variously of banality, condescension and the marginalization of Wales and Scotland. From mid-1940 a spate of programmes such as *My Day's Work, Everyman and the War, Go To It* and *We Speak for Ourselves* sought to shift the focus of 'national tributes' from the nation itself to its people, and were welcomed by progressive critics like *The Listener*'s W. E. Williams (later to become Director of the Army Bureau of Current Affairs) as providing a voice for the working class beyond that of 'gag-fodder for the Variety programmes'. Many listeners, however, found radio producers' attempts to represent a more comprehensive selection of regional dialects and class accents on air both stereotypical and tokenist, and LR was disconcerted to discover the ribaldry with which factory workers parodied the patriotic declamations of workers in such programmes as *Award for Industry*. Subsequent efforts at national representation tended to shift from Features (that is, where 'ordinary people' were presented to listeners in scripted contributions) to Variety (see below), where people throughout Britain presented *themselves* over the air.[37]

36. While the Ministry of Information certainly requested the BBC bring to an end Priestley's second *Postscripts* series in March 1941, his departure would probably have been only temporary had he not reacted so furiously to the suggestion that he take a rest and allow alternative viewpoints commensurate airtime. See S. Nicholas, '"Sly Demagogues" and Wartime Radio: J. B. Priestley and the BBC 1939–45', *20th Century British History*, 6 (1995), pp. 247–71.
37. See Nicholas, *Echo of War*, pp. 228–40; Cardiff and Scannell, '"Good Luck War Workers!"', pp. 102–3.

As for the maintenance of national culture and cultural standards in general, in almost every field of wartime broadcasting old aims and new needs vied for precedence. As pre-war cultural priorities were modified to accommodate audience preferences, listeners demonstrated a taste for both the serious and the more 'popular' that took producers by surprise. The Music Department 'lightened' its serious output by, for instance, shortening programmes and (a highly symbolic concession) avoiding in billing the dread words 'recital' and 'chamber music'.[38] With a certain patriotic logic it blacklisted composers whose copyright was held in enemy countries, but for the listeners' sake exempted particularly popular works such as Leoncavallo's *I Pagliacci*, a performance of which in September 1944 attracted an audience of over 25 per cent. Although the proportion of broadcast time devoted to classical music halved from over 17 per cent in 1938 to under 9 per cent in 1942, the substantial increase in total transmission time meant that the hours of classical music broadcast (increasingly on the Forces Programme as well as the Home Service) in fact remained approximately the same as before the war. Anecdotal evidence suggests that the audience for classical music rose throughout the war; the findings of LR are somewhat more equivocal, but indicate that serious music was especially popular in mid-war, and that the most popular items were well-known classics and (reflecting the popularity of the British people's favourite wartime ally) music from Russia. The Proms enjoyed unprecedented success, and such well-staged coups as the première of Shostakovich's 'Leningrad' Symphony in June 1942 (the score transported out of Russia by diplomatic bag) maintained the Music Department's high public profile.[39]

After a poor start, in which government information talks and exhortatory declamations seemed to dominate the schedules, the BBC Talks Department developed a broad range of offerings that stretched from straightforward 'cultural propaganda' to the most basic advice programmes. The unexpected willingness of intellectuals of both the Left and Right to participate in 'patriotic' propaganda provided Talks with almost an embarrassment of riches on which

38. A. C. Boult, 'Music Policy', 14 November 1939, BBC WAC R27/247.
39. See D. Cardiff and P. Scannell, 'Radio in World War II', *U203 Popular Culture*, Block 2, Unit 8 (Milton Keynes, Open UP, 1981) p. 35; Briggs, *War of Words*, pp. 581–3 and table, p. 596. See also LR music reports, BBC WAC R9/5/24.

to draw in promoting Britain's cultural achievements and heritage; highlights included E. M. Forster on Milton (celebrating the tercentenary of *Areopagitica* as a milestone in the British tradition of democracy and free speech).[40] A series of 'deliberately middlebrow' cultural talks, such as *Ariel in Wartime*, a general arts magazine, featured in the Saturday-night Forces Programme schedules. With books in both shorter supply and greater demand than ever before, a succession of book talks sought to balance the BBC's respective duties to 'the eternal verities' and to the newly discovered '2d library reader'.[41] None of these talks attracted audiences of more than 6 or 7 per cent (though even this, it was noted, represented some two million interested listeners), and Talks producers reluctantly conceded that they had failed to find a 'Middleton of books' and that the most powerful incitement to read a book was its mention on the *Brains Trust* (see below).[42] They were, however, annoyed to find the Variety Department running its own more overtly downmarket book talk, 'All for a tanner', in the Forces magazine programme *Ack-Ack, Beer Beer*. Daytime talks fared worse, with audiences of only around 4 per cent – with the remarkable exception (with audiences almost four times higher) of the daily early-morning *The Kitchen Front*, the first 'women's' programme on the BBC to find general approval among working-class housewives because of its practical treatment of basic wartime inconveniences such as rationing.[43] Where the Talks Department racked up its most impressive listener figures was in the topical talks slots scheduled directly after the nine o'clock news, notably *War Commentary* (seven million listeners) and *American* and *Russian Commentary* (six and four million respectively). Above all, the increasing use of 'ordinary people' in talks programmes of all kinds was an experiment that garnered great interest from critics and listeners alike (notably Leslie Merrion, a London bricklayer, who featured in several talks series and even presented an edition

40. See R. Weight, 'State, Intelligensia and the Promotion of National Culture in Britain, 1939–45', *Historical Research*, **69** (1996), pp. 83–101.
41. First Report of the Inter-Departmental Committee on Literary Output (Grigson/Potter), 31 May 1943, BBC WAC, R51/44/6.
42. Barnes memorandum, 23 February 1940, BBC WAC R51/44/3; reference is to C. H. Middleton, doyen of BBC gardening programmes.
43. See Nicholas, *Echo of War*, pp. 70–85. Paradoxically, one of *The Kitchen Front*'s most popular presenters was the archetypal middle-class male Freddie Grisewood ('A Man in the Kitchen').

of *A Week in Westminster*). But the most celebrated, and most eclectic, of all talks slots was the (post-Priestley) Sunday night *Postscript*, which featured a range of speakers from the American correspondent Quentin Reynolds (with his pungent diatribes against Hitler and Goebbels) to 'The Little Nurse', Joyce Castagnoli (who gave a talk of such dire sentimentality that the planned repeat broadcast was cancelled by public demand).[44]

The demand for radio drama during the war – and the breadth of that demand – took the BBC by surprise. Fearing the adverse effects of wartime scheduling, technical restrictions and fluctuating audiences, BBC Drama had defended its territory early in the war by arguing that it had an essential role in both the 'preservation of civilized culture' and 'national wartime activity'. The department was pleasantly surprised at the popularity of serious drama such as D. G. Bridson's bleak *Aaron's Field* (November 1939), Robert Ardrey's *Thunder Rock* (July 1940) and Eric Linklater's historical allegory *The Ship*, which received the unprecedented accolade of being broadcast three times in a week in May 1943. By contrast, Louis MacNiece's verse drama *Christopher Columbus* (October 1942), at two hours and twenty minutes the longest anniversary feature the BBC had ever produced, with a cast of 32 headed by Laurence Olivier, and music by William Walton, was lauded in artistic circles, but a *Daily Express* critic reported having met only two people who listened to the whole thing, one of whom had fallen asleep.[45]

However, it was classic serials (including a celebrated eight-part *War and Peace* in January 1943 that fed into the national pro-Russian mood), new 'middle-brow' drama slots such as *Saturday Night Theatre* on the Home Service and slick, short plays such as those featured in the innovative late-night horror series *Appointment with Fear* (modelled by writer/producer John Dickson Carr on American radio and narrated by doom-voiced 'Man in Black' Valentine Dyall) that won over the widest drama audiences. By the end of the war the department was producing 300–400 plays a year, from West End hits and popular film re-enactments to classical drama and contemporary literary adaptations, and audiences for radio drama had more

44. *Daily Mail*, 4 October 1943.
45. *Daily Express*, 15 October 1942. See also D. G. Bridson, *Prospero and Ariel. The Rise and Fall of Radio: A Personal Recollection* (London, Victor Gollancz, 1971), pp. 72–5 and ch. 3 passim; C. Holme, 'The Radio Drama of Louis MacNiece', in Drakakis, *British Radio Drama*, p. 41 and passim.

than doubled. A 'listener's popularity week' in October 1940 demonstrates the diversity of audience tastes: it included a repeat of
Aaron's Field, Noel Coward's *Cavalcade*, the Wodehouse adaptation
Crime Wave at Blandings and an all-star *Hamlet*. The latter production suffered the ignominy of being cut off in mid-scene after
overrunning by more than half an hour; it is unclear whether producers were appalled or gratified when listeners rang in to the BBC
demanding to know the ending.[46]

BBC Features, led by Laurence Gilliam, carved out an identity of
its own during the war years, as developments in recording technique
and the altered social conditions of war presented producers with
new subject areas to address. It made its mark almost immediately
with the documentary drama series *The Shadow of the Swastika*,
which provided ordinary listeners for the first time with a digest of
recent German history, and deliberately courted publicity by its
reluctance to reveal the identity of the actor portraying Hitler (Marius
Goring). In a four-page feature, *Picture Post* estimated that a third
of the nation had listened to the series ('In a certain barracks all
except two of the soldiers quartered there gave up their one night
out to listen').[47] BBC Features' output was often artificial and over-
produced (notably its industrial features), but its aspiration to be
the 'striking force of radio' led it into some powerful innovations,
notably *Marching On*, a dramatized 'news magazine' that modelled
its style on the American newsreel *The March of Time*, and *War
Report*, the groundbreaking nightly actuality report from the front
line, produced in collaboration with News, by which audiences of
10–15 million followed the Allied advance from D-Day to VE-Day
in the company of war correspondents Frank Gillard, Stanley Maxted,
Wynford Vaughan-Thomas *et al.*[48]

IV

But it was in variety that BBC attitudes were most profoundly affected
by the search for more popular radio forms. The BBC's wartime

46. See *Evening News*, 5 September 1940; *Glasgow Herald*, 7 October 1940.
47. See *Picture Post*, 2 March 1940, pp. 22–5.
48. See J. Thomas, 'A History of the BBC Features Department 1924–1964',
    unpublished D.Phil. thesis, University of Oxford, 1993, ch. III.

Variety Department was alternately the hero and the whipping-boy of the Corporation. It was fêted for keeping the British people entertained, yet accused of appealing to the lowest common denominator; it was indicted for both cravenly aping American styles and shamefully ignoring the slick professionalism of its transatlantic associates. The establishment of the Forces Programme gave the Variety Department both an unprecedented challenge and an unrivalled opportunity. As the time accorded dance music doubled (from almost 5 per cent in 1938 to nearly 10 per cent in 1942), that for variety almost trebled, from just under 6 to almost 15 per cent, and the principle that each night should feature at least one major variety offering was established. A survey of listening in April and May 1944 shows that of the top ten programmes on the Home Service, the top three were variety; on the Forces Programme all the top ten were either comedy or dance music.[49]

In contrast to Music, Talks, and Features and Drama, on the outbreak of war the Variety Department declared a populist agenda, roundly defended 'vulgarity', and warned against infiltrating propaganda into entertainment.[50] In July 1940 Director of Variety John Watt went further, declaiming for the benefit of the press that the 'Variety Department of the BBC is the only department which has no moral values whatsoever'. Variety aimed to entertain the 82 per cent of the British public earning less than £4 per week, and had 'no desire to teach the public, to be good or kind to it, … its sole desire is to give the public what it likes'.[51] In fact, early wartime light entertainment was so discredited by jingoistic bravura that the department 'relaunched' its offerings early in 1940 (and again in April 1941 to cheer up munitions workers, and again in November 1941 to 'meet the needs of the US forces').[52] But while critics condemned the BBC's pandering to vulgar majority tastes, a succession of listener surveys in 1940 and 1941 found that two-thirds of listeners believed the BBC was by no means too vulgar, and a further 15 per cent felt the BBC was not vulgar enough.[53]

49. Figures from Cardiff and Scannell, 'Radio in World War II', p. 35; Briggs, *War of Words*, table, p. 595.
50. Briggs, *War of Words*, pp. 106–22.
51. *Liverpool Echo*, 15 September 1940.
52. *Daily Sketch*, 31 April 1941; *Daily Express*, 25 November 1941.
53. See, for instance, LR/97, 4 March 1940; Silvey to CP, 28 February 1941, BBC WAC R9/15/1.

In wartime, ironically, the BBC found more stars available and willing to broadcast for it than ever before. The General Theatre Company's lifting in April 1940 of its discretionary ban (dating from 1933) on stage artists broadcasting for the BBC released to radio such stars as Flanagan and Allen, Max Miller, and the Americans Vic Oliver, Bebe Daniels and Ben Lyon. The latter three began broadcasting the first series of their enormously popular and long-running *Hi Gang!* just a month later.[54] Whereas pre-war BBC Variety was characterized by its music-hall origins, by May 1940, the *Daily Mirror* noted, 'seldom can you look at a music hall bill without finding some echo of the BBC in it'.[55] BBC Variety was boosted by imported American shows featuring Jack Benny, Bob Hope, and Edgar Bergen and Charlie McCarthy. More traditional 'British' fare was provided with Saturday night's *Music Hall* (first broadcast on the National Programme in 1932 and reintroduced on the Forces Programme in 1940) and the new Sunday-night *Happidrome* (Forces Programme, from 1941), whose 'English ... hearty obviousness of humour' (the antithesis to the quickfire *Hi Gang!* that preceded it in the schedules) was, unusually, praised by critics.[56]

Yet even in the Variety Department old habits died hard. The traditional BBC policy of removing programmes from schedules at their peak of popularity continued (for instance, with the Saturday-night Home Service favourite *In Town Tonight*) in the teeth of public criticism.[57] The department's ambivalence about whether to lead or follow audience tastes led it into a succession of controversies, notably the BBC's attempt to 'maintain standards' in popular music. Although LR found that roughly a third of the adult civilian listening public, predominantly female, working-class and young, were keen listeners to dance music, BBC popular music 'experts' (like their serious music counterparts) tended in almost every case to decry what the public liked best.[58] As the war increased the already excessive list of subjects, styles and lyrics which the BBC considered unsuitable for broadcast in popular musical form, the Variety Department's Dance Music Policy Committee found itself in the role of cultural

54. *Daily Mail*, 22 April 1940, 29 April 1940.
55. *Daily Mirror*, 7 May 1940.
56. Grace Wyndham Goldie, *The Listener*, 26 June 1941, p. 924; M. Gorham, *Sound and Fury* (London, Marshall, 1948), p. 171.
57. See Seton Margrave, *Daily Mail*, 16 November 1942.
58. LR/832, 21/4/42, BBC WAC R27/73/2.

arbiter, judging the respective merits of, for instance, *Praise the Lord
and Pass the Ammunition* (passed for broadcast, since allegedly based
on a true incident, and a march tune) and *Coming in on a Wing
and a Prayer* (not passed: a fatal combination of religion and foxtrot
rhythm). The popular hit *Paper Doll* was banned (the theme of
'feminine faithlessness' considered inappropriate at a time when
American GIs had just arrived in Britain) as was *I'll Be Home For
Christmas* (possibly upsetting to homesick servicemen and their
families). In June 1942 the committee decided to wage war against
the allegedly debilitating influence on servicemen's morale of
songs and singers (that is, the American-style 'crooners') considered
'anaemic', 'debilitated' or 'slushy in sentiment'. *When Daddy Comes
Home*, *Missing You* and *I Heard You Cried Last Night* were among
those excluded in what an enraged music press soon dubbed the
'Anti-Slush War'; the instruction went out to continuity announcers:
'when in doubt, err on the side of marches'.[59] The most celebrated
victim of the policy was the bandleader and singer Hutch; the most
notorious near-victim Vera Lynn, whose immensely popular BBC
'letter to the Forces', *Sincerely Yours – Vera Lynn*, was cited in
Parliament and by the BBC Board of Governors as a potential threat
to the national fibre.

Ironically, at the same time the Variety Department was engaged
in one of its most successful appeals to popular tastes, *Music While
You Work*, a twice-daily light music programme for war workers on
the Forces Programme, notable for being the BBC's first programme
designed to be nothing more nor less than background noise.[60] After
a less than happy start in June 1940 (during which producers discovered that varying the tempo of numbers and pausing between
tunes to retune instruments was not conducive to happy listening),
the series settled down under the supervision of the band leader
Wynford Reynolds to become a wartime institution, broadcasting a
morning and an afternoon half-hour of bright, familiar, rhythmic
live band music (augmented by a night-shift edition from August
1942), to an estimated daily audience of almost seven million (half
in factories, half at home). What was revolutionary was that, as the
BBC acknowledged in internal correspondence, they were 'asking

59. Frank Phillips to continuity announcers, 27 July 1942, BBC WAC R23/73/1.
60. For further details of *Music While You Work* see Nicholas, *Echo of War*,
    pp. 133–9.

for a *bad* piece of programme planning': 'These programmes are purely utilitarian; they do not need much contrast either in style or dynamics ... just try to make the period one of unrelieved BRIGHT-NESS AND CHEERFULNESS.'[61] Contrary to some accounts, the primary purpose of the programme was not so much to improve factory output (though anecdotal evidence to this effect was rife) as to lift the spirits of war workers, especially women new to factory work.[62] Since it was equally popular among non-factory listeners and among the forces, it also came to be seen as a link between servicemen, home front and factory front. The wide appeal of factory entertainment that steered clear of propaganda was further demonstrated in *Workers' Playtime*, broadcast through ENSA from factories across Britain, and *Works Wonders*, which featured amateur entertainment provided by the workers themselves (and so, like Vera Lynn, was deplored by critics at the same time as its popularity was noted), and attracted a regular audience of between seven and eight million, in factories, service quarters and homes.[63]

However, the most popular of all BBC wartime variety programmes, *It's That Man Again – ITMA –* was notable above all for transcending notions of 'highbrow' and 'lowbrow'. After an inauspicious debut in early 1939, the programme took off once war had broken out to become, in the words of Tom Harrisson, 'the best and most intelligent [of] variety shows that the BBC have put on ever'.[64] Written by New Zealander former medical student Ted Kavanagh and produced by Oxford graduate Francis Worsley, it made a national star of Liverpudlian music-hall veteran Tommy Handley, whose 'terrific vitality' was as essential to the programme's appeal as its elaborate joke structure, satirical edge (government officials took especial punishment), characters and catchphrases that became part of Britain's wartime vocabulary.[65] It successfully married

61. Hutchinson to Watt, 10 July 1940 (original emphasis); circular to all programme builders, 22 July 1940, BBC WAC R27/257/1.
62. Compare *Electrical Times*, 26 June 1941 with Reynolds, 'General Directive MWYW', June 1942, BBC WAC R27/257/3.
63. 'Who can assess the value of such stimulation to public morale?', *Manchester Guardian*, 25 November 1941.
64. Tom Harrisson to Stephen Potter, 1 April 1940, M-O Topic Collection Radio Box 3F.
65. See T. Harrisson, 'Second trial note for *New Statesman*', 1 February 1940, M-O Topic Collection 'Radio' Box 3B; also *The ITMA Years* (London, The Woburn Press, 1974).

snappy American production values (its producer claimed he wanted it to be a British version of the *Burns and Allen Show*) with British attitudes, jokes and fantastic situations. By the time of its celebrated tour of service bases in January 1944, Thursday evening's *ITMA* on the Home Service and its Sunday lunchtime repeat on the Forces Programme reached an estimated half the population, taking its undisputed place in 'the top flight of all the radio programmes of the world.' *ITMA* became a fixture of post-war light entertainment, and only came to an end with Handley's sudden death in January 1949, when, for the first time, Britain mourned a radio star as both national hero and lost friend.[66]

V

ITMA, The Shadow of the Swastika and other programmes showed with what success a public service broadcaster could negotiate a more populist approach within its broad remit to inform, educate and entertain. Yet the BBC's greatest success in uniting both the educative and the entertaining, *Any Questions* (better known by its original subtitle *The Brains Trust*), was an uncategorizable hybrid, whose successful bridging of elite and popular culture defied analysis. *The Brains Trust* ran from January 1941 almost without a break through-out the war (and afterwards), one of the very few series not to be taken off the air at the height of its popularity. It became a national sensation and the three original 'resident panellists', C. E. M. Joad, Professor of Philosophy and Psychology at Birkbeck College, London; Julian Huxley, Secretary of the London Zoo; and seafarer and raconteur Commander A. B. Campbell; together with the original chairman Donald McCullough, the most unlikely of national cele-brities. The reasons for the programme's popularity were hotly contested at the time, for they went to the heart of the question of what audiences wanted from the BBC and what the BBC was able or willing to offer in return.

The Brains Trust consisted of three resident panellists and two guests, marshalled by a chairman, answering questions of fact and opinion sent in by listeners. It had its origins in a plea from some

66. *News Chronicle*, 21 January 1944. For the extraordinary public response to Handley's death, see M-O Topic Collection 'Radio' Box 4D.

Figure 7   *The Brains Trust*, 1941, © BBC. (Left to right) Julian Huxley, W. D.
McCullough, G. E. M. Joad, Dr Malcolm Sargent, Miss Ellen Wilkinson MP,
Commander A. B. Campbell. Producer Howard Thomas is in the background.

servicemen for something more intellectually satisfying on the Forces
Programme than light comedy and dance music. Conceived therefore
as a broadly 'educational' experiment, the programme was, uniquely,
co-produced by a Variety producer, Howard Thomas (before the
war a successful advertising executive with experience in commercial
radio), and a Features producer, Douglas Cleverdon, later a leading
figure in the BBC Third Programme. It was an uneasy marriage of
convenience and the programme was not obviously fated to succeed:
Cleverdon (who originally nominated Joad and Huxley to the residents' panel) envisaged the series as presenting an analogy of the
brain at work, demonstrating on air the collaborative intellectual
exercise of finding the solution to a question through discussion
between panellists; Thomas (who nominated Campbell and McCullough) saw instead the entertainment potential of asking 'great brains'
to adjudicate bizarre claims or seemingly insoluble riddles. They did
not prove natural collaborators, and Cleverdon was happy to move

on to other things (though less so when Thomas began claiming sole parentage of the programme), but it is clear that if the programme would not have been the success it was without Thomas it certainly would not have taken the form it did without Cleverdon.[67]

The first programme attracted a small audience of about 5 per cent (1.5 million listeners), but within a month it had been decided to extend the planned six-week run and by August it had achieved the accolade of a *Picture Post* spread that described it as 'fast becoming something of a national institution', and was receiving 2,000 (eventually rising to 3,000) letters a week. The first questions sent in were from service personnel, but soon the producers were receiving questions from listeners of every class, age, locality and walk of life (including, it was claimed, the Royal Family). The type of questions featured (which ranged from the philosophical 'What is the meaning of democracy?' and the informational 'What causes colour-blindness?' to the notorious 'Why do flies land upside-down on the ceiling?') proved a compelling mixture. When it was moved to a Sunday 4 p.m. time slot (repeated on the Home Service on Tuesday evenings) the programme's audiences soared, and by 1944 it had an aggregate weekly audience of almost 40 per cent. The previously obscure phrase 'brains trust' swept the country, as the format was copied in barracks, town halls, villages, schools, local constituency party meetings – even prisoner-of-war camps overseas – and newspapers and magazines ran 'Brains Trust' columns. Not even children's literature was immune: the plot of Richmal Crompton's *William and the Brains Trust* (1945) centres on a case of mistaken identity involving a Joad-esque radio celebrity invited to the village's own brains trust and a comedian–impressionist appearing in a nearby Forces revue. The series itself featured Welsh, Scottish and Irish editions, transatlantic editions (with guests ranging from Jan Struther, author of *Mrs Miniver*, to New York Mayor Fiorello LaGuardia contributing from the BBC's New York studio) and Empire Service editions. To mark the programme's second anniversary a *Listeners' Brains Trust* reversed normal procedure and featured a cross-section of ordinary listeners answering questions sent in by the resident panellists. On the basis

67. See Thomas's popular but self-serving 'insider's account', *Britain's Brains Trust* (London, Chapman & Hall, 1944). The following discussion is based principally on *Brains Trust* files, BBC WAC R51/23/1–5. See also Briggs, *War of Words*, pp. 560–6; Seaton, 'Broadcasting and the Blitz', pp. 162–3; P. Black, *The Biggest Aspidistra in the World* (London, BBC Books, 1972), pp. 100–9.

of their broadcasting fame, Joad moved into popular journalism with a wartime newspaper column and Commander Campbell toured the music halls with a one-man show; Huxley, however, resigned his zoo position after complaints about his outside activities.[68]

What was the programme's appeal? Tom Harrisson, writing for the *Observer*, placed it above all in its spontaneity ('the rarest thing in radio'), and in Joad's giggle ('The giggle itself is a radio revolution no less. It underlines Joad's emancipation from those cautious disciplines which encircle and deodorise nine-tenths of BBC talk').[69] In a radio culture based on scripts, even for ostensibly spontaneous discussions, *The Brains Trust* was one of the very few genuinely unscripted BBC programmes (being recorded 'live' and edited before broadcast), and the effect on listeners of hearing lively and often heated impromptu debate – as well as the stumblings and hesitations of ordinary speech – was electric. The extent to which the programme's content determined its appeal was a more contested issue. Thomas attributed the programme's success to its light tone, and fought attempts to increase its serious content. The panellists themselves were equally certain that the programme's appeal lay in its serious agenda and capacity for intellectual debate (leavened by Campbell's 'common sense' and fund of anecdotes), and they periodically voiced disquiet at creeping elements of frivolity. Clearly it was entertaining to hear 'great minds' wrestle with the possible reasons why horses stood up front legs first but cows back legs first. But to have devoted the entire programme to such conundrums would have made it no more than a rather undignified parlour game, with a short life in broadcasting and a dwindling number of willing panellists. Instead, one of the most remarkable features of the programme was the willingness of the British intelligentsia to participate. The list of wartime panellists is a virtual roll-call of the nation's elite: Kenneth Clark, Augustus John, H. G. Wells, E. H. Carr, Leslie Howard, Sir William Beveridge and Edith Summerskill, among many others, plus such celebrities as West Indies cricketer Learie Constantine and theatrical impresario C. B. Cochran. The programme was also unusual in seeking to feature at least one woman panellist

68. *Picture Post*, 30 August 1941; LR/2847, 6 September 1944, BBC WAC R9/9/8 (this figure does not take account of 'double listening'); Thomas, *Britain's Brains Trust*, pp. 37–41, 168–78.
69. T. Harrisson, script, 10 November 1942, M-O Topic Collection 'Radio' Box 3B.

each week, despite Thomas's belief that the microphone was 'a man's instrument' and the brains trust format 'too difficult' for many women to deal with successfully.[70] Only a few people, recognizing their broadcast limitations, turned down the invitation to appear on *The Brains Trust* (among them E. M. Forster); perhaps the most striking absentee from the guest list was J. B. Priestley. The value placed by participants themselves on the programme's serious aspect was underlined when in 1943 Thomas attempted to adapt the format for an 'experts' quiz' in a new Variety show *Everybody's Mike*. The first team, six MPs (including *Brains Trust* regulars Jennie Lee and Quintin Hogg), walked out just before their 'turn', having seen a copy of the script which seemed designed principally to humiliate them in public. The show was cancelled a few weeks later and Thomas left the BBC shortly after.[71]

Above all, the programme's appeal lay in the debate it sparked, the sense of identification that its unscripted opinions prompted, and its remarkable power as a common reference point. As Briggs notes, it bore a striking similarity to *ITMA*, with its characters and catchphrases (Joad: 'It depends what you mean by ...'; Huxley: 'Surely ...'; Campbell: 'When I was in ...'), its combination of topicality and timelessness, its 'supremely "unofficial"' tone and its ability to attract every kind of listener.[72] No programme was so widely discussed after its broadcast, at home and at work, 'in trains, public houses and camps throughout the country'.[73] When the panel discussed 'Is Vera Lynn harmful to morale?', its comments were reported throughout both the general and trade press; when panel member Malcolm Sargent claimed swing music was inferior to classical (only Campbell begging to differ), the leader of the BBC's most popular house band and musical director of ENSA, Geraldo, publicly challenged Sargent to swap batons, to prove that dance

70. '[To] discover women guests for the Brains Trust, with all the virtues of feminine charm, fluency of speech, depth of knowledge, logical minds, plus being able to mix in something of an after-dinner manner with a company of men, was no easy matter' (Thomas, *Britain's Brains Trust*, p. 62).
71. For instance, compère Naunton Wayne's script introduced Jennie Lee MP as 'dark and sparkling and all eager to tear up the questions and me', and followed up a question on the Beveridge Report with the aside, 'This will show if they have read it or not' (note to Miss Fuller, 8 June 1943, BBC WAC R19/326; *The Star*, 9 June 1943).
72. Briggs, *War of Words*, p. 566.
73. Thomas, *Britain's Brains Trust*, p. 37.

musicians had as high a standard of technical ability and musicianship as classical players.[74] After Joad quoted the Confucian aphorism 'What economy is it to go to bed in order to save candlelight if the result be twins?' in a discussion of the relative merits as philosophers of Confucius and Plato, Parliament itself discussed this new manifestation of BBC vulgarity.[75]

Reith, one speculates, would have found it both trivial and undignified, but *The Brains Trust* did more to simultaneously entertain, educate and inform the listening public than any previous BBC programme. Indeed, although historians now question the popular contemporary belief that the war was making the public increasingly serious-minded, the popular response to such programmes as *The Brains Trust* presents an alternative perspective. The BBC steered clear of 'controversy' until nearly the end of the war, but news and topical talks were the backbone of wartime broadcasting, and listeners increasingly noted with disapproval *The Brains Trust*'s apparent reluctance to engage in topical or controversial political subjects. The extending of the resident panel to nine in 1942 and the splitting-up of the original threesome was defended by Thomas as a means of keeping listeners' attention, but was widely reported as having been carried out to ensure a less left-wing tone to the discussion. The panel itself protested to the Chairman of the BBC in January 1943 at the programme's studied avoidance of political and religious questions. Listener criticism mounted through 1943 and 1944 at the programme's failure to discuss reconstruction; an LR report in September 1944 noted a plea for questions that 'matter', and producer Peter Bax noted at the end of the fourth series in June 1945 the growing proportion of 'serious' questions among those sent in.[76] Hamstrung by a government that was embarrassed at the popularity of the Beveridge Report, and disconcerted by listener research that suggested strong levels of public cynicism about politicians' promises, the BBC stepped tentatively around such issues until late in the war.[77] But although much has recently been made of the British people's fears as opposed to hopes for the future in the last years

74. *Melody Maker*, 3 January 1942, p. 5; 21 February 1942, pp. 1, 3.
75. *Hansard*, Vol. 378, col. 209, 25 February 1942.
76. 'Everyone listens to the BT but everyone is dissatisfied with it', *Daily Herald*, 29 July 1944; LR/2847 6 September 1944, BBC WAC R9/9/8; Bax memorandum, 6 June 1945, R51/23/5.
77. LR/2553, 22 April 1944, BBC WAC R9/9/8.

of the war and leading up to the General Election of 1945, to interpret this hostility as indifference or apathy is misguided.[78] *Jobs for All*, an eight-part discussion series on the issue of post-war employment policy, broadcast on the Home Service over a two-week period in December 1944, was in tone and structure stilted, class-ridden and contrived. Yet it attracted audience figures of 26 per cent (over eight and a half million listeners), a quarter of whom (two million or more), it was found, had been unemployed before the war. Most remarkably, the series attracted higher audiences than the programmes scheduled against it on the General Forces Programme – including the ever-popular *Music Hall*.[79] How the *Brains Trust* panel might have tackled these issues is something the BBC never dared find out.

VII

It might have been thought that the BBC ended the war full of pride at its achievements and of anticipation at a new era of popular broadcasting. Yet, even before the war in Europe had ended, it was becoming fashionable to deplore the poor quality and simplistic and emotional appeal of wartime broadcasting, and to look to the post-war BBC to reintroduce intellectual stimulation and rigour to the airwaves. In *Horizon* Cyril Connolly disparaged the 'mediocrity' of the wartime BBC, while in a breathtakingly hostile *Listener* article Philip Hope-Wallace pronounced that 'To mere broadcastings of other people's enjoyments; to the amateur croonings of works-managers' daughters; to all tipsy-sentimental, idiot-nostalgic patter; to these and a thousand other feeblenesses we can no longer extend the justification that, somewhere, they might be helping to forget the war for a few minutes.'[80] While some within the BBC prided

---

78. See, for instance, S. Fielding, 'What Did "The People" Want?: The Meaning of the 1945 General Election', *Historical Journal*, 35 (1992), pp. 623–39; S. Fielding, P. Thompson and N. Tiratsoo, *'England Arise!': The Labour Party and Popular Politics in the 1940s* (Manchester, Manchester UP, 1995), ch. 2.
79. For two differing assessments of *Jobs for All*, see Cardiff and Scannell, 'Radio in World War II', pp. 56–9, and Nicholas, *Echo of War*, pp. 254–5.
80. C. Connolly, *Horizon*, December 1944, p. 367, quoted in P. Fussell, *Wartime: Understanding and Behaviour in the Second World War* (Oxford, Oxford UP, 1989), p. 219; *The Listener*, 29 March 1945, p. 360.

themselves on their wartime achievements, others deplored the war-time neglect of broadcasting's cultural role: Val Gielgud, head of BBC Drama, for instance, derided the wartime vogue for popular radio serials as the 'flattery of the ego of the common man'.[81] The post-war Third Programme was conceived by Director-General William Haley in part to restore to the airwaves that culturally elevating element seen as characteristic of British broadcasting.

Thus although the war years witnessed profound changes in the style and substance of British broadcasting (greater technical sophis-tication, a more professional approach to scheduling, more ambitious newsgathering, more popular and informal programme styles, and so on), the BBC's own culture was changed less than might have been thought by the war. There was never any intention of having a 'people's BBC': the inter-war preoccupation with 'elevating' persisted into the post-war period. Reithan aims were not so much removed as redefined, the aims left intact and only the method changed. Although Reith himself dismissed the Third Programme as no more than 'a sop to [the] moral conscience' of broadcasters who had abandoned their beliefs in public service broadcasting, Haley saw it as the keystone of a policy of progressive cultural education, envisaging a 'cultural pyramid' with the Light Programme at the base and the Third Programme at its apex, that would in time naturally invert itself as 'lowbrow' tastes were raised.[82]

It has often proved tempting to give the BBC credit for much it did not deserve, or achieved only by accident or force of circum-stance. It is also easy to decry the BBC's wartime achievements as far more apparent than real, its conspicuous successes merely high-lighting deeper inadequacies. The BBC during the war set out with a sense of responsibility to preserve national unity and national culture. When following this prescriptive remit, it rarely succeeded. Indeed it is possible to conclude that national unity was cemented at least as much by *Children's Hour* and record-request programmes as by patriotic tributes and/or classic drama. When it acknowledged that its listeners might in fact *need* the same things that they *wanted* (that is, entertainment, information and reliable news), the BBC found itself projecting a 'common culture' notable for its diversity

81. Gielgud, quoted in Drakakis, 'Introduction', p. 10.
82. *The Reith Diaries*, ed. C. Stuart (London, Collins, 1975), p. 474. Cf. Haley, quoted in Carpenter, *Envy of the World*, p. 6.

as much as its homogeneity. But there was no magic formula. No BBC programme created a common constituency more than *The Brains Trust*, but the reasons for its success were disputed by producers, panellists, critics and listeners. Like so much of the BBC's wartime policy, it owed its success as much to happy accident as to design.

In his *The Myth of the Blitz*, Angus Calder notes that, whatever the 'small facts' that cast shadows on the British wartime experience, the 'Big Facts' will always ultimately outshine them.[83] In this context, whatever faults the BBC had during the war (and there were many) serve above all to highlight the BBC's overall achievement in maintaining national unity and national morale during a time of unparallelled difficulty. The BBC certainly achieved less than it could have – but it also achieved more than might have been thought possible, given the broadcasting culture from which it came. Its achievement was less in sustaining a single national culture than in overseeing (at times despite itself) a national community of listeners characterized by the diversity of their lives, interests and cultural preferences. No one, least of all the BBC itself, could confirm the reasons behind its success. But the presentation of a rich and diverse public culture across a mass medium that formed part of the fabric of everyday life placed the BBC at the very heart of wartime Britain.

83. A. Calder, *The Myth of the Blitz* (London, Jonathan Cape, 1991), pp. 90, 120.

Was it the *Mirror* Wot Won it? The Development of the Tabloid Press During the Second World War

Michael Bromley

A n anecdote related by the former editor of *Picture Post*, Tom Hopkinson, remains many years later a potent symbol of the supposed radicalization of the British electorate in the first half of the 1940s, which has given a particular significance to the Second World War as 'the people's war'.[1] Following the general election of 1945 Hopkinson was accosted by a Conservative politician who insisted that it was Hopkinson's weekly illustrated magazine which had secured Labour's huge success. Hopkinson demurred: the *Daily Mirror* newspaper had been far more influential, he felt.[2] The story continues to have currency, and the idea that a left-wing press, in particular a combination of *Picture Post* and the *Mirror*, played a crucial role in establishing the agenda for post-war reconstruction has proved remarkably resilient.[3]

Contemporaries certainly believed that the press helped mobilize public support behind a project which some on the right saw as

I am grateful to Tom O'Malley, Nick Hayes and Jeff Hill for reading and commenting on a draft of this essay, and to Bruce Hanlin for the benefit of his advice derived from his many years of interest in Picture Post.

1. A. Calder, *The People's War: Britain 1939–45* (London, Jonathan Cape, 1969); S. Fielding. P. Thompson and N. Tiratsoo, *'England Arise!': The Labour Party and Popular Politics in 1940s Britain* (Manchester, Manchester UP, 1995), p. 19.
2. T. Hopkinson, *'Picture Post', 1938–50* (Harmondsworth, Penguin, 1984), p. 15.
3. P. Addison, 'Churchill and the price of victory: 1939–45', in *From Blitz*

taking Britain 'half-way to Moscow'.[4] George Orwell argued that
the press had been able to play this role because, as the war economy
was focused away from personal and household consumption, the
power of advertisers and other commercial interests over the press
waned, leaving them more 'controlled by journalists'. As a result,
Orwell sometimes felt the press demonstrated 'how very much
more thoughtful and also "left-wing" the non-highbrow public has
grown'.[5] Not all 'the sensational nonsense', 'stunt make-up' or
'screaming headlines' had been eliminated, but it did seem possible
to contemplate the arrival of a moment of cultural reformation.[6]
The challenge seemed to be to satisfy at one and the same time
popular tastes which existed for *both* 'light entertainment and high
thinking'.[7]

After 1945, the primacy of commercialism was reasserted, however.
Journalism, as a quasi-profession, was either unable or unwilling to
resist its own degrading, despite its pivotal role in the establishment
of the first Royal Commission on the Press in 1946. Journalists
and intellectuals on the left limited their ambitions for democratic

   to Blair: A New History of Britain since 1939, ed. N. Tiratsoo (London,
   Weidenfeld & Nicolson, 1997), pp. 67–8; see also P. Addison, *The Road to
   1945: British Politics and the Second World War* (London, Pimlico, 2nd edn,
   1994), p. 154.
4. The *Daily Telegraph* claimed Sir William Beveridge had said in an interview
   that his then still unpublished proposals for social security would take Britain
   'half-way to Moscow'. Beveridge denied the quote, which the newspaper later
   withdrew. See *Daily Telegraph*, 13 November 1942, p. 3; letter from Beveridge
   in *Daily Telegraph*, 18 November 1942, p. 4; and *Daily Telegraph*, 19
   November 1942, p. 3.
5. G. Orwell, letter to David H. Thompson, 8 March 1940, in *The Collected
   Essays, Journalism and Letters of George Orwell, Volume 1: An Age Like This,
   1920–1940*, eds S. Orwell and I. Angus (Harmondsworth, Penguin, 1968),
   p. 453; 'London Letter', *Partisan Review*, 15 April 1941, in *The Collected
   Essays, Journalism and Letters of George Orwell, Volume 2: My Country Right
   or Left, 1940–1943*, eds S. Orwell and I. Angus (Harmondsworth, Penguin,
   1970), p. 144.
6. G. Orwell, 'As I please', *Tribune*, 21 April 1944, in *The Collected Essays,
   Journalism and Letters of George Orwell, Volume 3: As I Please, 1943–1945*,
   eds S. Orwell and I. Angus (Harmondsworth, Penguin, 1970), p. 156; 'London
   Letter', *Partisan Review*, 15 April 1941, in *Collected Essays, Volume 2*,
   pp. 137–8.
7. Addison, *Road*, p. 152.

control of the press, accepting the principle of private ownership.[8] Furthermore, the Labour Party's participation in government from 1940 led to its attaining the 'commanding heights' of news management. Initiated by the exigences of war, and often dressed up as integral to the process of 'public accountability', by 1951 public relations was deeply embedded in government.[9] That the decade between the mid-1930s and mid-1940s is still regarded as a Golden Age of the popular press, in which 'the voice of the people' was truly heard *via* the mediation of independent journalism, may reflect responses to trends which have occurred since, rather than those of the period itself.[10] Other historical interpretations contend that in 1945 the British public was less in favour of the centrally planned economic and social innovations of Labour, and more concerned with registering its opposition to a Conservative Party associated with pre-war gross social inequality and the policy of appeasement – a hostility towards what the Labour politician Hugh Dalton called 'The Thoughtless Thirties and Workless Thirties'.[11]

Possibly no single event provided a better opportunity for the press to demonstrate its 'popular' credentials than the publication of the Beveridge Report in December 1942. The report was completed after Churchill had announced 'the end of the beginning' of the war and reconstruction had begun to emerge as the dominant theme of the war effort. Hundreds of thousands of copies of the report itself, and a cheap summary published for the purpose, were sold: here, it seemed, was a chance to show that 'the day of the common people had arrived'. In the midst of 'the people's war' came 'the people's Beveridge'.[12]

Picture Post's detailed and lengthy advocacy of Beveridge's proposals for a more comprehensive welfare state has coloured

8. Orwell, 'As I please', T. O'Malley, 'Labour and the 1947–9 Royal Commission on the Press', in *A Journalism Reader*, eds M. Bromley and T. O'Malley (London, Routledge, 1997), p. 129; p. 154.

9. H. Morrison, *Government and Parliament: A Survey from the Inside* (London, Oxford UP, 1954), pp. 268–72.

10. See G. Cox, 'The editor who made love – and great news', *British Journalism Review*, 7:3 (1996), pp. 16–24.

11. See S. Fielding, 'What did the people want? The meaning of the 1945 General Election', *Historical Journal*, 35 (1992), pp. 623–39; *The Times*, 19 October 1942, p. 2.

12. Addison, *Road*, p. 154; T. Hopkinson, *Of This Our Time: A Journalist's Story, 1905–1950* (London, Hutchinson, 1982), p. 211.

many recollections of the war. Similarly, the *Mirror*'s coverage of
Beveridge has received a considerable amount of attention. There
were connections between them. For example, the *Mirror*, having
wind of a possible Cabinet fudge over the report, ran a pre-emptive
editorial on 21 November 1942 urging its immediate publication in
full. A week later, Edward Hulton, the proprietor of *Picture Post*,
used his regular column in the magazine to add his support to the
Mirror's campaign.[13] Hulton, although formally a Conservative, and
Cecil King, who was instrumental in forging the *Mirror*'s editorial
identity in the late 1930s, largely shared a vision of reconstruction.
Yet this is to obscure the fundamental differences between the two
publications. Orwell was among those who recognized that the press
offered and invited different interpretations of content and presentation founded in social experience.[14] While the *Mirror*'s approach was
to establish the immediate links between Beveridge's proposals and
the everyday lives of its readers, *Picture Post* was more inclined
to explore the ideological ground which lay behind the report.
Beveridge, the *Mirror* announced, 'tells how to BANISH WANT': *Picture
Post* posed the question, 'Do we want more State planning?' The
Mirror's pragmatic view of the social egalitarianism behind the report
was that it meant 'All pay – all benefit.' *Picture Post*'s more idealistic
vision was of a 'Changing Britain'.[15]

In this essay it will be argued that an analysis which depends too
heavily on the categorization of the press during the Second World
War on the basis of its political alignments is misleading. The press
in the 1940s addressed and appealed to audiences segmented on a
variety of often overlapping levels – age, gender, income, leisure
interests, class, as well as politics – which were not simply subsumed
by the experiences of war. Mass-Observation (M-O) found it difficult
to trace simple qualitative relationships between the press and its
readers; political commitment appeared to be only one of several
significant factors.[16] A comparison will be offered here of the coverage

13. M. Edelman, *The 'Mirror': A Political History* (London, Hamish Hamilton,
    1966), p. 135; E. Hulton, 'A new social services charter', *Picture Post*, 28
    November 1942, p. 26.
14. G. Orwell, 'London Letter', p. 153.
15. *Daily Mirror*, 2 December 1942, p. 1; *Picture Post*, 20 February 1943, pp. 24–6,
    2 January 1943, pp. 1–30.
16. Mass-Observation, *The Press and Its Readers* (London, Art & Technics, 1949),
    esp. pp. 110–17.

of the publication of the Beveridge Report in a number of newspapers and weekly magazines whose editorial approaches were designed to appeal to differing configurations of readers. This, it is argued, will identify distinguishing characteristics of individual titles which transcended, although did not necessarily contest, their politics. All the publications broadly supported the Beveridge proposals and their early implementation. Moreover, given newsprint rationing, the further pressure on space from competing news from the military fronts, and a tendency towards the 'straight' reporting of official pronouncements, it is not surprising that there were many similarities in the content of the Beveridge coverage. Yet at a time when the tabloid newspaper (a description which applied as much to style, and the use of 'bright, snappy stories, big pictures and bold headlines', as to size [17]) was still a novelty, but exerting a growing influence, the treatment of the Beveridge story (for example, the balance struck between graphic and 'objective', or between actuality and background, reporting), it will be argued, was of particular significance.[18]

It is in this treatment that there can be found distinguishing differences between the *Mirror*, which was Britain's first truly tabloid newspaper, and the 'popular' orthodox broadsheet newspaper of the Labour movement, the *Daily Herald*, and also, more incongruously, connections between the Labourite *Mirror* and the Conservative *News of the World*. Equally, the *News of the World* can be seen to display critical, although still inchoate differences from another 'popular' broadsheet Sunday paper, the Co-operative *Reynolds News*. Finally, the analysis is extended beyond newspapers to include *Picture Post* and a rival weekly illustrated magazine with a more populist approach, *John Bull*. The editorial positioning of the two weeklies, both individually and in relationship to each other, in many respects paralleled those of newspapers beginning to arrange themselves along a 'popular'-tabloid axis.[19] In not only presentation,

17. A. C. H. Smith, *Paper Voices: The Popular Press and Social Change, 1935–1965* (London: Chatto & Windus, 1975), p. 64 passim; D. Griffiths (ed.), *The Encylopedia of the British Press, 1492–1992* (London, Macmillan, 1992), p. 50; p. 183; p. 185.
18. S. Hall, 'A world at one with itself', in *The Manufacture of News. Deviance, Social Problems and the Mass Media*, eds S. Cohen and J. Young (London, Constable, 1977), pp. 85–6.
19. D. Reed, *The Popular Magazine in Britain and the United States, 1880–1960* (London, British Library, 1997), pp. 185–6.

but also extent of coverage, tone, sources of information, engagement with readers, and comment, a clear distinction, which owed little or nothing to politics, can be drawn among both newspapers and magazines between a broadly tabloid approach and the older 'popular' journalism of social commentary.

I

The newspapers which characterized the 1930s were the 'popular' titles (particularly among the dailies, the *Mail, Herald, Express* and *News Chronicle*), whose sales comprised more than 70 per cent of the aggregate circulations of the national press. The tabloid newspaper appeared in mid-decade in the form of the *Daily Mirror*, and by 1937 it and the other tabloid, the *Daily Sketch*, accounted for about a fifth of the daily market. This rose to nearly 30 per cent over the next ten years, and coincided with an expansion of readerships, particularly among the working class. The aggregate circulations of the national press tripled between 1920 and 1947.[20] Across all titles, from *The Times* to the *News of the World*, content, presentation and style were tailored to appeal to a widening spectrum of readers.[21] Some 'popular' papers had larger numbers of middle-class readers than elements of what was commonly called the 'intelligent' or 'class' press (*The Times*, the *Telegraph*). In 1939 even the tabloid *Mirror* attracted significant numbers of middle-class readers, and of the daily newspapers only the *Herald* had an overwhelmingly working-class readership. By the end of the war, proportionately as many Labour voters took the Conservative *News of the World* as the Labour *Sunday Pictorial*, and almost as many took the Liberal *News Chronicle* as the *Mirror*.[22] This presented difficulties for the 'popular' press. At the *Herald*, editors debated the competing claims to space of the traditional coverage of current

20. R. Williams, *The Long Revolution* (London, Chatto & Windus, 1961), pp. 173–213.
21. C. Seymour-Ure, *The British Press and Broadcasting Since 1945* (Oxford, Blackwell, 2nd edn, 1996), pp. 148–50.
22. T. Jeffrey and K. McClelland, 'A world fit to live in: the *Daily Mail* and the middle classes, 1918–1939', in *Impacts and Influences: Essays on Media Power in the Twentieth Century*, eds J. Curran, A. Smith and P. Wingate (London, Methuen, 1987), p. 38; Mass-Observation, *Press*, tables 46 and 47, p. 126.

affairs and items about such apparent frivolities as 'a queerly-shaped potato dug out of an Ilford allotment'.[23]

The press entered the war in many respects discredited. It was accused of being paradoxically secretive, even censorial, socially deferential and insensitive. It was widely felt to be exploitatively irresponsible and, above all, motivated by the 'self-serving attempts to obtain personal recognition, political leverage, and especially commercial advantage' of its owners and managers. '[L]eft to their own devices' by Conservative governments,[24] papers did not publish anything 'actually offensive to the governing class ... at least in any place where large numbers of people are likely to read it'.[25] Analysts of the press, such as the organization Political and Economic Planning (PEP), believed that the accelerated commercialization of the press which had occurred in the 1930s was inimical to its democratic role. Claud Cockburn resigned from *The Times* to start his own paper, *The Week*, in 1932 because he believed the press's cosy relationship with the Establishment resulted in the suppression of information, and newspapers full of 'tight-lipped drabness'.[26] A number of prominent journalists, including a former editor of *The Times*, the editor of the *New Statesman* and a former president of the National Union of Journalists (NUJ), published critiques of the commercialism in newspapers, which had manifested itself most notoriously in the 'circulation wars' of the early 1930s, but which was also seen as being responsible for dubious journalistic practices, trivialization and sensationalism.[27] Such complaints formed the basis of the terms of reference of the Royal Commission which began work in 1947.[28] Orwell's view, which was

23. H. Richards, *The Bloody Circus: The 'Daily Herald' and the Left* (London, Pluto, 1997), p. 133.
24. S. Koss, *The Rise and Fall of the Political Press in Britain* (London, Fontana, 1990), pp. 980–1.
25. G. Orwell, 'As I please', pp. 211–12.
26. C. Cockburn, *Cockburn Sums Up* (London, Quartet, 1981), pp. 92–3.
27. O'Malley, 'Labour', pp. 131–6; Hugh Stephenson, 'Tickle the public: consumerism rules', in *Sex, Lies and Democracy: The Press and the Public*, eds M. Bromley and H. Stephenson (Harlow, Longman, 1998), pp. 13–24; H. Wickham Steed, *The Press* (Harmondsworth, Penguin, 1938); F. J. Mansfield, *'Gentlemen, The Press!' Chronicles of a Crusade* (London, W. H. Allen, 1943); K. Martin, *The Press and Public Wants* (London, The Hogarth Press, 1947).
28. Royal Commission on the Press, *Report* (London, HMSO, 1949), Cmd 7700, p. iii.

shared by many, was that in the 1920s and 1930s the press had been corrupted by commercialism; however, he believed this process had been assisted by the fact that Britain was a 'low-brow country ... [in which] the printed word doesn't matter greatly'.[29]

Orwell, who was nothing if not ambivalent about such matters, felt that the English public – 'the masses' – were largely inclined to 'philistinism'.[30] Even before the Royal Commission sat, Kingsley Martin sought to remind the public that in instituting the so-called newspaper revolution in the 1890s, Lord Northcliffe had hit on war, sex, crime, sport and a mix of the 'trivial and informative' as what sold newspapers most effectively to an increasingly mass market. Martin ridiculed the 'human interest' approach:

> Any flapper may become headline news if she makes the acquaintance of an eccentric clergyman; there is not one of us, however obscure, who may not become famous overnight if we care to throw ourselves from a window overlooking Piccadilly or arrange to strangle our sweethearts in sordid circumstances.[31]

It was felt in some quarters that 'pictures, "snippets", "human stories", the antics of film stars, football competitions and the profits of professional bruisers' had squeezed the serious reporting and consideration of politics from the columns of newspapers.[32] More thoughtfully, Orwell, charting 'the decline of the English murder', recognized the influence of the tradition of the Sunday newspaper in exposing the hypocrisy of stable (middle-class) domesticity to the apparently endless fascination, and social satisfaction, of a (mainly working-class) readership.[33] The challenge, as many saw it, was to combine a 'reflect[ion] of the distractions of modern life no less faithfully than existing papers reflect them ... [with] the truths behind these appearances ... [and] care for public affairs'.[34]

29. G. Orwell, 'A farthing newspaper', in *The Collected Essays, Journalism and Letters of George Orwell, Volume 1*, p. 37; 'London Letter', p. 144.
30. G. Orwell, 'The English people', in *The Collected Essays, Journalism and Letters of George Orwell, Volume 3*, pp. 53–5.
31. Martin, *Press*, pp. 56–67.
32. Wickham Steed, *Press*, pp. 170–1.
33. G. Orwell, 'The decline of the English murder', *Tribune*, 15 February 1946, in *The Collected Essays, Journalism and Letters of George Orwell, Volume 4: In Front of Your Nose, 1945–1950*, eds S. Orwell and I. Angus (Harmondsworth, Penguin, 1970), p. 124–8.
34. Wickham Steed, *Press*, pp. 246–8.

Inherent in the human-interest story was personalisation. 'The average man', Orwell reflected, 'is not directly interested in politics and, when he reads, he wants the current struggles of the world to be translated into a simple story about individuals.'[35] Left-wing journalists, such as Hannen Swaffer, argued for a more human-interest approach in the 'serious' press.[36] A good newspaper could be 'technically well-made, trustworthy, news-giving, hard-hitting [and] full of vim and drive'.[37] In the 1930s the primary model of 'vim and drive' was the *Daily Express*, the first London morning paper to carry news on the front page, to use banner headlines and openly to espouse substantially different editorial values by giving prominence to 'good news'. Its success was indicated by its claim to have the world's largest daily sale.[38] By 1947 less than 30 per cent of the editorial space of the *Express* was devoted to news. The *News Chronicle*, which carried the highest proportion of news among all the 'popular' morning papers, had 34 per cent, while the *Daily Mirror* gave over less than a quarter of its editorial columns to news. Even so, these 'more serious parts of the morning papers seem[ed] to be read sketchily and without much interest by a high proportion of "ordinary" people'. News was even less important to the readers of Sunday papers. Moreover, orthodox definitions did not always correspond to the readers' ideas that 'gossip and scandal' equated to news. The real attraction of news, M-O surmised in 1949, was its sensational character, and genuine interest in '*serious* news' was confined to probably no more than 27 per cent of all readers of the press.[39]

Only 17 per cent of *Daily Mirror* readers said that for them news was a main attraction of the paper. Nearly half the readers of the *News of the World* were attracted by the paper's coverage of gossip. Differences in the interest shown in politics were marked. More than a fifth of the *Herald*'s readers were attracted principally by the paper's political line. The figure for *Reynolds News* was 17 per cent (the largest among all the Sunday papers). Among *Mirror* and *News of the World* readers there was almost no interest at all in the papers'

35. G. Orwell, 'Raffles and Miss Blandish', *Horizon*, October 1944, in *The Collected Essays, Journalism and Letters of George Orwell, Volume 3*, p. 259.
36. Richards, *Bloody Circus*, pp. 154–5.
37. Wickham Steed, *Press*, p. 248 (my emphasis).
38. Williams, *Long Revolution*, p. 205; *Daily Express*, 14 April 1900, p. 1.
39. Mass-Observation, *Press*, pp. 26–7; p. 36; pp. 39–40; p. 46 (original emphasis).

politics. The two politicized papers of the Left (the *Herald* and *Reynolds News*) had, as might be expected, high proportions of Labour voters among their readers, and few uncommitted readers. The numbers of uncommitted readers of the *Mirror* and *News of the World* were significantly greater (20 per cent and 24 per cent, respectively). Almost a third of *Mirror* readers were actually unaware of its politics (see Table 1).[40]

Table 1: Newspaper readers' interest in news and politics
(% proportion of the total readerships of each title)

Newspaper	Interest in news	Interest in gossip	Interest in leading articles	Interest in paper's political line	Labour voters	Uncommitted voters
Daily Herald	25	2	4	21	81	10
Daily Mirror	17	1	3	3	58	24
News of the World	26	41	1	—	53	20
Reynolds News	9	—	4	17	65	14

Source: M-O (1949).

Despite drawing on the same broad working-class constituency, these four papers did not appeal to identical groups of readers. In 1939, the *Herald* and the *Mirror* were read by similar numbers of young people. A decade later the *Herald* (and *Reynolds News*) readers were older overall. The *Mirror* and *News of the World* readerships were on the whole younger and more evenly distributed between the sexes. In 1943 about 49 per cent of *Mirror* readers were women; 42 per cent were aged under 45.[41] Although less precisely determined, the *Herald* and *Reynolds News* almost certainly appealed more to organized workers in the old staple industries, while the *Mirror* and *News of the World* drew more of their readers from among the workers in the newer, lighter industries which emerged in the inter-war period. In 1939 nearly two-thirds of *Mirror* readers lived in the south-east of England – almost twice the number for the *Herald*.[42] These readership configurations had implications, not only for the

40. Ibid., tables 43–6, pp. 124–6.
41. H. Cudlipp, *Publish and Be Damned!* (London, Andrew Dakers, 1953), p. 122.
42. Jeffrey and McClelland, 'A world', p. 39; Richards, *Bloody Circus*, pp. 161–2.

politics of the individual titles, but also for the way in which newspaper content was treated.

The older, more politically committed readers of the *Herald* and *Reynolds News* showed a predilection for 'serious' news equivalent to that of those taking papers like the *Daily Express*, *Daily Mail*, *Observer* and *Sunday Times*. By comparison, the content of the *Mirror* and *News of the World* was skewed towards providing amusement, entertainment and the bizarre; for example, the *News of the World* carried a George Formby 'laughter column'.[43] Not only were the *Mirror* and *News of the World* readers far less interested in 'serious' news (and marginally more *Mirror* readers took it for its pictures than its news), but they were likely to be attracted by the style of presentation, which in the case of the *Mirror* was 'simple and lively'. Non-editorial material also ranked highly, and 27 per cent of *Mirror* readers regarded the comics and strip cartoons, which were such a feature of the paper in the 1930s and 1940s, as its most attractive feature. Nevertheless, the *Mirror* was no 'political lightweight'. Its achievement was to combine the popularity of the Sunday newspaper (the *News of the World* was 'the dominant newspaper' of the period, and its sales rose 110 per cent in the decade after 1938) with the aspirations to political influence of the daily.[44]

Orwell believed that there was no demonstrable mass demand for an 'intelligent' press, or, particularly among the young, for a 'serious' paper of the Left. The *Herald*, which was widely known as the 'miracle of Fleet Street', struggled for most of the period. Its circulation peaked in 1937 and was actually falling when war was declared.[45] In the 1940s the circulation of *Reynolds News*, which had once been one of the most widely read newspapers in Britain, was less than twice what it had been in the 1870s. After flirting briefly (and relatively successfully) with a content of 'crime and sex', the paper reverted to a 'serious popular' approach. This was felt to be a more fitting reflection of the 'interest and prestige' of its controllers, the Co-op. The *Herald*'s Labour connections prevented even such limited experimentation.[46] For example, in the 1930s it

43. *Popular Newspapers during World War II* (Marlborough, Adam Matthew, 1993), Parts 1 to 5: 1930–45, pp. 12–15.
44. Ibid., p. 51; Cudlipp, *Publish*, pp. 257–8.
45. Richards, *Bloody Circus*, pp. 144–61.
46. F. Williams, *Dangerous Estate: The Anatomy of Newspapers* (London, Arrow, 1959), p. 171; p. 201.

refused to carry comic strips, and ignored the craze for astrology, being the only 'popular' paper not to publish horoscopes.[47] Hugh Cudlipp called it 'the *Telegraph* of the left'. The difference in tone between it and the tabloid *Mirror* can be gauged from its occasional disdain for the latter's 'high-pitched and distasteful language' and 'silly' leaders.[48] This at a time when Orwell was justifiably complaining that leading articles, particularly in the mainstream newspapers of the Left, were written 'in an inflated bombastic style with a tendency to fall back on archaic words … which no normal person would ever think of using'.[49] Even among readers of the politicized press of the Left, there was very little interest in the papers' editorials (see Table 1).

The *Mirror*'s success was founded primarily on an extension of the commercialization of the press to secure huge numbers of mainly working-class readers by adopting the 'miscellany' approach of the Sunday papers, allied to the use of photographs, and aping the American tabloid.[50] This fundamental derivativeness should not obscure the reputation it gained for transforming the daily newspaper. Francis Williams thought its 'new kind of popular daily journalism' opened the door on to a different world. The *Mirror* redefined what news was, and employed a different type of journalist to provide it. This was not just a matter of tabloid presentation, but involved the adoption of the language and topics of 'four-ale bars, works canteens, shopping queues, fish-and-chip saloons, dance halls and jug and bottle departments'.[51] Cudlipp called it 'vivacity and a youthful attitude to life'. Alongside, the paper developed a social conscience, although only slowly. The shift from backing the Tories in 1935 reflected the anti-elitism of the paper's editorial director, Harry Guy Bartholomew, and King's radicalism. Yet it was only in 1943 that the paper began systematically to cover the political, social and economic issues of reconstruction. The *Mirror*'s reputation was based foremost on its campaigning stories on the price of cups of tea in

47. R. Graves and A. Hodge, *The Long Week-End: A Social History of Great Britain, 1918–1939* (London, Hutchinson, 1940, 1985), p. 430.
48. Cudlipp, *Publish*, p. 186; p. 189; p. 259.
49. G. Orwell, 'Propaganda and demotic speech', April 1944, in *The Collected Essays, Journalism and Letters of George Orwell, Volume 3*, p. 162.
50. H. Cudlipp, 'The godfather of the British tabloids', *British Journalism Review*, 8:2 (1997), p. 39.
51. Williams, *Dangerous Estate*, pp. 170–1; pp. 193–8.

cafés and cruelty to greyhounds, the exposure of King Edward VIII's intention to marry Mrs Simpson, its pin-ups, and, above all, its coverage of sex and crime. The paper was deliberately targeted at service personnel, factory workers and housewives, on the basis that these groups were interested most of all in 'their own appetites and the misfortunes of their neighbours'. The predominant treatment the *Mirror* gave to stories was an unabashed sensationalism.[52]

Picture Post was quite different. Launched in 1938 with realistic expectations of a circulation of no more than 150,000, within five months it was selling 1,350,000 copies a week. Unlike the *Mirror*, it did not treat stories sensationally.[53] The journalists believed they were in control of the magazine, where editorial excellence super- seded commercial objectives, to the extent that they 'did not think of *Picture Post* as being the property of Edward Hulton'. The maga- zine was claimed to have 'a unique rapport with its readers who came to look upon it as their mouthpiece'.[54] In it, 'Life as people recognized it, and not as it passed them by, was shown as interesting', it was claimed. *Picture Post*, unlike the *Mirror*, which was regularly criticized, quickly became a paradigm of 'journalistic excellence'.[55]

The *Mirror* obstensibly had no proprietor at all. It was run by a board after being sold by the Northcliffe family, and was created, the historian A. J. P. Taylor asscrted, by 'ordinary people'. At last, he argued, 'The English people found their voice.'[56] From the late 1930s the *Mirror* began to facilitate (chiefly through a variety of correspondence columns) the meaningful participation of a growing readership on the basis of 'a daily rehearsal of ... everyday life, of Us, the neighbours'.[57] *Picture Post*'s readership was far less prole- tarian. It appealed to the new suburbanites, chiefly in the south-east of England – 'technicians and the higher-paid skilled workers, the airmen and their mechanics, the radio experts, the film producers, popular journalists and industrial chemists ... [representing] wide

52. Edelman, *'Mirror'*, pp. 38–49.
53. J. Cameron, *Point of Departure* (London, Grafton, 1986), p. 149.
54. T. Hopkinson, 'When Britain armed itself with a camera', *Guardian* supple- ment, 11 February 1989.
55. R. Kee, *The 'Picture Post' Album* (London, Barrie & Jenkins, 1989), n.p.; G. Weightman, *'Picture Post' Britain* (London, Collins & Brown, 1990).
56. A. J. P. Taylor, *English History, 1914–1945* (Oxford, Clarendon Press, 1965), pp. 548–9.
57. Smith, *Paper Voices*, pp. 99–110; Cudlipp, *Publish*, pp. 265–70.

gradations of income, but ... the same kind of life'. Orwell felt the magazine traded in a 'classlessness' which attempted to avoid the politics of Left and Right, but shared a concern with a general malaise registered among largely apolitical 'multitudes'.[58] It attempted to connect particularly with 'the intelligent man in the street', holding 'ordinary commonsense views', who felt a certain alienation from party politics.[59] Its content was dominated by coverage of current affairs, and especially, after 1939, war news. Its intent was to provide information at the appropriate level as an aid to understanding. Its tone has been described as 'soft'.

By comparison, *John Bull*, which had been the best-selling weekly magazine in the 1920s, was far harsher, adopting a deliberately confrontational approach and courting controversy. It was aimed at 'the man in the street' (presumably without intellectual pretensions), and its advertising claimed it reached 'that mass of the people in the mass market'.[60] Like the *Mirror*, it made a point of being critical of public figures in the cause of 'ordinary people'. It published open letters (usually written by journalists) addressed challengingly 'to those in power', and invited service personnel to exercise the 'voice of the troops'. Its editor's leading article, which touched each week on a variety of topics, was called 'Straight from the shoulder'. Only a fifth of its content could be described as addressing 'public affairs'. It carried fiction and a large amount of historical material, as well as up to two pages of competitions. *John Bull*'s populism, which placed it somewhere between a more traditional illustrated weekly and a women's magazine, increased following the creation of *Picture Post*. It dropped much of its 'peripheral' content (for example, coverage of the arts).[61] Long after the war, *John Bull* retained a reputation for focusing on 'the lower levels of public taste ... [and] striking all the well-worn clichés of sensation'.[62]

The *Mirror* and *Picture Post* occupied separate positions along an axis which ran from, at one end, the hypercommercialized tabloid

58. G. Orwell, 'The lion and the unicorn: socialism and the English genius', in *The Collected Essays, Journalism and Letters of George Orwell, Volume 2*, p. 98; p. 122.
59. Graves and Hodge, *Long Week-End*, p. 331; pp. 427–31.
60. *Mitchell's Newspaper Directory 1940* (London, C. Mitchell, 1940), p. 76; p. 324.
61. Reed, *Popular Magazine*, pp. 171–2; pp. 184–6; pp. 210–12.
62. R. Holles, 'Death of a magazine: the end of *John Bull*', *Encounter* 15 (August 1960), pp. 45–6.

newspaper, to at the other, the licensed autonomy of 'popular' journalism. Orwell's view that by the spring of 1941 even 'the most lowbrow section of the press [by which he specifically meant the *Mirror*] ... [had] all grown politically serious ... and most of the tripe has vanished' seems unduly optimistic.[63] The *Mirror* was a slick, professional journalistic organ of mediation which directed its readers on the topics of the day, rather than encouraging debate. It positioned itself in contrast to 'The intellectuals of the Fabian Society ... and the Communist intellectuals of the older universities who wrote proletarian prose ... or poetry of social realism ... and hardly made any impact on the mass electorate'.[64] By the early 1940s the influence of this new tabloid approach was beginning to manifest itself in more traditional titles like the *News of the World* and *John Bull*. On the other hand, the attitude at *Picture Post* was more redolent of that of the 'popular' daily newspaper.

The magazine, edited throughout the war years by Hopkinson, with an agenda of egalitarianism and the pursuit of 'the justice, health and happiness of the people',[65] became, in the view of Kee, who joined the staff in 1948, 'something like the popular wing of an aspiring new establishment'.[66] The *Herald*, and even the Communist *Daily Worker*, might carry considerable amounts of, usually excellent, sports news, yet, despite the commercialization of the *Herald* after 1930, a commitment remained to 'intellectual' matters, such as the arts and literature.[67] This ambivalence was epitomized by *Picture Post*'s attitude towards glamour, sex and celebrity. Founded on the notion that 'the lives of ordinary people could be rewarding to curiosity', it did not ignore the rich and famous, leavening its 'high-mindedness' with a 'canny populism' which permitted the magazine to publish its quota of pin-up pictures.[68] The *Mirror*, 'loud-mouthed and radical',[69] was obsessed with sex, not overly fastidious with 'the facts', and professed greater social concern, for which it

63. Orwell, 'London Letter', pp. 137–8.
64. Edelman, *'Mirror'*, p. 47.
65. J. Hartley, *Popular Reality: Journalism, Modernity, Popular Culture* (London, Arnold, 1996), pp. 220–31.
66. Kee, *'Picture Post'*, n.p.
67. Graves and Hodge, *Long Week-End*, p. 333; Richards, *Bloody Circus*, pp. 134–5 passim.
68. J. Savage, *'Picture Post' Idols* (London, Collins & Brown, 1992), p. 6.
69. Williams, *Dangerous Estate*, p. 201.

is sometimes lionized, 'partly through luck', and only as the war drew to a close.[70] The assumption that lay behind the journalism of the *Mirror*, as we shall see, was that its readers felt not that they were shaping the post-war world, but that they were 'most exposed to unforeseen events, both good and bad, less able to understand their origins and implications, less able to control them'.[71]

II

The conundrum posed for the Left was what actually comprised 'working-class news', and how was it to be supplied. The war seemed to present opportunities which had been denied previously to address the issue. During the 1930s, in the negotiation which went on between the few suppliers and the increasingly mass audience, almost all power lay with the press barons. The press was not 'the voice of the people' but a voice *to* the people, or, as the poet Stephen Spender argued, the *ear* of the people. The war effort of the Ministry of Information, with its focus on the home front and reconstruction, and its acknowledgement that the crudest forms of propaganda would not meet its objectives, helped change the climate of opinion. The Left was co-opted, by various means, to provide a credible, critical edge for a public which, it was recognized, was likely to be sceptical. Apart from the hundreds of writers and journalists recruited into State public relations work, Whitehall co-operated, often secretly, with publications, including *Picture Post*.[72] This seemed to offer an opportunity to outmanoeuvre the press barons, and to subvert their commercialization of journalism.

Much of the opposition to the commercialized press had been articulated in a Labour Party pamphlet in 1936, which, although partisan, identified more broadly held concerns about the close

70. M. Engel, *Tickle the Public: One Hundred Years of the Popular Press* (London, Gollancz, 1996), pp. 164–9. Typical *Mirror* headlines of the early 1940s were 'ONE-EYED CRIPPLE DUPED WOMEN WITH THE SAME £2 RING' and 'REVELLER VANISHED FOR DAYS – COMES BACK AS POP-EYED DRAGON' (cited in Engel, p. 165).

71. Smith, *Paper Voices*, p. 232 passim.

72. K. Williams, *British Writers and the Media, 1930–45* (Basingstoke, Macmillan, 1996), pp. 15–17; p. 22; p. 49; pp. 181–8; A. James, *Informing the People: How the Government Won Hearts and Minds to Win WW2* (London, HMSO, 1996), p. 9.

relationship of the press to Conservative economic, political and social structures.[73] The performance of the press in relation to three major events of the 1930s – the Slump, the abdication and appeasement – was of enormous importance, but what served to coalesce the opposition was the handling of the opening months of war by Chamberlain's government. The Left seized the moment to embark on a concerted campaign to ensure that after the war there would be no 'return to normalcy' – or 'the old-time balderdash', as the Labour MP Manny Shinwell called it.[74]

Beveridge, a former journalist, utilized the media to pave the way for his report with personal contributions and appearances.[75] He was undoubtedly helped in this by sympathetic key media figures, such as King, Hulton, Hopkinson, J. B. Priestley, Gerald Barry (the editor of the *News Chronicle*), Francis Williams, David Astor (of the *Observer*) and E. H. Carr (at *The Times*), most of whom belonged to interlocking networks of reforming journalists, intellectuals and politicians.[76] In March 1942, *Picture Post* had taken up Beveridge's grievance that, despite his appointment to the chairmanship of the Social Insurance Committee, he was still waiting for 'another job even more worthy of his powers'.[77] Beveridge's report was completed by mid-October, and items hinting at its contents began appearing in the press.[78] Supporters were also alerted to likely obstruction to the Beveridge plans from Conservatives in the coalition government. In November the Lord Privy Seal and Leader of the House, Sir Stafford Cripps, enlisted the assistance of King in forcing the Cabinet's hand. The day after the *Mirror*'s leading article on Beveridge

73. O'Malley, 'Labour', p. 137.
74. E. Shinwell, *When the Men Come Home* (London, Victor Gollancz, 1944), p. 5. The key text in this series of extended pamphlets published in hardback editions was *Guilty Men* (1940), written under the pseudonym Cato by three London *Evening Standard* journalists, Michael Foot, Frank Owen and Peter Howard. It sold more than 200,000 copies. See S. Fielding, 'The good war: 1939–1945', in *From Blitz to Blair*, pp. 31–2.
75. N. Timmins, *The Five Giants: A Biography of the Welfare State* (London, Fontana, 1996), p. 41; J. Harris, *William Beveridge: A Biography* (Oxford, Clarendon Press, 1977), p. 421.
76. R. Cockett, *David Astor and the 'Observer'* (London, André Deutsch, 1991), pp. 72–5; pp. 90–2; pp. 97–8; p. 106.
77. C. Fenby, 'Beveridge, the man-power expert, is being wasted himself', *Picture Post* (7 March 1942), pp. 22–3; Harris, *Beveridge*, p. 376.
78. For examples, see *The Times*, 19 October 1942, p. 2 and 21 October 1942, p. 7.

appeared, Cripps left the war Cabinet.[79] In any event, the public was well prepared for the report, and its imminent publication had been trailed since at least mid-November. The *Daily Telegraph* had already suggested 26 November as the likely date.[80] Hopkinson was certainly well briefed beforehand.[81] The final report was officially issued to the press before formal publication (and before MPs received copies), on the grounds that journalists needed time to absorb it.[82]

The *Herald* previewed the report on the morning of publication (on 1 December), promising its readers 'a complete summary of every section' of the 120,000-word report the following day. The paper did not lead with the story on 2 December, giving it second place to the advances of the Eighth Army in North Africa. It did run a picture of Beveridge taken the previous day in St James's Park in London. The *Mirror* splashed the story, however, in the process popularizing the phrase 'from the cradle to the grave'. Both papers carried spreads inside: the *Herald* ran items over pages 2 and 3 of the four-page issue, while the *Mirror* had reports on pages 4, 5 and 7 (of an eight-page paper). The news reporting in the two papers was similar, a factor which was evident over the rest of the month. Nevertheless, the *Herald*'s coverage tended to be more comprehensive and earnest, and it seemed to give the topic greater priority.[83] It is in the other, background and contextualizing treatment of the matter, which, unlike news stories, was likely to have been more consciously formulated in the papers' editorial offices, that the significant differences in approach and tone began to make themselves apparent, however.

Both papers set out to offer their readers a concise guide to the content of the report, highlighting the main points. Each concentrated on what Beveridge would mean in cash terms to individuals and families. The *Herald* methodically divided the report into nine sections, with separate articles on individual aspects such as pensions, unemployment and children's allowances. It ran a leading article, which was only to be expected, and over the rest of the month

79. Edelman, '*Mirror*', p. 135; *The Times*, 23 November 1942, p. 2.
80. See *Daily Telegraph*, 13 November 1942, p. 3.
81. Hopkinson, *Of This*, p. 215.
82. A. Bevan, *Why Not Trust the Tories?* (London, Victor Gollancz, 1944), pp. 30–46; *The Times*, 2 December 1942, p. 2.
83. See *Daily Herald*, 7, 18 and 24 December 1942.

Figure 8   The social security 'balance sheet', *Daily Mirror*, 2 December 1942.

published three more. On 2 December it reproduced much of Beveridge's own introduction to the report. In the following days it sought the views on Beveridge of public figures, chiefly from the Labour movement, of course. For instance, on 31 December it ran a feature written by the secretary of the TUC's social insurance department. The *Herald*, like other 'popular' papers, ran cartoons and there was one on 'tackling the five giants' on 2 December, but the main graphical presentation consisted of a box with three tables of figures (see Figure 9). Similar tables appeared in nearly all the national newspapers that day.[84] Other tables in the *Herald* contained the complex bureaucratic classifications of contributors and welfare recipients suggested by Beveridge. The order, as well as the language, in which they were presented may have made sense to bureaucrats, but they made few concessions to the paper's readers. The *Herald* reproduced what were in effect government statistics applying to an impersonal 'typical family of man, wife and two children', using the clipped language of Whitehall in which the indefinite article was routinely omitted, so that people appeared simply as 'married couple'. The order in which the proposed benefits were listed seemed almost random – for example, widow's benefits preceding maternity benefits.

The *Mirror*'s treatment of the story differed quite significantly at a number of points. Its focus was on the everyday impact of the report. It ran no editorial on the issue on 2 December (and only one during the whole month), but presented much of the information

84. See *The Times*, 2 December 1942, p. 8; *Daily Sketch*, 2 December 1942, p. 5; *Daily Telegraph*, 2 December 1942, p. 3.

Figure 9
Details of the
Beveridge
proposals in
tabular form,
Daily Herald,
2 December
1942.

WHAT A FAMILY GETS

THE benefits payable to a typical family of man, wife, and two
children are shown below. Benefits under the Beveridge Plan
are in **black type**. Pre-war benefits are in *italics*.

UNEMPLOYMENT **56s. a week for unlimited time—no means test—possible training.**
33s. a week for 26 weeks—then means test.

INDUSTRIAL
DISABILITY .. **56s. a week for 13 weeks—then pension of 2-3rds earnings (max. 76s., min. 56s.); no compounding.**
30s. a week maximum, or half earnings.

OTHER
DISABILITY .. **56s. a week—no time limit—no means test.**
15s. for 26 weeks, then 7s. 6d. (may be extra benefits).

Other Benefits Compared

OLD AGE .... **40s. a week retirement pension for married couple, plus 2s. per week each year retirement postponed.**
20s. a week.

WIDOW ...... **52s. clear for first 13 weeks, then 40s. per week reduced by part of any earnings.**
18s. a week.

MATERNITY .... **80s. lump sum, plus 36s. per week for 13 weeks if wife working.**
40s. lump sum, plus 40s. extra if wife working.

FUNERAL ...... **£20, but smaller sums for children.**
Nil

MEDICAL
TREATMENT ...... **Comprehensive for whole family. Includes hospital, dental, ophthalmic, nursing, and convalescent homes, and rehabilitation.**
General practitioner for man only. Additional treatment in some cases.

Social Security Budget

Below is how the Beveridge Budget would be spent—in the
first year and when it got into full swing.
And how the cost would be met.

COST	1945	1965	INCOME	1945	1965
	Million £s			Million £s	
Retirement Pensions ..	126	300	Workers'		
Unemployment	110	107	Contributions ..	194	192
Disability Benefits	72	86	Employers'		
Other Benefits	41	42	Contributions ..	137	132
			Exchequer Share..	351	519
Total Social Insur.	£349	£535	Interest on Funds	15	15
National Assistance	44	30			
Children's Allowances..	110	100			
Cost of Administration	24	23			
Health Services	170	170			
	£697	£858		£697	£858

Figure 10   Beveridge-for-all: an explanatory graphic, *Daily Mirror*, December 1942.

in graphical form (see Figures 8 and 10). In particular, it published a simple guide to 'What the plan does for everyone'. The mode of address was unmistakable. The *Mirror* addressed its readers directly as 'you'. The language was far more informal, and the paper took its readers through the Beveridge proposals step-by-step from marriage, through childbirth and child care, to death and widowhood.

In the best traditions of tabloid alliterative headlines, this was 'How to be born, bred and buried by Beveridge', accessibly packaged. The *Mirror* was the quintessential graphic newspaper of the 1930s and early 1940s. It pioneered the publication of comic strips, which were taking up 12 per cent of its total space in 1947. Between 85 per cent and 90 per cent of *Mirror* readers looked at the comic strip 'Jane' during the war.[85] The paper purported also to present the views of 'ordinary man and woman', and on the day the Beveridge Report was published, it canvassed the responses of a panel of troops serving in the Middle East, publishing their comments the following day. On 4 December it inaugurated a helpline guide to social security, and invited inquiries from readers.

On 3 December the *Herald* offered its own personalization of Beveridge, under the title 'Life in Beveridge Britain', taking the form of a fictional account of the progress of the Johnson family from 1944.[86] The article filled an entire column on page 3, and was made up of text with no illustrations. It followed Bill and Mary Johnson, a working-class couple, from the early years of their marriage, through the birth of four children, to old age. Throughout, they 'manage nicely', thanks to social security. Parenthood, illness, bereavement were all 'simpler and nicer'. Yet, unlike the *Mirror*'s graphics, which worked from the premise that people were primarily interested in what social security would cost them and what they could hope to receive in terms of benefits, this was essentially a story with a moral. Some time in the future – beyond the 1960s – Mary Johnson recalls for her grandchildren when 'there wasn't any Social Security plan ... people often hadn't the barest necessities of life, and if you had a baby you never knew whether you would be able to feed it properly'. From the imaginary perspective of the 1970s, the reporter Hugh Pilcher concluded, 'It didn't seem credible.'

The initial conclusions to be drawn from this small-scale comparison might be that, while the *Mirror* professed to privilege 'the voice of the people', the *Herald* was far more hidebound by its formal connections with Labour and the Trades Union Congress (TUC). Like any other paper, the *Herald* 'packaged' the news, but its approach was didactic, and it slipped less easily into a more informal mode of address. On another level, however, it was involved

85. Cudlipp, *Publish*, pp. 69–77.
86. See Richards, *Bloody Circus*, p. 160.

in amplifying the debate around Beveridge. It published a guide to the report which was sold through newsagents, and its political correspondent discussed 'social security and the State' in an edition of the BBC radio series *Westminster and Beyond*.[87] It also carried readers' letters on the topic throughout December. The *Mirror*, on the other hand, was less interested in stimulating a more open public debate. It carried relatively few readers' letters on Beveridge, and the mainly question-and-answer helpline feature (mentioned above) ran only once more in December (on the 15th). Even then, there was no evidence that the questions had actually come from genuine readers; certainly none was identified. In the meantime, the government had raised another issue of more appeal to the *Mirror*'s sensationalist streak, and to which it duly paid close attention – official concerns over the incidence of venereal disease among British forces.[88]

A similar broad distinction can be made about the coverage of the Beveridge report by the Sunday newspapers, the *News of the World* and *Reynolds News*. On 6 December the *News of the World* published a leading article (supporting the proposals) and a news item on the coming Commons debate. It did not return to the topic again for the remainder of the month. While *Reynolds News*'s initial coverage was similar (a leader and a news story), it published further articles on Beveridge in its next two issues. There was an interview with Beatrice Webb (6 December) and signed articles by Seebohm Rowntree (6 December) and the chairman of the Co-operative Party (13 December). The paper also published readers' letters on the subject. The attention these two papers gave to the Beveridge Report largely mirrored that of the two dailies. Of course, neither was a tabloid in size, but the way in which the *News of the World* treated the Beveridge report suggests it shared at least some of the approach of the *Daily Mirror*, and was less attached to established forms of 'popular' journalism.

What was without doubt the most celebrated journalism on the Beveridge Report appeared in *Picture Post*. It took the magazine until January 1943 to give the issue its full attention. (In December, it published only Hulton's comments and a number of readers' letters on Beveridge.) Then, on 2 January, *Picture Post* published a 'special

87. *Daily Herald*, 8 December 1942, p. 2.
88. Cudlipp, *Publish*, p. 251.

issue', called 'Changing Britain'. The cover carried a photograph of a 'war baby ... the child who has never known peace'. The leading article linked the child's future to implementation of the Beveridge plan. There were features on various aspects of Britain contributed by, among others, Julian Huxley, Charles Madge, Earl De La Warr, Professor J. M. Mackintosh and, centrally, Frank Packenham, who had been Beveridge's assistant, writing about 'Social Security: The New Deal'. This was a repeat of the tactic the magazine had used exactly two years before. Then in an issue called 'A Plan for Britain', the magazine had drawn up an early blueprint for reconstruction. The project was supposedly instigated by letters Hopkinson had received from service personnel dissatisfied with the government's refusal to discuss reconstruction. The special issue, and a number of subsequent articles, prompted the public to send *Picture Post* nearly 2,000 more letters, and resulted in a conference attended by readers and experts.[89] One of the aims of the magazine's founder and first editor, Stefan Lorant, had been to encourage readers' letters, which, it was claimed, were printed more or less unedited.[90] On 4 January 1943 there was a BBC broadcast on the magazine's 'Changing Britain' issue.[91] Yet this was still not quite 'the people's voice' (Hulton called it 'the clamour of the people').[92]

The magazine felt it had identified a groundswell of public opinion in favour of the Beveridge plan, even before its publication.[93] Over the first three months of 1943 it hammered the message home, with an illustrated feature on the opposition to Beveridge in the Society of Individualists (6 February), a debate on state planning (20 February) and six pages devoted to 'The Beveridge fight' (6 March). Yet from its beginnings in 1938 all its attempts to stimulate an 'intelligent' response from general readers had met with a 'discouraging' response.[94] As well as appearing as 'expert' contributors, the well-qualified, well-placed and well-heeled were heavily represented in its correspondence columns. Following the magazine's invitation to readers to write in about 'Changing Britain', and the

89. Hartley, *Popular Reality*, pp. 220–31.
90. M. Hallett, *The Real Story of 'Picture Post'* (Birmingham, ARTicle Press, 1994), n.p.
91. *Picture Post*, 23 January 1943, p. 25.
92. E. Hulton, 'Struggle for progress', *Picture Post*, 27 February 1943, p. 26.
93. Timmins, *Five Giants*, p. 36.
94. Graves and Hodge, *Long Week-End*, p. 432.

related articles, *Picture Post* published letters in nine subsequent issues. The first four printed on 9 January had been submitted by the playwright Sean O'Casey (he had also written in response to the 'Plan for Britain'); Will Lawther, the mineworkers' union president; Dean W. R. Inge, an MP; and the chair of the Women's Liberal Federation. Over the coming weeks the correspondents included the parliamentary secretary at the Ministry of Works and Planning, the author Walter Greenwood, the Bishop of Truro, the Dean of Canterbury, Harry Pollitt (the leading Communist), Margaret Cole (of the Fabian Society), Lord Hinchinbrooke, Lady Violet Bonham-Carter, and the suffragist Emmeline Pethwick-Lawrence. In total, the magazine printed letters from 17 Members of Parliament. Letters were sometimes published across two pages under headlines such as 'Beveridge: Readers Write'. In such cases, up to 60 per cent (16 out of 27 letters on 20 March) were from politicians and other public figures. Those whose letters were headed 'a soldier', 'a sailor', 'a wage-earner', and even 'the people' were in danger of being swamped.[95] Malcolm Muggeridge believed the egalitarianism espoused by *Picture Post* and others was betrayed by their infatuation with 'the eminent'. As a result society had not become 'less snobbish', but one in which 'Social position and wealth have come to have an almost mystical significance.'[96]

The 'common people', as Robert Graves called them, responded in a 'dead-alive' fashion to the 'vital topics' raised by *Picture Post*: they were more interested in the issues raised in Lorant's other magazine, the monthly *Lilliput*.[97] Founded, too, on a belief in the intelligence of the general public and a desire to provide a platform for 'the outstanding writers of the world', the magazine was taken over by Hulton in 1938 and edited by Hopkinson between 1941 and 1946, when it became far better known for its 'relatively undemanding text ... its jokes and occasional nudes' (almost a thousand photographs of women were published in the first hundred

95. *Picture Post*, 9 January 1943, p. 3; p. 17; p. 26; 16 January 1943, p. 3; pp. 24–5; 23 January 1943, p. 25; 30 January 1943, p. 2; 6 February 1943, p. 3; pp. 22–3; 13 February 1943, p. 3; 20 February 1943, p. 3; pp. 24–6; 27 February 1943, p. 3; 6 March 1943, p. 3; pp. 7–11; p. 20; 20 March 1943, pp. 24–5; 27 March 1943, p. 3; p. 25; 3 April 1943, p. 3; p. 26.
96. M. Muggeridge, *The Thirties: 1930–40 in Great Britain* (London, Hamish Hamilton, 1940), p. 269.
97. Graves and Hodge, *Long Week-End*, p. 432.

issues).[98] Unlike *John Bull*, *Lilliput* 'did not attack or criticize'.[99] *John Bull* also had a far fiercer reputation for its development of promotion stunts, having acted as a kind of prototype for the high commercialization of the newspaper of the 1930s.[100] All the same, it showed relatively little interest in the Beveridge Report, which was raised as a subject twice in the editor's leading article (on 5 and 12 December) and once in a column written by Swaffer, who also wrote about Beveridge himself on a further occasion. Only one reader's letter was published on the topic. The magazine, like the *Mirror*, appeared to be more interested in 'righteous indignation, a strong stiffening of economics-and-social-reform-made-easy' than the detailed examination of policy. Another description applied to the *Mirror* ('pugnaciously populist') seems equally appropriate for *John Bull*.[101]

Where the *Mirror* was 'brash' and inconoclastic, *Picture Post* tried to steer a middle course between tradition and modernity.[102] It claimed to seek out the 'intelligence, common sense, courage and humour ... in the ordinary people',[103] but on issues like the Beveridge report even its correspondence columns were crowded with 'experts'. *Picture Post* was supposed to have established a unique equilibrium between the old 'popular' and the new populist journalism, which allowed it to 'tell it as it was – all of it'. The magazine's journalists were reportedly dispatched into the field free to exercize their individual judgement. Yet was such autonomy real? Interference-free proprietorship and the primacy of journalistic intuitive excellence always amounted to 'a myth', another journalist recalled.[104] When Ken Allsop joined the magazine in 1950, he found 'a rather cloying

98. Hallett, *Real Story*, n.p.; K. Webb (ed.), *'Lilliput' Goes to War* (London, Hutchinson, 1985), pp. 3–4; p. 245.
99. Hopkinson, *Of This*, p. 227.
100. Richards, *Bloody Circus*, p. 136.
101. H. Hopkins, *The New Look: A Social History of the Forties and Fifties* (London, Secker & Warburg, 1964), pp. 23–4; Koss, *Rise and Fall*, p. 1046.
102. J. Taylor, *War Photography: Realism in the British Press* (London, Comedia, 1991), pp. 74–5.
103. T. Hopkinson, 'Readers work on the Plan for Britain', *Picture Post*, 8 March 1941, cited in Hartley, *Popular Reality*, pp. 224–6.
104. Lionel Birch, Ted Castle and Fyfe Robertson, three of the magazine's journalists, quoted in J. Ormond, 'How Hulton and the Hungarian made picture history', *Listener*, **98** (1 September 1977), p. 261; p. 263.

mist of nostalgia and legend'. He decided that 'there never was such a place for legend-spinning'.[105]

Picture Post thrived during what have been described as 'the great periodical decades', and it harnessed one of the elements which made the tabloid *Daily Mirror* so successful – pictorial journalism.[106] Tabloid journalism was defined by more than its graphic form, however. When *Picture Post* used a graphic in its Beveridge coverage, ostensibly to explain 'What a Minister of Social Security would mean to the ordinary citizen', it was not to guide its readers, as potential welfare recipients, through the new system, but primarily to expose the 'absurdity' of the existing bureaucracy; and its focus was the rationalism of centralized planning in the provision of welfare. It praised Beveridge for having 'pointed out a clear, simple way' through the bureaucratic 'maze'. The fictional subject of the illustrated story, a recipient of welfare, John Jones, was a 64-year-old unemployed man, who appeared as one of 'them' – complete with cloth cap – the literally dumb victim buffeted by a labyrinthine officialdom. His was 'an extreme case' – one, it seems, which ought to elicit the sympathy of the more fortunate; and the government's responsibility was to act efficiently when faced with 'a man fallen on evil times who must be lifted up again' (see Figure 11).

The magazine was, if Orwell is to be believed, favoured, like the *Mirror*, by the burgeoning suburbanized southern half of England. It did relatively well out of wartime paper rationing, and its 40-page issues selling at 3*d* represented good value at a time when the daily and Sunday newspapers were restricted to as few as four and six pages, and cost 1*d*.[107] Although the magazine's run-ins with the authorities in the early years of the war have been well documented,[108] it also struck deals with the government, and it remains a matter of conjecture precisely how enmeshed it was in the expanding activities of the state's information services. Orwell, who had something of an insider's view, of course, warned, 'We shall have a serious and truthful press when public opinion actively demands it. Till

105. K. Allsop, '*Picture Post*', *Spectator*, **205** (25 November 1960), p. 813; p. 815.
106. A. J. Burkhart, 'Recent trends in periodical publishing', *Journal of Industrial Economics*, **13** (November 1964), p. 12; p. 16.
107. I am grateful to Bruce Hanlin for pointing this out.
108. Hopkinson, *Of This*, p. 176 passim.

Figure 11 The case for a single Ministry of Social Security, put graphically by *Picture Post*, 6 March 1943

then, if the news is not distorted by businessmen it will be distorted by bureaucrats, who are only one degree better.'[109]

III

A key aspect of the press during the Second World War was the extent to which large numbers of working-class people had become regular readers of national daily newspapers. Since the 1930s, the press had been developing more conversational styles of journalism and innovative forms of presentation, including, in the case of the *Daily Mirror*, the tabloid format. Nevertheless, there was concern at the extent to which a commercialized press reflected or manipulated mass demand for entertainment above 'reliable news on which ... [to] form sound opinions on current events'.[110] Left-inclined intellectuals and journalists in particular attempted to establish simple connections between an idealized Fourth Estate and an expanding working-class readership, which could demonstrate the capacity of the press to lead Britain towards a greater popular participatory democracy. This project, it seemed, was being frustrated by the commercializing tendencies of newspaper magnates. The war appeared to offer a moment of escape from the grip of the press barons. 'Popular' journalism was already serving the Left in newspapers like the *Daily Herald* and *Reynolds News*. This was an educative press, and the Left, as much as the Right, regarded the process as chiefly a top-down one of the few addressing the many. During the war other newspapers and magazines, such as the *News of the World* and *John Bull*, began to adopt some of the tabloid characteristics of the *Mirror*. The formal associations of the *Herald* and *Reynolds News* inhibited their ability to become more tabloid-like, and they continued in the 'popular' tradition. Thus the press was beginning to fragment, irrespective of politics, across the divide between the two approaches.

The claims of the 'popular' press to be 'the voice of the people' lay to a large extent in its close, often formal, connections with political structures and its ability to draw on well-placed 'experts' to inform its journalism; its reasonably comprehensive and explanatory

109. G. Orwell, 'As I please', p. 281.
110. Political and Economic Planning, *The British Press* (London, PEP, 1938), p. 32.

reporting, particularly of the background to the news; and the primacy it placed on constructive debate, facilitated by a relatively loosely mediated access it offered to its readers. Faced with the Beveridge proposals, the inclination of the 'popular' press, therefore, was to provide space in its columns for first, the expression of 'expert' opinion and, in a subsidiary role, the views of ordinary readers, principally in the traditional form of rather dense expanses of text, and to an established agenda. By comparison, the tabloid-inclined press asserted its right to be considered 'the voice of the people' by supposedly actively seeking out the opinions of ordinary people. It provided them with additional opportunities to state their cases, views and grievances, and it reported on the topics they were interested in, but which previously had not always been aired because they were not considered 'nice'.[111] The foundations of the tabloid press lay, however, in the exploitation of a mix of sensationalism and gossip, more often than not focused on some aspect of sex. Its relationships with its readers were more overtly commercialized. The channels through which it addressed them were more closely policed, and readers' views were more mediated. This explains why, despite its proclivity for publishing all manner of readers' letters, the Mirror in particular privileged its own professionalized, and often graphic, versions of the Beveridge debate to the almost total exclusion of the readers' authentic voice.

Picture Post appeared to ally the discursive nature of 'popular' journalism to the more accessible but formulaic approach of the tabloid. The analysis offered here suggests that in most important respects Picture Post remained firmly located in the tradition of 'popular' journalism. The claims made for the magazine are that it actually attained what Orwell sought – a partnership between 'good' journalism and a receptive readership in pursuit of a clearly defined and broadly agreed set of social objectives. Part of the myth of Picture Post is that during the war its readers accepted, and helped shape, its political and social project. The quid pro quo was the magazine's non-discriminatory acceptance and portrayal of all levels of culture. Presumptions about the educative function of 'popular' newspapers and magazines led, at a time of a general expansion in working-class consumption of print, to the equation of a sizeable

111. A word used by the Mirror's war-time editor, Cecil Thomas, cited in Cudlipp, Publish, p. 249.

readership for *Picture Post* with a rise in political awareness and ideological commitment. If this assumption could be applied to the *Daily Mirror*, then it was clear that a leftist press was in some way articulating popular support for a radical post-war settlement. This did not allow, however, for the significiant shift in journalism inherent in the tabloid press, and the complex relationship with popular sentiment associated with it.

There is no gainsaying the magnitude of the support for the Beveridge proposals among the British population in the winter of 1942 and spring of 1943. Yet, while almost every person in the UK was aware of the Beveridge Report, far fewer had any detailed knowledge of its contents. This, it has been suggested, reflected an ingrained popular apathy, a distaste for 'political abstractions', and a preference for instant, personal and material gratification rather than national projects for welfare provision;[112] but which should also be viewed within the context of the growth of the mass media.[113] *Picture Post* and the *Mirror* represented these tensions which lay behind Beveridge – in the case of *Picture Post*, support for the idealism of centralized state planning, and in the *Mirror*, the everyday benefits of welfare. This distinction was evident in the treatment each gave to the topic – the predominance of 'objective' and 'expert' background analysis and debate in *Picture Post*, and of graphic and immediate reporting, and determinativeness in the *Mirror*. The division was constitutive of the particularities of, respectively, the declining 'popular' press and the emergent tabloid, and of their readerships. In this respect, the tabloid-inclined press, given its larger, more youthful and more female audience, drawn to a greater extent from the more economically prosperous areas of England, was liable, as Hopkinson suggested, to have had a greater impact on post-war politics. Any such influence would be derived principally from the formulae of tabloid journalism, however. The impact of the *Mirror* is more likely to have been a measure of its tabloidism than its socialism. Its appeal, as a former editor of the *Herald* noted, was to the emerging working-class consumer who was 'crude, sentimental, self-sacrificing, selfish'. During the General Election campaign of

112. Fielding *et al.*, '*England Arise!*', p. 9; pp. 33–9.
113. R. Brookes, '"Everything in the garden is lovely": the representation of national identity in Sidney Strube's *Daily Express* cartoons in the 1930s', *Oxford Art Journal*, 13:2 (1990), esp. p. 32.

1945 it carefully steered a course somewhere between the class-based invective of the *Herald* and the rational (albeit occasionally passionate) radicalism of *Picture Post*.[114] As such, it established a dimension to British politics – the role of the tabloid press – which over the next 50 years was increasingly to occupy a central and problematical place in public debate.

114. Richards, *Bloody Circus*, pp. 161–2.

A More Even Playing Field?
Sport During and After the War

Norman Baker

In October 1943, in an address to the International Sports Fellowship, Philip Noel-Baker anticipated that 'we shall need more games, more sport, more physical training and recreation in this country when the war is over than ever we had before'. Although, in the same address, he claimed that games had been 'the great leveller of men', he was later to express the wish that participation in sporting competition should not be 'reserved for those who are rich enough to afford the necessary time'.[1] Noel-Baker hoped, not only for a post-war growth in sporting and recreational activity, but also that the socially-progressive role he believed sport to have played in the past would be continued in the future, so that the ways in which the divisions of social class determined who could or could not play a sport at any given level would diminish. He looked not only to an upsurge in sporting activity but also to its uplifting influence within a more egalitarian society. How far was this dual hope fulfilled?

The character of English sport was to be significantly influenced by an ongoing struggle between several different concepts as to the true purpose of sport, and how, and by whom, sports programmes should be administered. This struggle neither began nor ended with the Second World War. The distinctions within this conflict of ideas were by no means clear cut and Noel-Baker himself represented

---

1. Churchill College Archives, Cambridge, NBKR 8/61/4, draft address by Philip Noel-Baker, 10 October 1943. NBKR 6/3/1, Noel-Baker, quoted in *Sporting Life*, 26 August 1946. There are distinctions of sporting culture that make it difficult to generalize about Britain. Scotland, Wales and Northern Ireland have separate governing bodies in several of the major sports and my familiarity is with the records of the English organizations. For these various reasons, I will focus on England except where, as in the case of the Olympics, representation was British.

some of the ambiguities and confusions that were involved. An athlete as an undergraduate at Cambridge, Noel-Baker later won the silver medal in the 1,500 metres at the 1920 Antwerp Olympics. In the 1920s he was closely involved with the Achilles Athletic Club, made up of former Oxford and Cambridge athletes. He believed that it was this club 'on which the real prosperity of British track athletics rests'.[2] From this background Noel-Baker developed a powerful empathy for what might be termed the 'Corinthian' ideal, the code of true amateurism under which sport was pursued for sports' sake without ulterior political, social or economic motive. On the other hand, as a Labour politician, holding office in the wartime coalition and then in the post-war government, he did not support the exclusiveness of the gentlemen amateurs. He looked to a more inclusive philosophy which would extend the benefits of sporting activity and the virtues of true amateurism to a much broader constituency. By the late 1930s he was a vice-president of the British Workers' Sports Association (BWSA), whose 'comradely' ideal was to create sporting and recreational opportunities for the workers through organizations they themselves controlled.[3]

Though distanced politically and socially, the Corinthian and comradely ideals shared a preference for participation over spectatorship and a strong dislike for the commercialization and professionalization of established English sports that intensified during the inter-war years. The amateur gentleman saw in such developments the end of sport for sports' sake and the coming of professionalism 'and the evils which automatically follow'.[4] For their part, the advocates of

2. NBKR 6/2/1, draft of an article for the *Sunday Times*, March 1947. *Concise Dictionary of National Biography* (Oxford, Oxford UP, 1992), Vol. III.
3. In the context of modern English sport, the term 'Corinthian' derives from the pre-eminent football team of the late nineteenth and early twentieth centuries, renowned for their skills, but even more so for their sportsmanship. A serious question surrounds whether or not this ideal was, in reality, ever widely followed. W. Vamplew, *Pay Up and Play the Game: Professional Sport in Britain, 1875–1914* (Cambridge, Cambridge UP, 1988). For the history of the BWSA and its predecessors, see S. G. Jones, *Sport, Politics and the Working Class: Organised Labour and Sport in Inter-war Britain* (Manchester, Manchester UP, 1988) and, by the same author, 'The British Worker's Sports Federation, 1923–35', in *The Story of Worker Sport*, ed. A. Kruger and J. Riordan (Champaign, Ill, Human Kinetics, 1996).
4. *Athletics*, 2:16 (March 1947), p. 3. Mass-Observation (M-O) Archives, University of Sussex, File Report 3045, October 1948, Table VII.

workers' sports were alienated by what they believed to be capitalist exploitation of members of the working class; of players as employees, of spectators and punters as consumers. From either point of view, concerns were intensified by the development of sports such as speedway racing and ice hockey, where spectatorship was far removed from participatory experience and the appeal was thus more simply entertainment. Even more alarming to some was the growth of gambling, particularly on greyhound racing and through the football pools.

For Noel-Baker, as for others, commercialized sport presented a quandary. If only because it placed watching before playing, such a development was suspect. On the other hand, he was uncomfortable denying to large numbers of people that which they enjoyed; leisure was something that, within reason, people should be left to enjoy as they pleased. For Noel-Baker, a pacifist who had boycotted the 1936 Olympics 'on a matter of principle and conscience', a much more serious threat was presented by the use of sport for nationalistic purposes. He abhorred the efforts of Mussolini and Hitler to 'turn athletes into professionals for the purpose of national prestige'. Such an aim ran counter to Noel-Baker's belief in sport as a medium for international fellowship.[5]

How far were Philip Noel-Baker's hopes for growth and 'regeneration' of sport to be fulfilled during and after the Second World War? Further, was any one of the contending sporting ideals to gain ascendancy as a result of the war? This essay attempts to address these questions, first, through a description of the practical difficulties experienced in maintaining sports during and after the war and consideration of the wartime debate over 'appropriateness', then through review of post-war planning by sporting organizations and some judgement of subsequent policy on a number of socially relevant issues. Finally, I will make some assessment of why sport was, or was not, the object of fundamental change. My conclusion is that, on balance, continuity prevailed over change in the practice and organization of sport in the immediate post-war period.

5. NBKR 6/3/1, Minutes of the Special Congress of the International Amateur Athletic Federation (IAAF), 9 June 1947, p. 2.

I

Through the last week of August 1939, while all around preparations for war were going on, the major events of the English sporting summer continued to be staged. Symbolically, it was not until the end of the month that paintings were taken down in the Long Room at Lords and 'relics removed'.[6] Even more remarkably, English oarsmen, sailors, golfers, swimmers and athletes continued to compete with Germans. As late as 20 August, an English athletics team competed before a crowd of 60,000 in Cologne, where 'everyone was in good humour'.[7]

There existed significant continuity between the persistent refusal to abandon normalcy displayed in August 1939 and the value placed on efforts to 'carry on' through the ensuing six years of war. A dogged endeavour to maintain sporting practices in general and certain events in particular also gave 'carrying on' an aura of victory over adverse circumstances and thus over those who had imposed them, the enemy.

A government order 'closing all places of entertainment and outdoor sports meetings' issued at the outbreak of hostilities was quickly rescinded amid charges of undue panic. Through the autumn of 1939 many of the main spectator sports resumed activities, albeit in limited form. For example, Football League teams were playing friendly matches by mid-September and regionalized competition was under way a month later. The football pools were back in business under the Unity Pools format in November 1939.[8] Thereafter, the extent of success in maintaining programmes of competition varied considerably between sports and over time. Some of the county cricket clubs occasionally fielded sides against representative service teams and a reasonably full programme of games was played at Lord's, featuring such teams as London Counties and the British Empire XI. However, most of these games were one-day affairs and there was no attempt to stage three-day county championship cricket.

6. *The Times*, 2, 7, 8, 14, 22 and 28 August 1939.
7. Ibid., 7, 8, 10, 12, 17 and 21 August 1939.
8. Ibid., 5, 11, 16, 18 and 19 September and 2 and 3 October 1939; Football Association (FA) Council Minutes, 8 and 13 September 1939 and Memo No. 3, 'Football in Time of War', 21 September 1939; PRO CAB 71/19, 13 July 1945, p.9.

Cricket moved back closer to normal in the summer of 1945 with the well-supported Victory Test series against the Australian Services XI. Games between representative service teams provided the highlights of what Rugby Union and Rugby League competition was sustained. In the case of the Union code, both Richmond and Rosslyn Park 'nobly nursed' the game by maintaining partial fixture lists. Although in reduced form, professional boxing, including championship fights, continued to be staged throughout the war. Except for the Classics, all staged at Newmarket, flat racing, and for that matter the National Hunt, were limited to a modest programme of regionally based meetings for much of the war. Other sports were even less successful in staging major public events. Tennis was largely confined to the Queen's Club in London and speedway racing to Belle Vue, Manchester.[9]

Particularly in the case of major spectator sports, government policy played a variable but important part in restricting activity. The gradual resumption of sports during the phoney war of 1939–40 was dramatically reversed in face of Dunkirk and the Battle of Britain. A modest revival took place from the end of 1940 but, after the fall of Singapore and the changes in the War Cabinet in the early spring of 1942, government imposed a policy of severe restrictions. Thereafter, as the war situation gradually improved, restrictions were eased and in 1945, even before victory was finally achieved, there was a marked shift back towards peacetime levels of activity.

Participation in local amateur sports was largely dependent on access to facilities. Initial attempts to protect playing fields from government requisitioning were doomed to failure as food production and other wartime needs demanded higher and higher priority. Golf courses were ploughed up, allotments encroached on to parks and playing fields, and other sports facilities were requisitioned for various official uses. Where facilities escaped such fates, government redirection of labour made maintenance problematic. Because of their heavy use of fuel for heating, swimming baths were frequently shut down.[10]

9. T. McCarthy, *War Games: The Story of Sport in World War Two* (London, Queen Anne Press, 1989), pp. 54, 104–8; *The Times*, 3 January 1942, Review of 1941; MO File Report 13, December 1939; *Daily Herald*, 6 July and 7 December 1945.

10. M-O, Topic Collection, Sport, Box 2, and File Report 698, May 1941, p. 4; *Hansard*, Vol. 370, col. 285, 20 March 1941 and Vol. 379, cols 759–60, 23 April 1942; Amateur Swimming Association (ASA), Annual Report 1943, p. 1.

For many amateur sports, equipment and uniforms began to wear out and replacement was often impossible. Even with such strategies as the repainting of golf balls and the reinflation of tennis balls, the equipment crisis deepened over the six years of the war.[11] Such equipment and sports clothing as were manufactured went almost exclusively to the armed forces, whose fitness and morale were deemed to benefit from the playing of sport.[12] The shortage of personal and public transport and the restriction of public activity imposed by blackout regulations had the effect of 'privatizing' leisure. Thus, darts, table tennis, whist drives and billiards/snooker were activities that grew in popularity during the war, among both civilians and service personnel.[13]

Efforts to overcome practical difficulties were pursued against the background of a vigorous debate over the appropriateness of playing and watching sport in general, and some sports in particular. Probably more than any other aspect of wartime popular culture, sport became a bone of contention. However, debate over this issue cut across party lines.

The positive case rested on the dual assumption that sport contributed to the morale and the physical fitness of civilians and military personnel and that both were vital to the war effort. The debate focused on the morale-building importance of spectator sports. Not surprisingly, those administering the major spectator sports took a positive view. The Football League asserted that 'first class football undoubtedly supplies a very necessary relaxation to thousands of workers engaged on National Service'. In a self-congratulatory manner, the Marylebone Cricket Club (MCC) expressed satisfaction at the end of the war over the pleasure cricket at Lord's had given the public.[14]

Sir John Anderson, Home Secretary in the Chamberlain government, expressed the essentials of what was to be the official position

11. M-O, Topic Collection, Sport, Box 2, Golf, 4 August 1940; Lawn Tennis Association (LTA), Report to Annual General Meeting, 12 December 1946; NBKR 6/15/1, Evan Hunter to Noel-Baker, 19 August 1947.
12. The monopoly granted to the NAAFI as supplier of priority equipment was a source of controversy for much of the war. *Hansard*, Vol. 382, cols 837–8, 4 August 1942.
13. M-O, File Reports 653, April 1941 and 1632, March 1943; McCarthy, *War Games*, p. 85; *Hansard*, Vol. 369, col. 375, 25 February 1941.
14. FA Council Minutes, War Emergency Committee, 4 March 1940; MCC Minute Book, 1944–48, p. 32, Annual General Meeting, 1945.

throughout the war. He believed that 'experience has proved that if workers are to maintain their efficiency for more than a very limited period, some measure of relaxation is essential'. In spring 1942, Herbert Morrison, as Anderson's successor, maintained this basic argument in the face of severe criticism. He emphasized that 'we have taken the view that there must be, within reasonable limitations, recreation for the people. I do not think that we had better too readily or extensively adopt the philosophy or policy of progressive misery.' Morrison maintained that there was little real evidence that the continuation of spectator sports adversely affected the war effort. On the contrary, he insisted, 'public entertainments act as a lubricant rather than a brake on the war machine'.[15]

Critics of the government's tolerant position argued that spectator sports in particular constituted an unjustified distraction from the serious business of war. Particularly during the darker periods of the war, it was suggested that, rather than symbolizing defiance, the continuation of sporting activities contributed to an atmosphere of less-than-total commitment to the war effort. In Parliament the attack reached its peak in late-February 1942 in a Commons' debate on the war situation; one that mirrored a rising press campaign for radical restriction of sport headed by the *Daily Express*.[16] Sir Stafford Cripps, who had recently taken over as Lord President and Leader of the House, summarized the debate. He argued that the motto could no longer be 'Business as Usual' or 'Pleasure as Usual'. It was his view that activities such as 'dog-racing and boxing displays ... are completely out of accord with the true spirit of determination of the people'. Such sports should 'no longer be allowed to offend the solid and serious intention of the country to achieve victory'.[17] This speech turned Cripps into a popular symbol of the intent to pursue the war effort more seriously.

In fact, James Griffiths, Labour MP for Llanelli, had earlier made much the same argument as Cripps and, further, had responded to 'the suggestion that workmen need circuses to enable them to do their best for the nation. That is an insult. The people of this country

15. *Hansard*, Vol. 361, col. 1657, 30 May 1940; Vol. 376, cols 1666–7, 11 December 1941; Vol. 377, cols 19–20, 8 January 1942, Vol. 378, cols 1177–80, 12 March 1942.
16. M-O, File Report 1139, March 1942.
17. *Hansard*, Vol. 378, cols 311–20, 25 February 1942.

will respond to calls for service.'[18] Griffiths's assertion that the people themselves would accept, even demanded, sacrifices was supported by other speakers and by a Mass-Observation (M-O) survey in which only 17 per cent of respondents were strongly opposed to the ending of greyhound racing. In another report, M-O observed that while 'many people are still deeply interested in sporting matters, they didn't feel able, or that it was proper, to indulge their feelings in the present time'. Even in the Commons, where there was a general tendency to support the coalition government, Morrison was obliged to concede that there was 'sharp division of opinion in the House'.[19]

In response to the February 1942 debate, Herbert Morrison tightened restrictions which had already reduced horse racing to 20 per cent and consumption of fodder to 17 per cent of pre-war levels.[20] As a result, sporting events were essentially confined to the weekends. At the same time, opposition was often linked to other long-standing causes and was not merely based on hostility to sport in time of war. Opponents of 'cruel' sports such as fox-hunting, cockfighting and coursing, defenders of an entertainment- and sport-free Sabbath, and critics of gambling on sport, all believed that the circumstances of war added strength to their already well-established campaigns. In July 1941, Morrison had observed that 'there is a disposition to accept the war as an opportunity to push personal opinion and, if I may say so, personal intolerance'. When Labour party colleague Emanuel Shinwell joined in an attack on greyhound racing, Morrison replied that 'with great respect, I think my honourable Friend is sub-consciously influenced by his dislike for this form of entertainment'. In February 1943, Morrison cautioned Conservative Sir Waldron Smithers that 'I really think it is wrong to exploit the war situation for the furtherance of peace-time policy.' In March 1942, Morrison had been supported in his contentions by Sir Leonard Lyle, Conservative MP for Bournemouth, who believed it 'a fact that a lot of people are trying to stop every form of sport

18. Ibid., Vol. 378, cols 48–50, 24 February 1942.
19. M-O, File Report 1632, 'Some Notes on the Use of Leisure,' March 1943. The middle-class bias of many who participated in Mass-Observation probably deflated this figure to some degree. M-O, File Report 724, 4 June 1941; *Hansard*, Vol. 372, col. 1462, 2 July 1941.
20. *Hansard*, Vol. 378, cols 1177–80, 12 March 1942; PRO POW 20/133, Minute, 17 March 1948.

of which they do not happen to patronise themselves'.[21] Such acrimony, combined with practical difficulties, did not create an atmosphere conducive to a reformation of sporting practices or principles.

Particularly for those in the armed forces, sports were validated not only as entertainment and relaxation, but because participation contributed to physical fitness. In the first few weeks of the war, many sporting organizations aligned themselves with this view. Among those offering facilities, coaches and 'organizational experience' were the Rugby Football Union (RFU), the English Cross-country Union and the Table Tennis Association. By March 1940, 154 Football Association (FA) nominees had been accepted as physical training instructors in the services.[22] In a more generalized sense, both amateur and professional sports organizations publicly identified themselves with the war effort. Thus, the RFU made the West Stand at Twickenham available as a public air-raid shelter, 'complete with canteen'.[23] From the very beginning of the war, a wide range of sporting events were staged for the Red Cross and other wartime charities. By 1943 over £1 million had been raised. In this way, although genuinely patriotic motives were undoubtedly involved, such contributions could, fortuitously, also serve to deflect criticism of the staging of major sporting events. Greyhound racing was one of the principal contributors to the Red Cross Fund, with donations totalling more than £50,000 by 1943.[24]

Just as sports sought to legitimize themselves and connect with the national war effort, so attempts were made to associate physical fitness with nationalistic endeavour: to make the 'Daily Dozen' a part of 'Doing One's Bit'. How far this resulted in a fitter population likely to keep up, or wish to increase, levels of physical recreation and games-playing in peace is not easy to assess. For those in the armed forces opportunities for sport or recreation obviously varied

21. Ibid., Vol. 372, cols 1354–64, 2 July 1941; Vol. 376, cols 1666–7, 11 December 1941, Vol. 386, col. 1434, 11 February 1942; Vol. 386, col. 1780, 12 March 1942.
22. Ibid., Vol. 356, cols 808–9, 25 January 1940; *The Times*, 11, 12, 16 and 18 September and 3 October 1939; FA Council Minutes, War Emergency Committee, 4 March 1940, item 5.
23. *The Times*, 19 September 1939.
24. FA Council, Reference Minute No. 7, 22 January 1940; FA Annual Report, 1943–44; MCC Annual Report, 1945; McCarthy, *War Games*, p. 85.

greatly, depending on the circumstances in which the individual was serving. During 1947 and 1948, the *Daily Herald* carried a series of mini-biographies of 'Olympic Probables', a surprising number of whom were reported to have been introduced to their events while serving in the forces during the war.[25] Clearly, the majority of women in the forces had greater opportunities, and more pressure put on them, to participate in sport and physical exercise than had been the case before the war. Yet M-O surveys of the late 1940s indicate that only between 10 and 20 per cent of the population actively participated in sport or physical recreation. Proportions were higher among the young and particularly among men.[26] One thing that is certain is that, at least in the army, official efforts were made to enforce the Corinthian ideal. The Army Sports Control Board, established in 1918 and committed to 'strict amateur principles', laid out in its handbook used during the Second World War six basic rules:

> a sportsman is one who: 1. Plays the game for the game's sake; 2. Plays for his side and not for himself; 3. Is a good winner and a good loser; 4. Accepts all decisions in a proper spirit; 5. Is chivalrous to a defeated opponent; 6. Is unselfish and always ready to help others to become proficient.[27]

The maintenance of skeletal programmes of sporting competition and the provision of recreational facilities for both civilians and service personnel were tasks not easily fulfilled during the war and the effort, in both spheres, to 'carry on' often demanded significant degrees of initiative and improvisation. It is, however, not at all clear that wartime circumstances provoked sustained innovation, that is to say, significant changes that carried over into the immediate post-war period, and radically distinguished the organization and practice of sport in the late 1940s from that of a decade earlier.

Practical difficulties did not end with the end of the war. They inhibited efforts to return to normal after 1945, as they had the earlier endeavour to 'carry on'. The circumstances prevailing in austerity Britain created problems with regard to the facilities, clothing and equipment necessary for a return to pre-war levels of sporting

25. *Athletics*, 2:7 (June 1946), p. 3.
26. M-O, File Report 3045, 'A Report on British Sport', October 1948, File Report 3067, 'Work and Leisure,' November 1948.
27. McCarthy, *War Games*, p. 127.

activity. Ingenuity continued to predominate over fundamental innovation in the pattern of response to practical problems. Certainly, in the case of the established spectator sports there was, despite the many problems and hesitations involved, a very successful post-war recovery. M-O's judgement, made early in the war, that 'the traditional national interest in sport is only dormant and temporarily submerged' was to prove well founded.[28] In the late 1940s, attendance records were set in league and cup football and in first-class cricket, particularly during the 1948 tour by Australia. Horse-race meetings, boxing tournaments, greyhound racing, major athletics meetings and speedway racing all attracted large crowds. The consumers of sporting entertainment appeared very happy with the familiar fare offered them. Ironically, this very success, as much as the problems that had to be overcome in order to achieve it, served to minimize any incentive for change. Success engendered a general sense of satisfaction, if not, as some argued, complacency, among the organizing bodies of the main British sports.[29]

II

During and after the war, shortages and a wide range of other problems inhibited any attempt to pursue economic and social change of a far-reaching nature. Yet from an early stage of the conflict post-war reconstruction was the object of close attention and a degree of ambitious thinking. Anticipation of improvement in English society had existed even though it was to be significantly frustrated in the post-war years. Can the aspiration for change, for what contemporaries sometimes referred to as 'uplift', be found in the planning undertaken by the governing bodies of major sports? During the Parliamentary discussion of post-war reconstruction in late 1941, questions were asked regarding the 'adequate reservations of playing fields and recreational spaces'.[30] However, the first sign of commitment to deliberative post-war planning by any of the governing bodies of sport came from the FA in May 1943. The War Emergency

28. M-O, File Report 724, 4 June 1941.
29. Some argued that the crowds were coming too easily. *Daily Herald*, 29 September 1947.
30. PRO HLG 109/3, Lord Derby to Arthur Greenwood, 5 August 1941, Memorial from London and Greater London Playing Fields Associations, 26 August 1941.

Committee submitted a memorial on 'Post-War Development' to the
FA Council. In many respects it was a cautious, conservative document, reflecting a powerful Corinthian influence, a distinct leaning
for a body with authority over both amateur and professional football.
Quantitatively, it looked to 'the extension of football', but it was in
its qualitative implications that the authors of the memorial revealed
a strong bias in favour of supposedly amateur values. It was the view
of the Committee that:

> it must be generally apparent that the tone of wartime football has
> been higher than that in evidence during the years immediately
> preceding the war; the players, all being engaged in some form of
> national service, have played the game for the game's sake, keeping
> it in perspective and looking upon it as recreation rather than as a
> profession. If, after the war, this same spirit can permeate both
> amateur and professional play, the reputation of the game will be
> enhanced and the standard of play will undoubtedly improve.[31]

In its conclusion the Committee returned to a similar theme, regretting
that, in the pre-war period, there had been times:

> when instead of friendly co-operation there has been aggressive rivalry,
> when commercialism has tended to mar the reputation of games. In
> future, the development of football must be prompted by ideals above
> reproach; only in this way can the game contribute its maximum
> quota to the welfare of the nation.

Despite the generally cautious tone, the Committee raised two issues
that were 'not given a very favourable reception' because they
departed radically from past practices. One was the suggested adoption of the Swedish scheme whereby monies from football pools
were earmarked by government for the development of grounds,
gymnasia and sports centres. The other was the idea of forming a
Sunday football association as part of the FA.

It was not until October 1944 that the Council itself formulated
an interim report on 'Post-War Development'. This document was
predicated on the assumption that much needed to be done, particularly on facilities, in order 'to meet the demand for football which

---

31. FA Minute Book, pp. 4–7, 'Post-War Development'. The tone adopted here
    is an almost precise echo of *The Times* observations regarding friendly matches
    being played early in the war. There, it was hoped that, free from the
    'hurly-burly' of competition, 'football, in fact, may return in spirit to an earlier,
    more delectable, and less strenuous age'. *The Times*, 23 September 1939.

there will be after the war'. However, the report vehemently rejected the earlier memorial on the pools issue, and remained ambivalent on Sunday play. On the first issue, it went so far in a contrary direction as to call on the government to prohibit football pools. It was recognized 'that football would be played on Sundays after the War' but at the same time that 'opinion was divided on the policy of widening the jurisdiction of the Football Association to embrace organisations promoting Sunday football'.[32]

Rejection of the two 'radical' proposals from the 1943 memorial was consistent with some revealing comments in the FA annual report for the 1943–44 season. There, satisfaction was expressed over 'the fact that no revolutionary changes appear to be necessary, either in the laws of the Game or in the administration of the Association's affairs'. The report recognized that, although it was necessary to 'move with the times, it is desirable that there should be no unnecessary innovations and that those who play and watch the game should do so only in accordance with its highest traditions'. Ultimately, at a full meeting of the Council in December 1945, the report on Post-War Development was formally withdrawn.[33]

In March 1945, an MCC select committee on post-war cricket published an interim report, which was subject to radically differing interpretations. The *Daily Herald* quoted R. W. V. Robins of Middlesex and England as being enthusiastic for a scheme for a knockout cup: 'I believe we have a chance to put on the map the kind of cricket a large section of the public have wanted for some time'. The *Herald* saw this proposal as a blow to the 'ultra-conservative elders of the game'. Such celebration was somewhat premature, as the Gillette Cup lay a decade and a half away. R. C. Robertson-Glasgow, writing in *Wisden* for 1945, was more realistic:

> While the fate of the world was being determined, English cricket was the scene of an interesting little battle, which ended in the rout of the 'hustlers' and the triumph of conservatism over the heresy that progress and speed are synonymous. The defeat of the *soi-disant* progressives, with their programme of one-day and time-limited matches for first class cricket, was a certainty so long as the issue of debate rested with the majority opinion of practising cricketers.

One outcome of the report was a September 1945 commitment to

32. FA Minute Book, 'Post-War Development: an Interim Report', October 1944.
33. FA Minute Book, item 32, 17 December 1945.

rewriting the rules of cricket; the intention being 'to meet the development of the modern game'. Again, any hopes, or fears, of a major revision were soon put to rest. At a special general meeting of the MCC in May 1946 it was emphasized that the aim regarding the laws was clarification and the avoidance of 'any attempt to alter the principles of the existing laws'.[34] Not surprisingly, the recommended changes were minimal. While there was something of a battle going on within the MCC at this time and the controlling influence of the 'old school' was being challenged, it is clear from the above that, at least in the immediate post-war era, it remained dominant.

What of sports where both conservative social interests and spectatorship were less important? In February 1944, the Amateur Athletic Association (AAA) adopted a 'Post-war Planning Scheme' in which a major administrative reorganization was recommended. The Annual Report of 1946 observed 'very little progress made' and a special conference on the subject in the summer of 1947 was marked by 'continuing conflict'. The entire reorganization project was formally abandoned in the autumn of 1947. On the other hand, the AAA began the development of a national coaching scheme.[35] The annual reports of the Amateur Swimming Association (ASA) for both 1943 and 1944 noted that 'the War has brought about a much greater realisation by Parliament and people alike of the value and importance of a knowledge of swimming'. This led to a commitment by the ASA that 'facilities to learn and practise swimming shall be provided in much increased measure at the conclusion of the war'. Consequently, the Association sought 'vigorously to press this policy in influential quarters'. One product of such pressure was an amendment to the 1944 Education Act strengthening the obligation of local authorities to provide school swimming baths. Much of this enthusiasm for the expansion of swimming as a recreational activity as well as a sport was frustrated by post-war conditions. The ASA annual reports for 1945 and 1946 emphasized the problem of facilities, recognizing that 'this state of affairs must be faced for some years to come'. Unanimous in its, albeit frustrated, enthusiasms for

34. MCC Minute Book, Annual Reports, 1946, p. 94 and 1947, p. 161; *Wisden*, 1945, pp. 46–7; *Daily Herald*, 23 March and 5 September 1945.
35. AAA, 'Post-war Planning Scheme', 5 February 1944, Annual Report 1946, General Committee, 3 May and 4 October 1947; Centre For Sports Science and History, University of Birmingham, Abrahams Papers, NCAL XXV H 27, 'Review of the AAA Coaching Scheme', p. 2.

expansion, the ASA remained divided over other issues, particularly those concerning its strict definition of amateurism, where minor concessions were won at the end of extensive debate.[36]

Like swimming, cycling was a sport with a strong basis as a recreational activity and the two sports were both distanced from social elitism. Cycling was affected by one of the most significant and lasting sports innovations of the Second World War. In June 1942 the National Cycling Union's (NCU) ban on massed-start road racing was defied when a race from Llangollen to Wolverhampton was staged. Suspended by the NCU, the organizers and participants formed, in November 1942, the British League of Racing Cyclists (BLRC). Nevertheless, the NCU and the Road Time-Trial Council (RTTC) continued their 'firm opposition' to massed-start racing on public roads. Their own innovations were confined to a relaxation of clothing regulations and a concession allowing bicycle accessories, though still not bicycles, to be given as prizes in competitive events held under their jurisdiction.[37]

Hypothetically, the British Workers' Sports Association might have become a catalyst for a sporting revolution: the establishment of 'democratic sports' under the control of neither a social elite nor commercial interests. Its agenda for the post-war era rang with optimism. In 1945, the organization declared itself 'anxious to take full advantage of the present increased interest in sport to achieve our long-cherished ambition to become the most important recreation Movement in the country'. Sadly for its small cadre of enthusiasts, the BWSA did not prosper. Despite, perhaps because of, the spectator boom of the late 1940s, the organization failed to attract significant support for its increasingly sparse programme of regional or national events. By the time of the 1949 Annual General Meeting, the president, addressing the twenty members present, hoped 'that delegates would not despair at the trend of events during the past year'.[38]

The Central Council of Recreative Physical Training had been

36. ASA Annual Reports, 1943, item 2, 1944, item 2, 1945, item 1, 1946, item 1 and 1947, item 25; *Swimming Times*, **23**:1 (February 1946), p. 21, and **24**:4 (April 1947), p. 91; *Hansard*, Vol. 391, cols 2005–6, 30 July 1943.

37. McCarthy, *War Games*, p. 98; *Daily Herald*, 8 January 1945 and 14 January 1946.

38. National Museum of Labour, Manchester, BWSA, Announcement of a Special Conference, October 1945, and Minutes of the Annual General Meeting, 14 May 1949; *Daily Herald*, 20 December 1946.

founded in 1935 with the intention of representing the collective interests of amateur sports in Britain. By the end of the Second World War, its title changed to the Central Council of Physical Recreation (CCPR), and the organization claimed the affiliation of 135 national bodies, including those administering 'nearly every game, sport and outdoor activity'. In September 1944, a memorandum on 'The Post-War Work of the CCPR' was approved by its executive committee. Like the FA and other bodies, the CCPR's anticipation was of quantitative growth and qualitative continuity: 'After the war, it is suggested that its main functions should remain unchanged, as any new developments which would arise from its proposed wider field of activity would call for an extension rather than a fundamental change in its present methods of working.'[39] The post-war planning of the several sports organizations considered here does not offer very much evidence of a dynamic of change stimulated by wartime experience. However, change need not be planned. Thus, it is also important to review the immediate post-war period to judge the influence of the war on a number of social issues relevant to sport: amateurism, gender, race, Sunday play and voluntarism.

III

The general effect of the war in supposedly breaking down the distinctions of social class was evidenced in sport by the erosion of some barriers between the amateur and professional. Separate changing rooms for the two classes of cricketers disappeared at Lord's. Professionals served alongside amateurs as officers, and amateurs with professionals as other ranks, in the services. In June 1942, when Pilot Officer Len Harvey and Flight Sergeant Freddie Mills met for the British light-heavyweight title, the rules prohibiting fights between officers and other ranks had to be changed. In part because of the bitterness engendered by the organizational split of 1895, the RFU ban on any contact between its amateurs and the professionals of the Rugby League was one of the most rigorously enforced regulations in the whole of sport. In this light, the November 1939 lifting of

39. NBKR 6/2/1, 'The Post-War Work of the Central Council for Physical Recreation', October 1944, p. 1.

the ban for the duration of the war might appear as a major breach in the wall separating professional and amateur. In reality, it was a minor fissure. The easing of the rule merely allowed affiliated clubs to compete against service teams in which League players were participating, and then only if the individuals concerned had had no contact with the League since enlistment.[40]

Was the wartime reduction in the barriers between amateur and professional continued with the coming of peace? In the short term at least, the answer is no. Walls did not come tumbling down. On the contrary, the adminstrators of several British sports sought to reinforce those that had seemed in danger of collapse. The slow pace of demobilization obliged the RFU to extend into the 1945–46 season the ruling that allowed for the 'mixing' of players on service teams. However, they firmly defended other long-established restrictions. Despite several appeals and the fact that he had reported himself to the authorities, Corporal J. A. Gregory of the Army was banned because he played one game, unpaid, for Huddersfield, a Rugby League club. Individuals' requests for reinstatement as amateurs were routinely rejected. In further efforts to keep clear the lines of demarcation between amateur and professional, the RFU forbade member clubs from making their grounds available for practice by visiting League tourists from New Zealand or by local professional soccer teams.[41]

Though amateur and professional cricketers now used the same changing rooms, other distinctions between them were either maintained or even reintroduced in the immediate post-war period. Even before the war was over, a proposal to the MCC Emergency Committee that the name of the annual Gentlemen versus Players match should be altered was soundly rejected. For one season after the war the initials of professionals appeared, like those of amateurs, in front of their names on scorecards at Lords. Then, for 1947, it was

40. D. Lemmon, *The Crisis of Captaincy: Servant and Master in English Cricket* (London, Christopher Helm, 1988), pp. 87–8; McCarthy, *War Games*, p. 106; *The Times*, 14, 15 and 22 November 1939.

41. For these and other examples of attempts to maintain amateur/professional discrimination, see N. Baker, 'The Amateur Ideal in a Society of Equality: Change and Continuity in post-Second World War British Sport, 1945–48', *International Journal of the History of Sport*, **12**:1 (April 1995), pp. 99–126; RFU Minutes, Full Committee, 18 January 1946, Full Committee and Annual General Meeting, 11 July 1947, Full Committee, 26 September 1947.

decided to revert to the old system where initials appeared after the names of professionals. Some professionals believed that after the war 'it could never be the same again' in terms of amateur/professional relationships. Yet in 1948, having been invited to play festival cricket for Leveson-Gower's XI, Jim Laker watched his eight amateur team-mates enter the president's marquee for lunch while he and the other two professionals were 'told in no uncertain terms ... that we were not welcome'.[42]

Even sports much less closely identified with the defence of well-established ways went to considerable lengths to assure that practices tolerated in war were no longer acceptable if they contravened strict interpretations of amateurism. The All-England Badminton Association put an end to participation by amateurs in exhibition matches on stages. At its 1945 annual meeting, the Amateur Boxing Association (ABA) became involved in a long and inconclusive debate over whether or not temporary physical training instructors should lose their amateur status.[43]

In athletics, amateur football, swimming and lawn tennis, post-war debate over amateurism focused on the issue of 'broken time'; whether or not an amateur could receive compensation for wages lost while competing. This was a crucial question because it largely determined who could or could not compete at the national and international levels. This was clearly seen as 'a form of class distinction'. Discussion of this issue was complicated for the domestic authorities because of the influence of international governing bodies, assumptions regarding foreign practices, and the desire to be competitive which was not always consistent with the maintenance of true amateurism. The AAA, with the aid of its American ally, Avery Brundage, managed to hold off any revision of the rules of the International Amateur Athletic Federation (IAAF) until after the 1948 Olympics. The FA decided to compete in those Games with a strictly amateur side. The ASA, after extensive debate, decided to permit broken-time payment for those swimmers and divers who were competing internationally. However, such payments were to

42. MCC Minute Book, pp. 30–1, 9 April 1945, p. 109, 17 June 1946 and p. 139, 9 December 1946; *Daily Herald*, 17 July 1947; M. Marshall, *Gentlemen and Players* (London, Grafton Books, 1987), pp. 129–31. Marshall very effectively depicts the admixture of change and continuity present in cricket at this time.

43. *The Times*, 2 and 17 October 1945.

be made by the competitor's employer and not the ASA. Further, they were subject to prior approval on a case-by-case basis. The issue for the Lawn Tennis Association (LTA) focused on what was known as the eight-week rule. This permitted the payment of travel and living expenses to amateur players for a maximum of eight weeks each year. It had been introduced by the Americans in 1934 and adopted by the International Lawn Tennis Federation shortly thereafter. The British had been 'among the few dissentients' on the grounds that 'it was inconsistent with the true spirit of amateurism'. From discussion leading up to the reversal of this position and the LTA's acceptance of the eight-week rule in 1947, it is evident that the main motivating factor was competitiveness, or more precisely in terms of British performances, lack thereof. Similarly, it was concern over how well British rowers would be able to perform in the 1948 Olympics against intensively prepared foreigners that initiated discussion, though no action, by the Amateur Rowing Association (ARA) on possible rule changes. Although there were some token references to the spirit of the times, it is clear that it was the desire to be competitive internationally that levered such change as did occur.[44]

The appointment of Walter Winterbottom as full-time manager of the England XI in 1946 was similarly motivated by the desire to keep English football on top and represented a step away from the amateur principle of limited preparation which, up to that point, had influenced even professional players.[45] Such changes were part of a long-term, incremental, often resisted, drift away from Corinthian idealism, *not* the product of some fundamental shift in social values stimulated by the experiences of the Second World War. The contested and qualified nature of such change is evident in the adoption of coaching schemes by the AAA and the LTA. The appointment of Geoff Dyson as the first full-time national coach was followed by the addition of several regional coaches, whose positions, like that of Dyson, were largely funded by grants from the Ministry of Education. Thus, as pointed out in the AAA's annual report for

44. *Daily Herald*, 11 December 1947; AAA, General Committee, 12 October 1946, item (e), 7 December 1946, item (e), and 28 October 1948, item (d); ASA Annual Report 1947, p. 22; J. Crump, 'Athletics', in *Sport in Britain: A Social History*, ed. T. Mason (Cambridge, Cambridge UP, 1989), pp. 53–5; *British Lawn Tennis*, **16**:163 (November 1946), p. 11.
45. *Daily Herald*, 19 December 1945 and 27 September 1946.

1948, their primary responsibilites were for the training of other coaches, particularly among schoolteachers. Similarly, the LTA launched a coaching scheme with Ministry of Education grants. The image of tennis as a 'snobbish' sport was hardly threatened by the decision to use grant money to fund coaching at 25 public schools while denying support to county associations on the grounds of economy. From a different perspective, the LTA was criticized on the grounds that its coaching scheme did not target a smaller number of superior players and thus more rapidly address Britain's poor record in international competition.[46]

Did any change in amateur/professional relations improve the treatment of professional athletes? During the war, professional footballers had received 30s (£1.50) per appearance, whether playing for the club of their original registration or guesting. The attempt of the Football League not only to maintain club control over players once the war was over and even introduce a greater degree of semi-professionalism, but also to reimpose the maximum wage at pre-war levels, was almost certain to draw a response from the players, and it did. Record crowds were attending games and record transfer fees were being paid for players who received no part of them. At the same time the wages of the majority of workers were rising appreciably. The result was a strong upward pressure on the maximum wage, a series of strike threats, charges that conditions of employment were 'archaic, unjust and repressive' and, at one stage, arbitration by the Ministry of Labour. However, although it rose by over 50 per cent in the early years of peace, a maximium wage remained in place and, despite individual resistance such as that of Wilf Mannion, professional players remained tied to their clubs. In the struggle with their players, clubs of the professional Football League even used the rhetoric of Corinthianism to bolster their case. Players were said to be fortunate to be playing for a living and should participate for the sake of the game. The maximum wage was even justified on the grounds that it assured team play, while to lift it would encourage individualism. Old forms of labour relations in professional football were validated not only in terms of amateur values but also by de-emphasizing commercialism. In

46. AAA Annual Report 1948, p. 7; Lawn Tennis Association (LTA), Report of Council, 12 December 1946, item 14, and 11 December 1947, item 14; *British Lawn Tennis*, **16**:161 (September 1946), p. 7.

1945, during Parliamentary debates over the entertainment tax, it was argued that 'professional clubs are not commercial concerns in the ordinary sense of the word'; 'Directors are directors on account of their interest in the game, and for some of them it is a costly interest.'[47]

Just as the war was assumed to have broken down barriers based on class, so it was widely believed to have diminished differences in social and economic roles based on gender.[48] Certainly, the war drew many women into the services and industrial occupations and thus out of narrowly domestic roles. It is probably correct to assume that such a transition must have obliged some women, and provided opportunities for others, to participate in various forms of sport and physical recreation. There was significant proliferation of sports among female factory workers, netball being particularly popular. Sport was reported to be valued among these women 'as a relaxation and a contrast to long hours at war work'. Initially, the end of the war sent many women back into domesticity as men returned from the services to fill their old jobs. It was the export drive and an acute shortage of labour that, from 1947, led the government to encourage women back into industry.[49]

However motivated, was there any comparable stimulation of change in the world of sport? If M-O surveys are to be believed, the assumption that, in terms of both participation and interest, sport was a male province continued into the post-war era.[50] In practice, women's opportunities to participate in competitive sport continued to vary considerably by social class and from sport to sport. In sports such as lawn tennis, hockey and golf there was, as there had been before the war, significant female participation and prominence. However, even the development of municipal facilities in tennis and golf in the inter-war period had not significantly

47. *Daily Herald*, 4 July 1947; PRO LAB 3/575, Proceedings of the National Arbitration Tribunal, 27 March 1947.
48. M-O, File Report 698, May 1941, p. 2.
49. McCarthy, *War Games*, pp. 70, 84, 131–2; M-O, File Report 290, July 1940; NBKR 6/2/1, CCPR Memo, 'Physical recreation for Adult Industrial Workers' September 1944; P. Summerfield, *Women Workers in the Second World War: Production and Patriarchy in Conflict* (London, Croom Helm, 1984); J. Hargreaves, *Sporting Females: Critical Issues in the History and Sociology of Women's Sports* (London, Routledge, 1994).
50. M-O, File Reports 3045, October 1948 and 3141, July 1949, and Directive Box 136, A–K.

increased working-class participation in either sport. By contrast, cycling and swimming, though mainly administered by men, were both accessible to women of all classes and this characteristic, evident before the war, strengthened after 1945. In the first three years of peace, there was a proliferation of record-breaking rides by women cyclists, ranging from that for 25 miles to the standard for 12 hours. In swimming and diving, the virtual parity with men, achieved in 1936, in terms of number of events, was maintained at the London Olympics of 1948. Furthermore, the men and women of the British team participated together in a series of practice sessions prior to the Games.[51] In other sports, notably netball, participation and administration were almost exclusively female. Such autonomy was bought at the price of virtual invisibility to the eyes of the press and the male sporting public.

In sports such as Association Football and rugby, long entrenched at the core of concepts of masculinity, the total exclusion of women was maintained in the post-war era. In the case of football, such exclusion was expressly confirmed. In December 1946, 'it having been brought to the notice of the Council that so-called Football by women players is in contemplation in various parts of the country', the FA recorded continuing approval of its own resolution of 1921:

> Complaints having been made as to football being played by women, the Council feel impelled to express their strong opinion that the game of football is quite unsuitable for females and ought not to be encouraged. For this reason the Council request the clubs belonging to the Association to refuse the use of their grounds for such matches.[52]

Somewhere between the qualified approval given to women in some sports and the total exclusion applied in others, lay athletics, where grudgingly accorded concessions were admixed with outright hostility. While some men in athletic administration supported the efforts of the Women's Amateur Athletic Association (WAAA) to expand female opportunities in the sport, there remained many men who had difficulty in accepting the concept and the reality of the woman

---

51. *Daily Herald*, 22 July and 19 August 1946, 21 July, 4 and 25 August, 8 and 22 September and 29 December 1947, and 6 September and 12 October 1948; M. Tyler (ed.), *The History of the Olympics* (London, Marshall Cavendish, 1975), pp. 40, 47; ASA, Annual Report 1949, pp. 31–2.
52. FA Council Minutes, 16 December 1946.

athlete. This accounted for what one AAA administrator described as the 'thinly-veiled contempt in which the older male legislator has regarded them in the past few years'.[53] Resistance was expressed in several forms; denial of femininity, calls for the restriction or elimination of female participation in athletics, and the adoption of language stressing the other 'real' roles of women athletes. Press reference to 'the problem of half-sex entrants' and the categorization of women competitors by body type, big or hefty as against dainty or petite, served to imply that, although the term 'lesbian' was not used, some women athletes were less than 'real' women. The addition of the 200 metres, the long-jump and the shot in 1948 raised the number of Olympic athetics events for women to nine. However, that total was only slightly above a third of the number of events for men, and 200 metres was the longest race women were allowed to run. Even that was too much for some in the British press, who believed that athletics should be 'a matter for men and the little girls, largely, would be better occupied at home sewing their big brother's pants'. This would be for their own good, obviating 'the unnatural strain imposed on women by untimely competition'. Even four gold medals did not spare Fanny Blankers-Koen from the press insistence on a female athlete's 'real' persona. Thus, she was described as the 'lanky Dutch housewife, mother of two, with sink-stained hands, [who] came from the shopping queues of an Amsterdam suburb'. Readers were reminded that 'apart from her running, she lives the life of a housewife, sewing and darning and looking after her home and children'. It would be hard to argue that models of female domesticity had been shattered by the experiences of the Second World War.[54]

Before the Second World War, most of the English regarded race in sport or in society generally as a remote issue, relevant in foreign affairs and vaguely in the imperial context, but not domestically. Race, sport and politics began to intersect for the English during the war. In July 1941 Home Secretary Herbert Morrison was asked if he was aware that a British-born subject serving in the Royal Air

53. J. Crump in *World Sports* (September 1948), p. 22.
54. *Athletics*, 2:27 (February 1948), pp. 15–16 and 2:35 (October 1948), p. 12; Tyler, *Olympics*, pp. 40, 47; Hargreaves, *Sporting Females*, p. 264; *Daily Herald*, 3, 4, 9 and 10 August 1948; *Daily Express*, 19 July, 5, 8 and 12 August 1948. The 'medical' rationale for female non-participation had a long history: see P. Vertinsky, *The Eternally Wounded Woman: Women, Doctors and Exercise in the Late Nineteenth Century* (Manchester, Manchester UP, 1990).

Force had been barred by the British Boxing Board of Control (BBBofC) from competing in British boxing competitions on the ground of colour. Morrison was asked to discourage such discrimination 'having regard to the harmful reactions to the war effort among our many coloured subjects'. Morrison declared himself in 'entire sympathy' with his questioner and opposed to any discrimination on the basis of colour. However, he went on to reflect some of the strained ambiguity prevalent in the era on this issue: 'I understand that there are differences of opinion on the question whether spectacular fights between opponents of different colour ought to be encouraged; and that it is for this reason and not from any prejudice against coloured boxers that there is a rule of the BBBofC.' Morrison also pointed out that the rule did not apply to all competitions, but only those for a British Championship.[55]

The issue of a colour bar, though not so specifically related to sport, was raised again in 1943 following an incident at a London hotel where Learie Constantine, test cricketer and pre-war star in the Lancashire League, was asked, along with six other West Indians, to leave on the grounds of colour. This led to further Parliamentary statements deploring discrimination, again accompanied by some rather contradictory opinions. These included a denial that any colour bar existed and the assertion that it was a 'social' question 'in which it is very difficult for Governments or Legislatures to interfere'. Any discrimination was to be deplored because 'we want to have, as a nation, the love and respect of our children from overseas'.[56]

In the spring of 1947 Labour MP John Lewis mounted a campaign to have the BBBofC's colour bar lifted. Lewis received strong support from different sections of the press and from boxing promoter Jack Solomon who, in June 1947, staged a programme which involved five fights pitting white against coloured boxers. All five whites lost, including the popular Freddie Mills, knocked out in five rounds by the American Lloyd Marshall. Interestingly, Lewis's initial Parliamentary question was not addressed to the Home Secretary, the minister with general oversight of sporting matters, but to the Colonial Secretary. Later in the campaign it was reported in the press that the

55. *Hansard*, Vol. 373, cols 1548–9, 31 July 1941.
56. Ibid., Vol. 393, col. 1465, 13 November 1943 and Vol. 395, cols 1910–12 and 1921–2, 17 December 1943.

Colonial Office was bringing pressure for change to bear on the BBBofC. Even for those who took a progressive position, race was still being viewed as an imperial/colonial, not a domestic, issue. It was not until twelve months after Lewis raised the issue that the BBBofC was persuaded to change the offending rule.[57]

It was not only the continuing colonial context of race that tempered any sense of progress but also the language of the time, common to sections of the press with markedly different political sympathies. A cricketer who was 'coal-black', sprinters who were described as 'a Flash of Black Lightning', or more simply just as a 'Black Flash', a footballer whom it was felt could be a 'Black Bombshell', were all the objects of language usage prevalent in the 1940s. At times, the press went beyond such simply descriptive language to make judgements about the characteristics of coloured athletes. In November 1948, the 'fuzzy-haired' Bunda Bangurati from Sierra Leone, 'probably the only Negro playing amateur soccer in England', was described by an offical of his club, Leyton, as having 'the speed of a greyhound and (he) followed the ball everywhere: positional play just did not suit him'. This same emphasis on natural, untrained, physical gifts of the coloured athlete was also evident in a *Daily Express* pre-Olympic discussion of the anticipated non-white domination of the sprinting events, to be explained by the speed necessary to survive in the jungle.[58] As in the case of gender, grudgingly granted concessions did not equate to a radical uprooting of prejudice based on race.

As they had tested attitudes on race and gender, so wartime

57. The relevant rule was not technically based on colour. It limited participation in British Championship fights to boxers whose fathers had been British born. *De facto*, as late as the 1940s this ruled out the great majority of coloured boxers. When changed, the rule only required that the fighter himself be British born and normally domiciled in the UK. *Daily Herald*, 27 March 1947, 3 April and 29 June 1948; *Daily Express*, 20 May, 4 June and 11 September 1947 and 3 February 1948. Interestingly, the Home Office claimed to have no jurisdiction over the BBBofC, but the Colonial Office negotiated directly with the boxing authorities over the colour bar. *Hansard*, Vol. 435, col. 231(wa), 27 March 1947, and col. 196(wa), 26 March 1947.

58. *Daily Herald*, 23 February, 24 March and 13 November 1948; *Daily Express*, 27 November 1947, 17 March and 12 May 1948. For an extended discussion of the history of such perspectives on race and physicality, see J. Hoberman, *Darwin's Athletes: How Sport has Damaged Black America and Preserved the Myth of Race* (New York, Houghton Mifflin, 1997).

conditions brought public and official attention to bear on the practice of the 'Victorian' Sunday; the Sabbatarian endeavour to minimize public activities which would divert from the commitment of the day to religion and religious thoughts. The constraints of shift work and military service made Sunday the only day of relaxation for many, which stimulated demands for greater latitude in using that free time. Wartime Parliamentary debates on Sunday observance focused on the opening of cinemas, but they reflected positions relevant to the issue of Sunday sport. Those who wished to see a general relaxation of Sabbatarian rules argued the absurdity of the variations in local regulations and of troops being denied Sunday entertainment when they could well be asked to fight, and possibly die, on Sundays. Labelling defenders of a restrictive Sunday as 'woefully antedeluvian', those favouring relaxation argued that it was 'out of keeping with our democratic professions', when the estimated 20 per cent of the population who were regular churchgoers could dictate to the other 80 per cent. However, even those who insisted on the need for more leisure opportunities were opposed to the 'commercialisation of Sunday', and to what was termed 'the Continental Sunday'.[59]

Those defending the traditional Sunday argued that there still existed a 'deep-rooted feeling of reverence for religion' and that 'our people are, at heart, as truly religious as ever'. Because of this surviving religiosity it was argued of an open Sunday that 'it would hurt the feelings of a great mass of people in this country who are devoted to keeping the Sabbath holy'. Some viewed the war as having strengthened rather than weakened such sensibilities.[60]

During the war there was no significant effort to permit the staging of major professional spectator sports on Sundays. Some local amateur play had long been permitted, for example, in cricket. In other amateur sports there was no such established and sanctioned play on Sundays. It was on one such sport, football, that the circumstances of war brought to bear pressure for change. The focal point of such

59. *Hansard*, Vol. 357, cols 927–8, 15 February 1940, Vol. 358, col. 1365, 14 March 1940, Vol. 371, cols 1248–9, 15 May 1941, Vol. 374, col. 334, 11 September 1941, Vol. 396, cols 1516–26, 3 February 1944, Vol. 397, 6–7, 15 February 1944, cols 645–6, 22 February 1944 and cols 1642–4, 2 March 1944.
60. Ibid., Vol. 370, cols 932–3, 1 April 1941, and Vol. 415, col. 758, 1 November 1945; *Daily Herald*, 20 March 1947.

pressure was the FA's rule 25 which, since 1910, had denied recognition to clubs or players participating in competition on Sundays. In October 1939, the FA declared itself 'unable officially to recognise Sunday Football'. However, during the course of the war some relaxation was permitted in regard to shift workers and other special groups, such as the Civil Defence, when they were unable to play on other days of the week. A special subcommittee of the FA's post-war planning group, recognizing the probability of a peacetime growth of Sunday football, recommended further, permanent, relaxation of rule 25, giving the FA Council discretion to waive the rule when clubs could only play on Sunday. In August 1945, having received some very negative reaction from County FAs, the special committee dropped the recommendation and merely suggested that wartime relaxation be continued 'for the time-being'. This modest proposal was formally adopted by the FA Council itself in October 1945.[61]

The issue of Sunday play could not easily be put to one side with the end of the war. If anything, the situation became more difficult for the FA as pressure increased on a limited number of playing fields. The production drive and the consequent increase in shift work added to the problem. At a conference of chairmen and secretaries of county associations held in October 1946, there was reportedly 'stimulating controversy' over Sunday play. The proponents of change argued that the shortage of grounds had intensified since the end of the war and this had forced increased Sunday play. They contended that, if the FA continued to forbid such play, 50 per cent of participants would be forced into 'unaffiliated' football. With no recognized officials running Sunday play it was feared the game would be marked by 'the stigma which might result from unprincipled organisation'. Against this essentially pragmatic and jurisdictional case there was posed a more 'moralistic' argument. The points made by the opponents of relaxation ranged from public-house sponsorship of Sunday play to the belief that 90 per cent of those playing on Sunday could in fact play on other days. Tactically, it was argued that 'once the breach was open' it would be impossible to impose any limits at all. The most basic argument was that

There is in this country a substantial section of the public which holds a conscientious objection to the Continental Sunday. It would be

61. FA Minutes, War Emergency Committee, 30 October 1939, Memoranda from the Special sub-Committee on Sunday Football, June 1943 and October 1945.

wrong for the Football Association to offend this conscience by abrogating a ruling of an important principle which has been defended for such a long time.

By May 1948 the Conference refused even to discuss Sunday football. In the meantime, the FA Council was moving toward a position that it should have discretion to relax rule 25, 'pending the resumption of normal conditions'. However, at its Annual General Meeting in June 1948 this proposal was defeated and rule 25 reaffirmed.[62] Thus, the governing body of the most watched and played sport in England was successfully confronted by a strong, resistant traditionalism which drew upon the nationalistic sentiment hostile to the 'Continental Sunday'. Such resistance was not reflective of public opinion, if M-O surveys showing a 62 per cent approval of Sunday play are to be accepted.[63]

From the second half of the nineteenth century to the eve of the Second World War, the dominating principle of sports organization in England had been voluntarism. Honorary, that is, unpaid, elected officials, usually former players of the relevant sports, made up the governing committees of all the major sports. Demands on time and personal resources served to ensure that the elderly or the well-off, or both, dominated most of these sports organizations. That government, national or local, should be, so to speak, on the sidelines, fitted both long-standing notions of *laissez-faire* and the concept that sport and politics should be isolated, the one from the other. Such distinctions were difficult to maintain, in part because of claims that sports played an important role in the health and education of the nation. Nevertheless, for much of the inter-war period, government's function was limited to that of facilitator, and that primarily at the local level. Where co-ordination at the national level became necessary, it was undertaken by independent bodies such as the National Playing Fields Association (NPFA) and the CCPR.

The first Parliamentary measure which could be deemed any sort

62. FA Minutes, Reports on the Conferences of County Chairmen and Secretaries, 12 October 1946, 27 September 1947 and May 1948; Report of the Annual General Meeting, June 1948. There was similar resistance to swimming competition on Sundays. ASA Annual Report 1947, p. 109; *The Times*, 10 March 1947. The AAA did make a few special concessions, on the wartime principle of no other day for competition. AAA General Committee, 4 December 1948, item (c).
63. M-O, File Report 3045, 'A Report on British Sport', October 1948, p. 5.

of threat to the voluntarist tradition was the Physical Training and Recreation Act of 1937. The Act provided £2 million over three years in the form of grants, partly for programmes in coaching, and it also created the National Fitness Council (NFC), with regional and national offices staffed by government-employed experts in physical education. From the outset the NFC drew opposition because it threatened established organizations, it challenged the tradition of voluntarism and, to some, it smacked of militarism.[64]

Even though the war led to significant regulation of sporting events, much of that was to be rescinded by August 1945 and the principle of voluntarism was to prove remarkably resilient. In fact, the NFC was one of the first casualties of the war. It was disbanded in September 1939. A wartime perception of a need for physical fitness led to an adjustment in policy in the autumn of 1940. The Board of Education established a Directorate for Physical Training and Recreation, targeting youths between 14 and 18 years of age. The ultimate aim was to provide young workers with release time for physical training. In order to avoid the kind of criticism raised by the NFC this subsequent proposal was couched in very modest terms, yet still provoked the accusation that it introduced 'the Hitler system for youth'.[65] During a Commons debate on the 1944 Education Act, the government was obliged to give assurance that the work of voluntary youth organizations would not be diminished or ignored as the formal commitment to physical education within the schools was expanded.[66] Before, during and after the war proposals for a Ministry of Sport, or even more modest plans for an increased government role regarding sport, failed in the face of opposition from both sides of the House.[67]

The post-war Labour Government offered no serious challenge to the principles of voluntarism. Individual cabinet members such as James Chuter-Ede and Emanuel Shinwell expressed opposition to

64. D. Birley, *Playing the Game: Sport and British Society, 1910–1945* (Manchester, Manchester UP, 1995), pp. 302–3.
65. *Hansard*, Vol. 351, col. 1038, 20 September 1939, Vol. 356, cols 808–9, 25 January 1940, Vol. 364, cols 1471–5, 22 August 1940 and Vol. 365, cols 739–64, 16 October 1940.
66. Ibid., Vol. 398, cols 1181–6, 23 March 1944.
67. Birley, *Playing the Game*, p. 303; *Daily Herald*, 9 August 1948; *The Times*, 23 July 1948; N. Fishwick, *English Football and Society, 1910–1950* (Manchester, Manchester UP, 1988), p. 11.

government involvement in sport and there is no evidence in party publications or in annual conference reports that theirs was a minority position. Twice in the late 1940s the government chose not to pursue opportunities to play a more intrusive role. The recommendation of the official enquiry into the 1946 Bolton Disaster that the government legislate regarding the safety of sports grounds was not followed. Second, when the intense economic crisis of early 1947 made it necessary to discourage midweek sport, the government proceeded through negotiation with the organizing bodies of the major sports, not by legislative initiative.[68]

Reflective of a bipartisan support for voluntarism, there was a nationalistic tone in the rejection of state involvement as something foreign to the English. Such state activity was associated with the Nazis and later the Russians. Even Western democracies such as Sweden and France were disparaged for state subsidization of sport.[69]

IV

The maintenance of the principle of voluntarism with regard to the administration of sport is of particular importance in advancing 'play as usual' as the principal characteristic of sport in the late 1940s. It also provides a basic key to understanding why there was no major infusion of radically new ideas into the adminstration or playing of sport during or immediately after the Second World War. Even at a time when the two main parties believed they were offering sharply contrasting programmes, the lines drawn by political ideology did not correspond to those that distinguished one sporting philosophy from another. Sporting issues were non-party issues, not merely because of the widely professed desire to keep sport and politics

68. *The Times*, 15 April 1946 and 22 March 1947; *Daily Herald*, 10 July and 10 September 1947; Labour Party Archives, John Smith House, Labour Party Publications, 1945–48, and Annual Reports to Conference, 1945–48; N. Baker, 'Have They Forgotten Bolton?', *Sports Historian*, 18 (1998) pp. 120–51; and 'Going to the Dogs – Hostility to Greyhound Racing in Britain: Puritanism, Socialism and Pragmatism', *Journal of Sport History*, 23 (1996), pp. 97–118.
69. NBKR 6/3/1, Minutes of the Special Congress of the IAAF, June 1947, pp. 2–3; *Athletics*, 2:12 (November 1946), p. 3; *The Times*, 24 September and 18 November 1946, and 1 May 1947; J. Crump, *Running Round the World* (London, 1966), p. 72.

apart, but, equally importantly, because supporters of Corinthian and Commercial ideals, and for that matter those of muddled amalgams of the two, could be found on either side of the House. The great majority of Labour politicians, like the Conservatives who preceded them in power, believed in voluntarism, in the autonomy of the main sporting associations. For the duration of the war most of those organizations were administered by emergency committees with personnel drawn from their pre-war leadership. At the end of the war there were power struggles within some of the governing bodies of sport, but no general elections were held to alter radically the personnel at the head of these organizations. Generally, continuity of personnel meant continuity of ideas. For the Corinthian, change was inherently problematical and for the advocates of commercial spectator sports it was, at least for a time, unnecessary while attendances boomed in the late 1940s. With its regular seasons of competition, its recurring calendar of major events and its treasured records of past achievements, individual and collective, sport was valued for its routine and its familiarity. Administrators who struggled to overcome the myriad of problems that beset the resumption of sporting activity found large numbers of followers happy to play or watch that which they had been used to in the ways that they had been used to. There was not the time, the inclination, the pressure or the incentive to undertake rethinking or reform of established ways. If there was a leverage for change, it arose not from any new perspective on sport but from the age-old concern to be competitive at a time when, internationally, this was proving harder and harder. However, recognition of this problem was slow to come and effective reaction slower still.

Certainly, profound change lay in the future of English sport but if there was a watershed it came not during the war but at the end of the 1950s and into the 1960s. The end of the Gentlemen v. Players fixtures, an open Wimbledon, the beginning of one-day cricket, the FA's recognition of Sunday football, the end of the maximum wage, the Eastham case, the establishment of the Sports Council, declining numbers on the terraces, and the direct and indirect impact of television that reached a majority of English homes, *these* were really landmark changes in the social and economic history of English sport. They also marked the practical demise of the Corinthian ideal and the conclusive ascendancy of an increasingly thorough commercialization.

A Time for Hard Writers: The Impact of War on Women Writers

Johanna Alberti

A ngus Calder has suggested 'that we, born since, have ignored how frightening and confusing the period from April 1940 through to June 1941 was for the British people. Perhaps we simply cannot comprehend that fear and confusion imaginatively.'[1] It may be especially the case that we cannot comprehend life in London in the Blitz, and the writing, which this essay explores, is often haunted by images of that city as embodying the experience of the Blitz. This essay is focused on the impact of the outbreak of the Second World War and the Blitz on some women writers who were then in their forties and fifties and had made a name for themselves in the preceding decades. Their understanding of what Nick Hayes has described in the introduction to this book as 'a defining episode' was recorded, reconstructed, re-created in a variety of sorts of writing: diaries, letters, autobiography, articles and novels. That understanding was complex and subtle, often anguished – they took themselves very seriously – and always individual.

The singularity and immediacy of responses to the war contained in these writings is the main focus of this essay. My contention is that the authors' skill as writers enabled them to capture for us a historical moment of dislocation with unusual intensity. These women writers were also aware of their own political and social contexts, so that their reactions and reflections are often consciously placed within a broader framework. They gave expression to their ideas about gender, patriotism, culture and their sense of identity as writers in wartime. As successful women writers they had reached a position before the war of feeling part of a shared culture, and

---

1. A. Calder, *The Myth of the Blitz* (London, Cape, 1991), p. 18.

none of them claimed to write 'as a woman'. The stability of their place within the culture of which they were a publicly visible part was challenged by the war: war faced them with a crisis which destabilized their sense of identity as writers. This destabilization is the focus of the first section of this essay. The middle section concentrates on the complex feelings of personal and communal responsibility for the preservation of cultural values with which these writers wrestled within a context of terror and destruction. The third part contains a reading of the writers' understanding of the war's relevance to class and gender.

I

> Leaving one still with the intolerable wrestle/ with words and
> meanings.[2]

Implicit in what these women wrote is an unshaken faith in the capacity of art to transcend. In *Black Lamb and Grey Falcon* Rebecca West views the Blitz as a time 'to test the artistic process, and judge whether it is a tool that does honest work, or whether it simply makes toys for the childish'. Art passes the test: precisely, an aria from *The Marriage of Figaro*, 'the small white star of light', can 'unknot' the writhing bowels and draw attention from 'the huge red star of light that is a high-explosive bomb'.[3] In a far less grandiloquent tone, Elizabeth Bowen advocated the reading of the classics at a time when there was evident 'an inability to obtain the focus necessary for art'. She found that 'These years rebuff the imagination as much by being fragmentary as by being violent. It is by dislocation, by recurrent checks to his desire for meaning, that the writer is most thrown out.'[4] Vera Brittain agreed that when it came to the creation, rather than the reception of art, danger destroyed concentration on 'ideas, books, music, philosophy'.[5] Brittain saw artists as exceptional people, uniquely 'penalised' by war. They had no need for crisis to 'give them excitement or provide them with occupation'; war was

2. T. S. Eliot, *Four Quartets* (London, Faber & Faber, 1944), p. 26.
3. R. West, *Black Lamb and Grey Falcon* (Edinburgh, Canongate, 1995), pp. 1126–7.
4. E. Bowen, Review of V. S. Pritchett essays, *New Statesman and Nation*, 23 May 1942, p. 340.
5. V. Brittain, *England's Hour* (London, Futura Publications, 1982), p. 183.

a 'tragic interruption' for them. She devoted the entire contents of one of her 'Letters to Peace Lovers' to Virginia Woolf soon after the latter's death, and suggested in it that Woolf's suicide in 1941 might have been a 'deliberate protest' against the impact of war on literature.[6]

Vera Brittain's answer to the question of what the writer should do in wartime was ambitious: she obeyed her own dictum to explore the problems to which war gave rise and to suggest possible solutions. Later she wrote of her work as 'an attempt to enlarge "the consciousness of humanity"'.[7] Rebecca West also saw herself as fulfilling a portentous task, that of following the 'dark waters' of the war 'back to its source'.[8] West created an image that insinuates a more general, and profoundly ambitious, role for art. On the vision of an old woman walking in the mountains of Montenegro, asking why she had been subject to terrible tragedies, West invested the search for a meaning, the desire to 'understand ... the mystery of process', which, she averred, is the 'sole justification' for both art and science.[9] In the same vein, Storm Jameson described 'the writer's function' laconically as 'that of uncynical sceptic, Socratic questioner'.[10] At the very end of her autobiography she asserted that 'Many people are competent to tell us what to do to survive. Only the artist ... can tell us how, in what conditions, men can survive as human beings.'[11]

It was far from easy to retain this confidence during wartime. In her 'Provincial Lady' stories published in *Time & Tide*, E. M. Delafield provided humorous comment on the function of storytelling: 'Enquire of Robert whether he does not think that, in view of times in which we live, diary of daily events might be of ultimate historical value.' Robert's responses force her 'to realise that Cook's gas-mask is intrinsically of greater importance than problematical contribution to literature by myself'. She is also ironic about the ambition of writers to do more than entertain: she has the Provincial Lady

6. V. Brittain, *Testament of a Peace Lover: Letters from Vera Brittain* (London, Virago, 1988), pp. 67–70, 24 April 1941.

7. V. Brittain, *Testament of Experience* (London, Virago, 1979), p. 472.

8. West, *Black Lamb*, pp. 1088–9.

9. Ibid., p. 1012.

10. S. Jameson, *Journey from the North* (London, Collins and Harvill Press, 1970), p. 73.

11. Ibid., p. 143.

suggest to a writer that people in war are likely to 'fall back on reading. Realize too late that this is not very happily expressed.'[12] The other women whose words are used here retained their faith in the significance of writing in some form in wartime.

Each of these women had lived through the Great War and were haunted by its ghosts in various forms. Virginia Woolf wrote in May 1938: 'The 4th August may come next week.' When dismissing the meaning of the war that was looming as 'merely a housemaid's dream', she adds: 'And we woke from that dream & have the Cenotaph to remind us of the fruits.'[13] Vera Brittain had enjoyed a huge public success when she reconstructed her tragic experience of the First World War in a book published only six years before the outbreak of the Second World War. Listening to the announcement of war by Neville Chamberlain, she understood it in terms of the struggle she had engaged in over the previous 20 years to 'overcome the brute force of evil'. Fourteen months later she toured London to observe the effects of the Blitz, and saw the 'still untouched' Cenotaph as mocking the war dead whom it commemorates for 'their confident faith that they were preventing the next'. Her mind often slipped back, so that she found herself thinking she was experiencing the earlier war.[14] In the early months of 1941, Storm Jameson could only let herself 'cry over the last war'.[15] Naomi Mitchison at times saw her experiences through the lens of that war. Visiting her son Murdoch at Oxford, she wrote of him and his friends:

> I wish one could know them. I wish there were tokens to tell. The fortunate fellows that now one can ever discern, and then one might talk with them friendly and wish them farewell, and watch them depart on the road that they will not return. It was all so hellishly like last time.[16]

The war years can be read not as a discontinuity but as a continuation of an extended international tragedy. The Second World War was

12. E. M. Delafield, 'The Provincial Lady in Wartime', *Time & Tide*, 7 October 1939, p. 1304; 28 October 1939, p. 1389.
13. A. Bell (ed.), *The Diary of Virginia Woolf* (London, Hogarth Press, 1984), Vol. V, 24 May 1938; 5 September 1938.
14. Brittain, *England's Hour*, pp. 17, 208, 137.
15. Jameson, *Journey*, p. 196.
16. D. Sheridan (ed.), *Among You Taking Notes: The Wartime Diaries of Naomi Mitchison, 1939–1945* (Oxford, Oxford UP, 1986) p. 187, 15 February 1942.

anticipated to varying degrees by these women writers, and their perspectives on it were already partly shaped by their political experience of the inter-war years. Dorothy Sayers suggested in an article in *Time & Tide*: 'We cannot be thoroughly and whole-heartedly prepared in advance for war without abandoning the very things we are prepared to fight for.' [17] Virginia Woolf's diaries provide vivid images of the way the threat of war gradually pressed in on her consciousness during the 1930s. In March 1936 she commented on the closeness of 'the guns' to 'our private life'. [18] At the time she was writing *Three Guineas*, finishing it in October 1937. The book expressed her rejection of a society still steeped in 'the fear which forbids freedom in the private house'. [19] The feelings expressed in the book again 'flamed up' in her when there was discussion of the military prospects. She had 'wanted – how violently – how persistently, pressingly compulsorily I cant say – to write this book; & have a quiet composed feeling; as if I had said my say; take it or leave it; I'm quit of that.' But the threat of war led her to imagine the book as 'a moth dancing over a bonfire – consumed in less than a second'. [20]

For very many Britons, Munich brought a 'feeling of relief' that 'had the effect of recovery from an illness, & going out of the house for the first time. Everything looks wonderful.' These words are Ray Strachey's, yet she detected in others 'a rage of criticism', and predicted that 'all the intellectuals' would soon range up against Chamberlain. [21] Five days later Sylvia Townsend Warner wrote that Munich 'has given us ... the burden of a guilt too heavy to bear'. [22] Naomi Mitchison shared this sense of shame. She had always seen herself as one of a select number of people of her own generation who carried the responsibility for developing and practising a new politics after the First World War. [23] At the time of Munich, she

17. D. Sayers, 'Notes on the Way', *Time & Tide*, 22 June 1940, p. 656.
18. *Diary of Virginia Woolf*, 13 March 1936.
19. V. Woolf, *Three Guineas* (London, Penguin, 1982), p. 162.
20. *Diary of Virginia Woolf*, 12 April 1938. Apostrophes are generally omitted in Woolf's original manuscript and have therefore likewise been omitted throughout this essay.
21. H. W. Smith mss, Lilly Library, University of Indiana, Bloomington, Indiana, Letter from Ray Strachey to Mary Berenson, 3 October 1938.
22. S. T. Warner, Letter to the Editor, *Time & Tide*, 8 October 1938, p. 1375.
23. Haldane Papers, National Library of Scotland, 6033 f295, Letter from N. Mitchison to E. Haldane, 1928.

became agonizingly aware of a sense of betrayal. She wrote to Aldous Huxley: 'I think all of us are partly to blame for it.' During the 'crisis week', she could see no 'obvious good or right course to follow', but the 'terrible fears' which were prevalent led her to conclude: 'And *that* is what we with our anti-war propaganda have done; we've just made people afraid, so that everyone was enormously relieved to think that Nazi methods had won again and it was only Czecho-Slovakia which was being done in.' Now 'we are laden with such an intolerable burden of shame that its hard to take any action or even think ... I simply don't know what to do with myself. I feel we have behaved so badly that we deserve almost anything.' [24]

The experience of Munich as a nadir of despair took the edge off the shock of war a year later: the tone of contributions to *Time & Tide* in the first eight months of 1939 is apocalyptic. In July Rose Macaulay compared the atmosphere to 'standing poised diver-fashion on the rim of a volcano wondering when we shall get the signal to jump'.[25] Ray Strachey, whose code of femininity was invariably brisk and unheroic, wrote in a letter to her mother: 'its most curious to be living under the shadow of war ... Its not exactly a *crisis* feeling, but such a deep uncertainty about the stability of anything.' [26] Even on the eve of war, however, writers' pens were poised: these very articulate women and their friends immediately expressed this sensation in imagery, giving it shape and significance. Woolf wrote: 'Everyone's writing I suppose about this last day ... . How to go on, through war? – thats the question.' [27] Naomi Mitchison wrote a lengthy entry to her Mass-Observation diary on the day war was declared, noting conversations which took place in her house. During one of these, the writer Joan Rendel 'said she was on a small island of sand with everything cut off before and behind ... . We all agreed that it was queer to feel the past so cut-off, everything had different meaning now.' Mitchison and her friends saw reality through the lens of literature: 'We all kept on noticing how these last two days have been a parody of all the Auden-Isherwood stuff; we might have been *On The Frontier*.' [28]

24. Mitchison Papers, National Library of Scotland, Acc. 8185, Letter from N. Mitchison to A. Huxley, 17 October 1938.
25. R. Macaulay, 'Notes on the Way', *Time & Tide*, 8 July 1939.
26. H. W. Smith mss, Ray Strachey to Mary Berenson, 15 April 1939.
27. *Diary of Virginia Woolf*, 28 August 1939.
28. Mitchison, *Among You Taking Notes*, pp. 36–7, 3 September 1939.

In early October, Woolf observed: 'Its odd how those first days of complete nullity when war broke out – have given place to such a pressure of ideas & work.'[29] Nor did Woolf's voracious reading stop with the outbreak of war; she continued to search for the appropriate book for her state of mind, using words to calm or to set her mind swinging.[30] Words provided Mitchison, also, with a sense of reality; she tried 'to bring things into consciousness, into words, into something I can be sure of – though why should I feel more sure of words?' She answers her own question ontologically, and hesitantly: 'Because of being a writer perhaps.' But being a writer also meant being 'aware that one never speaks the real truth', and knowing 'that you can die for a thing, but all the same that won't make it completely valid, at least for the double-minded, the fully conscious, who are perhaps the ones that matter in any generation'.[31]

War sharpened the awareness of writing as a choice of action. As war threatened, Storm Jameson continued to write a novel, feeling an 'intense happiness', and ignoring a voice, which came from 'the darkness at the back of my skull: You may not see your son again'. 'A writer, even a minor writer,' she concluded, 'is something of a monster.'[32] Woolf's portrayal of Miss Latrobe, the author of the pageant in *Between the Acts*, is of a monstrous, obsessed, yet creative woman. When war broke out Jameson decided it was 'unlikely, as well as slightly indecent, to think of earning a living as a novelist'. Yet by the summer of 1940, her only reason for not writing was that she had just finished a novel and saw no point in beginning a book that might never be finished.[33] War's impact was not constant, it could suffocate, but it could also liberate. Within a week of the outbreak of war, Mitchison had decided: 'I think one sees things more vividly, storing them up, insisting on the moment, at these times. If one is wise.'[34] Woolf observed: 'The war is like desperate illness. For one day it entirely obsesses; then the feeling faculty gives out; next day one is disembodied, in the air.' She used the image

29. *Diary of Virginia Woolf*, 7 October 1939.
30. Ibid., 29 March 1940.
31. Mitchison, *Among You Taking Notes*, p. 85, 21 August 1940; p. 51, 28 October 1939.
32. Jameson, *Journey*, pp. 26–7.
33. Ibid., pp. 28, 77.
34. Mitchison, *Among You Taking Notes*, p. 39, 9 September 1939.

of war destroying 'the outer wall of security' so that 'no echo comes
back' to convey the impact of war on her writing: the walls 'wear
so terribly thin' that 'there is no standard to write for'. Yet it inspired
in her 'a certain energy and recklessness', and she thought: 'perhaps
the walls, if violently beaten against, will finally contain me'.[35]

So they wrote, but continued to wrestle with the question of
what to write during wartime: war seemed to demand a place within
their writing. Rebecca West and Vera Brittain self-consciously expressed particular wartime tasks for themselves. Mitchison wrote in
some despair: 'The only thing I can do is write. And the only
people who can write now are the really successful professionals
like Priestley and co, or the equally whole-hearted antis, who can
write against.'[36] Woolf had earlier observed Priestley's project of
using words to give himself a role as 'the helper in the cause of
common life' and acknowledged its necessity – and her own dislike
of it.[37] E. M. Delafield made a sardonic comment on the desire of
writers to use their skills to some national purpose. She has an
innocent character ask of the Provincial Lady and a 'well-known
writer and broadcaster': 'Why can't they be used for propaganda?',
to which the writers 'with one voice – assure her that every author
in the United Kingdom has had exactly this idea, and has laid it
before the MoI [Ministry of Information] and has been told to
return to Stand By for the present'.[38] Storm Jameson described in
her wartime diary going to Hugh Walpole's flat to discuss a scheme
which Priestley had come up with – 'does he want to be our First
Minister of Culture?' – to force Ministries to employ writers.
Jameson had taken a voluntary job with the Ministry of Labour
sorting files of letters which, connected with the 'Special Register',
included many from intellectuals. She wrote: 'Nothing will come
of it. If Hugh or J.B.P. had worked on the Special Register he
would know that the last thing the authorities want to do is to
employ writers; any writer they give a post to will have been
commended for other qualities than his status as a novelist or poet.'
Later she did agree to edit, somewhat reluctantly, a volume of

35. *Diary of Virginia Woolf*, 20 May 1940; 27 June 1940; 24 July 1940.
36. Mitchison, *Among You Taking Notes*, p. 72, 4–7 July 1940.
37. *Diary of Virginia Woolf*, 6 September 1939.
38. E. M. Delafield, 'The Provincial Lady in Wartime', *Time & Tide*, 28 October
    1939, p. 1389.

stories written by English writers for American readers with the purpose of cementing Anglo-American relations.[39]

'Should one write novels?' Naomi Mitchison enquired of E. M. Forster, meeting him 'in his old school muffler at the corner of St James Square'.[40] Storm Jameson had asked the same question of a friend who, like E. M. Forster, replied in the affirmative; behind his reply there seemed to lie an apocalyptic sense that such an activity would not be possible for much longer.[41] In London it seemed impossible to Mitchison

> to think seriously of writing any non-immediate book. No chance of publishing of course ... . The quality of life here is different; one can't think long except in terms of war, nor take any long view at all ... . There is not fear, but acute apprehension. In the face of that one must be ashamed to do anything or think anything outside it; one cannot break the solidarity.[42]

Yet she had already begun a new novel in the summer of 1940 which she wrote on trains and in hotels and whenever she was able to find time, however brief, to do so.

II

And the fire and the rose are one.[43]

In May 1940, Virginia Woolf wrote laconically 'Well, the bomb terror. Going to London to be bombed.'[44] There is a certain satisfaction in the way Storm Jameson describes graphically her enjoyment of London, or Vera Brittain writes: 'The Front is no distant battlefield', and 'the war is always with us whether we want it or not'.[45] For Jameson, London in wartime, 'air-raids apart', was 'infinitely pleasanter than it has ever been since, shabby, quiet, friendly, and magnificently alive'.[46] Was this precisely because, as Virginia Woolf

39. Jameson, *Journey*, pp. 80, 117–18.
40. Mitchison, *Among You Taking Notes*, p. 118, 12 February 1941.
41. Jameson, *Journey*, p. 35.
42. Mitchison, *Among You Taking Notes*, pp. 113–14, 2 February 1941.
43. Eliot, *Four Quartets*, p. 59.
44. *Diary of Virginia Woolf*, 20 May 1940.
45. Brittain, *England's Hour*, pp. 38, 126.
46. Jameson, *Journey*, p. 111.

put it: 'You never escape the war in London'? [47] As the Blitz began, Mitchison reported that her friends in London were 'doing things, and comparing notes about raids. Nobody seems much frightened.' [48] Elizabeth Bowen lived in London throughout the war, apart from official visits to Ireland on behalf of the MoI, and wrote a celebrated description in *The Heat of the Day* of how the experience of living in London in the autumn of 1940 could give relish to the moment: 'Never had any season been more felt; one bought the poetic sense of it with the sense of death.' [49]

As the violence of war drew closer, Naomi Mitchison had found it difficult to maintain her sense of the importance of her decision to stay in her farm at Carradale on the west coast of Scotland and work in the face of the guilt of feeling safe: 'I should like just to have a taste of London atmosphere; it is too safe here to understand.' [50] When her friends Douglas and Margaret Cole came to stay at Carradale, together with her husband, the disjunction between her life and theirs in London was discomfiting.

> They are all clear-cut and grown-up, at least I suppose they are, they have definite jobs: I'm *desoeuvree*, at least nothing I have to do counts, and I have these woolly Scottish ideas about the whole end of man. And I'm so out of the London political and departmental life that I don't understand what they're talking about, nor what the various committees and things are. [51]

She was impressed by the attitude of Stevie Smith, who had not been out of London except for four days, and remained 'quite unshaken. "Never had such quiet nights – no dogs, no motor cars, no babies crying." She really doesn't seem to worry at all.' [52] Leaving London meant exclusion from the communality of experience and memory which Jan Montefiore has described, and Elizabeth Bowen recreated ironically in her wartime short story, *Careless Talk*. [53]

Bowen's Londoners were 'people whom the climate of danger

47. *Diary of Virginia Woolf*, 22 October 1929.
48. Mitchison, *Among You Taking Notes*, p. 88, 5 September 1940.
49. E. Bowen, *The Heat of the Day* (London, Penguin, 1962), p. 90.
50. Mitchison, *Among You Taking Notes*, p. 61, 25 May 1940.
51. Ibid., p. 84, 17 August 1940.
52. Ibid., p. 115, 6 February 1941.
53. J. Montefiore, *Men and Women Writers of the 1930s: The Dangerous Flood of History* (London, Routledge, 1996), p. 9.

suited'.[54] It is in Vera Brittain's writing that fear during the Blitz is most raw. It is also probably the case that she came closest to death during the Blitz when the house she was in was struck by 'a blow such as I have never known even in nightmares', and she was 'swept off my feet and out of my senses'. Brittain was acutely conscious of what she termed – quoting from Winifred Holtby's *The Comforter* – 'the horror of immunity'.[55] She refused to go to the USA with her children, and chose to 'identify myself with this country in its time of adversity, to submit myself to perils which I might have avoided, and to volunteer for various humanitarian jobs'.[56] She remained in London despite her fears, and elevated the experience to a high plane. She came to understand the idea of remaining in danger, of accepting avoidable suffering, as rooted in the Christian injunction to overcome evil with good.[57]

Naomi Mitchison and Virginia Woolf visited London but were relatively detached from the somewhat unreal sense of community engendered by terror, exhaustion and exhilaration which Mitchison described as 'the solidarity' of London in the Blitz. Complete detachment was not possible, and it was not detachment they sought, but some degree of distance. Mitchison's novels were almost invariably set in the quite distant past; for her, in T. S Eliot's construction, there was the possibility of freedom in history.[58] Virginia Woolf gave a paper to the Workers' Educational Association in Brighton in May 1940, in which a 200-year survey of the importance of context to writers was an essential part of her argument. She identified as a significant and admirable characteristic of nineteenth-century writers the 'immunity from war'.[59] For Woolf, immunity was what the outsider could cherish, 'an exalted calm desirable state'; 'a deep blue quiet space'. War provided the opportunity for Woolf to achieve immunity in 'the contraction of life to the village radius', the uninterrupted peacefulness of 'our lovely free autumn island'. She was

54. Bowen, *Heat of the Day*, p. 94.
55. Brittain, *England's Hour*, p. 122; *Testament of a Peace Lover*, p. 90, 25 September 1941.
56. Letter from V. Brittain to S. Jameson, quoted in P. Berry and M. Bostridge, *Vera Brittain: A Life* (London, Chatto & Windus, 1995), p. 403.
57. Brittain, *Testament of a Peace Lover*, pp. 95–6, 29 November 1941.
58. Eliot, *Four Quartets*, p. 55.
59. V. Woolf, 'The Leaning Tower', in *Collected Essays*, ed. L. Woolf (London, Chatto & Windus, 1966–67), p. 162.

aware of a 'growing detachment from the hierarchy, the patriarchy.[60] Fear and hate, she believed, were 'sterile, unfertile. Directly that fear passes, the mind reaches out and instinctively revives itself by trying to create.'[61]

The war impinged on writing in ways which made these women more acutely aware of a sense of responsibility as writers. Vera Brittain's public and somewhat sententious statement was that she wrote her letters to Peace Lovers in order 'to help in the important task ... of keeping alive decent values at a time when these are undergoing the maximum strain'.[62] She believed she was one of those who was performing 'the outstanding duties of detached thought and humanitarian co-operation'.[63] Virginia Woolf struggled in private to express her sense of the connection between the war and her writing: 'So intense are my feelings ... yet the circumference (the war) seems to make a hoop round them. No, I cant get the odd incongruity of feeling intensely & at the same time knowing there's no importance in that feeling. Or is there, as I sometimes think, more importance than ever?' Two days later she wrote: 'Thinking is my fighting.'[64] Naomi Mitchison had made a public statement of her understanding of politics as concerned with 'treating and imagining people simply as other people and not, as we commonly do, as means to some end of our own', in a book published at the time of Munich.[65] During the war, she tentatively expressed her sense of responsibility as a political writer in terms of a search to 'keep alive certain ideas of freedom which might easily be destroyed in the course of this totalitarian war'. As the violence of war drew closer in the summer of 1940 she expressed her anxiety about a different sort of betrayal, the *'trahison des clercs'* contained in the pages of *New Statesman* and *Tribune* which were 'going all militarist, blaming the Government because it "postponed conscription to the last moment"'. Resistance to this involved trying to 'keep some intellectual values, some aesthetic values,

60. *Diary of Virginia Woolf*, 14 July 1932; 9 April 1937; 12 October 1940; 29 December 1940.
61. V. Woolf, 'Thoughts on Peace in an Air Raid', in Woolf, *Collected Essays*, Vol. IV, p. 176.
62. Brittain, *Testament of a Peace Lover*, p. 2, 4 October 1939.
63. Brittain, *England's Hour*, p. 39.
64. *Diary of Virginia Woolf*, 13 May 1940; 15 May 1940.
65. N. Mitchison, *The Moral Basis of Politics* (London, Constable, 1938), p. 9.

even?'[66] What this task might involve in practice haunts her diaries. Like Mitchison, Storm Jameson was tentative in expressing the hope that it was valid to write about 'the need to save a few ideas, the idea of brotherly respect, the common man's instinctive mistrust of authority, the need to doubt'.[67]

Mitchison, Woolf, Brittain and Jameson were resolved not to suffer the fate which Adam Piete has identified as befalling British culture in general in the war: to allow the 'fabrications' of the war machine to enforce their 'complicity in the double-dealing of its rhetoric and history-making'.[68] Naomi Mitchison wrote a letter to *Time & Tide* in November 1939 expressing 'horror and astonishment' at the paper's 'blind acceptance of war: of the thesis that it is possible to do direct good by direct evil'. Rebecca West responded in the letter columns of the paper, attacking Mitchison's letter for its contradictions, and an intense correspondence ensued which drew in other readers. West and Mitchison accused each other of lacking historical sense and of inconsistency, and West implied that Mitchison lacked moral and political responsibility. Mitchison commented that she and West were 'being pushed into extremes' as war led people to use 'certain classes of words as drugs ... . It is the job of the writer to see through that romanticism and muddiness and expose it now.' She withdrew first from the correspondence, and continued to be 'quite unable to be anything but anti-war', referring frequently to 'this bloody silly war'.[69]

The intense significance which Storm Jameson and Vera Brittain placed on their attitudes to the war is apparent in the resulting collapse of their friendship. They were members together of the Peace Pledge Union in the 1930s, but in the war Jameson concluded: 'The way of reasoning together is not open to us. What is open to us is submission, the concentration camp ... . When my reason forced me to see the choice I was unhappy. I could not choose

---

66. Mitchison, *Among You Taking Notes*, p. 42, 26 September 1939; p. 62, 2 June 1940.
67. Jameson, *Journey*, pp. 27–8.
68. A. Piete, *Imagination at War: British Fiction and Poetry 1939–1945* (Basingstoke, Macmillan, 1995), p. 2.
69. N. Mitchison and R. West, *Letters to the Editor, Time & Tide*, p. 1436, 11 November 1939; pp. 1466–7, 18 November 1939; pp. 1488–9, 25 November 1939; pp. 1519–20, 2 December 1939; p. 1584, 9 December 1939; p. 1606, 16 December 1939; p. 1651, 30 December 1940.

submission.'[70] Vera Brittain conceded that those who believed that their efforts could stop the war were inhabiting 'a realm of fantasy'. She believed that the task for the pacifist was the high-minded one of pointing 'ceaselessly to the ideals of a nobler community'.[71] Jameson expressed a similar determination when she wrote that she would not 'push out of sight the misery of poor women unable to pay their rent, the children running loose in London with gas-masks knocking against their skinny shoulder-blades, the anger of young men, the useless deaths'.[72] Virginia Woolf, too, after visiting a bombed London in September 1940, thought of 'the very grimy lodging house keepers ... with another night to face; old wretched women standing at their doors; dirty, miserable'.[73]

Behind their perspective on war lay complex feelings about Britain, or, as they mainly wrote, England. These women were travellers, now confined to the island of their birth, a country under siege, and their writings evince signs of an almost reluctant patriotism. Storm Jameson was heavily involved with refugees and her feelings for her own country were mediated by her contact with them. In early May 1940, Jameson heard of the landing of Nazi troops in Norway from a Norwegian broadcaster who was very angry about what he saw as the British desertion of his country. She listened with him and other Scandinavian friends to Chamberlain's broadcast; 'It was a painful hearing.' As she travelled home:

> Grief and a feeling of shame raged in me. And yet ... . *We* are not defeated, I thought.
> Is it absurd to say that I have never felt the life of England stronger in me and in the people I passed in the street and sat opposite in the underground than on that evening of the 2nd May 1940?[74]

For Naomi Mitchison, patriotism in the sense of a willingness to die for a country 'was finished between 1914 and 1918'.[75] Later she wrote:

> I am wondering whether nationalism is entirely a bad thing. We have

---

70. S. Jameson, *The End of This War* (London, George Allen & Unwin, 1941), p. 25.
71. Brittain, *Testament of a Peace Lover*, pp. 102, 103, 18 December 1941.
72. Jameson, *Journey*, p. 38.
73. *Diary of Virginia Woolf*, 10 September 1940.
74. Jameson, *Journey*, p. 44.
75. Mitchison, *Among You Taking Notes*, p. 59, 23 May 1940.

been led to suppose so and I would call myself an internationalist . . . .
But I am almost sure that nationalism is on the whole good for people,
that it corresponds with something they want, and that it is not
incompatible with internationalism and peace.[76]

In *Bull Calves* she put together her growing fascination with Scottish
nationalism, her desire to present its tradition to her community,
and her response to the war. The writing of it helped her, spasmod-
ically, both to escape from 'England' and to retain her sense of herself
as a writer. Rebecca West also presented a strikingly positive understanding of nationalism in *Black Lamb and Grey Falcon*.

> nationalism is simply the determination of a people to cultivate its
> own soul, to follow the customs bequeathed to it by its ancestors, to
> develop its traditions according to its own instincts. It is the national
> equivalent of the individual's determination not to be a slave.[77]

Perhaps because rather than in spite of her pacifism, Vera Brittain's
patriotism is the most romantic. In her 'Letters to Peace Lovers', she
personified London as a beautiful woman who is facing 'an ordeal'
and 'putting on her loveliest aspect in order to ask her citizens to
endure for her sake'. Her England is shaped in bucolic images of
'dewdrops sparkling on English gorse'; 'chimneys of little red-roofed
houses ... smoking in the chill October air'; 'the roots of apples
trees still golden in the orchards'.[78] From our perspective such images
may seem sentimental, and poems published in *Time & Tide* in the
period between September 1940 and June 1941 were invariably
imbued with a nostalgia for the countryside, the farmyard and the
garden. Yet a profound attachment to the English landscape can be
understood as 'the thirst for grace' which Adam Piete has identified
as a 'natural feature of the wartime imagination'.[79] It was shared by
Virginia Woolf, whose attitude to the war was detached and sceptical.
In the summer of 1940 she wrote that she disliked all 'the feelings
war breeds: patriotism; the communal &c., all sentimental and emotional parodies of our real feelings'. But she also noted her 'individual,
not communal BBC dictated feeling' of wishing luck as British fighter
planes passed over one evening. At the end of that year she reflected:
'How England consoles & warms one, in these deep hollows, where

76. Ibid., p. 78, 4 August 1940.
77. West, *Black Lamb*, p. 1101.
78. Brittain, *England's Hour*, pp. 120–1, 194–5.
79. Piete, *Imagination at War*, p. 106.

the past stands almost stagnant. And the little spire across the fields.'
Woolf's deepest patriotism was roused by images of London: 'Odd
how often I think with what is love I suppose of the City: of the
walk to the Tower: that is my England; I mean, if a bomb destroyed
one of those little alleys with brass bound curtains & the river smell
& the old woman reading I should feel – well, what the patriots
feel.' After the heavy raids of late December 1940, she walked in
the bombed City among 'the desolate ruins of my old squares ... all
that completeness ravished & demolished'.[80] Rebecca West expressed
the same feelings in less subtle images, reminiscent of Brittain's ardent
personification:

> those who see the city where they were born in flames find to their
> own astonishment that the sight touches deep sources of pain that
> will not listen to reason ... . We may recognise that the streets that
> are burned are mean and may be replaced by better, but it is of no
> avail to point out to a son weeping for his mother that she was old
> and plain.[81]

For her, as for Elizabeth Bowen, the heart of London lay in the
rose-garden in Regent's park.

III

'Yes, but whose play? Ah, that's the question.' [82]

Virginia Woolf was aware of 'the community feeling' which the
threat of war inculcated through 'all England thinking the same thing
– this horror of war – at the same moment'.[83] The seduction of
communality was potent: yet any reading of how unified, how
inclusive was that collectivity is unstable. In describing Regent's Park
in the summer of 1940, Rebecca West referred to 'the people' who
'sat on the seats among the roses': they were those who in the autumn
exhibited a 'new form of heroism':

> bombs dropped; many were maimed and killed, and made homeless,
> and all knew the humiliating pain of fear. Then they began to laugh ...

80. *Diary of Virginia Woolf*, 12 July 1940; 24 December 1940; 2 February 1940;
    15 January 1941.
81. West, *Black Lamb*, p. 1126.
82. V. Woolf, *Between the Acts* (London, Penguin, 1953), p. 138.
83. *Diary of Virginia Woolf*, 15 April 1939.

though their knees knocked together, though their eyes were glassy with horror, they joked from sunset, when the sirens unfurled their long flag of sound, till dawn, when the light showed them the annihilation of dear and familiar things.[84]

Vera Brittain also made use of a heroic image of the 'bombed and menaced population' who 'resolutely' took possession of the London Underground.[85] Yet West and Brittain stand outside 'the people' and the 'population'. There is admiration for 'them', but 'they' are different.

Naomi Mitchison had her own conception of a common culture, one that combined a longing for inclusiveness with her continued sense of being different. Her dream was of a culture she could share with the fishermen and farmers of Carradale whom she could both learn from and 'set ... on to creation'. She put on a play – not unlike the pageant in *Between The Acts* – which she wrote herself. It was acted by the local people, and there was a second May Day performance in Tarbert when Mitchison closed the evening with 'a short speech, emphasising that we could do this kind of thing all over Scotland, that the Nazis wanted to make people into machines, but we were refusing to be, we were individuals, this was part of democracy, etc.' By then she was also working on *Bull Calves*, about which she later asked rhetorically: 'what is this book of mine going to be but service to Scotland, or rather, to the dumb Scots, the ones who need to be given pride and assurance and kindness'. When exposed to wartime popular culture she was horrified. An enthusiastic film-goer, she watched a film which featured an '"all-girl orchestra" in technicolour, crooning', and was led to recollect 'sympathetically the words of Goering – was it – when I hear the word culture I draw my revolver. If this is culture, what the hell are we fighting for anyway? How willingly I would see the producers, musical directors etc, of Quickies, put into concentration camps.'[86]

Like Mitchison, Woolf was married to an active Labour Party member. In *Three Guineas* she had delivered a scathing attack in a note on those who obtain 'emotional relief' from adopting 'the working-class cause without sacrificing middle-class capital, or

84. West, *Black Lamb*, p. 1130.
85. Brittain, *Testament of a Peace Lover*, pp. 158–9, 12 August 1943.
86. Mitchison, *Among You Taking Notes*, p. 41, 21 September 1939; p. 142, 2 May 1941; p. 179, 21 January 1942; p. 166, 14 October 1941.

sharing working-class experience'.[87] Speaking to the Workers' Educational Association during the war, she alluded to a future classless society that would produce a stronger and more varied literature. Her paper finished with the image of literature as common land, not 'private ground', a country which 'commoners and outsiders like ourselves' would make their own. But she laid restriction on what could grow on that land; not 'detective stories' and 'patriotic songs'.[88] In her diary she is more candid in expressing her distaste for the culture a visiting Labour candidate appeared to her to envisage; the collecting of 'mice' and 'matchboxes'. In the summer of 1940 she assisted in the production of plays by the local Women's Institute:

> My contribution to the war is the sacrifice of pleasure: I'm bored: bored & appalled by the readymade commonplaceness of these plays: they cant act unless we help. I mean, the minds so cheap, compared with ours, like a bad novel – thats my contribution – to have my mind smeared by the village & WEA mind; & to endure it.

For Woolf the problem lay in 'the conventionality – not the coarseness. So that its all lulled & dulled. The very opposite of "common" or working class.' Her vision is of possibilities beyond the conventional. She collected in her diary the words of the gardener, her maid, people she overheard in shops relating stories about the war, and she commented: 'what a surplus of unused imagination we possess. We – the educated – check it.'[89]

Woolf's 'we' places educated men and women together in opposition to the working class. There are few reminders in her wartime diary entries of the exclusion of 'the daughters of educated men'. A reading of this sample of women's writing suggests a more ambiguous understanding of the impact of war on gender relations than is to be found in Susan Gubar's assertion that 'the literature women wrote about World War II needs to be understood as a documentation of women's sense that the war was a blitz on them'.[90] Woolf's deeply felt critique of patriarchy does emerge at moments during the war.

87. Woolf, *Three Guineas*, p. 196.
88. Woolf, 'Leaning Tower', pp. 182, 180.
89. *Diary of Virginia Woolf*, 10 September 1938, 29 May 1940, 31 May 1940.
90. S. Gubar, '"This is My Rifle, This is My Gun": World War II and the Blitz on Women', in *Behind the Lines: Gender and the Two World Wars*, ed. M. Higonnet (New Haven, Yale UP, 1987), p. 359.

The businessmen in the third class railway compartment, as she portrayed them in her diary, are 'contemptuous & indifferent to the feminine', and provide 'Not a chink through which one can see art, or books. They play cross words when insurance shop fails.'[91] In an essay written during the war for American readers she asked how far an Englishwoman could 'fight for freedom without firearms'. In answering her own question she insisted that 'private thinking, tea-table thinking' could be used to resist the pressure of propaganda which constructed Hitler as the only impediment to freedom. 'Let us drag into consciousness the subconscious Hitlerism that holds us down. It is the desire for aggression; the desire to dominate and enslave.' And it was 'access to creative feelings' which could be offered to men to compensate for 'the loss of his glory and his gun'.[92]

Naomi Mitchison perceived the pressures of war in gender terms in snatches, but did not suggest that war was an attack by men on women. Like Woolf, she placed intellectual activity in opposition to the violent behaviour which war legitimized: 'I think it's dangerous if women start admiring men for being brutal, taking risks and generally living in an unintellectual and insensitive way.' She wanted to combine with her writing other sorts of creativity: 'I think my farming and all that is important, I'm not just a potato factory. But also I'm an artist, I'm aware. I'm an adventurer.' In this struggle, she longed for the companionship of women of her own age, class and profession; women, she thought, were 'more likely to be sane than men, less certain of themselves, less arrogant, more able to see two sides to any question. Perhaps if they had men's power they'd become destructive, though'. This longing was especially acute when her baby died in July 1940 after only a few hours of life. The death made her aware of how the idea of a child had made sense of her decision to stay at Carradale. 'I feel I shall get landed with agricultural work that would have been tolerable and even delightful with a background of a baby – of creation. To some extent too, I had used this as an excuse to be out of the war, out of destruction, still on the side of creation; now that's over.'[93]

Rebecca West and Vera Brittain wrote in more sweeping terms

---

91. *Diary of Virginia Woolf*, 6 October 1939.
92. Woolf, 'Thoughts on Peace in an Air Raid', pp. 173–5.
93. Mitchison, *Among You Taking Notes*, p. 250, 9 July 1943; p. 179, 21 January 1942; p. 65, 13 June 1940; p. 72, 7 July 1940.

of the relationship between gender and war. Brittain described history as a struggle between the masculine and the feminine principles, and claimed that the former 'expresses itself through the rule of power and the tyranny of the strong'.[94] However, she was not there associating the masculine principle exclusively with men, and does not see war as an attack on women. West was obsessed at this time by 'the study of original sin', 'our inherent disposition to choose death when we ought to choose life'. She described the frame of mind which had led to the war as 'a compulsion to suicide', an attitude of mind which she compared to that of the desire to be the lamb of sacrifice. This is not a gendered construction: her understanding of the difference between men and women lies athwart this vision. Women's 'defect' is an 'idiocy' which leads them to focus on their private lives and ignore the public; men's 'lunacy' leads them to be 'obsessed by public affairs'. It is not clear which trait is more responsible for war, and there is no gender distinction in her celebration of the moment when 'England' lost the 'willingness to serve as the butchered victim' and chose to defend itself.[95]

One aspect of war experience for these women is from our perspective indubitably gendered, although none of these writers, with the possible exception of Mitchison, analysed it in those terms. Mitchison was consciously trying during the war to put into practice what she saw as a better 'New Order', a community based on more equal relationships. Such an order she knew in theory and found in practice involved much domestic work and '*no* time to write'.[96] Each of these women observed the changes war brought to their level of involvement in domestic work, an experience rooted in class. Woolf lists the changes war had made to the life of her household.[97] Storm Jameson wrote most productively and happily in the war when she did not have 'the responsibility of running a household'.[98] She moved into London partly in order to avoid this – as did Delafield's Provincial Lady.[99] Mitchison deplored the way trying 'to be enthusiastic and competent about saving fat and similar idiocies' prevented her

94. Brittain, *Testament of a Peace Lover*, p. 160, 9 September 1943.
95. R. West, Review; *Time & Tide*, p. 933, 1 November 1941; *Black Lamb*, p. 1121; p. 3; p. 1125.
96. Mitchison, *Among You Taking Notes*, p. 270, 17 February 1944.
97. *Diary of Virginia Woolf*, 19 December 1940.
98. Jameson, *Journey*, p. 60.
99. *Time & Tide*, p. 1304, 7 October 1939.

friend Joan Rendel from writing, as well as making her feel incompetent.[100] Brittain's response to the prospect of running a household without servants was to move into a service flat. When an Equal Citizenship Bill was proposed in the summer of 1943, she asserted that for women 'with special powers or gifts' marriage should not be associated with domesticity and child care.[101]

These women knew that those who were in most danger most often were young men. Woolf's reflections on the destruction of war invariably brought her nephew Quentin to mind; her older nephew Julian had died in the Spanish Civil War. On the eve of war, she is haunted by images of 'young men torn to bits' and mothers experiencing the same terrible pain that her sister had felt two years before.[102] Mitchison had expressed her terror at the prospect of one of her sons becoming a combatant at the time of Munich: she did not have to face this because he was a medical student and the threat to him was limited, in comparative terms, to living and working in London. When he left for London she wrote: 'I shall miss him horribly, but of course he's right to go, at least I suppose so.' She then seems to confirm Rebecca West's identification of the desire for sacrifice: 'If only one could be the sacrifice for someone else.' But the idea is quickly brushed aside, followed by a recognition that her son does not share her desolation: 'He of course feels that there will be a future; he's full of hope underneath. I feel I must carry on, but the underneath hope isn't there. I see endurance, but no happiness. I try to tell people that it will be a world full of building and excitement and new things but not for me.'[103] For those who were in most danger the war could be a stimulant; the anguish was perhaps felt most acutely by those who remained comparatively safe.

IV

By the summer of 1942, enduring the war had led to 'a deadened acclimatization'.[104] Mitchison found that war had become a habit –

100. Mitchison, *Among You Taking Notes*, p. 270, 17 February 1944.
101. Brittain, *Testament of a Peace Lover*, p. 162.
102. *Diary of Virginia Woolf*, 25 August 1939.
103. Mitchison, *Among You Taking Notes*, p. 74, 9 July 1940.
104. Bowen, *Heat of the Day*, p. 92.

'that's the way total war is'.[105] The first year of the war had been a time when writers wrestled with words to make meanings, as the growing storm, to use Walter Benjamin's image, irresistibly propelled them into the future. When death came closer in the autumn of 1940, there came a time when 'feeling stood at full tide'.[106] A poem by Mitchison was published in February 1941 which is taut with life and vigour, consciously reining energy in so as 'Not to be too glad this Spring'.[107] Elizabeth Bowen found in Ivy Compton-Burnett's *Parents and Children*, published in the spring of 1941, 'a book for *now*', hearing in its pages 'the sound of glass being swept up, one of these London mornings, after the blitz'. She concluded that 'This is a time for *hard* writers and this is one.'[108]

Bowen's most intense admiration was reserved for *Between the Acts*, which Woolf completed in March 1941. Woolf seemed to her to provide a 'reconciliation' through the organic integration of 'plot and vision'. In place of Woolf's accustomed speculation, she found a 'perceiving certainty'.[109] *Between the Acts* juxtaposed the menace of violence, the threat of dispersal and of a return to barbarism with a fragile but fertile sense of possibility. Bowen's review of the book can be read as a declaration of her faith in the possibilities of the moment in history in which it appeared. Bowen wrote as if the book embodied for her a time when 'calmness, anguish, desire, surprise have reached rim-level: the miracle is that they are contained'.

This containment occurs within an English landscape and culture, and there are signs in Woolf's writing, as there are in those of Mitchison, Jameson and perhaps even Bowen, of the 'neo-romanticism' Robert Hewison detects in post-war writing and sees as a harvest of the war.[110] If there are traces of nostalgia in such writing it is not a fabricated emotion, nor did it lead to the 'enforced complicity' with the 'rhetoric and history making' of the 'war machine' to which Piete refers. Hewison has suggested that to many writers during the war, the necessary link between their values and those of the society in which their work was done had been

105. Mitchison, *Among You Taking Notes*, p. 198, 29 May 1942.
106. Bowen, *Heat of the Day*, p. 96.
107. N. Mitchison, 'Spring', *New Statesman and Nation*, p. 109, 1 February 1941.
108. E. Bowen, Review, *New Statesman and Nation*, p. 536, 24 May 1941.
109. E. Bowen, Review, *New Statesman and Nation*, p. 63, 19 July 1941.
110. R. Hewison, *Culture and Consensus; England, Art and Politics since 1940* (London, Methuen, 1995), p. 23.

broken.[111] This, I think, is true of the writers to whom I refer, but I have also found a sense of continuity with a more specifically feminine culture. Alison Light has identified new codes of femininity in inter-war writing by women: 'Ironic dismissal, worldly wisdom, brisk competence, and heroic disavowal.'[112] These codes were well-suited to war, yet war put extreme pressure on them. Where there is irony in the writing of the first two years of the war, it is most often a protective shell for an acute perception of the fragility of life.

Piette has argued that there was 'some obscure guilt within British culture about its own isolation from the real horrors of war'.[113] For these mature women writers, this was not the case: the Blitz included them in a way that was understood as destroying the distinction between combatant and non-combatant. As the mouthpiece of the Women's Publicity Planning Association, a major feminist co-ordinating group put it, 'Bombs don't discriminate'; and women were 'in the front line'.[114] Nor did the women writers who appear on these pages suffer the spiritual exhaustion which Piete detects in British wartime culture.[115] Their writing does, however, suggest that they experienced the pressure to perceive of Britain at war as one nation, and that such a notion was discomfiting to Woolf, Bowen and Mitchison. Although these writers did not conceive of the war in terms of gender, their attitudes at a time when danger was most acute were informed by the code of stoicism Alison Light has identified in women's writing in the inter-war period. A discernment that such a moment was one which also offered creative possibilities came from Woolf, the writer who was perhaps most detached from that moment.

111. R. Hewison, *Under Siege: Literary Life in London 1939–1945* (London, Weidenfeld & Nicolson, 1977), p. 94.
112. A. Light, *Forever England: Femininity, Literature and Conservatism Between the Wars* (London, Routledge, 1991), p. 210.
113. Piete, *Imagination at War*, p. 1.
114. Piete, *Imagination at War*, p. 2.
115. Ibid.

Safe and Sound:
New Music in Wartime Britain

Robert Mackay

Of all images of the composer in wartime, none is better known or more compelling than that of the half-starved Dmitri Shostakovich sitting in his unheated room in Leningrad writing his Seventh Symphony, while the Germans pounded the besieged city. An image of Ralph Vaughan Williams, at that very time completing his Fifth Symphony in the relative peace and comfort of his Dorking home, somehow does not have the same heroic drama. And yet there is an underlying similarity in the situation of the two men. Neither could ignore the war; this was total war, after all. Nor did they want to ignore it: as creative artists both willingly placed their art at the service of the nation at war.

Like Shostakovich, Vaughan Williams was the leading musical figure of his country. Some years before, he had delivered a down-to-earth message to his fellow-composers: 'The composer must not shut himself up and think about art; he must live with his fellows and make his art the expression of the whole life of the community.' And, more famously: 'The art of music above all the other arts is the expression of the soul of the nation.'[1] The implications for composers when war came to command the 'whole life' and perhaps even 'the soul' of the British people were clear, not least to Vaughan Williams himself. For most composers in the period 1939–45, at least, those who chose to remain composers, it meant accepting commissions from official or quasi-official sources to write music that would help sustain the war effort; thus did total war mobilize and channel the nation's 'creative resources'. Most commonly, the work entailed writing music for documentary and feature films, but there were commissions, too, to write for radio features and to

1. R. Vaughan Williams, *National Music and other Essays* (London, Oxford UP, 1963), pp. 10, 68.

produce works for ceremonial or martial occasions and concerts for the forces and war-workers. Some composers, of course, were of an age that made them liable for military service; for these, whether called up or conditionally exempted, composition was to a degree bound by the same official needs and preferences.[2]

The war was more than an organizer of people's lives, however. It was also a disturber of feelings. In one way or another, as much through its intrinsically destructive and dehumanizing character as through its capacity to bring out the best in human beings, the war forced itself upon everyone's sensibilities and conditioned the performance of whatever roles they were called upon to fulfil. Composers were no more immune from this than anyone else. As Frank Howes, music critic of *The Times*, put it: 'Composers do not live in ivory towers, nor are they spiders spinning silk threads out of their own guts. They live in the world and their minds are nourished by events in the world, and their emotions are stirred as other men's are.'[3]

This essay takes as its subject the effects of the existence and circumstances of war on the production of new music. It will examine music that was written to order and music that was not, asking whether the former impeded the latter and to what extent the imprint of war rests on both. It will also assess the role of the war in the longer-term development of musical composition in Britain.[4]

I

It has become a convention to describe the 60 years up to the start of the Second World War as the period of the English musical renaissance.[5] At its start British composers were few in number and of the principal figures – Hubert Parry, Charles Stanford, Arthur

2. For some the call-up meant an extended lay-off from composition; as a serving naval officer, Arnold Cooke effectively had to stop composing for the duration of the war.
3. F. Howes, *The Music of Ralph Vaughan Williams* (Oxford, Oxford UP, 1954), p. 52.
4. It will be evident from the allusions already made that the ambit of this essay is 'classical' or 'serious' music, and that no consideration will therefore be given to other categories, such as light music, jazz, dance music and popular song.
5. The leading texts for this are F. Howes, *The English Musical Renaissance*

Sullivan, Alexander Mackenzie and Frederic Cowen – none had the talent or the international reputation of the leading European composers of the time, such as Brahms, Dvořák, Tchaikovsky and Verdi.[6] This was hardly a new state of affairs: one needed to go back 200 years to Henry Purcell to find in English music a composer whose genius was universally acknowledged. Since his death such composers that appeared were by and large musical craftsmen, contributing nothing original to the art of composition and meekly submitting to foreign influences, be they Italian, French or German. It is clear that in the last two decades of the nineteenth century this long period of creative mediocrity was finally coming to an end and that the 'Land without Music' was again engendering in music, artists whose output was comparable in quality to that of its best poets and novelists.[7] Nor was this merely a passing phase: the revival that began with Edward Elgar, Frederick Delius, Gustav Holst and Ralph Vaughan Williams was later consolidated by William Walton, Benjamin Britten and Michael Tippett, composers of the front rank, alongside whom there were many more of widely acknowledged merit. Not since Tudor times had there been such a flowering of creative musical talent. Preceding this phenomenon, and almost certainly contributing to it, was the establishment of a conservatoire system comparable to that found in most European countries. The founding of the Royal Colleges' of Music in 1883 and the modernization of the Royal Academy of Music soon after was at the heart of this. Stanford and Parry were foundation members of the College's teaching staff and among their pupils were Holst, Vaughan Williams, George Dyson, Eugene Goossens, John Ireland and Herbert Howells.

The search for a distinctive national style was common to composers working in this period but it did not lead to an 'English

(London, Secker & Warburg, 1966); P. Pirie, *The English Musical Renaissance: Twentieth Century British Composers and their Works* (London, Victor Gollancz, 1979); M. Trend, *The Music Makers: the English Musical Renaissance from Elgar to Britten* (London, Weidenfeld & Nicolson, 1985).

6. Although it might justifiably be pointed out that two of the composers given here as heading the English musical renaissance (Stanford and Mackenzie), were not, in fact, English, the convention of so designating the revival has been retained. Similarly, no affront to Scottish, Irish or Welsh sensibilities is intended in deferring to the usage 'Englishness' in music.

7. The origin of the phrase *Das Land Ohne Musik* is obscure; Pirie and Trend simply refer to it as 'the old German jibe'.

School' working in a single idiom. Perhaps the nearest the renaissance came to this was in the way that a number of composers turned for inspiration to folk music, Tudor polyphony and the music of Purcell. It is thus possible to discern a 'historical–pastoral' stream in English music, lasting to the Second World War and beyond, that shook off the German symphonic tradition and renewed itself by rediscovering its roots in the rural landscape and the pre-modern past. Besides its principal begetter, Vaughan Williams, this stream included Holst, George Butterworth, John Ireland, Edmund Rubbra, Gerald Finzi, E. J. Moeran and Peter Warlock. But another broad stream, flowing away from the Vaughan Williams route to a national music, established itself among the generation born mostly after the start of the century: Arthur Bliss, Constant Lambert, Gordon Jacob, William Walton, Malcolm Arnold, Alan Rawsthorne and Benjamin Britten. These composers saw the folk-song and Tudor inheritance as something their elders had needed to rediscover in order to stake out the ground of the new age of English music. Its explicit or even organic presence in their own idiom, however, was vestigial at most, existing, as indeed Vaughan Williams taught that it should in the ideal national style of the future, as an unconscious, immanent presence. The 'modern' group was as much in rebellion against the late Romanticism of Parry, Stanford and Elgar as Vaughan Williams and Holst had been, but they were much more interested than the latter in what was going on in Europe, especially the teachings of Nadia Boulanger in France and the extended tonality to be heard in Stravinsky's music.

The phrase 'extended tonality', while serving to differentiate the 'moderns' from the traditionalists in English music, nevertheless reflects the fact that both groups spoke the common language of the European tradition established in the seventeenth century. It also separated them from a third, much smaller, group of composers that to a greater or lesser degree followed the revolutionary departure from that tradition, made in Vienna from 1914 by Arnold Schoenberg, Alban Berg and Anton Webern.

Since about 1600 Western music confirmed the dominance of two ways, or 'modes', of ordering a scale of notes: the major (or Ionian) and the minor (or Aeolian). This dominance gradually rendered obsolete the other ten modes that had been used in Church plainsong and in folk song. When a piece was set mainly in one of the twelve major or minor keys, its melodic and harmonic development would proceed according to aural expectations that were influenced by the nearness or remoteness of other keys to the dominant key. Under 'extended tonality' this development was stretched beyond the conventions of key modulation, producing tensions and dissonances that nevertheless were normally resolved by an ending that returned to the keynote (or Tonic). Schoenberg's system abandoned these concepts of tonality and instead organized composition on 'serial' lines. In place of the hierarchy, in any key, of Tonic, Dominant, Subdominant, etc., all twelve semitones of the scale carried equal importance for the way the composition developed. One of the effects of this system on the sound of the music was that the musical intervals had none of the tonal implications and none of the emotional associations carried by those intervals under the traditional key system. As Michael Tippett put it: 'The "discords" are not just "wrong notes", they are simply the sounds which our stomachs cannot respond to in the traditional manner. No tones, no stomachs; music is to be only in the head.'[8]

Most British composers did not adopt the techniques of the Second Viennese School, although most were interested in this development and a few, notably Humphrey Searle and Elizabeth Lutyens, became true 'converts'. In years to come many of the country's leading composers were to embrace serialism, including Benjamin Frankel, Alexander Goehr, Richard Rodney Bennett, Iain Hamilton and Gordon Crosse. But before the war there was generally much less attachment to it in Britain than in most European countries. Delius had called Schoenberg and his followers the 'wrong note' school, and he probably spoke for most of his countrymen, composers and audiences alike, when he said of Schoenberg: 'When a man has to write about his methods of composition you may be sure he has nothing to say.'[9] Although it was no longer true to say that English music was stuck in the historical–pastoral mode that partly characterized its revival, its mainstream in 1939 was nonetheless still rather conservatively located within the less extreme extensions of the traditional tonal system. Insofar as it was inspired by literature it was not to the contemporary avant-garde of Eliot, Pound, Auden, Spender, MacNeice and Isherwood that English composers turned,

8. M. Tippett, 'Music and Life', *Monthly Musical Record*, July/August 1938.
9. Quoted in Trend, *Music Makers*, p. 187.

but to pre modernists like Kipling and Hardy or to Georgians like Housman, Bridges, de la Mare and Masefield.

II

If composers had been apprehensive about the disruption that war would bring to their work, in the event things were not so bad. Because of the government's policy of keeping the arts alive and healthy in order to sustain popular morale and to counter the cultural propaganda of the enemy, there were in fact new opportunities for composers. While patronage from non-governmental sources shrank as expected, from government and quasi-government agencies it actually increased. Naturally, there were strings attached. When it came to paying composers to compose, there was no room for doubt that what was required of the recipient was music with a 'patriotic' resonance, music that would promote the national identity and at the same time sustain the spirit of the people. This might take on some unexpected forms when the basic brief encompassed high policy. While it was thus to be expected that the Poet Laureate (John Masefield) and the Master of the King's Musick (Arnold Bax) should be asked to produce a tribute to the Red Army for the occasion in February 1943 when the Sword of Honour was to be presented to Stalingrad, it was a surprise to William Walton that he was asked to write two fanfares for the same event. He obliged, but baulked at a BBC commission in November 1943 for a 'victory anthem', which came with the condition that it should be symbolic of all the freedom-fighting nations and not last for more than five minutes! [10] More to his liking was a commission that came in the same year to compose the music for a new 'patriotic' ballet, *The Quest*. The Sadler's Wells Company was the sponsor, although it, too, was clearly cutting its coat according to its cloth by devising a work suitable for a morale-raising tour of the provinces, as indeed was the choreographer Frederick Ashton, given special leave for the purpose by the Royal Air Force (RAF). [11] Composers had reason to be grateful that at the Entertainments National Service Association (ENSA) the person responsible for organizing concerts for the forces and war-workers

10. M. Kennedy, *Portrait of Walton* (Oxford, Oxford UP, 1989), p. 125.
11. Ibid., pp. 121–2.

was Walter Legge, who was not only an enthusiast for serious music, but was also keen to promote new compositions. He commissioned work from Alan Rawsthorne, E. J. Moeran, Arnold Bax and William Walton, with little more by way of remit than that the music should be cheering and optimistic.

Although the BBC was formally independent of the government, a commission from the Corporation was held to have the official stamp, more so during the war than before it. At the suggestion of the Minister of Information, Sir John Reith, it invited four leading composers, including Vaughan Williams, each to write a patriotic hymn. To Vaughan Williams, who, according to Ursula Wood, his future wife, felt 'desperate for useful work' when war broke out, the task was entirely congenial; several years before he had said, 'Why should not the musician be the servant of the state and build national monuments like the painter, the writer, or the archi-tect?' [12] The price of accepting the role soon became apparent, however, when the master acted in a way that the servant could not stomach. Learning that the work of his fellow-composer Alan Bush, who was a Communist, was to be denied airtime, Vaughan Williams withdrew his acceptance of the commission and forwent his fee. But the episode did not change his view of the patriotic duty of the composer in wartime. When he appeared as a character witness in the trial in June 1943 of Michael Tippett (charged with failure to conform to a work order, following his conscientious objection to military service), Vaughan Williams described Tippett as a 'national asset' and went on to say: 'We know music is forming a great part in national life now: more since the war than ever before, and every one able to help on with that work is doing work of national importance.' [13] By then, the BBC had relented and adopted a more liberal policy towards nonconforming artists. In turn, Vaughan Williams relented and fulfilled the commission, not demurring at the very conservative nature of its terms, that is, in Adrian Boult's words: 'It is certainly the "Jerusalem" brand that we want.' [14] Appropriately, when the BBC celebrated his 70th birthday on 12

12. U. Vaughan Williams, *RVW: A Biography of Ralph Vaughan Williams* (Oxford, Oxford UP, 1964), p. 231; Vaughan Williams, *National Music*, p. 10.
13. *The Times*, 22 June 1943.
14. Letter from Adrian Boult to R. Vaughan Williams, 9 September 1940, cited in *From Parry to Britten: British Music in Letters 1900–1945*, ed. L. Foreman (London, Batsford, 1987), p. 232.

October 1942, among the musical items commissioned for the occasion and broadcast that evening was a work by Alan Bush. And if conscientious objectors experienced official contempt and felt generally unloved at this time, the BBC seemed in 1944 to be making a point when it commissioned a work from Michael Tippett.[15] The BBC also commissioned a patriotic march from John Ireland, eventually entitled *Epic March*, and a choral work from Vaughan Williams for use when victory finally came, which he produced under the title *Thanksgiving for Victory*. This was intended for the same purpose as the abortive commission to Walton mentioned above. Vaughan Williams, too, had disliked the restrictive terms of the commission and successfully negotiated his own, that is, complete freedom in the choice of words to be set and in the length of the work.[16] In the event his choices and, indeed, the resulting composition, involved no further problems with the BBC. The piece was recorded in November 1944 and put in store for transmission as soon as Germany was defeated.[17]

Most official commissions were for music to accompany films made for or sponsored by the Ministry of Information, where the form and character of the music were naturally closely dictated by the screenplay and the visual images. The constraints for composers of this situation echoed those bearing on the industry as a whole. Since the government controlled film stock and studio space, there was on the part of film-makers a necessary degree of conformity to official preferences on what sort of films were made and the messages they carried for audiences. Those responsible for presenting Britain's case at home and abroad and for maintaining popular morale had a preconceived idea of the national identity that was translated into the scripts of all types of films, escapist comedies and costume dramas, as much as the documentaries and dramas that featured the armed services, the civil defence services or ordinary citizens

---

15. *The Weeping Babe*, a setting for soprano and chorus of Edith Sitwell's poem. The BBC had, moreover, provided a testimonial for Britten at the tribunal considering his conscientious objection to military service in 1942.
16. M. Kennedy, *The Works of Ralph Vaughan Williams* (London, Oxford UP, 2nd edn, 1973), p. 285.
17. Roy Douglas, whom Vaughan Williams asked to make a reduced score of the work for Oxford University Press, said of the BBC: 'doubtless they had received a Message from Above that we were going to win in the following year'. R. Douglas, *Working with R V W* (Oxford, Oxford UP, 1972), p. 7.

participating in 'the people's war'. Composers therefore often found themselves working to briefs that carried musically-limiting expectations, typically for sequences that sounded hopeful, confident, patriotic, heroic or simply 'English'.[18] Many British composers were commissioned for this work; they included leading figures such as Vaughan Williams, Ireland, Bax and Walton and younger or lesser-known people like Malcolm Arnold, Constant Lambert, Lennox Berkeley, Lord Berners, William Alwyn, Alan Rawsthorne, Frederick Austin, Gordon Jacob and Richard Addinsell. The writing of music for films best exemplifies the 'serving' composer in wartime, and it was one of the principal ways in which music had its place in the mobilization of the nation's resources. Even so, not all composers succeeded in getting film work. Most had in any case depended for their livelihood on other sources of income, principally teaching, either privately or in music colleges and university music departments. Although there was some contraction in the number of music students, the institutions carried on and so there was still work for composers. Getting new compositions performed was more difficult than in peacetime, but most of the established composers were nevertheless able to achieve this. Even large works entailing extra rehearsal made their debuts: Britten's *Sinfonia da Requiem* in 1942, Vaughan Williams's Fifth Symphony in 1943, Tippett's *A Child of Our Time* in 1944.

Another aspect of the war that changed the context of music production was the extended period of isolation from Europe. Writing about painters and sculptors, Robert Hewison has argued that this isolation meant being cut off from the 'energy-source of the modern movement' and that its effect was to 'turn British art back on itself, rather as poets and writers turned to introspection'.[19] Richard Weight endorsed this point thus: 'Stranded on a besieged island, unable to travel abroad, intellectuals were forced back to the British scene for inspiration in their work.'[20] Music, like painting and writing, depends to a degree on international cultural intercourse, and if it is true that during the war British painters and writers felt

---

18. I. MacLaine gave the title *Ministry of Morale* to his monograph on the Ministry of Information.
19. R. Hewison, *Under Siege: Literary Life in London 1939–45* (London, Weidenfeld & Nicolson, 1977), p. 144.
20. R. Weight, 'State, Intelligentsia and the Promotion of National Culture in Britain, 1939–45', *Historical Research*, **69** (1996), p. 91.

impelled to reach back to the national romantic tradition, 'the pic-
turesque, the mystical and the visionary', then one might reasonably
expect to discern a similar shift of emphasis in the work of their
composer contemporaries.

Two who might have found this situation claustrophobic in fact
chose to return to Britain from the USA. Their cases are revealing.
Arthur Bliss had every reason to stay in the USA – there was plenty
of work for him there, his wife was American, his family was with
him, he was advised that crossing the Atlantic had become dangerous,
and, as a distinguished veteran of the First World War, he owed
no patriotic debts. He was nonetheless torn by the conflict of duty
to family and country: 'I was haunted by the thought of what our
absent friends in England were enduring and wondering what was
the right thing for me to do.' He admitted to being 'too disturbed
in my mind' to write any music.[21] When an invitation came to work
at the BBC he hesitated no longer. Benjamin Britten was also working
in the USA when the war came. By early 1941 he was planning to
become a naturalized citizen. Then, in July of that year he abruptly
changed his mind. The occasion of this turnabout was the chance
reading of an article by E. M. Forster on the Suffolk poet George
Crabbe in *The Listener* of 29 May 1941. In this Forster evoked
Crabbe's (and Britten's) native landscape: 'To think of Crabbe is to
think of England. ... Aldeburgh huddles round a flint-towered church
and sprawls down to the North Sea – and what a wallop the sea
makes as it pounds at the shingle! ... Crabbe is entirely of England.
Aldeburgh stamped him for ever.' These words reached out to Britten
in his Californian exile with an emotional pull that he could not
resist. As Britten recalled: 'I suddenly realized where I belonged and
what I lacked ... I had become without roots.'[22] Although that same
Suffolk coast was by this time a place of pillboxes, barbed wire and
tank-traps, Britten, like Bliss, instinctively knew that his life and
work would only have meaning if he returned to his 'roots'. Both
men were moved to act by their sense of belonging; if threatened
and battered Britain was where their work had to be done, then so
be it: the soft and secure life of exile would be relinquished.

Bliss's temporary affliction with 'composer's block' serves to
illustrate how composition depends as much on the composer's state

21. A. Bliss, *As I Remember* (London, Faber & Faber, 1970), pp. 122, 130.
22. Quoted in M. Oliver, *Benjamin Britten* (London, Phaidon, 1996), p. 90.

of mind as on the physical constraints imposed by changing external realities. While some, like Vaughan Williams and Walton, were able to adapt and continue to compose, others were adversely affected by the upheaval and the uncertainty that the war brought. Arnold Bax was the most distinguished casualty. Four months into the war he wrote: 'All these fearful events are very distracting ... I cannot adapt myself very well to the conditions. I have written nothing at all since August and I doubt if anyone else has either.'[23] That little of a 'fearful' nature had up to this point occurred only underlines the war's intimidatory power to paralyse the creative impulse.[24] In Bax's case the incapacity persisted. Taking the advice of friends, he filled the void by writing his autobiography. Being made Master of the King's Musick in 1942 only highlighted his difficulties, especially as the passed-over Vaughan Willams was at this time particularly prolific. Even when the block eventually shifted a little, his meagre and lightweight output did nothing to maintain the reputation of a post that has been described as 'a focal point of national musical tendencies and a repository of characteristic national culture'.[25]

In summary, the pervasive reality of the war could affect the work of the composer by reordering his objective and subjective states. Since the normal sources of commission (orchestral societies, cultural foundations, individuals) tended to be replaced by state or quasi-state organizations such as the Ministry of Information, the BBC, ENSA and the Council for the Encouragement of Music and the Arts (CEMA), there was a consequent shift in demand towards music that would inspire and uplift; in other words, music that would serve the purpose of sustaining national morale. The likelihood that such music would eschew experiment and follow well-tried examples from the past was inherent in this situation. This, it might be added, was perhaps what people wanted in the anxious upheaval of wartime. As William Glock put it: '[Since September 1939] audiences have wished, not unnaturally, to be sustained rather than challenged by

23. Letter to Tilly Fleischmann, 27 December 1939, quoted in L. Foreman, *Bax: A Composer and His Times* (London, Scolar Press, 1983), pp. 321–2.
24. E. J. Moeran, like Bax, afflicted with composer's block, blamed the war: 'I found I could do no work at all when the war started for some weeks.' But his recovery was quicker: 'I have now stealed myself to the task and am pegging away.' Letter to May Harrison, 4 November 1939, cited in Foreman, *From Parry to Britten*, p. 224.
25. C. Scott-Sutherland, *Arnold Bax* (London, J. M. Dent & Sons, 1973), p. 181.

the music they heard.'[26] The implication, however, is that 'normal' artistic development was thereby halted, or at least distorted. Furthermore, isolation from European musical influences, coinciding with an awakened sense of the traditions making up the national identity – intensified by the sustained period of crisis and threat that followed the retreat at Dunkirk and the fall of France – seemed likely to produce music of a self-consciously 'national' character, traditionally conceived. Composers were no different from their fellow human beings in experiencing the intense emotions of war: pride, optimism and sense of fulfilment as much as fear, anxiety, grief and despair. In *The Listener*, during the dark days of 1941, Frank Howes mused on this: 'Life is indeed one, and composers are no exception to the general rule that there are no absolutely watertight compartments of the mind.'[27] Writing music in the abnormal circumstances of the Second World War was still possible, then, but there was little chance that what was produced would be uninfluenced by those circumstances.

III

The music that most clearly showed the mark of war was that written to official order. When the BBC asked John Ireland to write a patriotic piece, it suggested a stirring march on the lines of Elgar's *Pomp and Circumstance*. This was not Ireland's preferred idiom, but he loyally fulfilled the brief and in April 1942 his *Epic March* was ready for performance. Its main tune, with its steady stride and optimistic rising thirds and fifths, did indeed evoke the Edwardian imperial world associated with the Elgar marches. In its opening bars, moreover, was a figure in the rhythm of the Morse sign for V ('V for Victory'), thereby anticipating the BBC's own adoption of this as the call signal for its broadcasts to occupied Europe. The march was evidently exactly what its commissioners had wanted; it was much used by the BBC and was heard on numerous official occasions throughout the war, then falling into near-total oblivion, its purpose achieved, its mood no longer in tune with the times.

Vaughan Williams's 1943 commission *Thanksgiving for Victory*

26. *Horizon*, IV:22, October 1941.
27. *The Listener*, 6 November 1941.

(later renamed *A Song of Thanksgiving*) for soprano, speaker, mixed
chorus and orchestra, likewise turned out to be perfectly judged in
mood and idiom for the time it was first heard, 13 May 1945. The
composer chose to set lines from Shakespeare's *Henry V*, Kipling's
Puck of Pook's Hill, and from three biblical sources: Chronicles,
Isaiah and the Apocrypha (the songs of the Three Holy Children).
It is not a concert piece but a public celebration. Frank Howes
described it as 'music engaged in social service'.[28] Its total absence
of triumphalism, and spirit of gratitude and optimism about the
future make it an occasional work that yet transcends the occasion.
Although it begins with a fanfare for six trumpets and large orchestra,
it ends with a quiet benediction sung by the soprano alone. It
contains several memorable tunes of broad, diatonic, hymn-like
quality, the last of which, a setting of Kipling's 'Land of our birth
we pledge to thee / Our love and toil in the years to be', is begun
by children's voices and then taken up by the whole chorus. With
sounds that had a traditional 'English' resonance, the composer was
thus able to give expression to the nation's thanks, without the
bombast or jingoism that Kipling's name might have evoked. The
work continued to be performed, alongside Elgar's *For the Fallen*,
at Armistice commemorations for several years after the war.

In completing his scores for *For the Red Army* and *The Quest*,
Walton's idiom was more or less ordained. Fanfares played by massed
military bands have an inbuilt character of bright, heroic splendour;
St George (Britain) will set out to kill the dragon (Nazism) and
rescue the maiden (Europe) to sounds that acknowledge no uncertainty of outcome. His ENSA commission, however, came apparently
without strings. The *Sinfonia Concertante* (1943), perhaps because
it was essentially a revision of a piece written in the 1920s, owes
nothing at all to the circumstances in which it was produced. There
is no indication that ENSA was disappointed. After all, with its
lightheartedness, sweet lyricism and jazzy humour, the piece could
serve well as a cheer-raiser for ENSA audiences in the weary fourth
year of the war.

According to Ernest Irving, the wartime musical director of Ealing
Studios, music written for films merits serious consideration only in
terms of its role in underpinning the moods created by the images
and script: 'the music must always be subsidiary and ancillary and

28. Howes, *Music of Ralph Vaughan Williams*, p. 194.

cannot be allowed to develop on formal lines for musical reasons only; it is not being played at a concert, its principal effect should be upon the subconscious mind, and if the film is a good film the music will be felt rather than listened to.'[29] A film score will typically underline and punctuate the action, point up the mood and heighten the emotion. Music composed for itself, on the other hand, will have a structure of exposition, development, recapitulation, etc., that is at odds with these episodic, linear needs. The implication is that film music and art music are different entities and that in appraising them one ought to respect this distinction. It is true that some of the film scores written during the war were successfully converted into suites for concert performance. In this form the composer could work the same musical ideas into a structure that was musically coherent and which therefore could stand on its own. Few survived the adaptation and retained a place in the concert repertoire, however. Of those that did, most were unlike the typical film score in the first place, having already a suite-like form of several musically coherent episodes heard in succession. Alternatively, the enduring scores are those that had an 'overture' to accompany the film title and credits, which could easily be detached from the rest for concert performance. Walton and Vaughan Williams alone (perhaps not just for the reasons suggested above) succeeded in producing enduring music that started life as an adjunct to a film.[30]

Walton wrote music for 14 films in all, four before, six during and four after the war. He was generally active in the war effort, not only writing music for morale-boosting films, but taking on the role of civilian music adviser to the Army Film Unit. This work, even though it diverted him from his intention to write chamber music, was more congenial than life in the forces. Walton was just young enough to be called up and it was due to the intervention of Jack Beddington, director of the films division of the Ministry of Information, and a music-lover, that he was exempted from military service, on condition that he would write music for films

29. E. Irving, *Cue for Music: An Autobiography* (London, D. Dodson, 1959), p. 163.
30. Bax enjoyed a brief success with the concert piece arranged from his score for the Crown Film Unit documentary *Malta GC*. But it is a mediocre piece that was for Bax 'entirely impersonal' and detracted from his more personal works. In a letter to his brother he wrote: 'I can't say I derived much pleasure from the writing.' Quoted in Foreman, *Bax*, pp. 326–7.

deemed to be 'of national importance'.[31] His attitude to film music was exactly that of Ernest Irving, quoted above: 'Film music is not good film music if it can be used for any other purpose. ... The music should never be heard without the film.'[32] And yet, no other British composer's film music has the place that Walton's has in the concert repertoire, in its arranged form, at least. In his score for *The First of the Few*, Leslie Howard's film about the designer of the Spitfire, R. J. Mitchell, the march that accompanied the opening credits and the fugue that so aptly ran behind the factory scenes of aircraft parts being assembled were so immediately popular with audiences that the BBC was pressed to broadcast the music for a year before it was able to do so, following the recording in August 1943 of a concert version that Walton was persuaded to make. With its stirring Elgarian big tune and unstoppable energy, it recalled the heroic days of the Battle of Britain, when the sense of national unity was at its strongest. In writing this sort of music Walton was increasingly seen by the general public as taking on the mantle of Elgar. He had already, in 1937, written a spacious, patriotic march *Crown Imperial* for the coronation of George VI. *The Spitfire Prelude and Fugue* was another spoonful from that pot, brilliantly crafted, tuneful, but essentially music from a past time. The film came out at a bad time in the war. News from the war fronts was largely negative: in June Tobruk had fallen to the Axis and British forces had retreated in Libya. For three gloomy months, therefore, until the great victory at El Alamein, Walton's music served the vital patriotic purpose of helping to prop up drooping morale. In its style and mood it is the complement to Ireland's *Epic March*, which coincidentally reached the public during the same period. For the film of Shakespeare's *Henry V*, directed by Laurence Olivier (1944), Walton composed no less than 55 minutes of music. He found the task difficult but he did it because he needed the money. And yet the music he produced is of lasting quality. Olivier said he thought it 'the most wonderful music I've ever heard for a film. In fact, for me the music actually made the film. The charge scene [Agincourt] is really made by William's music.'[33] *Henry V* had great patriotic resonance in 1944, and Walton showed he could write to order

31. Kennedy, *Portrait of Walton*, p. 112.
32. Ibid., p. 117.
33. Ibid., p. 125.

music that was its complement. Many of the elements that go to make up an immediately recognizable 'English' sound are worked into the score. In the opening scenes of the Globe Playhouse in the 1590s the music is mock-Tudor, with lute, tabor and harpsichord in the instrumentation. Two ravishingly valetudinarian melodies for strings mark the episodes of the death of Sir John Falstaff and Pistol's farewell to Mistress Quickly, at the lines 'Touch her soft lips and part.' For the first of these Walton chose the evocatively archaic form of the chaconne and skilfully married it to the tune of an old folk song, *Watkin's Ale*. The cadences of the *Agincourt Song* stirringly call up an heroic past time when England was, as in 1944, locked in a struggle with a continental foe. As a suite, the music for *Henry V* is still frequently played. Musically, it is akin to other consciously out-of-period suites such as Warlock's *Capriole Suite*, Grieg's *Holberg Suite* and Fauré's *Masques et Bergamasques*. It thus stands somewhat apart from its time and from the composer's musical development.

Walton wrote the music for *Henry V* as a response to the text, before he had seen any of the film (which may partly account for its musical coherence). This was also Vaughan Williams's preferred approach. He worked from a script and a set of cues, but without waiting to see rough-cuts of the film's scenes. As he put it in his 1945 essay *Composing for Films*: 'ignore the details and intensify the spirit of the whole situation by a continuous stream of music'.[34] In this way he was able to produce an unbroken flow of music that ran parallel to the action rather than, Hollywood-style, precisely reinforcing each bit of the action. A score produced in this way was less fragmented and episodic than most film scores. In consequence, it was altogether more coherent musically and, perhaps with some subsequent slight modification, was capable of standing on its own. Several of Vaughan Williams's film scores were success-fully turned into concert suites in his way. Vaughan Williams was 70 when the war began, the leading figure in British musical life and a composer of international standing. He had never written music for the cinema and certainly had no need to turn to it to support himself. And yet, during the war years he wrote the scores for five films: *49th Parallel* (1941) for Powell and Pressburger, financed by the Ministry of Information, *Coastal Command* (1942)

34. Royal College of Music Magazine, 1945, reprinted in Vaughan Williams, *National Music*, p. 161.

for the Crown Film Unit, *The Flemish Farm* (1943) for the Air Ministry, *The People's Land* (1943) for the National Trust and *Stricken Peninsula* (1945) for the Army Film Unit. For him the work represented one of the ways he could contribute to the war effort. It gave him a new opportunity to live the philosophy he had so long professed, whereby the composer was organically part of the community in which he lived. By this means his music could become the embodiment of the wartime spirit that would be the saving of the nation. What better way, moreover, of underlining the English identity of his music than by associating it with films that were about the struggle for human rights and resistance to tyrannical government? Working in what was for him a completely new medium he was, then, entirely 'in his element'.

As befitted the time at which it was written (1941), the score for the feature film *49th Parallel* contains music of reassuring optimism, notably in the Prelude and in the final section. Its incorporation of the anthem O *Canada* (the action is set in Canada) served to remind audiences that Britain was not fighting alone. *Coastal Command* was a documentary showing how the RAF protected Britain's coastal waters. Jeffrey Richards has described it as 'a study in British character'.[35] Vaughan Williams's music served this brief partly through the use of expansive, confident, heroic melodies and themes suggestive of quiet determination, and partly by working into the score motifs of a folk-song character. Music that celebrated heroism and self-sacrifice for one's country was the main requirement for the feature film *The Flemish Farm*, and again, Vaughan Williams produced it to order. Without ever descending to overwrought bombast, the music has a stirring, elevating quality, underlining the film's message that though the worst was past, heroism came in many forms and none need feel unchallenged. It was also in 1943 that Vaughan Williams wrote the musical score for the short National Trust documentary, *The People's Land*. The title was literal, for the main thrust of the film was that it was 'the people' that the Trust embodied: they founded it, they used its buildings and land; it was their heritage. This was a theme after Vaughan Williams's own heart. His score incorporates folk tunes like *As I Walked Out*, children's rhymes like *Pop Goes the Weasel* and *Boys and Girls Come Out to*

35. J. Richards, *Film and British National Identity* (Manchester, Manchester UP, 1997), p. 296.

Play, and popular songs like The *Spring-time of the Year*. These are enclosed in a richly-scored evocation of the beauty and peacefulness of the English countryside.

Much of the music Vaughan Williams wrote for the cinema was, like that of other composers, of a solid, journeyman character, serving a specific, practical function, but having slight intrinsic merit. And it is generally the case that the scores of wartime films are dismissed as trivia by their begetters. Musicologists on the whole give them scant attention, except in the odd instance where the germs of a 'legitimate' opus are to be traced in a film score written earlier.[36] Exceptionally, the suites from *Coastal Command* and *The Flemish Farm* and the ten-minute score for *The People's Land*, like Walton's arrangements, have earned a lasting place in the concert repertoire. It must be conceded, however, that that place does not depend wholly on their musical merits but to some degree on their extra-musical associations. They are the musical testimony of a historic period in national history, recalling the mood and emotions of the time, and valued accordingly.

IV

If official commissions inevitably produced music that was to a greater or lesser degree 'war music', to what extent did the music written under no more constraint than the fact that 'there was a war on' emerge bearing its imprint?

A small number of works have an obvious relationship to the war or have been acknowledged by their authors to be so linked. Bliss's *Phoenix March* was his reaction to the news of the liberation of Paris in August 1944; it predictably suggests a Gallic rebirth in an uplifting, if conventional, manner. When the critic E. Sackville-West heard Britten's *Sinfonia da Requiem*, written during the composer's three-year stay in America, he thought it his 'least English' work but one that reflected the 'European tragedy of 1940'.[37] Britten had in fact acknowledged this in a radio talk he gave in July 1942: 'the

---

36. In his 1989 monograph, *Vaughan Williams and the Vision of Albion* (London, Barrie & Jenkins), Wilfrid Mellers briefly mentions just one film, *The Flemish Farm*, and only then as a contributory source for the Oboe Concerto.
37. *Horizon*, July 1944, X:55.

external stimulus was the death of my mother. ... To this personal tragedy were soon added the more general world tragedies of the Spanish and present wars.'[38] The implication of a programme given by the title is reinforced by the subtitles given to the three movements, *Lacrymosa*, *Dies Irae* and *Requiem Aeternam*, as appropriate to a work about the horror of war as to one about mourning. In its dramatic development the music evokes irreconcilable conflict, in the first movement; fury, terror and grief in the second; consolation and transcendent hope in the last. Britten had already, before the war, been moved to respond in his work to public events. In 1938–39 he had written *Advance Democracy* for unaccompanied chorus to a text by Randal Swingler, and *Ballad of Heroes* for tenor, chorus and orchestra, to a text by W. H. Auden, as a tribute to British volunteers killed in the Spanish Civil War. The *Sinfonia*, then, coming just a year later, can be seen as part of that response, itself submerging until its striking reappearance in the *War Requiem* in 1962.

Three works by Vaughan Williams, appearing in 1940–41, represent the practical expression of his view that composers could use their skills and creative imagination to serve their country. He turned first to song because, as he put it: 'no bombs or blockades can rob us of our vocal chords; there will always remain for us the greatest of musical instruments, the human voice'.[39] The *Six Choral Songs to be Sung in Time of War* (1939) were scored for unison chorus with piano or orchestra (or neither). Their purpose is clear in their titles: *A Song of Courage*; *A Song of Liberty*; *A Song of Healing*; *A Song of Victory*; *A Song of Pity, Peace and Love*; *A Song of the New Age*. The setting of Shelley's words is rather severe, but the last song has 'the blazing contrast of A minor and A major, made to express hopes of a fairer future which the unquenchable spirit of man contrives to extract from the disaster of war'.[40] Unison settings being easier for amateurs, Vaughan Williams deliberately offered this form for *England My England*, a choral song to words by W. E. Henley for baritone, double chorus (in parts or unison voices) and orchestra or piano; and for three hymns: *The Airmen's Hymn*, *A Hymn of Freedom*, and *A Call to the Free Nations* (all 1942). He also had the amateur in mind when he wrote *Household Music: Three Preludes on Welsh Hymn Tunes* (1940) for string quartet or alternative

38. *The Listener*, 30 July 1942.
39. 'The Composer in Wartime', *The Listener*, 16 May 1940.
40. Howes, *Music of Ralph Vaughan Williams*, p. 242.

instruments, and optional horn: his first offering towards 'music for every fortuitous combination of instruments which may happen to be assembled in a parlour or a dug-out, with a part for anyone who happens to drop in'.[41] This simple music, with its traditional melodies and flexible instrumentation, symbolizes that period of the war when the nation was forced in on itself, the sense of national identity was strong and 'carrying on' was what people did. It has to be said, however, that other composers did not follow Vaughan Williams's lead and that he himself turned to other ways of serving his country when the crisis of the early years had passed.

The inception of Michael Tippett's oratorio *A Child of Our Time* (1939–41) is best explained in the words of the composer:

> Although the artist appears to be locked away, doing his own particular thing, one could not, at that time, but be aware of what was going on. ... The Jews were the particular scapegoats of everything. They stood for every kind of outcast, whether in Russia or America or even in England. For these people I knew somehow I had to sing songs. Suddenly, in fact the day after war broke out, the whole thing welled up in me in a way which I can remember exactly. I simply had to go and begin to write *A Child of Our Time*.[42]

The sense of urgency, he elsewhere acknowledges, was increased by a fear about being unable to write what he wanted before the war killed him – he was no different from anyone else in believing that war would mean mass bombing and great loss of life. It is nonetheless clear that the coming of war was for him a sign that human depravity would reach new depths before things got better. The original stimulus was the *Kristallnacht* pogrom in November 1938, the Nazis' response to the shooting of a German diplomat in Paris by a young Polish Jew, driven to despair over the plight of his parents in Germany. He became the hero of *A Child of Our Time*, a symbolic figure, standing for all outcasts and persecuted people. This was clearly apparent to *Times* critic, present at the first performance in March 1944: 'Tippett has succeeded to quite a remarkable extent in creating a powerful work out of contemplation of the evil abroad in the world of yesterday and today ... combining the force of the particular with the significance of the universal.'[43] Tippett believed

41. 'Composer in Wartime'.
42. M. Tippett, *Moving into Aquarius* (London, Paladin, 2nd edn 1974), pp. 152–3.
43. *The Times*, 20 March 1944.

that art should aspire and compensate, and not simply reflect, its subject. Music, by virtue of its power to disclose the deeper levels of common humanity, might induce reconciliation and healing. It was also important to him to produce a work that was accessible to a wide audience and that was not very difficult to perform: 'I felt I had to express *collective* feelings and that could only be done by *collective* tunes, such as Negro spirituals, for these tunes contain a deposit of generations of common experience.'[44] The presence of the spirituals affects the general musical style of the oratorio. Tippett explained: 'I used the interval of a minor third (produced so characteristically in the melodies of the spirituals when moving from the fifth of the tonic to the flat seventh) as a basic interval of the whole work – sometimes on its own, sometimes superimposed upon the open fifth below the whole note.'[45] The broad appeal of the resulting music together with the theme – 'The simple-hearted shall exult in the end' – ensured an instant and enduring success for the work. As Maurice Edelman put it at the time: '[It] speaks the inexpressible thoughts of us all, children of our time, brothers and sisters in the modern agony.'[46]

In his biography of Tippett, Meirion Bowen points out that the composition of *A Child of Our Time* came uncharacteristically close to the events that inspired it; more often, Tippett did not produce an immediate response to his experience. He preferred to detach himself from an affecting episode, recollecting at a later point the emotion he had felt. The work would then emerge 'embodying a wider perspective'.[47] It was thus not until 1950–51 that Tippett wrote *The Heart's Assurance*, transmuting into music the feelings he had had five years earlier. The work is a song-cycle for high voice and piano, being a setting of poems by Alun Lewis and Sidney Keyes, both killed in the war. It relates to Tippett's grief for his friend Francesca Allinson, who killed herself in 1945, and was written when 'the personal wound began to heal, and, more importantly, as the very real wounds of the war healed'.[48] The theme is 'love under the shadow of death'. In the last song *Remember Your Lovers*,

44. Tippett, *Moving into Aquarius*, p. 153.
45. Ibid., pp. 121–3.
46. *Picture Post*, 3 March 1945.
47. M. Bowen, *Michael Tippett* (London, Robson Books, 1982), pp. 49–50.
48. M. Tippett, *Those Twentieth Century Blues: An Autobiography* (London, Hutchinson, 1991), p. 187.

each verse begins with a Last Post-like motif, answered by a bugle-and-drum figure in the piano, to be swallowed up each time by the florid lyricism of the voice part. When the motif makes its final appearance voice and piano at once come together and, in a striking moment, the perfect fifth of the Last Post is symbolically raised a semitone. Love conquers all, even war, even, in the end, death itself. This passionate music is more than a private expression of love and remembrance; it stands for the pity of lives blighted by man's collective destructiveness.

Not all music written 'under the shadow of war' advertised its provenance by title or by attachment to a literary text. The creative imagination of composers was influenced by the pervasiveness of this social context, nonetheless, and this was as evident in their unprogrammed as in their programmed works. Three instrumental works by Tippett, spanning the war years, have caused commentators to make inferences relating to the war: the *Fantasia on a Theme of Handel* (1944–45), the String Quartet No. 2 (1941–42) and the Symphony No. 1 (1944–45). Tippett was working on the *Fantasia* (for piano and orchestra) in 1939 when the war began, and broke off to write *A Child of Our Time*. When he returned to the piece, according to David Matthews, himself a composer, Tippett was strongly influenced by the war and the new and more sombre world of *A Child of Our Time*.[49] He introduced the *Dies Irae* theme into the last section and ended the work with a long and serious fugue. Matthews also hears the influence of the war in the string quartet, written in the winter of 1941–42, when the military tide had yet to turn and life on the home front was dreary: 'In the tortuous chromatic lines of the slow fugue that forms the second movement, and in the stern mood of much of the finale, we may feel a response to the immediate grimness of the world around him.'[50] Finally, the composer in Matthews reacts in much the same way to the second movement of the Symphony No. 1: 'This movement, which alternates dark, brooding music with grimly passionate out-bursts, is a deeply-felt response to the suffering of the war.'[51] In this reading, some cautious support comes from the music academic Ian Kemp (despite his preferred view of music as an essentially non-referential art). He

49. D. Matthews, *Michael Tippett: An Introductory Study* (London, Faber & Faber, 1980), p. 37.
50. Ibid., p. 37.
51. Ibid., p. 42.

compares the movement's 'sombre and harrowing' mood to the brooding slow movements of the later symphonies of Shostakovich. In the fragmentary figures in variations three and four, and the distant fanfares that follow, he detects something of a programme: 'it is impossible to avoid the conclusion that ... the movement is a direct comment on war'.[52] As one might expect, the composer of *A Child of Our Time* does not communicate despair; rather, the mood conveyed is one of optimism about the ultimate resilience of human beings.

After the first performance of Vaughan Williams's Fifth Symphony at a Promenade Concert in 1943, Adrian Boult, who conducted it, said: 'I feel that its serene loveliness is completely satisfying in these times and shows, as only music can, what we must work for when this madness is over.'[53] The contrast in mood with the Fourth Symphony (1934) could not have been greater. Whereas the Fifth, in D major, has a calm, life-affirming character, the earlier work, set in F minor, a key associated with darkness, death and hell, is full of tumultuous discord. This contrast has prompted some to see the two symphonies as linked comment on public affairs: the Fourth, composed alongside *Dona Nobis Pacem*, whose text explicitly relates to war, as a peacetime appeal for the renunciation of war; the Fifth as an appeal for peace in the midst of war. Wilfrid Mellers reminds us that the second half of the Fifth's finale, a *passacaglia* (a form that was historically a musical synonym for unity), and still more its transformation in the epilogue, evokes the alleluias in Vaughan Williams's great hymn *Sine Nomine*: 'We know the New Jerusalem does not, cannot, exist in social reality; whereas in the Symphony the validity of art for a moment makes the vision true.'[54] The spiritual quality of the work had great appeal, perhaps, as Boult sensed, by virtue of the contrast with the anxious and chaotic times in which it appeared.

Vaughan Williams began work on his Sixth Symphony in 1944 and completed it in 1947. For Frank Howes, although it bears no title, its provenance is unambiguous: 'the implicit programme declares itself to anyone who lived through the period during which the composer was writing it ... to anyone who is not deaf or doctrinaire

52. I. Kemp, *Tippett: the Composer and his Music* (London, Ernst Eulenberg, 1984), p. 201.
53. Quoted in Vaughan Williams, *RVW*, p. 254.
54. Mellers, *Vaughan Williams*, p. 186.

this symphony spells a word of three letters – WAR'.[55] Two pre-
liminary points are worth making here. The first is that the opening
themes of the second and fourth movements have their origin in
music of an undeniably 'war' character: the score for the film *The
Flemish Farm*. The second is that the key of the symphony, E minor,
is symbolic: E minor was Bach's key of Crucifixion and, as Mellers
points out, it is the negative minor of the paradisal E major.[56] Analysis
of the movements reveals features that are strongly suggestive of a
programme. In the first, turbulent, clashing of irreconcilable ideas,
confusion of key-centres, and threatening brass passages bring to
mind the stress and fury of war. Then there is a transforming shift
to E major and a passage with an unusual scoring for harps and
trombones, that is of lyrical tranquillity, strong and radiant and
carrying the paradisal associations of the key. Howes hears this as
'the assurance of victory', the musical equivalent of Churchill's
speeches in the 'finest hour' of 1940.[57] The second movement has
a decidedly military character in the prominence of trumpets and
drums, and the tumult of war continues in the insistent rhythm and
swirling scale passages. In the third, the scoring is heavy and its
aggressively stomping march suggests the mechanized brutality of
battle. The last movement, entitled *Epilogue*, is quiet and slow,
drawing out the implications of the previous movements. '[It is] the
conclusion of the anger of the first movement, the conflict of the
second, the battery of the third.'[58] It suggests the bleak insecurity
of the world that emerged in 1945 from the destructive upheaval
of war. As Howes puts it: 'To me his Epilogue spells out the
emotional significance of the word "aftermath". The end of war is
not triumph but dead-sea fruit.' Mellers agrees, though relating it
also to Vaughan Williams's own exploration of the Unknown Region,
concluding that it denotes that 'man is alone, in the dark, cold and
empty desolation. Acceptance brings to this strange music a serene
insecurity: a courageous testament of our frightful century.'[59] And
because, as he puts it, Vaughan Williams 'had become, rather more
than most composers, our representative', the symphony stands as
a social testament.

55. Howes, *Music of Ralph Vaughan Williams*, p. 53.
56. Mellers, *Vaughan Williams*, p. 188.
57. Howes, *Music of Vaughan Williams*, pp. 56–7.
58. Ibid., p. 62.
59. Mellers, *Vaughan Williams*, p. 194.

V

It was suggested above that one of the by-products of the shift in the sources of commissions for new music was the discouragement of experiment and the consolidation of well-tried traits in what was produced. It is arguable, however, that much of the music written during the war demonstrated a degree of introspective conservatism independently of official influence. The clearest indication of this is the near-absence of works from composers who had embraced the techniques of the Second Viennese School and the failure of that particular stream of the avant-garde to widen during the war years. And in the meantime, Vaughan Williams was apparently leading the way back to the past: in his Fifth Symphony the radical path set out by the Fourth was abandoned in favour of a return to the style of his early symphonies. Compared with the harmonic asperities of the Fourth, which, on its appearance in 1935, caused some critics to suspect that Vaughan Williams was succumbing to atonalism, the Fifth was closer to the aural world of Parry. The harmonies and chordal progressions are blandly conventional and the overall sound is at times almost cloyingly sweet.

Another facet of wartime conservatism is the extra lease of life given to 'Englishness', or the historical–pastoral. In writing his piano suite *Sarnia*, John Ireland was consciously attempting a nostalgic evocation of the Channel Islands, that part of Britain where the English way of life was roughly subjected to the untender mercies of the *Wehrmacht*. Julius Harrison gave to his rhapsody for violin and orchestra the title *Bredon Hill*, after the poem by Housman. When this piece, written in 1941, but sounding like something from before 1914 (that is, 'historical' as well as 'pastoral'), was broadcast on the BBC's Overseas Service, the presenter, without irony, introduced it thus: 'Julius Harrison, Worcestershire-born of many generations of countrymen, lives in sight of Bredon Hill ... . He has the love of our English countryside in his veins ... . It is a fact remarkable in itself that such music comes out of the present time. That it does, is perhaps the best witness of the eternal spirit of England.'[60] When Edmund Rubbra, heavily involved as a performer for ENSA and CEMA, took time off to write, he looked to an

60. Foreman, *From Parry to Britten*, p. 241.

Elizabethan madrigalist for inspiration, his opus 50 being *Improvisations on Virginal Pieces by Giles Farnaby*. Admittedly, Rubbra had always had a strong sense of English tradition and had often used modal harmony in his music. But Malcolm Arnold, who was in fact interested in, and had experimented with, serial techniques, also looked to a familiar aural past when he wrote *Three Shanties for Wind Quintet* in 1943 for performance by his colleagues in the London Philharmonic Orchestra on their regional tours. The idea of the British as a seafaring 'island race' was, of course, a salient element in the national self-concept promoted by official agencies concerned with popular morale and national unity.

In 1939 Benjamin Britten was what Michael Kennedy has described as a 'conservative composer' who was yet never conservative in outlook; always innovative, but with no intention of becoming the English Schoenberg.[61] At the same time, he did not feel himself to be part of the stream of English music associated with Vaughan Williams and the historical–pastoral tendency. During the war years, his music nevertheless came to express an Englishness that was previously absent. It is perhaps significant that the emergence of this element in his music coincided with his return to England from America in April 1942. If the pre-1942 works, such as *Les Illuminations*, the *Seven Sonnets of Michelangelo* and the Violin Concerto are European in their influences, those written after that point insistently resonate with England and Englishness. Of *A Ceremony of Carols* and *Hymn to St Cecilia*, Michael Kennedy writes that Britten 'seems deliberately to be holding out an olive branch to the English tradition, without sacrificing his individuality'.[62] Firstly, he was using the medium of unaccompanied choir (though with harp in the *Carols*), which he had previously avoided, perhaps because of its associations with English part-songs and nineteenth- and twentieth-century church music. Secondly, the texts are decidedly English: medieval and sixteenth-century verses and the plainsong antiphon from the Christmas Eve Vespers for the *Ceremony of Carols*, Auden's lines for the *Hymn to St Cecilia*. Thirdly, these pieces deploy fragments of the ancient modes: Lydian in the *Hymn*, Aeolian, Dorian, Lydian and Mixolydian in the *Carols*. Britten continued to explore modality in old or entirely new scale constructions to provide the

61. M. Kennedy, *Britten* (London, Dent, 1981), p. 149.
62. Ibid., p. 164.

basis for a technique that had popular appeal, a style easily grasped by audiences. Through this consciously-forged link with the Golden Age of English music the 'modernity' of his music had a comforting familiarity. In his 1945 opera *Peter Grimes* the Lydian and Phrygian modes are again in evidence. Not that the Englishness of that work depends on the device. In every sense, the score is permeated by the English spirit and landscape, in apt complement to the source of the libretto, the poem *The Borough* by the eighteenth-century Suffolk poet George Crabbe (Britten followed up that Forster stimulus of four years before). But by relating his music to his audiences' traditional musical experience Britten succeeded in writing a work of immediate popular appeal. This had been equally true of his 1943 composition the *Serenade for Tenor, Horn and Strings*, where again the strong emotional pull lay partly in the choice of text – poems by Cotton, Tennyson, Blake, Jonson and Keats. One of the last of his wartime compositions was his String Quartet No. 2. Even here, with no literary reference to help, the composer roots his utterance in his English background, in this case by writing the last movement as a chacony, in tribute to Henry Purcell, on the 250th anniversary of whose death the quartet was performed, on 21 November 1945.

Three compositions by Tippett indicate that he, too, (and who can doubt that in this most self-conscious of composers it was intentional?) was using musical devices to link his work with English tradition: *Plebs Angelica* (1943) for unaccompanied double chorus is itself a homage to the English church music tradition. This is evident in the Tallis-like eight-part harmony and in the false relations and chromatic turns associated with the period from Tallis to Purcell. In *Boyhood's End* (1943), for tenor and piano, Tippett consciously uses a Purcell-like melisma vocal technique.[63] For *The Weeping Babe* (1944), for soprano and mixed chorus, he uses melisma after the manner of the Elizabethan madrigalists, the whole piece being in the tradition of Byrd's polyphonic songs, even to the extent of using the device known as the English Cadence, a 'trade mark' of English music of that period that often differentiated it from that of the Continent.

63. i.e. five notes or more to a single syllable of text.

VI

A complete survey of music written during the war would disclose a number of works that evince no evidence of its influence. Strikingly, there are proportionally not many of them. Such as they are, they fall mainly into three categories: important pieces written or completed close to the start of the war and therefore to that extent not *of* the war (e.g. Britten's *Seven Sonnets of Michelangelo* and *Les Illuminations*, and Walton's Violin Concerto and his overture *Scapino*); revisions of earlier works (e.g. Rawsthorne's First Piano Concerto and Walton's *Sinfonia Concertante*); and lightweight or minor works (e.g. Moeran's *Sinfonietta* and *Serenade for Orchestra*, Bax's *Legend-Sonata* for cello and piano, and Rawsthorne's overture *Street Corner*).[64]

It is clear, then, that all but a very small part of the music written during the war, including those compositions that have an important place in the development of English music, bears the stamp of the war in one way or another. It is thus possible to speak of 'wartime music' and mean something more than music merely written during the war. All the leading figures in English music, and most of the rising figures, too, composed music that shows its wartime provenance.[65] In several instances (Vaughan Williams, Tippett, Britten, Walton) virtually their entire output in this period is war-related, within the meaning of this phrase as it has been used here. The best of their 'war music', moreover, stands in quality alongside the best of their peacetime compositions. Most also produced work of relatively mediocre quality; understandably, this was more often than not that written under the constraints attaching to commissions from official agencies for 'patriotic' music. This sort of work often diverted composers from their 'serious' work as, typically, they laboured to meet the requirements of a succession of screenplays. Some, like Vaughan Williams, nonetheless managed to do both. Others, William Walton being the most extreme example, found their creative energy was effectively absorbed by this work, to the point where their other

---

64. Bax, who had not found the war conducive to composition, revealingly said of his *Legend-Sonata*: '[It] gets about as far away from present day realities as it possibly could.' Foreman, *Bax*, p. 327.
65. Here, one would have to mention again the regrettable exception of Bax, reduced almost to silence by the upset of war.

writing plans were delayed until the war was over. In Walton's case, the loss is mitigated by the acknowledged excellence of his film music. Viewed as a whole, however, the commissioned music of the war years is not of enduring quality, is largely ignored in critical assessments of composers' work, and is rarely revived for performance or recording. It has historical rather than musical interest; a testimony to the reach of total war into the lives of all citizens, including composers of music. Its unseen, or rather, unheard consequence was a musical hiatus: the music that might have been written but was not.

The nudge of officialdom is no part of the explanation, however, for the appearance of works like *A Child of Our Time*, *Sinfonia da Requiem* and Vaughan Williams's Fifth and Sixth Symphonies. These are the creative artist's response to the dramatic, un-ignorable events that were taking place around him, whether consciously (as in the case of Britten and Tippett) or unconsciously (as in the case of Vaughan Williams). Nor is a 'patriotic' remit the whole explanation for the tendency of wartime composition to follow a relatively conservative, nationally introspective path. The isolation from outside (especially European) influences may have played a part in this, but probably of greater importance was the heightened emotional atmosphere created inside Britain as a result of the terrifying, and yet exciting, experience of the Dunkirk retreat, the Battle of Britain and the Blitz, followed by the years of gritty 'carrying on' through the long haul to victory. Music written to order in time of war was likely to have a 'national' feel to it, even if that was not explicitly in the brief. But the sharpened sense of national identity was more than the product of the propagandist's art; when music expressed its essential Englishness it did so because it was inwrought, the instinctive embodiment of core values under threat. In this way, the intrinsically personal and private activity of writing music effectively became for a time a communal or public activity, part, as it were, of a national project. As such it forms part of the distinctive musical legacy of the war.

A consequence of all this self-referential, introverted activity, it could be argued, was that the more conservative voices in English music were stronger at the end of the war than at its start. It is undeniable that in 1945 their standard-bearer, Vaughan Williams, dominated the musical scene. His music had embodied the wartime spirit of quiet patriotism and strength of will. He had matched the national mood and was regarded as a national treasure when the trial of war was over. Furthermore, the rising stars, Britten and Tippett, though 'modern' in ways that Vaughan Williams was not, were nonetheless firmly committed to tonality. Finally, the avant-garde, although never a leading force, had virtually atrophied during the war. Lutyens single-mindedly stuck to her serial guns, but not even the arrival in Britain in 1939 of the Catalan, Roberto Gerhard, a committed and productive serialist, was the stimulus it surely would have been in more normal times.

But if there was a suspicion of stagnation in 1945, it was not for long. To a large extent the status quo ante was restored; pervasive though the war's effect was at the time, it was in the end just a passing influence. In the post-war period, while the mainstream shook off much of the Deep England moss that had taken hold in the war, and widened its horizons once more to encompass the further reaches of extended tonality, the avant-garde gained new adherents, infiltrated the music colleges and university music departments and in the 1950s and 1960s was serving up its own English Musical Renaissance, this time with a distinctly Viennese flavour.[66]

66. Audiences were slow to respond, however. Even at the Cheltenham Festival, supposedly the showcase for new music, the programming for 10 years after the war reflected audiences' liking for the works of the more conservative, mainstream composers, in preference to the (admittedly more aurally challenging) products of the British atonalists and serialists.

More Than 'Music-While-You-Eat'[1]? Factory and Hostel Concerts, 'Good Culture' and the Workers

Nick Hayes

The Second World War, Kenneth Morgan suggests, proffered a release from that 'class-bound straight-jacket' which handicapped the arts in Britain before 1939: the 'people's war was generating a new people's culture, with clear radical implications'.[2] Whatever view one takes of recent criticisms against the emergence of a popularist social radicalism generally in wartime Britain, Morgan's comments undoubtedly capture the hopes of those influential left-of-centre educational improvers seeking to transform popular cultural practice during and after the war.[3] Nor contemporaneously was the circulation of such ideas restricted only to an inner sanctum of the chattering classes. *Picture Post* – perhaps the most influential popularizer of progressive opinion – regularly ran features celebrating an apparent social diffusion of the arts as it campaigned for cultural reconstruction. Beside Priestley's 1941 notorious condemnation of 'silly, passive style' popular amusements ran one such muscular call to battle. 'The soul', he prescribed, 'demands the arts as the body demands exercise ... . In the [new] Britain we want to build, then,

---

1. A phrase coined by CEMA regional staff to distinguish between their lunchtime factory performances and 'genuine concerts', PRO EL 3/1, Report by Eve Kisch, October 1944.
2. K. Morgan, *Labour in Power* (Oxford, Oxford UP, 1984), p. 318.
3. S. Fielding, P. Thompson and N. Tiratsoo, *'England Arise!': The Labour Party and Popular Politics in 1940s Britain* (Manchester, Manchester UP, 1995), pp. 135–8.

there will be plenty of art of every kind', for 'the enjoyment of good art demands some active co-operation on the part of the audience', and 'plenty of opportunity', not just for the few but also for the 'ordinary chap'.[4]

Two years later, in asking, 'Are we building a new culture?', *Picture Post* declared that in 'millions of men and women a new understanding and appreciation for the arts has grown up', part of the 'greatest movement ever known in adult education'. As W. E. Williams (Director, Army Bureau of Current Affairs) explained, the state-sponsored Council for the Encouragement of Music and the Arts (CEMA) had 'on an annual budget which just about buys a couple of bombers ... instigated a wide and catholic foretaste for the arts'.[5] Yet were Williams's and Priestley's hopes realized? Had cultures transcended class boundaries in the melting pot of war or were contemporary claims – subsequently endorsed by historians – for a newly discovered mass audience for the arts wildly exaggerated, essentially one further myth née propagandist line laid bare by wartime reality and post-war experience? Indeed, do CEMA's wartime activities warrant the label of 'exemplary success' still being attached to them?[6] This essay will examine the foundation of these assertions, focusing particularly on those areas of operation viewed consistently by CEMA itself as having priority: that is, its mission to take the arts to factory workers at their place of work or rest.

I

CEMA was established in December 1939, funded initially as an emergency measure by the Pilgrim Trust to which was added, pound for pound, a block Treasury grant. In its search for funding and status, from its earliest days CEMA naturally attested to its own successes and to the existence of a public hungry for its cultural provisions. Such a construction, while not necessarily a wholesale

4. J. B. Priestley, 'When Work is Over', *Picture Post (A Plan for Britain)*, 4 January 1941; for an earlier call for cultural eclecticism, see J. B. Priestley, 11 August 1940, *Postscripts* (London, Heinemann, 1940), pp. 49–53.
5. W. E. Williams, 'Are We Building a New British Culture?', *Picture Post*, 2 January 1943. See also H. C. Dent, *Education in Transition: A Sociological Study of the Impact of War on English Education 1939–1943* (London, Kegan Paul, 1944), pp. 148–50.
6. F. Leventhal, *Twentieth Century British History*, Vol. 8 (1997), p. 146.

distortion, was nevertheless also capable of serving a broader national wartime interest; conscripted as one of a number of icons (all deemed to have innate value) which, in summating Britain's heritage and past notable achievements, were pressed into service to codify and reinforce the nation's sense of self-identity. A truly eclectic audience for the arts bespoke an essentially egalitarian design, accentuating that the British people as a whole were fighting against Nazi barbarism and for the finest in their own and wider European cultural and civilized traditions. CEMA then set to making people 'believe intensely in the value and reality of their own cultural roots'.[7]

If any single representation epitomized this conception in the national consciousness, it was Myra Hess's 'shilling-a-time' National Gallery midday concerts (subsidized by CEMA). As *Picture Post* characteristically reported straightway in November 1939,

> at lunch-time every day you can see queues outside the Gallery which you never saw in the old days. There are men and women, young and old, rich and poor waiting patiently in the cold up the steps of the Gallery and along the pavements ... to hear Bach, Beethoven, Brahms, Chopin and Schuman .... Strange things happen in wartime.[8]

Present also was the Queen, 'enjoying herself, smiling and clapping ... in the front row among the rest of the audience' – overall signifying harmony and diffusion. It was this ubiquitous motif which inspired Humphrey Jennings's acclaimed aural and visual montage *Listen to Britain* (1942) which, in stressing the richness, diversity yet euphonic cultural resonances which in union symbolized the strength of British values, cut famously to Hess performing Mozart before Her Majesty and (as Calder points out) 'lots of ordinary people'.[9] Yet, typically, Gallery audiences consisted of city white-collar workers, not ordinary Londoners or Britons.[10] Indeed, as CEMA lamented of the equally

7. R. Weight, 'State, Intelligentsia and the Promotion of National Culture in Britain, 1939–45', *Historical Research*, **69** (1996), pp. 85–6.
8. 'Music among the Masters', *Picture Post*, 11 November 1939; for similar themes, see *Picture Post*, 'Shilling Ballet', 5 October 1940, 'Sadler's Wells Plays "Butterfly" in Burnley', 7 February 1942, 'London Goes Music Mad', 18 July 1942, 'Music Festival', 10 April 1943.
9. A. Calder, *The Myth of the Blitz* (London, Jonathan Cape, 1991), pp. 238–41; P. Stansky and W. Abrahams, *London's Burning: Life, Death and Art in the Second World War* (London, Constable, 1994), pp. 97–9.
10. P. Zeigler, *London at War, 1939–1945* (London, Sinclair-Stevenson, 1995), p. 191.

popular lunchtime recitals by Hess at the Royal Exchange, time and again 'leisured members of the public had queued up beforehand, and ... it was impossible [even] for any genuine City worker to find a seat'.[11] But then, with London's arts audiences starved of concerts and exhibitions, everything offered was eagerly consumed. It follows that had a larger menu been available, queues at the National Gallery and elsewhere – if not the wartime stories about those queues – would have been shorter.

There are other reasons, perhaps, to doubt the wholesale integrity of contemporary evidence supporting the wartime release of a classless, latent hunger for good music and the arts. The reputed existence of a strong, socially diverse and appreciative audience significantly bolstered the case for a continuing Treasury subsidy for the purposes of entertainment and morale. Moreover, it provided an egalitarian justification to underpin continuing state intervention in fostering a national culture both during and after the war. And aside from practitioners' own understandable zeal for promoting their arts, for the intelligentsia generally the act of high art to the people was all that survived of their pre-war ideals.[12] Nevertheless, historians have, by and large, broadly accepted as accurate the message placed before them by contemporary arts providers and enthusiasts. Typical is Paul Addison, who concludes that 'CEMA won a mass audience for drama, classical music, painting and sculpture. The secret of its success was that it literally took art to the people, that is out to the provinces and into popular venues ... factories and air-raid shelters', breaking down social barriers between audience and performer.[13]

11. PRO EL 1/6, CEMA minutes, 1 July 1942.
12. Weight, 'State, Intelligentsia', pp. 83–101; J. Minihan, *The Nationalization of Culture* (London, Hamish Hamilton, 1977), pp. 215–27.
13. P. Addison, *Now the War is Over* (London, Pimlico, 1995 edn), pp. 135–6; B. I. Evans and M. Glasgow, *The Arts in England* (London, Falcon, 1949), pp. 19, 42–5. The most comprehensive recent assessment, for example, concludes that 'during the six years of its existence CEMA had demonstrated that the receptivity of the public to the arts had exceeded all expectations', F. M. Leventhal, '"The Best for the Most": CEMA and State Sponsorship of the Arts in Wartime', *Twentieth Century British History*, 1 (1990), p. 316. See also A. Calder, *The People's War: Britain 1939–1945* (London, Jonathan Cape, 1969), pp. 372–3; A. Croft, 'Betrayed Spring: The Labour Government and British Literary Culture', in *Labour's Promised Land? Culture and Society in Labour Britain 1945–51*, ed. J. Fyrth (London, Lawrence & Wishart, 1995), pp. 199–203; Minihan, *Nationalization of Culture*, pp. 215–16, 225. A

Any assessment of wartime performance, of course, demands a recognition of pre-war attainment and its heritage. Certainly a strong tradition existed of community-based musical self-provision stretching back into the nineteenth century and beyond. Although professional/commercial entertainments had gained much ground by 1914, Dave Russell posits that, except for the very poorest in the community, 'the largest single element in the popular musical life of all ... was always provided by "the people" themselves': whether informally in the pub, street or house, or more formally in the concert hall or contest arena. (It was this tradition of self-provision which CEMA initially sought to stimulate and build upon.)[14] However, the social composition of those involved in formal, staged provision – the area where musical performance arguably breached the interface between the popular and classical repertoires – was more socially constricted: for brass bands, this meant the skilled and semi-skilled working class (and especially miners); and for choral societies the 'respectable lower classes' (that is, the lower-middle-class and worker elites), while audiences, at least at the larger concerts, were predominantly middle-class. During the inter-war period, participation became still more socially exclusive: with oratorio singing becoming increasingly a lower-middle-class rather than working-class activity, although brass-band playing remained a significant factor in the cultural lives of upper-working-class men.[15] Nevertheless, the popularity of these canons – which depended heavily on a standard repertoire – or the contemporary success of Richard Addinsell's *Warsaw Concerto* (composed for the film *Dangerous Moonlight*, 1941), attests only to the presence of a 'large and relatively unadventurous "middlebrow" musical audience of catholic rather than

(*note 13 continued*) dissenting view is offered by those commenting on wartime radio, who note the deliberate exclusion of good culture – as not being wanted – from the popularist Forces Programme: see D. Cardiff and P. Scannell, '"Good Luck Warworkers!" Class, politics and entertainment in wartime broadcasting', in *Popular Culture and Social Relations*, ed. T. Bennett, C. Mercer and J. Woolacott (Milton Keynes, Open UP, 1986), p. 99; and, more recently, by R. McKibbin, *Classes and Cultures: England 1918–1951* (Oxford, Oxford UP, 1998), p. 386.

14. D. Russell, *Popular Music in England, 1840–1914: A Social History* (Manchester, Manchester UP, 1987), p. 133; Leventhal, '"The Best for the Most"'.
15. Russell, *Popular Music*, pp. 170–1, 200–10; McKibbin, *Classes and Cultures*, pp. 388, 417.

discriminating taste'.[16] Likewise, the universal presence of 'popular classics' fitted together as 'light music' (well-loved ballads, 'the brilliant gems of Liszt', well-known overtures and symphonies) and played widely on the radio or at the cinema provides little evidence of a demand for 'serious' music. Contemporaries suggested (as they did during the Second World War) that it did, however, offer a potential bridge for cultural improvement; it is as likely that it simply reaffirmed the separate presence of a large 'middlebrow' constituency, and that, as such, 'popular' and 'high' culture were indeed 'almost completely divorced' by 1939.[17] Given that 'middlebrow' provision was also to form the staple diet of much that CEMA initially offered, a certain scepticism necessarily holds to any argument which claims a wartime originality here, or, moreover, for any dynamic conjuring up of a new mass arts audience during the Second World War, based as it was on more of the same.

CEMA officials, of course, acknowledged that, geographically, wartime isolation and dislocation provided a uniquely captive market for their product (or any mobile entertainment), to which the workers' long hours, transport shortages, and few alternative distractions all contributed. Other contemporaries, too, bore witness to the extraordinary circumstance of war. Basil Dean, as Director of the Entertainments National Service Association (ENSA), suggested that as the war progressed, basic 'Ensatainments [sing-song concert parties] were no longer adequate to [meet] the changed psychological atmosphere'; serious music, on the other hand, brought 'spiritual illumination' – focusing on 'a prophetic sense of the brevity of life'. Among practising artists, Stephen Spender was not alone in arguing that a 'revival of interest in the arts ... arose spontaneously and simply because people felt that music, the ballet, poetry and painting were concerned with a seriousness of living and dying with which they themselves had suddenly been confronted'.[18] Nonetheless,

16. McKibbin, *Classes and Cultures*, pp. 386–9, also citing E. D. Mackerness, *A Social History of Music* (London, Routledge & Kegan Paul, 1964).

17. Ibid.; P. Scannell and D. Cardiff, *A Social History of Broadcasting. Volume One 1922–1939, Serving the Nation* (Oxford, Blackwell, 1991), pp. 212–13; J. Stevenson, *British Society 1914–45* (Harmondsworth, Penguin, 1984), p. 438.

18. B. Dean, *The Theatre at War* (London, Harrap, 1956), pp. 375–6, 421; S. Spender, *World Within Worlds* (London, Hamish Hamilton, 1951), p. 286. For an examination of various aspects of a possible relationship between war and music, see B. Arnold, 'Music, Meaning and War: The Titles of War

politicians, arts administrators and practitioners, and commentators alike fully expected that wartime 'success' would lead to peacetime emulation. Underpinned by this presumption, both major political parties went on to endorse the principle and practice of state arts subsidy through the Arts Council as part and parcel of the new welfare state. Wartime triumphalism, however, was to counterpoise uncomfortably with a noted post-war failure to diffuse 'the best' in cultural provision. It was this failure, which ignored the enigma of wartime success, upon which critics and apologists alike alighted: thus the Arts Council, as CEMA's inheritor, was rebuked for its metropolitan bias or for neglecting education; for its inner conservatism in abandoning workplace performances or for an elitist focus which repudiated any broader definition of what constituted the arts.[19] Notwithstanding these shortcomings, a critical examination of the true and chequered foundation of this inheritance would, contextually, have been equally revealing in explaining post-war disappointments.

II

To argue that the war years saw the blossoming of a latent working-class demand for good culture is to accept also the contention of contemporary cultural providers that this process was essentially endogenously centred; or put another way, that good culture was not imposed from above in Reithian fashion in a ritual which largely ignored workers' own preferences. The matrix, of course, was never that precise. Sampling an innovatory programme of workplace performance, for example, was an introductory prerequisite which facilitated, rather than excluded, choice. And as we shall see, cultural

Compositions', *International Review of the Aesthetics and Sociology of Music*, **22** (1991), pp. 19–28; L. Botstein, 'Why Music in a Time of War?', *The New York Times*, 3 March 1991; A. Marwick, 'War and the Arts – Is There a Connection? The Case of the Two Total Wars', *War in History*, **2** (1995), pp. 65–86.

19. R. Shaw, *Arts and the People* (London, Jonathan Cape, 1987), pp. 30, 122–5; R. Hewison, *Culture and Consensus: England, Art and Politics Since 1940* (London, Methuen, 1995), pp. 48–9, 78–81; R. Hutchison, *The Politics of the Arts Council* (London, Sinclair Brown, 1982), passim; A. Sinfield, *Literature, Politics and Culture in Postwar Britain* (London, Basil Blackwell, 1989), pp. 39–58.

missionaries saw their role in terms of education and joint development, where both parties drew benefit. However, the pursuit of
institutional éclat also dictated paths other than those determined by
missionary sentiment or audience choice. Nor, necessarily, were
pre-war affinities to be readily abandoned by workers or providers.
All were likely, however, to have an important impact on the development or otherwise of a mass arts audience.

It was 'at the top' that the self-reinforcing pressures to conform
publicly to the positive values linking cultural provision to the allied
cause found clearest expression. This was particularly true of ENSA,
the true provider of live mobile entertainments *en masse*. The mutual
antipathy and rivalry that existed between ENSA and CEMA is well
known and illustrative; the former bitterly resented the widely held
view that, in concentrating on variety entertainments, it was pandering
to the 'lowest common denominator of taste, [while] CEMA was
synonymous only with the highest artistic integrity'. It was the latter's
offerings which Bevin and his Ministry of Labour welfare officials,
who directed Treasury funds for worker entertainment, originally
dismissed as being 'too highbrow' for factory audiences.[20] CEMA
officials, for their part, remained 'pique[d]' at being placed in a
'position of subservience to ENSA' when control of all factory entertainments – including its own musical initiatives – initially passed
into the hands of its rival until redeemed in March 1941. Sharing
billings with, or working under, ENSA had not suited CEMA's sense
of special purpose, and they subsequently 'refuse[d] to be associated
with work they [and artistes] considered to be unworthy', even
blackballing musicians who accepted ENSA engagements.[21]

By 1943, however, ENSA was also offering a repertoire of good
music and drama to the troops, and later to war workers. Characteristically, Mary Glasgow (CEMA's Secretary General) dismissed
this departure as an 'orchestral stunt' which, 'although tiresome',
would 'collapse before long'.[22] Dean's already noted comments

20. Dean, *Theatre at War*, pp. 134–5; PRO LAB 26/40, Godfrey Ince (Perm. Sec.
    Min. of Lab.) to Bullock (Min. of Lab.), 17 July 1940.
21. PRO LAB 26/35, notes by Rossetti (Min. of Lab.), 2 January 1941; EL 2/29,
    Glasgow to Kidd (Min. of Lab.), 1 February 1941; EL 1/7 CEMA minutes,
    19 October 1943; EL 1/16 CEMA Paper 169, 'Employment of Musicians for
    Factory Concerts'; Dean, *Theatre at War*, pp. 219–20.
22. PRO EL 2/38, Glasgow to Keynes, 6 November 1943.

attempt to set the change in a different context. As he explained to
Ministry officials, 'Ensatainment' was 'all very well in the early days
of strain when the provision of a certain amount of bright music
and fun during meal-times was a novelty'. Now concerts of a 'more
peaceful nature' were required to provide the 'necessary relaxation
that enables efficiency to be maintained'. Thus, while not 'necessarily
to be of a high-brow nature', future ENSA shows were increasingly
to be of a musical character. Nevertheless, shortly afterwards ENSA
launched its Symphony Concerts for War-Workers scheme to aug-
ment and replace mealtime variety performances.[23] This followed
the success of similar forces concerts, and of the regional record-
lending libraries and factory clubs established by Walter Legge,
ENSA's autocratic Director of Music, who throughout, vigorously
promoted the cause of classical performance.

However, ENSA's enthusiastic embrace of good music was neither
exactly altruistic nor internally driven. The armed services had consistently pressed for higher standards of performance, including more
serious music and drama. Politicians and the press were equally
critical of past offerings, and particularly (as befitted the guardians
of public morality) of the vulgarity deployed by ENSA's bedrock
comedians.[24] This was material which ENSA and the service chiefs
thought that British troops neither wanted, nor should have. Minis-
terial concern in March 1942 about an alleged further lowering of
standards saw Dean attempting to defuse further criticism by reducing
comedy and variety provision. Essentially he was also conforming
to that wider wartime discourse linking cultural provision to the
spiritually positive and uplifting. Yet the wholesale dismissal of Ensatainments remained quintessentially a 'from the top down' phen-
omena. Ministry of Labour Regional Welfare Officers reported that
while worker reactions to existing ENSA fare varied from week to

23. PRO LAB 26/42, Dean to Smith, 15 June 1942; LAB 26/42, Dean to Min.
    of Lab., 10 August 1942; Dean, *Theatre at War*, p. 376.
24. PRO EL 2/38, Glasgow to Keynes, 4 October 1943; 'Culture at Arms', *Punch*,
    16 February 1944; Dean, *Theatre at War*, pp. 201–3, 457; *Hansard*, Vol. 376,
    col. 2078, Vol. 385, cols 1722–3, Vol. 399, cols 8–9, Vol. 416, cols 1726–31.
    J. A Crang, 'The British Soldier on the Home Front: Army Morale Reports,
    1940–45', in *Time to Kill: The Soldier's Experience of War in the West
    1939–1945*, eds P. Addison and A. Calder (London, Pimlico, 1997), pp. 60–74,
    suggests that aside from hierarchical preoccupations with poor morale, the
    citizen-soldiers themselves thought ENSA offerings to be 'too low-brow and
    suggestive in tone'.

week (because of the poor quality of specific acts), generally the shows were still received favourably, while the mere suggestion that they be discontinued drew 'considerable opposition'.[25] Mass-Observation reported similarly favourable shop floor responses, where

> [ENSA] concerts were definitely looked forward to with considerable zest – perhaps more as a landmark in the week than for themselves .... But there was too a certain eagerness for the concert itself. There was a more frantic rush than usual to get up to the canteen and grab a place the moment the buzzer went, and afterwards there was always a lot of interesting talk and criticism.[26]

Such occasions could be boisterous affairs where enthusiasms found expression through banter and personal ribaldry between audience and performer, seen as a mark of approbation by the former, but frowned upon in certain quarters. It was these self-same managers, other middle-class employees and sectors of the skilled workforce who were also more likely to express dissatisfaction with the quality and content of the shows, and be to the fore in suggesting their replacement with CEMA-type performances of a more cultural nature.[27]

Not all shared the preoccupations of promoting good culture. Ministry welfare officials had more pressing priorities, the foremost of which was and remained shop-floor morale and productivity; it had little immediate concern or interest in cultural improvement or its associated broader themes. Ministry policy was, by necessity, geared 'to cheer up workers ... deprived ... of normal opportunities for seeing films, concerts, music-hall shows and so on' where success could 'be judged solely by the extent to which workers *are* cheered up'. By contrast, the provision of serious music was thought likely to exclude large numbers in working-class audiences. Indeed the Ministry's own reports of 1941 suggested that:

> There is increasing evidence ... that many of the CEMA concerts are failures. They are being given to workers who don't want them, and who – as one factory manager said – feel they have been cheated of their weekly fun. Another factory manager said that many of his men

25. PRO LAB 26/42, Smith to Regional Welfare Officers, 5 March 1942 and précis of replies; for a popularist endorsement, see Priestley, *Postscripts*, pp. 49–53, 11 August 1940.

26. Mass-Observation, *War Factory* (London, Gollancz, 1943), pp. 76–7.

27. Ibid., pp. 77–8; Mass-Observation, *People in Production: An Inquiry into British War Production* (London, John Murray, 1942), p. 219.

would appreciate good music but not in their meal-break when they are tired and dirty. To factories such as these CEMA concerts, from our standpoint (and we have thought from CEMA's also) should not go.[28]

A greater selectivity over venue and audience was later to contribute significantly to CEMA's reported success, reducing, as it did, the incidence of rejection. At the time, however, all touring parties were routed directly by ENSA's London headquarters with little prior consultation or benefit of local intelligence as to specific need or suitability. Petty jealousies aside, as Lord May's Interdepartmental Entertainments Board of Enquiry reported, 'this system has not worked too well ... [as] CEMA parties have been sent to factories where they have not been suitable to the audiences to be entertained'. When judged at first hand, therefore, evidence from within industry suggests no widespread preference existed for good music and against variety provision. Nor do such reports identify the ubiquitous presence of a mass arts audience at shop-floor level. Indeed, the Ministry rejected such premises by subsequently confining its own provision 'to entertainment of the type organized through ENSA, leaving such factory owners as may consider that their own work people would prefer CEMA type concerts free to make their own arrangements direct'.[29] In such negative circumstances did CEMA regain from ENSA its operational independence in the industrial sector.

Undoubtedly the severe shortage of professional talent during wartime, coupled with the far-reaching scale of ENSA's commitments, diluted further what critics like Priestley dubbed the already low standard of 'rubbishy light entertainment offered by theatre managers and the BBC' during peacetime; bluntly, it was the least talented that most welcomed the security of an ENSA contract. Complaints from below, however, centred on an absence of star acts and a lack of diversity, coupled with a preference for straight entertainments – or more particularly, fewer unfunny turns.[30] Moreover, if ENSA

28. PRO EL 2/29, Rossetti, summary of meeting between Min. of Lab. and CEMA, 3 March 1941; see also LAB 26/35, Kidd to Durst, 7 April 1941.
29. PRO LAB 26/41, Inter-Departmental Entertainments Board First Report, March 1941, para. 83.
30. J. B. Priestley, 'The Work of ENSA', *Picture Post*, 28 June 1941; Calder, *People's War*, p. 372; H. M. D. Parker, *Manpower: A Study of Wartime Policy and Administration* (London, Longman, 1957), pp. 409–11; PRO, LAB 26/42, Vincent to Smith, 9 March 1942 and North Midlands Region to Smith (see précis above).

standards remained fairly constant, quality was increasingly judged against nationally broadcasted factory entertainments such as *Workers' Playtime*. Such contrasts explain, in part at least, the popularity of ENSA's grandiose symphony recitals and perhaps also CEMA's successes, for anecdotal evidence suggested that certain factory audiences preferred 'from time to time a measure of good music' as a variant to ENSA's offerings. As Mary Glasgow (and even Ministry of Labour officials) appreciated, CEMA concerts could be sold to 'the workers as something special and out-of-the-ordinary'.[31]

CEMA's guiding ethic also changed considerably during the war. As Leventhal comments, 'there was an avowedly popularist tone to CEMA's early pronouncements' which posited that 'ordinary people experience art as practitioners, not as consumers' and where professionals played an auxiliary and enabling role.[32] This missionary emphasis, which saw arts for the people as a social and educational service for cultural self-improvement, was to be slowly whittled away amid much animosity and 'rumours of half-filled village halls and apathetic audiences'.[33] First support for amateur drama activity was curtailed and finally, by 1944, its itinerant music travellers, who toured the country stimulating local self-help groups, were discarded. Professional performance became the benchmark within an organizational culture which sought to preserve excellence during wartime. Keynes's accession to the chairmanship only reinforced this trend, as CEMA became progressively more metropolitan oriented, 'less popularist' and emphasized entertainment rather than education.[34]

Yet in one key area the missionary ethos was retained and expanded. From the start the 'importance of the canteen concert in factories was stressed, ... and it was agreed that during the present emergency the maximum effort of the council should be expended in this field'.[35] Nor was this simply the rhetoric of the centre. Eve

---

31. PRO LAB 26/41, Inter-Dept. Ent. Board, March 1941, para. 83; EL 1/16, CEMA Paper No. 172, minutes of Factory Concerts Conference, 1 December 1943; LAB 26/42, Smith aide-mémoire, 14 March 1942.
32. Leventhal, '"The Best for the Most"', esp. p. 295; see also Hewison, *Culture and Consensus*, pp. 33–42.
33. PRO EL 1/17, CEMA Paper No. 176, R. Vaughan Williams, 'CEMA and Rural Music', 25 January 1944; see also correspondence file PRO EL 2/73.
34. Leventhal, '"Best for the Most"', pp. 297, 305–7; E. White, *The Arts Council of Great Britain* (London, David Poynter, 1975), pp. 38–54.
35. PRO EL1/6, CEMA minutes, 28 May 1940.

Kisch, a provincial Regional Officer, recalled her arrival in early 1941 from London 'as a lonely missionary' when CEMA was 'almost completely unknown in the North-West ... . It is obvious that the diffident sales-talk and generous sample concerts of those early days met a genuine need', especially in the factories – which she saw as CEMA's 'chief war-work'.[36] Here, simultaneously the arts could 'do their bit' for the war effort and work to stimulate a future audience. For those in authority seeking to promote a national culture the canteen concert provided a guaranteed coincidence of workers and live performance. As Kisch's successor, the composer and musicologist Peter Crossley-Holland, ingenuously pointed out,

> few men and women will make the initial effort to seek out good music for themselves. Many people barely know of the existence of good music. The main way of creating conditions under which music will gain new converts is by taking music to a man's place of work. Works canteens supply these conditions. A concert given in a canteen during a meal can hardly be escaped ... . Although concert conditions are obviously better in a room set aside for the purpose, where quiet prevails, it is found that on the whole only the devoted attend.[37]

Notably the sums allocated to factory concerts, and earmarked specially for this purpose by the Treasury, increased through the war from some £5,000 in 1940 to £45,000 by 1944, so that finally a little under half of CEMA's expanding music budget was allocated to this programme.

Similarly, CEMA saw its subsidized hostel work, another area of protected growth, as providing 'not merely an amelioration of hostel living conditions' for war-workers separated from home and family, but centrally 'an opportunity [for] creating new audiences that will demand in future the good music, drama and painting they have enjoyed in wartime'. Hostel work was 'of more importance than anything else undertaken by the Drama Department,' CEMA declared, 'both from the point of view of the players and audience'.[38] For those educators seeking to renegotiate the relationship of artist to society, such work provided an extraordinary opportunity to break down the class barriers of mutual incomprehension that

36. PRO EL 3/1, report by Eve Kisch, October 1944.
37. PRO EL 3/1, report by Crossley-Holland, November 1944.
38. PRO EL 1/16, CEMA Paper No. 171, 1943, Paper No. 161, 'Plays in R.O.F., Industrial and Rural Hostels for Workers July 1942–June 1943'.

segregated audience and provider. On tour actors and artists lived, slept and ate with factory workers in the hostels in which they performed – although CEMA accepted that 'wise [hostel] managements will see that artists do get a little preferred treatment'! Before them CEMA saw a separated world wholly lacking in theatre etiquette or tradition, where only 2 per cent of its audience had seen a stage play before; here were workers – as Evans and Glasgow so tactfully put it – who 'hardly realised that the peopled stage before them was not an inanimate cinematographic screen'.[39]

Such guiding missionary zeal, however simplistic or misplaced, was significantly less apparent out in the field; here CEMA's artiste ambassadors provided music very much in perfunctory and traditional terms. At the most basic of levels, experience dictated that 'it was fatal if the artistes gave the impression that they were singing or talking down to the audience'; that this so obviously occurred is borne out by CEMA's request that 'frequent confidential reports should be sent by the hostels on the artistes and programmes'. Charles Landstone, CEMA's Assistant Drama Director, was more critical still. Landstone held special responsibility for hostel touring parties, which he considered vital in building a vibrant future repertory audience and which also received considerable and favourable press coverage. Yet in his view, CEMA under Keynes 'was always more interested in "glamour"' activities (especially in London), whereas hostel tours were thought mundane and unspectacular; consequently CEMA 'always approached them with the happy glow of an aristocratic lady going slumming'.[40] Nor was it just in hostels that this new relationship broke down. Internal CEMA reports on factory concerts noted one common fault to be an aloof separateness or 'old-fashioned outlook on the function of artistes in society' by organizers and performers alike, 'resulting in a faulty attitude to

39. Ibid.; Evans and Glasgow, *Arts in England*, p. 44 (also Dean, *Theatre at War*, p. 189); Jack Lindsay, cited in D. Watson, 'Where do we go from here?: Education, theatre and politics in the British Army, 1942–1945', *Labour History Review*, 59:3 (1994), p. 65.

40. PRO EL 1/16, CEMA Paper No. 163, 'Hostel Conference 24 June 1943'; Charles Landstone, *Off-Stage: A Personal Record of the First Twelve Years of State Sponsored Drama in Great Britain* (London, Elek, 1953), pp. 58–9; for CEMA's own self-confident published assessment see *The Arts in Wartime: A Report on the Work of CEMA 1942 & 1943* (London, CEMA, 1944), pp. 16–17.

workers' instead of the idealized rapport of 'one craftsman addressing a group of fellow craftsmen'.[41] Clearly, and to say the least, the practical transference of good culture across existing social barriers was, and remained, problematic. Below there was a ready acceptance of the traditionally and contemporaneously familiar, with no great demand for radical change. Among artistes existing prejudices and practices frequently remained firmly entrenched, the social barriers between audience and performers tenaciously intact. And above, while many could be deemed enthusiastic missionaries who, for a variety of reasons, were eager to enlighten, educate or impose (depending on the viewpoint adopted), cultural aloofness remained reputedly endemic and misunderstanding commonplace. Indeed, perhaps it would have been more surprising had this not been the case.

III

It would still be disingenuous, if not intellectually dishonest, to ignore contemporary testimony supporting the widespread belief that both CEMA and ENSA found new audiences, albeit temporarily and maybe by default, for the arts during the Second World War. A brief overview of the raw data indicates the scale of provision: ENSA gave 364 full-scale Symphony Concerts for War-Workers in the three seasons from October 1943 to May 1946 while, more spectacularly, the BBC Symphony Orchestra broke the record for Saturday night takings – previously held by Gracie Fields – at Aldershot barracks. By its high point of 1944 CEMA was providing 3,169 factory and 371 hostels concerts annually within an overall total of 6,140 directly provided performances.[42] If our attention is drawn to this (and other similar wartime experiences), it is in part because something out of the ordinary did occur: the arts, perhaps somewhat loosely defined, were taken directly to 'the people' who, in turn, responded in a way not altogether expected.

Viewing concert attendance and delivery as a conduit for patriotic

---

41. PRO EL 3/1, Jeanette Jackson (CEMA), 'Report on CEMA in Industry', 1944; EL 1/16, CEMA Paper No. 172, 'Mins of Factory Concert Conf. 1 Dec. 1943'.
42. Dean, *Theatre at War*, pp. 217, 229; CEMA, *The Fifth Year: The End of the Beginning. Report on the Work of CEMA for 1944* (London, CEMA, 1945), pp. 9, 31.

expression may, in part, help explain favourable wartime responses to the arts at a time when contemporary exaggeration and utilitarian necessity promoted – and inwardly reinforced – distorted images of conformity. Alan Sinfield, arguing that the Second World War 'was understood [and experienced] mainly through rumour, radio and writing' where the 'requirements of wartime "morale" transformed the relationship between the state and cultural production', posits that CEMA was one of these 'new organisations created to get people thinking along the right lines'.[43] Yet overall audiences responses were frequently unpredictable, contradictory, and less than mechanical. The personal attestation which recorded this (as distinct from the publicly reported testimony) sits uneasily with wartime representations of Britain as a nation of newly enfranchised high cultural consumers. It is this evidence, set alongside an evaluation of the concert content and scale of diffusion, which we will now explore.

Publicly, CEMA maintained that its programme had, 'with few exceptions', met 'enthusiastic and intelligent audiences, to an extent which confounds some critics' – or even that it had 'met with a success which was embarrassing'.[44] The reality was somewhat less conclusive, more variable, as an internal report on an early factory tour in Southampton during August 1940 indicates:

> Monday: This particular factory was said ... to provide an excellent audience from the ENSA point of view ... . [But] our party found the audience a little 'tough' and difficult to warm up.
>
> Tuesday/Wednesday: Tuesday cancelled because of air raids ... . Wednesday: turned up to find no arrangements had been made.
>
> Thursday: ... The first concert was given to a hall packed with 1,800 factory workers, mostly men ... . They clapped every item enthusiastically afterwards, and more important still, most of them seemed to be listening and enjoying themselves during the actual performance ... . [During an air raid] the girls in our shelter had a gramophone playing jazz; ... it was pretty clear that they did not want a[n emergency] concert from us ... . We emerged just in time to reach the next factory ... . Everyone was eating and clinking cups of tea and getting up to fetch more during the concert ... . [W]e stood unnoticed in the corner, wondering how to begin and feeling a little unwanted, but suddenly someone started clapping and it spread

43. Sinfield, *Literature, Politics*, pp. 23, 47.
44. CEMA, *Arts in Wartime*, p. 8; CEMA, *Fifth Year*, p. 13.

rapidly through the room to the accompaniment of cries of 'come on, get started' and so forth. After that all went well. We decided to stick to things that were simple and well-known.[45]

Such experiences were neither extraordinary nor confined to the first years of the war, when conditions were more haphazard. Operational independence from ENSA, which as intended brought a greater flexibility over the selection of venue, certainly promoted more favourable responses. Even the once sceptical Ministry of Labour now recorded that, within the boundaries of its expectation, overall from all regions and 'in every case the [CEMA factory] tours have been highly successful and greatly appreciated'.[46] Nevertheless, within this rubric of general approbation, individual audience responses, even to the same concert tour, remained unpredictably varied. A CEMA report from August 1941 on a Bristol tour noted that in one factory 'where we were warned to be prepared for a cold reception', we found instead it was 'uproarious', with 'great attention and an audience growing in numbers'. The following day and venue, however, they faced a 'very apathetic audience of about 70 which gradually warmed up to a moderate enthusiasm'. This nevertheless delighted the welfare officer, who promptly asked for a return visit. Later that week the group performed in an acoustically ill-suited room,

> holding about 500 men and a few girls, most of whom were being served from the service canteen during the first half of the programme. Very few of them seemed to have any inclination to listen – a small amount of applause, courteous enough, was the outcome and we all felt strongly that ENSA would best meet these peoples' wishes rather than ourselves.[47]

The typical CEMA factory concert party consisted of two singers and a pianist, or a singer, pianist and one other instrumentalist. The vast size of some canteens – really too big for accompanied soloists or trio ensembles when set against the disruption of mealtime clatter and chatter – poor factory and internal organization and, in the

45. PRO EL 1/12, CEMA Paper No. 68, 'Factory Concerts for ENSA', memo by E. M. Stokes, 12 September 1940 (for the repertoire played see text attached to n. 66).
46. PRO EL 2/29, Rossetti to Glasgow, 16 August 1941.
47. PRO EL 2/29, CEMA report on Bristol factory tour, August 1941.

earlier days, the variable quality of pianos and sound equipment, were just some of the many problems encountered. Nonetheless, such obstacles, along with an initial and natural reluctance to engage CEMA parties could be, and were, frequently overcome. As one Ministry official wrote of a concert at the Royal Ordinance Factory (ROF) in Hooton:

> I felt a bit diffident when the concert was first arranged as I was doubtful whether it would be appreciated by the majority of workers. The success, however, exceeded any expectation. The canteen was more crowded than usual; there was more attention, appreciation and applause. It was, no doubt, the most popular concert held in their works. I spoke to many of the employees afterwards and they told me how they would welcome further concerts of this nature.[48]

Transferring worker 'enthusiasm' for CEMA's musical repertoire beyond the factory gates (where performances were no longer inescapable or free) proved more problematic. This was true even of the semi-captive wartime environments of hostel life, where leisure activity remained collectively organized. Once one entered the sphere of private time and self-selected entertainment, it seems, resistance to the culturally challenging or alien found singularly fuller expression. Workers, CEMA's Regional Officer in the West Midlands recorded in 1944, remained

> very suspicious of anything that they think might be 'highbrow' and this may explain why our music has not been nearly as successful in these hostels as our plays, but it is difficult to understand why we have not succeeded in breaking down this prejudice in the hostels, as the residents all work in the factories where our concerts appear to be extremely popular.[49]

Interestingly, the West Midlands was deemed to have more than its 'fair share of stony ground' because it was 'so heavily industrialised'; indeed Kisch thought generally that the 'hardest public to please is that of industrial towns'![50] Yet a lack of transference was common elsewhere: in the South-West, for example, CEMA regional staff

48. PRO LAB 26/35, J. W. Brown (Labour Officer, ROF Hooton) to Percival (Min. of Lab.), 22 July 1941; for corroborating testimony, see Percival to B. W. Vincent, 25 July 1941.
49. PRO EL 3/1, report by Tom Harrison (CEMA Midlands Regional Officer), October 1944.
50. Ibid.; E. Kisch, 'Music in Wartime', *Our Time*, July 1943, p. 11.

reported that 'music in the hostels seems to have made little progress ... . Our concerts are wanted by a small minority only and this minority does not appear to grow'; the North Midlands noted that in contrast to factory provision, 'only a small proportion of the residents in industrial hostels seem to enjoy a concert of straight music', but added that 'once trained' they provided 'excellent material for a play – yes, even Shakespeare, Ibsen and Shaw – or for a comparatively "highbrow" variety show'.[51] That most audiences could not 'yet relish a "straight" concert' (but enjoyed drama and variety) was variously attributed, not to the music itself or the closer links between staged drama and traditional working-class entertainments, but to an 'exhaustion induced by wartime factory conditions' – for 'aural perception involves more strain than ocular' – and the frequent presence of 'all-female audiences' in hostels; or to unsympathetic hostel managements and 'indifferent (in some cases bad) presentation and badly chosen programmes'; or simply because 'these people are unable to concentrate or listen to any one thing for very long' belonging, as they do, to a 'class who had not yet learned to use their [sic] leisure'.[52]

Undoubtedly Ministry of Labour Welfare Officers did provide a critical link in the chain of factory evaluation and subsequent development, especially as initially CEMA lacked its own regional organization. And at the factory and hostel level CEMA continued to remain dependent. Indeed, all at CEMA agreed that 'much depends on the enthusiasm of the local welfare officer', not only in terms of securing invitations and in preparatory organization but also in generating an enthusiastic and compliant audience. Where this was lacking, or where the welfare officer or hostel management favoured alternative entertainments provision, CEMA performed badly. Again, in hostels particularly it was argued that staff showed little interest or had 'no idea how to sell our type of concert to the resident'.[53] Moreover, as Mass-Observation reported in 1942: 'Welfare to any extent [only] exists in about half of factories, ... [and] in a great

51. PRO EL 3/1, report by E. Kisch, October 1944; report by Cyril Wood (CEMA South-West Regional Officer), November 1944.
52. Ibid; report by Harrison, October 1944.
53. PRO EL 3/1, report by Crossley-Holland, November 1944; report by Carlisle, June 1944; report by Wood, November 1944; EL 1/16, CEMA Paper No. 161, 'Plays in ROF, Industrial and Rural Hostels for War-Workers, July 1942–June 1943'.

many of these it is thought of as something *purely physical* ... . It recognises that the worker has an inside (a stomach for instance)' but this 'recognition stops at the neck', excluding the mind. Overall, anyway, there existed a dearth of 'sympathetic and competent' welfare managers.[54] These were not particularly auspicious circumstances for those seeking to promote entirely new forms of workplace practice where active factory-based co-operation, indeed enthusiasm, was essential.

The criteria used to select suitable factories and hostels for CEMA's offerings were determined, in large part, by stereotypical expectation, added to the immediate experiences and predilections of the officials concerned. Broadly, audiences were partitioned into skilled and unskilled workers – reinforced by gender divisions – and by a company's leisure traditions. For example, ROF's were thought

> not particularly satisfactory ... they have no background and no future. The work is not particularly skilled and so the general standard of intelligence among employees is not particularly high. They are mainly 'transferred' war-workers and include a lot of poorly educated young girls, the most difficult audience in the world.[55]

This evaluation reflected CEMA's longer-term hopes of fermenting a workplace culture of arts appreciation after the war. In other ways also, when allocating limited resources, it not unrealistically viewed skilled workers as potentially sympathetic and the more likely converts. Even ENSA had noted that when its organizers sent CEMA parties to 'the rougher works ... the artistes suffered from a disastrous lack of appreciation'. Dean also held that as the war progressed and the age of service recruits rose, so too did the mean intelligence level – in part explaining the increased popularity of good music.[56] Nevertheless, as earlier testimony suggests, generalizations based on skill levels or age, or which saw mixed audiences as preferable because 'all-women audiences were often too emotional or hysterical', while those composed entirely of men were 'generally dull', were far from accurate predictors of audience reaction.[57]

54. Mass-Observation, *People in Production*, pp. 353–4, 357.
55. PRO EL 3/1, report by Harrison, October 1944.
56. Dean, *Theatre at War*, pp. 134–5, 212; PRO LAB 26/35, B. W. Vincent to Rossetti, 12 December 1940.
57. PRO EL 1/16, CEMA Paper No. 161, 'Plays in ROF, Industrial and Rural Hostels for War-Workers, July 1942–June 1943'.

CEMA had proclaimed privately to Ministry officials in early 1941 that it 'had no interest in providing factory concerts simply for the entertainment of workers'; instead it wanted to lead them, through repetition, reinforcement and refinement, to an appreciation of good music.[58] Its independence from ENSA thereafter restored, CEMA engaged in a continuing process of 'gradually weeding out' those factories to whom it was 'just another concert', instead concentrating on 'those who have shown that they really want and appreciate us'. Of the 28 factories initially selected as potentially sympathetic on Tyneside and Teesside (which between them received some 114 concerts over a 21-month period) five 'never progressed beyond the try-out stage', five others 'eventually proved unsuccessful', 16 'turned out really good' and two were 'outstanding'.[59] The West Midlands lacked even this sense of progress. CEMA's Regional Officer, writing in 1944, recalled:

> Even though CEMA has been going for four years we are still doing much pioneer work. Certainly the ground is softer now and centuries of industrial frost appear to be thawing – indeed many seeds have taken root. A first event of any description is always very discouraging. Then, very grudgingly and often ungraciously, we are asked to follow it up.[60]

That 'pioneer work' still dominated CEMA's agenda is hardly surprising when the frequency of visits to individual factories remained so low. Every factory on the Ministry of Labour's approved list received one or perhaps two ENSA concerts per week. Yet in the West Midlands, for example, CEMA parties visited selected factories about once every three months. Hostels, being fewer in number and more dependent, were slightly better accommodated: here a £1,250 per annum allocation to cover the region's 40 hostels allowed for occasional visits of drama and music once a month, while again ENSA visited each week. Such levels of service devalue further any claim that CEMA developed (or even discovered directly) a mass arts audience. Moreover, with regional and factory welfare officers consistently requesting significantly greater provision than was

58. PRO LAB 26/35, aide-mémoire, H. Kidd (Min. of Lab.), 15 January 1941.
59. PRO EL 3/1, report by Wood, November 1944; see also report by Anne Carlisle (CEMA Eastern Regional Officer), June 1944; Jackson, 'Report on CEMA in Industry'.
60. PRO EL 3/1, report by Harrison, October 1944.

available, ultimately it meant that CEMA remained an inefficient wartime diffuser of national culture.[61]

Even limited diffusion meant bringing together a mismatch of audience and repertoire, forcing a concentration on the popular and known, rather than the esoteric and innovative. In effect the border between 'the arts' and entertainment frequently became blurred, as CEMA variously sought to separate its provision from the 'variety' provided by ENSA, marry its own missionary and artistic imperatives, and cultivate an audience potentially resistant to, and unfamiliar with, its preferred product. Initially the repertoire offered was avowedly populist, with few concessions made to an overtly educationalist ethos. Commenting, for example, on one of the earliest concerts in March 1940 at Lockheed Brake, Leamington, the Industrial Welfare Society reported:

> the hall was packed, completely quiet and attentive during the half-hour recital. Mr Trefor Jones gave a delightful programme of ballads. [Romantic] Songs such as 'Rose of Tralee', 'Moyra My Girl', 'Here's to the Best of Us', 'Roll the Clouds Away', 'Singing along with You', were evidently well-known by most of the audience and the announcements were greeted with murmurs of approval. ... There was no attempt to make it a formal occasion; it was simply a works entertainment ... . The programme was not at all educative, in the sense that it contained nothing unfamiliar or difficult to appreciate, but it seemed to an outside observer that it gave emotional relief and refreshment to these factory workers as well as the experience, however unconscious, of good singing.[62]

CEMA generally advised a contrasting programme of half an hour, broken into five- or ten-minute slots, of music of the 'clearly rhythmic type that needs no close attention and adds vitality and good cheer', added to that which is 'simple and lovely and natural enough to command silence'. What was not required was 'clever or abstrusive music nor long programmes'.[63] Familiarity was the key. Particularly successful were those songs or classical excerpts already known by the audience through the cinema. In this way CEMA won itself a hearing.

61. Ibid.; Calder, *People's War*, p. 372; Weight, 'National Culture', p. 86.
62. PRO EL 1/11, CEMA Paper No. 42, Appendix.
63. PRO EL 1/10, CEMA Papers Nos. 20 and 26 by Sir Walford Davies, January and November 1940.

For some this approach was wholly unacceptable. An extremely popular concert in Wolverhampton, given by the well-known baritone George Baker and soprano Olive Groves, was described by the part-time local CEMA organizer as 'altogether odious'. He continued, 'I don't know what is generally given to factory audiences by CEMA, but if it is this type of stuff, I can see absolutely no point in differentiating between a CEMA and ENSA concert.' Mary Glasgow agreed that the programme was too populist but typically added:

> we really have got to be very careful of frightening our working-class audiences with apparently highbrow programmes. I am convinced from the concerts I have seen and from the reports and advice I have from all our people the best stuff 'gets across' – provided you don't tell the people what it is beforehand .... By the same token there is a very great deal of the 'best' which is genuinely easy and popular. ... We mustn't be afraid of being popular and simple in our efforts to avoid being vulgar and sentimental. Above all we mustn't let people call us highbrow.[64]

Voices from industry tended to reinforce Glasgow's interpretation. Congratulating CEMA on an earlier concert given by Groves, in which she performed a medley of well-known songs, the Managing Director of Vauxhall Motors commented that the 'men do appreciate a good singer, ... provided we realise that it is not advisable to get very far "over their heads"'. The Ministry of Labour, not surprisingly, supported this assessment. Concerts would be more popular still, it suggested, if artistes, for example, were instructed to substitute a '"straight" song for an operatic aria'.[65]

Typically, by the late 1940 CEMA's factory fare, advertised somewhat misleadingly as 'good light music', comprised of an interspersed concert of folk songs and well-known ballads (for example, *King Charles*, the *Volga Boat Song*), extracts from the populist repertoire (the *Prologue* from Leoncavallo's *Pagliacci* and the *Toreador's Song* from *Carmen*) and better-known instrumental pieces (*A Londonderry Air*, Kreisler's *Liebesleid*, a Mozart minuet).[66] Certain items, having once established themselves, became repertoire standards. Sarasate's

---

64. PRO EL 2/29, Jack Hollins to Glasgow and Glasgow to Hollins, 16 September and 1 October 1940.
65. PRO EL 2/31, C. J. Bartlett (Vauxhall Motors) to Glasgow, 26 April 1940; LAB 26/35, I. Thomas (Min. of Lab., Cardiff) to Kidd, 13 August 1941; EL 2/29, Rossetti to Glasgow, 16 August 1941.
66. PRO LAB 26/35, CEMA concert circular [c. December 1940].

Gypsy Airs was one such. Crossley-Holland, dismissing the piece as 'highly ornamented' and 'in poor taste', doubted he had 'been to a single factory concert which included a violinist in the programme in which this work has not been played. ... It is not by any means necessary to approach an audience by way of the familiar', although he added 'this is always a safe course'.[67]

Indeed there remained marked divisions over repertoire policy. Musicians, by and large, opted for safety first; a majority of programmes were offered *ad hoc* – some performers even took requests! Audience tastes also varied: according to one 'enlightened' industrial adviser, 'some want noise, others like a quiet programme'. Only later in the war, running somewhat behind its practice of grading factory venues, did CEMA offer graduated programming complementary to its educative philosophy, starting with elementary concerts (a vocal–piano recital) and developing upwards, through instrumental interludes, finally to a string quartet.[68] Indeed earlier CEMA attempts to take more substantive orchestral works to working people – the so called People's Concerts scheme – were quickly dropped after moving from well-known choral and orchestral highlights. ENSA's War-Workers' Symphony Concerts, also, were built on core popular classics, although it also offered a symphonic repertoire.[69] Reporting on such a concert given in Glasgow by the London Philharmonic in 1944, a local Co-operator offered the following assessment of co-workers:

> To most of them it was their first symphony! Few appreciated Tchaikovsky's No. 5. The Mastersingers Overture was 'familiar' therefore, favourably received, and obviously gave rise to the following questions and requests. Do symphony orchestras play any overture? e.g. Lilac Time [Berté, popularised by Noel Coward]; Madame Butterfly; Tannhäuser; Dance of the Hours [episode from Act 3 of

67. PRO EL 3/1, report by Crossley-Holland, November 1944, commenting particularly on a concert featuring the well-known violinist Ida Haendel and pianist Joan Davies. The full programme included the *Praeludium* and *Allegro* (Paganini-Kreisler), *Spanish Dance* (Manuel de Falla), *Toccata and Fugue in D minor* (Bach-Tausig) and *Gypsy Airs* (Sarasate).

68. *Picture Post*, 15 May 1943; PRO EL 3/1, talk by M. E. Trotter (Lab. Manager, Reynolds & Co.) at CEMA Conference on Music Speaks Scheme, 1944; Jackson, 'Report on CEMA in Industry', 1944; Kisch, 'Music in Wartime', p. 11.

69. PRO EL 1/13, CEMA Paper, 'Peoples' Concerts', 16 June 1941; Dean, *Theatre at War*, pp. 221–2; for a sample programme see LAB 26/35.

Ponchielli's *La Gioconda*]; Nutcracker Suite ... . [V]ery many requests are made for the popular Strauss Waltzes to be heard in their classic form. To summarize, I would state that the majority ... listened to the really high standard works of the programme with passive receptiveness, but that mood was replaced by active listening when the lighter items were rendered.[70]

That some names were known stands as part testament to the established listening habits (if continuing naiveté) of this new audience. Reports from Ministry of Labour regional officials in mid-1944 generally confirmed audiences' preference for the familiar, a sentiment which found resonance within ENSA's own musical advisory council.[71] When ENSA, however, staged a parallel programme of string orchestra concerts in smaller towns it played 'to houses in some cases not one quarter booked up' and the initiative was abandoned. Similarly Tom Harrison, CEMA's Regional Officer in the West Midlands, in explaining the lack of popularity of its musical provision in workers' hostels, concluded that the 'uninitiated' simply remain 'frightened of our concerts'. Workers flocked to ENSA symphony concerts, he thought, because they saw it as a 'natural development from their traditional brass bands'; but CEMA 'concerts are, of necessity, more of the chamber music type, and with these men, as with so many of the general public, there is an unreasonable prejudice against anything even suggestive of chamber music'.[72] The further, it seemed, one stepped from performance strongly linked to the culturally familiar towards the esoteric, the singularly more unfavourable the response.

IV

The evidence, both published and private, is frequently contradictory. Harrison, despite decrying the lack of a broader public for chamber music, notes occasions when factory audiences warmed to a string quartet. Spender and Dean, in testifying to a sea change in popular

70. PRO LAB 26/44, A. Black (Scottish CWS) to Hamilton (Min. of Lab.), 27 June 1944.
71. Dean, *Theatre at War*, pp. 227–9; for Regional Welfare Officers' responses to programme selection, see PRO LAB 26/44.
72. PRO LAB 26/44, Corbett (Min. of Lab., Newcastle) to Heighway (Min. of Lab.), 7 July 1945; EL 3/1, report by Harrison, October 1944.

tastes towards the arts as the war progressed, nevertheless both acknowledged that the 'ordinary chap' from the fire station, canteen and barrack room still preferred light and cheerful music – indeed, that only classical broadcasts caused the radio to be switched off.[73] Even *Picture Post*, a chief purveyor of the ideal of arts for the masses, was famously to conclude that the troops preferred to ogle the familiar feminine images from popular commercial culture to those of high art.[74]

How then should we interpret the evidence? The wartime climate of public conformity to positive and 'inclusive' depictions of British life – in this case arts for all – explains in part contemporary and subsequent distortions. Viewed in this light, ENSA's cultural reformation was first and foremost a reaction to well-publicized establishment and media criticism of its reputed low standards which stood outside what was expected. Promoting good music addressed this 'shortcoming', while decorously lifting its self-esteem. Yet ENSA's 'orchestral stunt' was also to be presented as further evidence of, and as a direct rejoinder to, a strongly articulated audience need. This verdict, however, was not passed first-hand by factory workers themselves; instead it was based largely on the selective mediated accounts promoted by arts enthusiasts and their wartime allies. Fostering the arts conformed to elite ideals which imagined a culturally enfranchised wartime community *en masse*, enjoying 'the best' of provision. Judged, however, by CEMA's own generally more sanguine internal appraisals, worker reaction to its lunchtime provision varied markedly (as, of course, did the composition of factory audiences). A minority (notably skilled male workers) was identified as potential converts; the majority, however, and for a variety of reasons, was effectively discarded. Moreover support for good music (although not for drama) became conspicuous by its wholesale absence among hostel audiences, or noticeably less marked among those who, unlike its captive 'music-while-you're-eating' public, retained an element of choice over attendance. Negative or nonconforming

---

73. PRO EL 3/1, report by Harrison, October 1944; Spender, *World Within Worlds*, p. 270; Dean, *Theatre at War*, p. 365.

74. *Picture Post*, 'What is a Pin-Up Girl?', 23 September 1944, a response to *Picture Post*, 'Art Goes to the Forces', 27 February 1943 and 'Modern Artists Paint for the Forces', 29 July 1944. For an excellent assessment, see M. Rothenstein, '"Can we be Educated up to Art?" Notes on Lecturing to the Army', *Horizon*, **40** (April 1943), pp. 270–7.

reviews, however, formed little part of contemporary published thinking.

Overall, this reassessment provides little foundation to support claims for the wartime emergence of a truly mass arts audience. At best the diffusion of CEMA's product remained partial and, for those workers fortuitously included on CEMA's lists, the frequency of concerts remained low. To argue that such provision, even had it been universally well received (which simply was not the case), exerted sufficient influence as to radically alter existing leisure practices or prejudices is less than tenable. In recognizing also the need significantly to improve programming standards beyond the already familiar 'middlebrow' and to abolish mealtime performances as being unsatisfactory, CEMA set benchmarks that we too should acknowledge, and against which we should temper wartime claims. Only if we judge potential, not performance, can we marry these findings with traditional assessments, and then only on the presumption that CEMA's qualified successes would be replicated and improved upon in those areas it had already deemed less promising, and which were left largely untouched by its wartime activity. Any judgement on post-war potential, moreover, would also have to acknowledge that wartime and peacetime conditions – in which the former on balance aided the process of cultural dissemination – differed substantially. In terms of creating a new arts audience, therefore, it was more likely a case of 'thousands' than 'millions like us'.

'When Work Is Over':
Labour, Leisure and Culture
in Wartime Britain

Jeff Hill

... the subject I have been given is practically a death trap.[1]

Towards the end of the momentous edition of *Picture Post* of 4 January 1941, after the arguments for reform in areas such as employment, health, education and housing, the writer and broadcaster J. B. Priestley turned his attention to the quality of life.[2] *Picture Post* was perhaps the most popular wartime forum for discussion of 'reconstruction', and its themes showed a marked convergence with sentiments expressed in the labour movement.[3] Though not itself an organ of the movement, many of its writers were people of progressive views. The 4 January edition, entitled 'A Plan For Britain', included contributions from A. D. Lindsay, Julian Huxley, the economist Thomas Balogh and the architect Maxwell Fry – all of whom would doubtless have subscribed to a 'social democratic consensus'. Priestley certainly did. There had been a hint of it as early as 1934 in his screenplay for the popular Gracie Fields film *Sing As We Go*. As an

1. J. B. Priestley, *The Arts Under Socialism* (London, Turnstile Press, 1947), p. 5.
2. J. B. Priestley, 'When Work Is Over', *Picture Post*, 4 January 1941. For similar sentiments see Herbert Read, *To Hell With Culture: Democratic Values Are New Values* (London, Kegan Paul, Trench, Trubner & Co., 1941), part of the series 'The Democratic Order' edited by Francis Williams. I am indebted to Nick Hayes for bringing this essay to my attention.
3. *Picture Post's* edition of 4 January 1941 was among the most influential issues the journal ever produced. The playwright Sean O'Casey wrote in to say so (18 January 1941) and the overwhelming sentiment in the many letters from readers printed over the next couple of months was supportive (though some readers cancelled their subscriptions, complaining of 'socialistic' influences). Fifteen-year-old Michael Dunnett wrote from Winchester College to say that 'it is the best thing done here since "Rights of Man"' (25 January).

established novelist, dramatist, journalist and (most recently) radio broadcaster who the BBC feared was attaining demagogic status in his 'Postscript' talks, his views carried great influence, especially with a 'popular' audience. He had, moreover, clear associations with the Left. By lending his weight to questions of leisure, recreation and culture there seemed a reasonable hope that such issues might be introduced into the labour movement's thinking on reconstruction, and that reforms in leisure might be added to those being considered on material problems. The questions to be posed by this essay are, therefore: did Labour's contribution to the discourse of reconstruction during the Second World War encompass the qualititative as well as the material aspects of life? And, if so, how did the labour movement propose to deal with leisure and culture? They are questions that historians, in the welter of debate on 'the people's war', have usually overlooked. The essay will argue that the wartime labour movement, and especially the Labour Party, evinced little interest in questions of leisure and the quality of life. In contrast with the immense attention directed at reconstruction in material life, and in view of the strong legacy bequeathed by the socialist movement in matters of recreation, issues of leisure and popular culture were generally felt to be safe in the hands of their traditional commercial and voluntary providers, helped along by the occasional intervention of a benevolent state.

I

In his contribution to *Picture Post* Priestley assumed a position on leisure that was not dissimilar to that of many labour critics. He attacked those who regarded leisure as a stupefying, do-nothing alternative to work, and urged instead a conception of leisure in which people (among whom he rightfully acknowledged a special problem for women) gained enjoyment through *creative* endeavour, by being engaged in pursuits and hobbies in which they exercised their own imagination and intelligence. Through creative leisure – 'recreation' in the true Victorian meaning of the term, as opposed to mere 'amusement' – Priestley imagined that people would find satisfaction and society would achieve stability. Indeed, he gave his argument immediacy by suggesting that the lack of an outlet for creative energies was the cause of much of the trouble in the world

– and instanced Hitler as a case of a 'creative artist who has gone wrong'. The contrast (explicit or implied) with Nazism was frequently used in wartime discussions of reconstruction, and in Priestley's article was reinforced by the use of a characteristic *Picture Post* framing device – the photograph. The essay was accompanied by an illustration of 'young people enjoying life at an Essex bathing pool'. It showed young swimmers in a setting of rustic clapboard houses shaded by trees. The juxtaposition suggested a harmony between people and environment, evoking a peculiarly English image of 'strength through joy'. It neatly underpinned Priestley's message. For the new, reconstructed Britain to be the utopia of which people dreamed, rather than the dystopia they might dread, a proper concern should be cultivated for the spiritual aspects of life.

The argument was only partly to do with the 'quality' of culture. Priestley was astute enough to recognize that a missionary attempt to improve the leisure habits of the working classes – a 'Third Programme' approach, as one post-war Labour writer was to put it – was not likely to have much impact. It was perhaps less quality and more *control* that concerned him. Though he was not above delivering, as the need arose, scathing critiques of popular pleasures – as when, for example, he upset the citizens of Nottingham in his *English Journey* (1934) with some especially caustic remarks, both on their beloved Goose Fair and on the good citizens themselves [4] – Priestley usually had a feel and a respect for what ordinary people liked doing in their spare time. In the same *English Journey* he had recalled (through a characteristically Priestleyian haze of nostalgia) the northern popular culture of his early years:

> When I was a boy in Yorkshire the men there who used to meet and sing part-songs in the upper rooms of taverns (they called themselves Glee Unions) were not being humbugged by any elaborate publicity scheme on the part of either music publishers or brewers, were not falling in with any general movement or fashion; they were singing glees over their beer because they liked to sing glees over their beer; it was their own idea of the way to spend an evening and they did not care tuppence whether it was anybody else's idea or not; they drank and yarned and roared away happy in the spontaneous expression of themselves. [5]

4. J. B. Priestley, *English Journey* (Harmondsworth, Penguin Books, 1977 edn), pp. 130–6.
5. Priestley, *English Journey*, p. 377.

It was precisely this ability to take control of their leisure – to engage in a 'spontaneous expression of themselves' – that Priestley admired and which formed the core of his plea of 1941.

In making it, he was drawing from a complex discourse on leisure and mass culture that had been articulated in various forms and from different quarters since the previous century. It contained a number of overlapping and sometimes contradictory ideas. Many of them circulated in the labour movement, which was the main ideological context for Priestley's thinking.

The British labour movement has had an enduring interest in questions about what workers do with their spare time.[6] In its early years the Labour Party inherited from the various branches of the socialist movement an intellectual baggage which placed the question of leisure in an explicitly political, indeed class, context. The research of the historian Chris Waters has shown very clearly that, in the quarter-century or so before the First World War, socialists were exceedingly sensitive to the influence of pubs, music halls, the popular press, sport and other forms of commercial leisure. These hedonistic pleasures were seen as a threat to the self-disciplined and self-improving socialist fellowship that movements like the Independent Labour Party (ILP), the Social-Democratic Federation (SDF) and its successor the Communist Party (CP), as well as the various groups formed into the Co-operative movement, were attempting to promote. Popular commercial culture was not, therefore, to be ignored. It was a key target in the battle waged by socialists against the evils of capitalist society. Commercial popular pastimes were felt to be inculcating 'capitalist values', not least among which was an inertia and indolence of mind on the part of the very workers whose support the socialist movement was seeking. For socialists, therefore, whether of a Marxist or an ethical persuasion, the struggle to change society was to be waged on cultural, as well as on economic and political, ground. The weapon to be used was an independent and assertive brand of socialist culture which fostered creativity, a communitarian spirit and a new socialist way of life.[7]

6. See R. McKibbin, 'Why Was There No Marxism in Great Britain?', *English Historical Review*, 99 (1984), pp. 297–331.
7. C. Waters, *British Socialists and the Politics of Popular Culture* (Manchester, Manchester UP, 1990), esp. ch. 6. See also S. Fielding, P. Thompson and N. Tiratsoo, *'England Arise!': The Labour Party and Popular Politics in 1940s Britain* (Manchester, Manchester UP, 1995), ch. 6. For the puritanical strain

However, it is doubtful whether much of this spirit remained in the labour movement, particularly at the centre of its increasingly national-based bureaucracy, by the eve of the Second World War. Alongside the anti-capitalist strain of thinking, the socialist movement itself had always contained other views and strategies on mass culture. Broadly speaking, there were two approaches: to use terms that have been applied in the rather different context of working-class education they might be described as 'substitutionist' and 'statist'. The 'substitutionists' proposed an alternative cultural form, built up from within the resources of the socialist and labour movement itself, whilst the 'statists' looked to the agencies of the state, often the municipality, as the mechanisms through which to provide a culture for workers better than that available in the commercial market-place.

By the 1930s the 'substitutionist' outlook had become marginal. It was most evident in those aggressively left-wing towns and villages, often in Scotland, Wales or the north of England, which were frequently associated with the Communist Party and sometimes known as 'Little Moscows'.[8] The borough of Nelson in Lancashire provides an interesting, if often overlooked, example where a combination of socialist culture and strong trade unionism produced a distinctively oppositional Labour stance. In 1939 the MP for the district, Sydney Silverman, was among the first to call for the inclusion of 'reconstruction' in the government's war aims.[9] Similarly aggressive and self-confident socialist attitudes could be found in other areas, often associated with the Communist Party and nurtured in left-wing educational initiatives like the Labour Colleges movement and the Plebs League. There was a recognition in such quarters that culture

(*note 7 continued*) that sometimes came into socialist thinking see N. Baker, '"Going to the Dogs" – Hostility to Greyhound Racing in Britain: Puritanism, Socialism and Pragmatism', *Journal of Sport History*, 22 (1996), pp. 97–119.

8. See S. Macintyre, *Little Moscows: Communism and Working Class Militance in Inter-War Britain* (London, Croom Helm, 1980). S. G. Jones, *Workers At Play: A Social and Economic History of Leisure 1918–1939* (London, Routledge & Kegan Paul, 1986).

9. See J. Hill, *Nelson: Politics, Economy, Community* (Edinburgh, Keele UP, 1997), chs 4 and 6; J. Liddington, *The Life and Times of a Respectable Rebel: Selina Cooper (1864–1946)* (London, Virago, 1984); E. O'Connor, 'Fighting for Peace, Waiting for War: Left-Wing Attitudes in Nelson to European Re-Armament', *Journal of the North West Labour History Group*, 22 (1997/98), pp. 48–60; *Nelson Gazette*, 21 November 1939.

and politics were inseparable, both in understanding the status quo and in opposing it.

Much more in evidence than these attitudes, however, was the 'statist' approach. It typified the labour movement in the Second World War. It placed a premium on the cultivation of mind and body through the provision of libraries, theatres, swimming baths, recreation grounds and community centres. It saw the state as an instrument, not for the oppression of the workers, but for enhancing voluntary leisure activity and curbing the worst excesses of commercial leisure provision. The inspiration for this was no less likely to come from the Left than it was for the 'substitutionist' approach. The veteran Social Democrat Dan Irving, for example, had produced a wonderfully detailed plan of municipal action for the pre-1914 SDF, including in it schools, libraries and theatres as part of the drive to bring 'comfort, convenience and healthful enjoyment to the common people'.[10] In the 1920s the ILP had expressed similar views in a pamphlet by Arthur Bourchier entitled *Art and Culture in Relation to Socialism*. Bourchier condemned the 'sordid, money-grubbing state of society' which failed to educate working people in anything other than vocational training. He claimed that society was afflicted generally by a lack of sensitivity to art and culture. 'It is painful to see that, as things are today, people live and die surrounded by ugliness; that the purer and more lasting joys never once enliven and enlighten their sordid, toilsome and monotonous lives.' The beauty to be found in music, painting and literature – though not, Bourchier felt, in the 'inane, vulgar and disappointingly trashy' American cinema – should be made available to all as 'common property', to create 'a race of happy, cultured people'.[11]

'Statism' brought the Labour Party close to a quite different strand of opinion, one which had developed largely outside the labour movement but which was to exercise considerable influence in wartime Britain. This might be characterized as a 'middle-class intellectual' concern with leisure. It had a long history, experienced something of a revival in the 1930s, and during the war was associated with writers and thinkers such as Priestley, George Orwell and Cyril Connolly, whose journal *Horizon* was a forum for much debate. The

10. D. Irving, *The Municipality From a Worker's Point of View* (London, Twentieth Century Press, n.d.), p. 15.
11. A. Bourchier, *Art and Culture in Relation to Socialism* (London, ILP Publication Department, 1926).

agenda for wartime discussions had been fashioned by some of the issues considered during the 1930s. Leisure, as R. H. Tawney put it, had become a 'common possession'.[12] But how it was to develop – whether as a blessing or a curse of modern society – was the fundamental question. Opinions varied. Some inclined towards the belief that it was a blessing. The academic Cecil Delisle Burns, a former member of the Joint Research Department of the Labour Party and Trades Union Congress (TUC) in the 1920s, warmly embraced the new leisure forms, seeing the motor car, cinema and radio, the passion for hiking and rambling, and even the old bogey of gambling, as pursuits that provided excitement and new ideas which would 'break the crust of acquiescence' in society.[13] But Burns was an exception. Most other commentators approached the subject more cautiously. Henry Durant, writing in the late 1930s, pointed to the need for a more rewarding form of work.[14] Tawney and the New Education Fellowship saw the problem as residing essentially in education, where changes were felt to be needed to enable children to think more for themselves; otherwise, leisure opportunities would be lost for want of a creative spirit. This was particularly felt in relation to the seemingly all-consuming medium of film. The desire, expressed frequently at this time, for film criticism to accompany literary criticism in the school curriculum stemmed from the feeling that films had the power to close off enquiry by diverting attention away from real issues and the means of solving them. William Farr of the British Film Institute, for example, warned of the 'vicarious resolutions' to familiar problems offered in escapist cinema. The danger, he claimed, was that people would come to accept submissively the 'vicarious satisfaction of instincts and desires which could and should be actually satisfied'.[15] It was in this vein that Roger Manvell, mindful of the ambiguous relationship of film to propaganda in wartime, produced one of the first attempts at serious yet popular film criticism, conceived in 1941 and published in 1944 – 'to raise the standards of the ordinary film-goer'. 'Entertainment', said Manvell, echoing one of

12. R. H. Tawney, introduction to W. Boyd and V. Ogilvie, *The Challenge of Leisure* (London, New Education Fellowship, 1936), pp. ix–xvi.
13. C. Delisle Burns, *Leisure in the Modern World* (London, George Allen & Unwin, 1932), esp. pp. 78–81.
14. H. Durant, *The Problem of Leisure* (London, George Routledge & Sons Ltd, 1938), pp. 31, 253.
15. Boyd and Ogilvie, *Challenge of Leisure*, pp. 131–4.

Priestley's main sentiments, 'should re-invigorate and re-create its customers. We look for pictures which serve such recreation.' [16] Manvell's work provides a good example of how pre-war issues were injected with vigour by the context of the war. The problem of leisure, conceived in the 1930s as a problem of people ill-prepared for a life in which work did not consume their entire energy, became in the 1940s a topic in which matters of democracy and national identity were increasingly seen to be present.

II

If there was one labour arena in wartime Britain where these themes were taken seriously it was the trade union movement. The TUC had long been associated with a number of ventures, expressed in weekend and summer schools, which had at their core the interlinked themes of education, leisure and culture. It acted as a forum for a number of convergent initiatives within the labour movement. H. H. Elvin, Secretary of the Clerks and Administrative Workers' Union and a member of the General Council, played a particularly active part in drawing the various strands together. A vignette of this world of labour recreation was provided in the critical month of May 1940 when, with Dunkirk in the offing, the annual workers' lawn tennis championships were held for the last time during the Labour Party conference at Bournemouth.[17]

As far as was possible, bearing in mind the many physical obstacles the war placed in the way of normal associational life, the trade union movement sought to carry on 'business as usual' in its educational and recreational work. But the war emergency was not normal, and many new issues came to the fore. Typical of these was the concern with women workers, illustrated in the series of day and weekend schools arranged throughout the country from 1942 onwards. They were organized by local trades councils and aimed specifically at women, many of whom had come into the labour market for the first time as a result of the war. The schools usually justified themselves in terms of attendance. At Bolton in May

16. R. Manvell, *Film* (Harmondsworth, Penguin Books, 1950 edn), pp. 9, 21, 243–7.
17. Trades Union Congress, *Annual Congress Report* (London, TUC, 1940), p. 11.

1943, for example, Florence Hancock, Chair of the TUC's Women's Advisory Committee, spoke to a group of 50 women on the theme of 'Women's War and Post-War Problems'.[18] Thus an established educational method was infused with a new topic occasioned by the war situation. Similarly, the TUC continued to be in contact and to give encouragement by way of speakers and delegates (and some financial aid) to bodies such as The Workers' Educational Association (WEA), the National Council of Labour Colleges (NCLC), the extra-mural studies bodies of Oxford and Cambridge, Ruskin College (though its TUC scholarships were suspended in 1940), the Wood-craft Folk and the Youth Service Volunteers (YSV), of which the General Secretary of the TUC, Walter Citrine, was a trustee. Except for the YSV, all were existing initiatives which in wartime found a new topic of concern in the problem of youth.

In this respect the YSV was particularly interesting. It reveals a number of cultural themes which were specific to the war situation. The scheme encouraged young people in their mid- to late teens to combine a summer holiday with work of national importance. Felling timber for pit-props, harvesting and fruit picking were the most common, usually with a marked gender division of functions. It sought to promote the virtues of a healthy outdoor existence, in contrast to the boredom and negativity that were claimed to be part of adolescent life during school holidays or when awaiting call-up. Its promotional literature foregrounded the theme of national unity. The volunteer camps attempted to draw together people of all social classes, educational backgrounds and geographic regions into a melt-ing pot of national service based on hard work and camaraderie. It was a youthful microcosm of the nation pulling together in the right use of leisure, and served a valuable purpose in propagating the idea of national unity.[19]

Youth and education were two aspects of culture that commanded much attention at the TUC in the early stages of the war. They were linked to a fear, often implicit rather than outrightly expressed, of the causal connection between wartime disruption and juvenile delinquency. The General Council, for example, had been concerned that the raising of the school-leaving age to 15, scheduled in the

---

18. TUC Archive, Modern Records Centre, University of Warwick (hereafter MRC), MSS 292/819.31, 14–16.

19. Youth Service Volunteers, *Report*, Summer, 1943 (MRC, MSS 292/826.28/3).

Education Act of 1936 for 1 September 1939, had been postponed because of the war emergency. In addition to its general anxiety over the delay, the TUC evinced great concern over the educational plight of children from evacuated areas, where the schools had been closed. There were many children who had not been evacuated, and equally many evacuees who had returned to their homes. All these children had been lost, not only to teaching and learning, but to provisions such as school medical supervision and meals. A great many, it was felt, were also likely to have found their way into employment below the statutory age. Some opportunities to intervene in the handling of these matters were provided by new arrangements made by the Board of Education. Committees at both national and local levels had been created to advise on the welfare, physical training and recreation of young people, and the TUC successfully lobbied for trade union representation on these committees alongside employers. Concerns over youth and education also filtered into the Labour Party, where the problems were sometimes voiced in more alarmist language. Speaking at the annual conference of 1941, Harold Davies of Leek alluded to the danger of juvenile delinquency resulting from deficiencies in the education system, especially in the bigger cities. In the same forum two years later Professor Joad, a distinguished member of the popular radio programme *The Brains Trust*, referring to the problem of large classes and overworked teachers, said: 'it seems to me ... that we are bringing up in this country ... a generation of little gangsters and barbarians, because they are not being properly taught and supervised at school'.[20]

Out of this kind of thinking and campaigning had grown the realization that the war was presenting the opportunity to inaugurate major changes. As early as January 1940, for example, an internal memorandum in the TUC's Educational Committee, setting out a draft for a brochure on adult education, made the point very plainly:

> When the war is over there will be no easy resumption of the normal ways of life, for they will have disappeared into history. International Relations and trade, political and economic organisation, the

20. TUC, *Annual Congress Reports*, 1940, pp. 135–8; 1941, p. 144; 1943, p. 199. These concerns had a parallel in the USA at much the same time. See C. Gilbert Wrenn and D. L. Harley, *Time on their Hands: A Report on Leisure, Recreation, and Young People* (Washington, DC, American Council of Education, 1941). The authors feared that youth might not be willing to fight to defend democracy if it felt it had no stake in it.

distribution of wealth and plans for social progress – all will start from a new level with new problems and opportunities ahead.[21]

By the time Mr Attlee addressed Congress in the autumn of 1941 the issue was open for discussion: 'the principles for which the Trade Unions have fought throughout their history have now been recognised as something fundamental to civilization ... the claim for economic and social security is made, not for some, but for all'.[22] The following year the Educational Committee's report to Congress noted that 'Perhaps no aspect of reconstruction is more discussed than that of education, and from every quarter come proposals for the post-war period.'[23]

One quarter was that of the TUC itself. By 1943 it had turned its collective thoughts to the related question of leisure. The Southport Congress, held in the wake of the Beveridge Report and the growing interest in reconstruction, discussed a number of post-war reforms. Among them was 'the problem and right utilisation of leisure'. It was undoubtedly the major initiative on this theme from the labour movement in the war years. It began with a proposal from Tom O'Brien, Secretary of the Theatrical and Kine Employees and a member of the General Council. O'Brien, whose members worked in the leisure industry, felt that leisure time was usually disregarded, in contrast to the attention now being given by both state and trade unions to such matters as working conditions, education and, following Beveridge, social services. Mindful of foreign totalitarian practices, O'Brien was quick to dispel any notion that 'correct' leisure forms should be prescribed: 'they wanted no regimentation in this country, no State marionettes, no frustration of individuality'. The TUC had already expressed its hostility to a report coming out of Conservative Party headquarters in which, it was alleged, compulsory physical training was being proposed as a means of 'toughening' youth. This was regarded by the TUC as a 'very long step towards the Nazification of the young citizen'. But O'Brien nonetheless pointedly directed his concern at the adolescent population.

21. Memorandum of Education Committee (9 January 1940) marked 'Private and Confidential' (MRC, MSS 292/812.2). See also speech of Ernest Bevin to 1940 Congress (*Annual Congress Report*, p. 322–8).
22. TUC, *Annual Congress Report*, 1941, pp. 265–8.
23. TUC, *Annual Congress Report*, 1942, p. 48; also p. 283.

Were they, at ... the most important years of their lives, to hand over their leisure hours to irresponsible purveyors of pleasure and education, to have their minds distorted for profit-making motives only? All the great work of the movement and of the State for youth and adults could be torpedoed and lost by indifference in this manner.[24]

O'Brien's speech contained echoes of the old socialist, anti-commercial theme. This was to be expected. There was a strong left-wing presence in the Theatrical and Kine Employees.[25] But there was also a new element in O'Brien's argument which had parallels in other wartime circles. It concerned the relationship of leisure and war. Leisure was not simply another item to be added to the reconstruction shopping list. It took on a new significance in wartime. Its *right* use was essential for the maintenance of democratic freedoms. There were many implications embedded in this type of thinking. What is noteworthy in much of the discussion of reconstruction – we have already seen it in Priestley – is the comparison with Nazi Germany. This might assume different guises: on the one hand, the idea that state power could be used for good, as against evil, purposes; on the other, that unless a decent society of responsible citizens could be created, the threat of fascism to society would be ever present. Moreover, there might also be a motive of self-interest in reconstruction. In O'Brien's resolution the 'irresponsible purveyors of pleasure' were not Nazi propagandists but businessmen, possibly American, and especially film-makers. O'Brien's trade union had been engaged in a lengthy battle during the 1930s to secure some protection from the state against foreign influences. O'Brien himself had called for the protection of 'British cultural and educational standards from alien disparagement and infiltration' in a speech to the TUC six years earlier.[26] At this time it had been fear of European influences that prompted his demands. By 1943, with an eye to the post-war years and the possibility of a return to unemployment, it may well have been the fear of American competition that was behind O'Brien's plea for attention to leisure. There was, ingrained in the notion of the *right* use of leisure, a sense of that leisure being *British*. This was one way in which wartime leisure discourse continued to

24. TUC, *Annual Congress Report*, 1943, p. 304; also pp. 71, 303.
25. See S. G. Jones, *The British Labour Movement and Film, 1918–39* (London, Routledge & Kegan Paul, 1987).
26. Quoted in ibid., p. 71.

shift attention in the labour movement away from any vestiges of 'substitutionist' thinking, and towards the idea of leisure as a national possession.

In practical terms, there were three consequences of Congress's acceptance of the O'Brien proposal. First, the drafting of a policy statement – 'The Problem of Leisure'.[27] Its philosophy was compounded of three key principles: responsibility, judgement and voluntarism. Since trade unionism itself was felt to be the product of active citizenship, so it was felt that mental inertia should not influence leisure pursuits: 'the mass of the population shall not be merely passive recipients of provided entertainments and pastimes'. The document made no attempt to prescribe what was to be enjoyed, but it did show concern that the public should be capable of discriminating about the value of what was being offered to it, especially by commercial producers. For this reason, much emphasis was placed upon the part to be played by voluntary organizations – 'especially characteristic of the social life of this country' – in providing leisure. Though commercial provision was not objected to – 'to the limit desired by the public' – the ideal of associational leisure, neither over-commercialized nor state-controlled, nor even (as in the old model of the German Socialist Party) Labour-controlled, was fundamental. '[P]eople should not have done for them things which they can do for themselves.' Fears were strong of the standardization of leisure resulting from a centralized provision. Voluntary associations were felt to be the guarantee of diversity and variety against 'dominance by a single hand'. As with Priestley, and the later musings on a similar theme of T. S. Eliot,[28] the question of culture in democracies could not be separated from the dangers perceived in fascist or other totalitarian cultural systems.

Second, in pursuing this issue Congress had agreed that a number of labour movement bodies with interests in leisure should be contacted for their responses to the draft document before it was finalized. These were received during the summer and autumn of 1944. They reveal interesting perspectives, and an insight into other work being carried out within the labour movement on the broad

27. Originally intended to be put before Congress in 1944, its completion was delayed and the final version of the document not printed until 1947. (*The Problem of Leisure*, Introduction by V. Tewson, London, TUC, n.d.)
28. T. S. Eliot, *Notes Towards the Definition of Culture* (London, Faber & Faber, 1948).

issue of 'culture'. In general terms, the responses agreed with the stance taken in 'The Problem of Leisure'. The WEA, for example, was warm in its reception of the TUC line, agreeing on the role of continuing education as a means of securing freedom and initiative for young people. The WEA had, in fact, pioneered a scheme in 1936 with a grant from the Carnegie Trust to promote youth education in a number of industrial areas, working alongside the Labour League, the Toc H, and the Young Communist League to introduce social and political issues to young people.[29] Equally supportive of the TUC was the Co-operative Union, which sent a copy of its pamphlet *Co-operative Youth Movement*, an earnest attempt to promote active leisure for children through bodies such as the Playways Group, aimed at 7–10-year-olds. The 'Playways Promise' was an interesting, if pious, attempt at a reformation of manners through leisure:

> In all things I do I will try to be a worthy member of my Playways Group.
> I will love my playmates.
> I will tell the truth.
> I will always do my best.
> I will be clean.
> I will be kind to birds and animals.
> I will think of children in other countries as my friends.[30]

This approach characterized the Co-op's general outlook on leisure – it was a route to responsibility and good citizenship, something that promoted enjoyment but also 'informal education': 'an interest in drama, an interest in camping, in music, in outdoor activities, may be the cause of an awareness of other people or a responsibility to the community'.[31]

Education emerged as a strong theme in the response of the Workers' Film Association (WFA), a body closely involved with the Labour Party and keenly aware of the power and influence of commercial popular culture, as well as of the lowly critical status accorded to film as an artistic medium. It had been active in organizing circuits and distributing films during the early stages of the war.

29. MRC, MSS 292/812.2, Memo dated June 1944 from WEA.
30. *Co-operative Youth Movement* (MRC, MSS 292/812.2).
31. MRC, MSS 292/812.2, Memo from Co-operative Union, Holyoake House, August 1944.

Not surprisingly, the WFA called for the educating of the public into an appreciation of film and its potential. This being so, it emphasized rather more than other labour bodies the role of the state – in providing 'correct training', film appreciation through the educational curriculum, funds for schools to purchase sound projectors and films, and for the creation of a national film library.[32]

In complete contrast, yet representing an equally important aspect of working-class leisure, was a response from the Club and Institute Union (CIU). This was one of the oldest working men's organizations, established in the 1860s and having almost 3,000 affiliated clubs by the 1940s. It was overwhelmingly a male-centred body. Its Secretary acknowledged that women were generally not admitted in their own right, attending only as guests of the men. In his response he clearly felt obligated to stress the educational activities of the CIU, though this was not easy, since its main purpose was relaxation, especially drinking.

> [T]he great majority of working men, perhaps because their school education finished at the early age of 14, or possibly before then, are not inclined, having reached manhood, to engage in any form of education which involves study, and the promotion of education by the Union has been an uphill struggle.[33]

The Secretary went on to point out that games and sports, both indoor and outdoor, along with concerts, flower shows and dances, aroused the greatest interest among members. It is significant that he expressed all this in a defensive, almost apologetic, tone, making every effort to draw out the 'improving' side of the CIU mission. 'Every endeavour is made to develop the spirit of sportsmanship and tolerance, and a right sense of neighbourliness and civic duty and responsibility.'[34] For all this, the CIU's was perhaps the most authentic of all the responses received by the TUC in revealing what 'leisure' really meant to working men. It differed markedly from that of the NCLC, which came from its Secretary, the left-winger J. P. M. Millar, and which conceived of leisure as a means to an end. For Millar there was no such thing as 'mere recreation' – spare time was a way of stimulating interest in trade unionism and the labour movement, and thus of counteracting the apathy that he claimed existed among

32. MRC, MSS 292/812.2, Memo from WEA, June 1944.
33. MRC, MSS 292/812.2, Memo from CIU, September 1944.
34. Ibid.

many nominal members. Though not a Communist, Millar exhibited some of the earnest attitudes about leisure usually found on the far Left, and his idea that the working man's social life should be built around the trade union did not coincide with the general line of the TUC.[35]

The third outcome of the 1943 Congress resolution was contact with a simultaneous initiative in a related field. The Youth Advisory Council of the Board of Education, in planning for the post-war youth service, had invited the TUC to submit observations on the training of adolescents through leisure activities. The TUC responded with a lengthy memorandum which contained a restatement of the sentiments outlined in 'The Problem of Leisure'. The Youth Service, and the proposed Young People's Colleges, were seen as a service at a stage in continuing education when encouragement and premises should be given to permit adolescents to organize their own leisure. 'It is ... not desirable that Education Authorities should do for young people through the Youth Service those things they may be expected to do for themselves.'[36] Thus, the authority could make available a swimming-pool, but the swimming club should be organized and administered by young people themselves. A philosophy was evolving which drew together state and voluntary initiatives. It was to be the characteristic feature of Labour thinking on leisure in the years to come.

How far were these ideas taken up by the Labour Party itself? The authors of a recent study of the Labour Party and popular politics in the 1940s claim that many Labour leaders and activists wanted to reform popular leisure. It is argued that when the party won power in 1945 it embarked on a crusade, only to be defeated by popular resistance. The attempt served to give Labour a reputation as, to use the authors' phrase, 'the wowser's party'.[37] As far as the war years were concerned, however, little of this appears to have surfaced. In fact, there was little indication of any strong desire by the Labour Party, as a party, to take a principled stand on qualitative issues of culture and leisure. This was the case at various levels of the party. Constituency organizations do not seem to have asserted

35. MRC, MSS 292/812.2, Memo from NCLC, November 1944. The TUC did take up this idea in the form of Centre 42 in the early 1960s, but with no great success (TUC, *Annual Congress Reports*, 1960, p. 435; 1961, pp. 453–5).
36. TUC, *Annual Congress Report*, 1944, p. 78.
37. Fielding et al., *'England Arise!'*, p. 161 and ch. 6 passim.

themselves on this matter.[38] Even such a lively labour movement as
that of Nelson came up with few direct statements on leisure. The
local party was unrelenting in its pursuit of reconstruction – Silverman
even calling for the *immediate* implementation of the Beveridge
Report – but this was conceived almost entirely in material terms.
The main issues in 1945 were seen by the local Labour press as
being social security, education, housing, employment, health and a
lasting peace.[39] Nor was there very much discussion nationally in
the Labour-inclined press. The *Daily Herald*, in its otherwise full
coverage of the Southport TUC of 1943, did not comment on
O'Brien's resolution.[40] The *New Statesman* provided little on any
aspects of leisure. *Tribune* was more assertive, especially Orwell's
column. *Horizon*, not officially a Labour journal, carried some lively
material, notably Orwell's influential essay 'Raffles and Miss Blandish', which appeared in the autumn of 1944 and contained some
censorious remarks on the reading habits of the people. It explored
some of the themes present in O'Brien's speech to the TUC of the
previous year, subtly weaving together interconnections between
morality, totalitarianism and the influence of America. There was a
distinct post-war relevance to Orwell's argument, which seemed to
amount to the view that totalitarianism did not reside only in fascism
or communism. The target of his attack, *No Orchids For Miss
Blandish*, a novel about American gangsters by the popular writer
James Hadley Chase, had all the hallmarks of contemporary pulp
fiction, principally a lack of moral centre. Orwell pointedly contrasted
this version of the genre with the earlier ethical stories of Raffles
by E. W. Hornung, whose hero was a cricketer, with all the ideological
connotations that sport communicated. The sting in the tail of
Orwell's essay was the revelation that the amoral world of American
gangsters and police portrayed in *No Orchids for Miss Blandish*

38. There is a need for more detailed research on constituency organization during
    wartime.
39. *Nelson Gazette*, 22 December 1942; 5, 19 June 1945.
40. See *Daily Herald*, 6–9 September 1943; 1 October 1943. The *New Statesman
    and Nation* put full employment 'right in the forefront' of reconstruction (28
    April 1945), and closed the year in which Labour had swept into power with
    the pessimistic comment: 'We have never seen any reason to believe that the
    violent deaths of millions and the social upheavals of continents would produce
    any kind of Utopia. Why should they?' (22 December 1945).

sprang from an uncomfortably close imagination: James Hadley Chase was an Englishman.[41]

The views of intellectuals are one thing; their influence on political thinking is harder to judge. Early formulations of policy, such as *Labour's Home Policy*, inspired by Attlee in the spring of 1940, were sphinxlike. The document concentrated on the need for material improvements and only briefly, in pointing out various 'opportunities' presented by the war for the building of a new society, did it refer to the 'creative use of leisure'.[42] Some five years later, only a muted voice was heard in Labour's manifesto for the 1945 general election, *Let Us Face The Future*. Drawn up under the guidance of Herbert Morrison (a former member, we should recall, of both the SDF and the ILP), this document offered a pertinent statement of Labour's wartime and proposed post-war trajectory. As a programme of action for a future Labour government it not surprisingly threw its emphasis on material issues – food, work and homes. Morrison was aware that the votes not only of traditional Labour supporters but also of the uncommitted were necessary to return his party to power.[43] For this reason *Let Us Face The Future* adopted a populist language, fusing ideas of 'the people' with those of 'the nation' in a nebulous but very clever way. In a tone strongly reminiscent of nineteenth-century radicalism the text positioned its readers on the side of the many, 'the people'. Their efforts were deemed to have secured victory for Britain. As against the many were the few, whose 'sectional interests' had in the past prevailed, with all the consequences of unemployment and misery of which the people were all too well aware. These interests were likely, if unchecked, once more to jeopardize the peace. It was an 'us' and 'them' contrast – 'us' very plainly being *not* simply the working class, nor even the middle class. Such terms were eschewed in favour of language which evoked a national unity. At the end of the manifesto the many were brought together politically as the 'progressives' whose unity would secure the future. As a piece of political polemic it remains an object-lesson

41. S. Orwell and I. Angus (eds), *The Collected Essays, Journalism and Letters of George Orwell* (Harmondsworth, Penguin, 1970), vol. III, pp. 246–60.
42. *Report of the 39th Annual Conference* (Labour Party, London, 1940), pp. 191–5. Also S. Brooke, *Labour's War: the Labour Party During the Second World War* (Oxford, Clarendon Press, 1992), p. 43.
43. H. Pelling, 'The 1945 General Election Reconsidered', *Historical Journal*, 23 (1980), pp. 399–414.

to all manifesto writers. It also stands in contrast to the Labour Party's previous essay in reconstruction, *Labour and the New Social Order*, produced for the general election of 1918 by Arthur Henderson and Sidney Webb. Though the 1918 manifesto explicitly denied that it offered a class-based analysis of society, its language was much harsher, especially in its welcoming of the 'death of a European civilisation' which, it proclaimed, Labour would not be seeking to revivify. *Let Us Face The Future*, in fashioning its image of the nation, had a more communitarian tone. This further closed off some of the socialist heritage of the party. Though prepared to acknowledge its ideological inheritance – 'The Labour Party is a Socialist Party, and proud of it ... . Its ultimate purpose at home is the establishment of the Socialist Commonwealth' – the manifesto suppressed any notions of *class* and *class conflict* in favour of the older radical image of 'the people' against the rich few. This meant that in the brief references to educational and recreational objectives there was nothing of the sense of cultural struggle that the old socialist groups had once injected into this field. Leisure was not marked out as a battleground on which the war against capitalism would be fought. Nor, even, was it expressed as a specific problem for *workers*. Recreation, in fact, emerged from *Let Us Face The Future* as a material problem alongside all the other proposals for jobs, houses and social insurance: something to be 'provided' for the benefit of all.

> National and local authorities should co-operate to enable people to enjoy their leisure to the full, to have opportunities for healthy recreation. By the provision of concert halls, modern libraries, theatres and suitable civic centres, we desire to assure to our people full access to the great heritage of culture in this nation.[44]

An unkind verdict on this would see it as the work of the 'wowsers' party'; exactly the kind of mentality that turned the working class in droves to football matches and the cinema. To be sure, the tone was rather more 'highbrow' than Priestley's, and in speaking of leisure, the populist language of the manifesto momentarily slipped into a more patronizing register: 'our people' being given access to

44. *Let Us Face the Future: A Declaration of Labour Policy for the Consideration of the Nation* (Labour Party, London, 1945), p. 9 and passim. See also *Labour and the New Social Order: A Report on Reconstruction* (Labour Party, London, 1918), esp. p. 19.

'the great heritage of culture' sounded like having a dose of what was good for them. To be fair to Morrison and his co-authors of the manifesto, though, there were no objections raised when *Let Us Face The Future* was intensively debated at the Blackpool conference in May 1945. Morrison's lengthy introduction concentrated on domestic economic matters, and from the conference floor speaker after speaker followed his lead.[45]

Labour's standpoint of 1945 was consistent with the statist approach that had come to dominate the party before the war. The main purpose of the party was not so much to reform leisure habits as to provide opportunities to all people to enjoy their leisure. If leisure could create responsible citizens, all well and good, but for every effort to reform there was also a concern to enrich. What came more into prominence after the war was an element of pragmatism about leisure. It had been present previously. Walter Citrine had expressed it as clearly as anyone before the war in making his very able presentation of the case for holidays with pay:

> Whatever the effect of it in industry it would result in a very much better type of service than they [the employers] got now; from men who have been away for a fortnight with their families without the anxiety of no pay. They would come back in a sense much better and fitter to do their work.[46]

But in the economic climate of the later 1940s, with a government committed to boosting exports and earning dollars, Citrine's sentiments took on added importance. The mood of the period was neatly captured in Ferdinand Zweig's classic study of working-class mores; underpinning much of his discussion of 'secondary poverty' was the sense that many working people used their spare time wrongly. The 'right' use of leisure was something in which they needed, for sound economic reasons, to be educated:

> The problem of leisure in modern communities is crucial ... . It has a definite bearing on the problem of manpower, efficiency, wages, industrial choice, saving and investment ... more leisure time means also claims for higher wages, and it is quite true that those who

45. *Report of the 44th Annual Conference* (Labour Party, London, 1945), pp. 89–106. The exception was Professor R. S. T. Chorley of Northwich, who called attention to the education and recreation section of the manifesto, but mainly to emphasize the need for more scientific research.
46. TUC, *Holidays for All* (TUC, London, 1937).

make the worst use of their leisure make the loudest claims for more wages.[47]

This struck at the heart of the matter. Industrial efficiency and output were the watchwords of the period. Similar perceptions were present in a draft document of 1947, 'The Enjoyment of Leisure', prepared for consideration by the Policy Committee as part of Labour's strategy for the next general election.[48] 'The Enjoyment of Leisure' saw the subject as important for two reasons: it was connected to the pursuit of 'full enjoyment', and also provided an incentive for higher output. On the first of these there was undoubtedly a sense that people's current leisure provision did not allow for a balanced personality capable, in Lewis Mumford's phrase, of 'attacking life at more than one point'. A shortage of facilities was identified in certain areas, especially rural ones, as was a need to extend the range of leisure available. At the same time there was no intention of forcing a 'Third Programme policy upon unreceptive citizens'. However, in keeping with the interventionist philosophy behind the welfare state, it was felt that the state's role should assume bigger proportions in the area of leisure. Traditionally, public involvement had been regulatory – 'to keep people out of mischief' – and, more recently, to maintain morale in wartime. Now, the policy document proposed, a new stance was required: a national policy 'which should aim solely at helping the citizens of Britain to live full and varied lives through the different ways of spending leisure'. These were acknowledged to be many and varied and not rigidly categorizable by, for example, social class. There was almost a glorification of the regional diversity of sports and leisure activities, and certainly a resistance to any suggestions of standardizing provision. The authors of the document therefore opted for what (had the broadcasting metaphor been continued) might have been termed 'mixed programming'. The state's place in all this was to be complementary to that of voluntary associations, and in this the Labour Party strongly reinforced the point made four years earlier by the TUC in its statement on leisure. Again, the document was cautious about over-centralization and though it favoured a public corporation model for leisure activity, it rejected the example of the BBC in favour of one which would

47. F. Zweig, *Labour, Life and Poverty* (EP Publishing, East Ardsley, Wakefield, 1975 edn), p. 123.
48. MRC, MSS 292.812.21, 'The Enjoyment of Leisure', 24 March 1947.

combine national and regional levels of influence. The eventual Sports Council, as developed in the 1970s, was perhaps to come closest to what the framers of the document had in mind. Local authorities were also to play a part alongside voluntary groups, providing finance and administrative expertise rather than becoming involved in the content of leisure, except 'to supply a healthy corrective to any tendencies towards over-specialisation and "cultural snobbery" that may appear'.

In relation to private commercial leisure, the bugbear of the old Socialists, the document adopted the same line that the Labour government had taken towards private industry. If it could not provide for profit the services needed by the community, there was no reason why those services should not be brought into public control. Cinemas in rural areas, for example, or pubs on housing estates, could be made available through public or voluntary effort if the profit motive for setting them up was absent.

Policy was generally conducted in this spirit. Though J. B. Priestley was critical of Labour's post-war attitude to culture,[49] the record of Labour governments of 1945–51 has usually been hailed as positive. Minihan's verdict, for example, on Attlee's first administration is generous: 'It was more concerned to enrich the country's cultural life, and to bring it within the reach of the people, than any previous Government in the nation's history.'[50] The 'statist' strategies adopted to achieve this enrichment varied in emphasis, but there was a strong sense of the state as facilitator. Pride was taken in the fact that no Ministry of Culture was formed, and that, indeed, the very conception was alien to British thinking.[51] Much of what was achieved, however, affected 'elite' cultural activities more than the leisure of the masses. The impact of the Arts Council, the National Theatre Act, the permissive clause in the 1948 Local Government Act enabling local authorities to finance cultural activities in their areas – all these measures tended to work in favour of 'good culture' and minority interests. Rather more populist was the work of Harold Wilson at the Board of Trade in attempting to support the film industry, and Lewis Silkin's National Parks and Countryside Act of 1949 which

49. Priestley, *Arts Under Socialism*.
50. J. Minihan, *The Nationalization of Culture* (London, Hamish Hamilton, 1977), p. 235.
51. Ibid.

took up the socialist cause of open access from the 1930s.[52] Conversely, some important areas of public culture remained unresponsive either to voluntary or even substantial democratic control. The notable example was the BBC, hailed as a beacon of democracy in wartime. Good at 'presenting the people to the people' (a phrase used in the popular Wilfred Pickles radio programme *Have a Go*), the BBC was an organization which, paradoxically, allowed for no control by the people themselves over the content of its programmes. Left-wing Labour MPs had railed against this, and in particular against its Director-General John Reith, in the Commons before the war. According to the Clydeside ILPer Campbell Stephen, the BBC was 'run very largely by people ... who do not know the working class, do not understand the working class point of view, but are seeking, evidently, to mould the working class'.[53] There was more than an echo here of an older socialist conception of culture. After the war, even though there was a return in some measure to cultural elitism after the BBC's wartime populism, such criticisms evaporated. The Labour leadership did not seek to revive them. The BBC was even used as the model for the newly nationalized industries and services of the welfare state. Old socialists may well have claimed that, under Labour, the cultural challenge to capitalism had been replaced with an arts policy.

III

Though an enduring issue in the labour movement leisure was never, as Stephen Jones has pointed out, a primary concern.[54] This seems to have been as true of wartime as it was of the inter-war years that were the subject of Jones's own extensive research. Whereas the war presented new opportunities for both discussion and action on material issues such as social security, on matters concerning the quality of life there was nothing like the same interest. In spite of the undoubted interest in reconstruction and the building of a new society after the war, the issue of leisure figured in it only marginally. If

---

52. See *Parliamentary Debates*, Hansard 457 H.C., Deb. 5s (London, HMSO, 1948), col. 33; B. Pimlott, *Harold Wilson* (London, HarperCollins, 1993 edn), pp. 118–20.
53. Minihan, *Nationalization of Culture*, pp. 212–13.
54. Jones, *Workers at Play*, p. 160.

1945 represented any kind of revolution in British society, there were certainly no signs of one in the field of leisure and recreation. The subject merited little more than a footnote in the 1945 election manifesto. At first sight, therefore, the war appears not to have been an especially significant episode in the labour movement's stance on this matter.

Labour's wartime stance was determined by what had gone before. To begin with, most sections of the labour movement had ceased to think in terms of alternatives to existing provision in leisure and culture. The 'substitutionist' approach once evident in the work of early Socialists had not captured the mainstream of the movement, and had certainly been banished to the margins in the Labour Party itself. This meant that, although some local groups still nurtured the counter-cultural mentalities of early socialism, there was by the 1940s no alternative being offered by the Labour Party or trade unions to voluntary or commercial popular culture. Indeed, the idea of Labour adopting an autonomous workers' culture of the kind promoted by the pre-1933 German socialists would probably have seemed alien to many Labour voters of the late 1930s, and distinctly ludicrous to the many more who voted Labour in 1945. Furthermore, in company with its general approach to material problems, the Labour position on matters of leisure was 'statist'. There was a consistent theme on this running through Labour Party policy statements from 1918 to 1945: leisure, recreation and culture were matters for a degree of government intervention, either to supplement what people did for themselves, rectify what was flawed, or provide what was absent.

The war affected this stance in subtle ways. Previously leisure had been thought about in terms similar to those in which material questions were approached: as deficiencies in the existing order. The war superimposed upon this a new rhetoric. Leisure became part of a discourse on nationality, an icon of a British way of life which was being defended most obviously against Nazi tyranny but also (and increasingly as the war continued) against Americanism. The function performed by leisure was to identify the organic unity of British life – its unity in diversity – and to guarantee British liberties and democratic freedoms.[55] How people, especially young

55. See also R. Weight, 'State, Intelligentsia and the Promotion of National Culture in Britain, 1939–45', *Historical Research*, **69** (1996), pp. 83–101. Weight

people, spent their leisure time became an important issue because democracy depended, so the rhetoric went, on people thinking for themselves. Hence the emphasis, from Priestley's 1941 message to the TUC debates of 1943, on the *right* use of leisure. This reinforced the 'statist' approach, implemented in a particular form. Because the discourse was framed in the context of totalitarianism it resulted, for the most part, in an ideology of minimal state intervention in culture. Labour policy in the later 1940s clearly reflected this. There was to be no Ministry of Culture. The 1949 manifesto *Labour Believes in Britain* summed it up: 'The use of leisure is something personal. We do not want exhortation or interference. We do want greater richness of opportunity for the individual.' [56]

In any event, there was a body of opinion that had convinced itself that wartime cultural tastes were improving. Julian Huxley was one of many who had subscribed to it.[57] Priestley was also part of it. Speaking at the *Daily Worker* conference, convened in May 1945 to consider the paper's role in the post-war world, he launched into an attack on the proprietors of the capitalist press who, he claimed, were reluctant to feed their readers any real ideas. As against this:

> the success of the Brains Trust and similar features suggests ... that there is now a big public for the discussion of social and artistic problems in a popular style. It is very important ... that the new *Daily Worker* ... should examine the relation between our economic and cultural life, e.g. what is happening about films and theatres – and I believe this would attract a great deal of attention.[58]

This optimisitic view of the improving effect of the war's cultural changes sat well with the idea of minimal government responsibility in leisure. The 1945 manifesto offered little on this because, it seemed, there was little that needed to be offered.

(*note 55 continued*) argues that left/liberal intellectuals did not always use their influence to promote the idea of reconstruction and a Labour post-war world; instead they 'promoted British culture specifically in order to defend the traditions and achievements of the nation rather than to look forward to how they might be built upon in the future' (pp. 83–4).

56. *Labour Believes in Britain* (Labour Party, London, 1949), esp. pp. 20–1.
57. See his series of articles in the *Daily Herald* in the autumn of 1943, especially that of 1 October, in which he called for 'a decent cultural foundation for life ... the Russians have done this on a large scale, and CEMA and similar bodies have made a good beginning here'.
58. *Daily Worker*, 14 May 1945.

Not Just a Case of Baths, Canteens and Rehabilitation Centres: The Second World War and the Recreational Provision of the Miners' Welfare Commission in Coalmining Communities[1]

Colin Griffin

The impact of the Second World War on social change has long been a subject of much controversy.[2] The centre of debate has, however, recently moved from perennial favourites, such as the role of women or the nation's health, to the People's Culture: the effect of the war on popular leisure, recreation, the arts and lifestyles generally. Did the war, for example, cause 'people to be favourably disposed to "improving" pastimes',[3] a people's culture for a people's war, which quickly reverted to what Priestley characterized as the 'silly, passive-style amusement' of peacetime?[4] Alternatively, is the judgement of Pat Kirkham and David Thoms that wartime disruption

1. The Miners' Welfare Commission took over the function of the Miners' Welfare Committee in 1939. It was charged with the administration of the welfare fund which was, by 1939, providing pit-head baths and canteens, rehabilitation centres, medical treatment, education and research, in addition to recreation.
2. Much stimulated by Arthur Marwick's interventions and provocations in works such as *War and Social Change in the Twentieth Century* (London, Macmillan, 1974), particularly ch. 5.
3. J. Fryth (ed.), *Labour's Promised Land? Culture and Society in Labour Britain 1945–51* (London, Lawrence & Wishart, 1995), particularly part 3.
4. J. B. Priestley, 'When Work Is Over', *Picture Post* (*A Plan For Britain*), 4 January 1941.

'ensured that British society and culture were fundamentally altered by the experience of war' convincing?[5] These are large questions that will not be addressed in the round here. Rather the spotlight will focus on a single actor in the wider drama of events: the recreational provision and activity of the Miners' Welfare Commission (MWC), financed by a fund raised through levies on coal output with a remit to provide improvements in the 'social well-being, recreation and conditions of living' in mining communities.[6] The recreational provision of the MWC is a highly appropriate site to address the impact of the conflict of 1939–45, because it was a unique experiment in state initiated and sponsored welfare provision in a private-sector industry which served the needs of one of the most significant sections of the working class from 1920 into the era of coal industry nationalization. Also, the mining population comprised about one-eighth of the British population and was both geographically dispersed and, despite its popular image as 'a race apart' from its compatriots, resident in all types of settlement from single-industry village to industrially diverse city.[7] In some senses, then, the MWC was a social institution serving a cross-section of Britain.

I

A two-tier system of administration for the allocation of expenditure of the Miners' Welfare Fund quickly emerged following the Fund's creation in 1920: a national committee, with overall responsibility,

5. P. Kirkham and D. Thoms (eds), *War: Culture Social Change and Changing Experience in World War Two* (London, Lawrence & Wishart, 1995), p. x.

6. The miners' welfare programme has also been regarded, correctly, as an experiment in industrial welfare capitalism designed to improve labour relations and worker efficiency and assist the recruitment of juvenile labour. This ideological and industrial relations perspective provides the underlying context of the discussion which follows, though a detailed discussion of it is beyond the scope of this modest account.

7. Miners' Welfare Committee Annual Report 1938 (hereafter MWC Ann. Rpt); M. Benney, 'The Legacy of Mining', in *Mining and Social Change*, ed. M. Bulmer (London, Croom Helm, 1978), p. 49, who viewed Durham miners in 1944–45 as 'a tribe of Englishmen so distinctive in their way of life that, had they been situated on a remote island in the South Seas, would have been the subject of a dozen ethnographic monographs'.

and 25 (one for each coal district/coalfield) local committees which, in practice, assumed responsibility for developing their own local programmes under the general aegis of the national body. Representatives of both sides of industry served at national and local levels whilst the Fund itself advanced from temporary to permanent status, with an initial levy of 1*d* a ton being reduced to ½*d* in 1932 and being restored to 1*d* in 1939. This was increased to 3*d* on nationalization of the industry, and miners also contributed from their pay-packets for their own pit welfare schemes.[8] One of the most important consequences of giving district welfare committees responsibility for expenditure is that they adopted widely different priorities, and it was relatively easy for recreational provision to be squeezed out by the expenditure on, for instance, utilitarian pit-head baths and rehabilitation centres. A decade after its inception Lancashire and Ayrshire had spent nothing on recreation, while North Staffordshire and South Derbyshire had spent 7 per cent and 8 per cent of their allocations respectively. Other districts, such as Warwickshire, Cumberland and the Lothians, had spent virtually the whole of their allocations on recreational provision.[9] South Wales, with an expenditure of over £900,000 on recreation (63.4 per cent), was regarded as a model and it was estimated that £3,300,000 would have to be spent in other coalfields to bring recreational provision up to South Wales standards.[10] At the outbreak of war Ayrshire was still devoid of a recreational scheme while Lancashire now had one (a youth club), at a cost of £2,043 (the national average cost per scheme was £4,000). Indeed, the league table remained much the same as in 1931 as recreational expenditure climbed from £4,236,717 to £5,763,108, from 48.1 per cent to 54.5 per cent of total district expenditure.[11] Decentralization had also resulted in large recreational schemes developing at collieries with an urban or semi-urban location,

8. W. J. Morgan, 'The Miners' Welfare Fund in Britain 1920–1952', *Social Policy and Administration*, **24**:3 (1990), pp. 199–211. Between 1921 and 1952 expenditure on miners' welfare was £30,103,398, of which £6,856,403 (22.8 per cent) was spent on recreational provision. Income for each colliery scheme was also raised from lettings, subscriptions from non-mineworkers, receipts from wage levies and bar sales (where provided).
9. MWC Ann. Rpt 1931.
10. PRO POWE 26/222 Miners' Welfare Act 1931. Extension of Period of the Fund Discussion Paper.
11. MWC Ann. Rpt 1939.

where alternative leisure provision was available, whilst remote, rural mining communities might have little or no provision.

There was also tremendous variety in other respects: some collieries possessed magnificent, multi-purpose, architect-designed social centres catering for all members of the mining community whilst the poorest provision comprised a wooden hut which served as a miner-only drinking den.[12] This huge variety of provision and lack of uniformity – a characteristic of coalmining in general – became a challenge to the national committee and its professional officials once the funding was established on a permanent basis in 1934. There was a call for the submission of comprehensive five-year plans from the districts, which were also constantly lectured on their responsibilities to provide comprehensive recreational facilities by the national welfare adviser, Commander B. T. Coote RN, Rtd.[13] He also regularly provided them with advice and guidance from headquarters and offered the services of the Committee's impressive architecture and design department.[14] Provision for the whole family became the central concern and the way forward was exemplified by two model schemes which came to fruition as the war clouds gathered: the Kells Community and Miners' Welfare Centre, Whitehaven, Cumberland and the Derbyshire Miners' Holiday Camp on the Lincolnshire coast at Skegness. The former was planned to serve 'several social and welfare organisations' co-operating with the local miners' welfare committee and it provided facilities for all kinds of crafts and hobbies; dressing-rooms for outdoor and indoor sports; a gym; an assembly hall and stage which could be converted into a theatre, dance hall or cinema; a library; a billiard hall; reading rooms; boys', girls' and women's rooms, including a nursery and a refreshment room with a sun terrace.[15] The origins of the latter are to be found in the 1938 paid-holiday legislation. The bulk of the miners thereafter were granted an annual week's paid holiday, but the cost of lodgings made it impossible for many families 'to pass their holidays in the different surroundings and health-giving conditions' to which they were entitled. Derbyshire quickly decided to

12. Mines Department, *Miners' Welfare Fund. Departmental Committee of Enquiry (1931). Report to the Secretary of Mines*, January 1933 (HMSO, Cmd. 4236); MWC Ann. Rpt 1934.
13. MWC Ann. Rpt 1934; Morgan, 'Miners' Welfare Fund', p. 205.
14. MWC Ann. Rpt 1935.
15. MWC Ann. Rpt 1939.

build a holiday camp offering subsidized holidays to their members and persuaded the Commission that the experience of the recently established Butlin's holiday camps indicated that it would be a great success. The community and family ethos would be encouraged because, unlike the organized, commercial provision at Butlin's, the Derbyshire camp would provide 'The freedom and friendly atmosphere in which visitors join together to make their own amusements', with the minimum of commercial entertainment provided. The chalets and public spaces, such as dining-halls and dance-floors, would match commercial provision within a carefully planned layout on an attractive site next to the sand dunes.[16]

At the outbreak of war only one district plan (from Nottinghamshire) had been submitted whilst Leicestershire, more typically, had not progressed beyond merely noting that it 'might be advisable to consider the adoption of a long-term policy related to the District fund as the Committee was not pursuing any settled policy and the various local schemes were developing along adhoc lines'.[17] Nonetheless the MWC pronounced that grants had been distributed to

> more than 14,000 schemes of various sizes ... from the park and the recreation ground for all sports, complete with pavilion, children's play ground and perhaps a swimming-pool, to the village football field; from the modern structure of architectural merit comprising rooms for library, reading, billiards, table games, meetings etc., a gymnasium, a hall for dances and dramatics, and even a cinema, to the modest hut which serves for all social purposes in community.[18]

The MWC's target of levering the quality of recreational provision up to the highest standards throughout the coalfields was still a long way from fulfilment.

16. MWC Ann. Rpt 1938. On Butlin's and similar commercial holiday camps see S. Fielding, P. Thompson and N. Tiratsoo, 'England Arise!': The Labour Party and Popular Politics in 1940s Britain (Manchester, Manchester UP, 1995), pp. 150–2.
17. Leicestershire Record Office (hereafter LRO), Leicestershire District Miners' Welfare Committee Minute Book, DE1177/33, 25 July 1939.
18. MWC Ann. Rpt 1939.

II

Since at the outbreak of war miners were expected to be 'soldiers of the home front', the MWC considered that it was its duty to continue 'business as usual' in view of the importance of its work to the war effort. It soon found difficulty in doing so as a large number of its buildings were requisitioned for civil defence, such as air-raid precautions or the billeting of troops, and in the confusion 'communal life tended to disintegrate and activity at miners' welfare institutes and halls suffered a temporary decline'. The Derbyshire holiday camp was an early and permanent casualty, though institutes in South Wales and other districts were recaptured from the military and local authorities after the MWC had emphasized to the government 'the importance of miners to the war effort' and the significance of social functions to the maintenance of morale in mining communities. Certainly during the so-called 'phoney war', as the blackout and transport restrictions obliged mining communities 'to look near home for their leisure hour interests and pastimes', the welfare indoor schemes came to be increasingly appreciated. Nottinghamshire, for instance, congratulated itself on the use of its facilities

> as centres of communal life of the villages. In several of the newer villages, which before the war were simply dormitories in so much as social life and entertainments were obtained in the larger towns, such as Nottingham and Mansfield, there was a great danger that during the blackout there might be a blackout of social life also. Statistics alone could not demonstrate the work that the institutes in such places have done to prevent this and to maintain the morale of the people.[19]

Nottinghamshire also introduced a district fête and gala for the 1941 August Bank Holiday. Entertainment for the 20,000-strong crowd included boxing, tennis and bowls championships, and Gracie Fields was the star attraction.[20] The fall of France produced another problem for the MWC, since unemployment mounted in exporting districts like South Wales and Durham and institutes were required to intensify their activities 'to maintain the interest and morale of those unemployed', as they had in the darkest days of pre-war depression. Since

19. Ibid.
20. PRO POWE 1/36, October 1941.

loss of output and unemployment automatically reduced district funds they sought assistance from central funds. This was a challenge to MWC pre-war practice and 'was open to grave objections' since it discouraged self-help among the unemployed and 'People do not appreciate welfare facilities which they get for nothing.' Central funds were also only sufficient for assisting with the capital costs and 'landlord' maintenance of institutes.[21] The military conscription of the bulk of the unemployed miners solved the MWC's dilemma, though it was soon to contribute to the grave labour shortage that gripped the industry within a few months.

Although annual average expenditure on recreational welfare in the period 1940–45 was only about one-tenth that of the 1930s,[22] it was still, given the virtual cessation of building and construction work, considerable and reflected the trend established during the 'phoney war' for indoor facilities to be increasingly used for social gatherings, hobbies, and multifarious leisure and cultural pursuits. The halls and institutes, moreover, acquired more the character of community centres as gender and age participation widened. Women increasingly accompanied their 'menfolk' to the bar and institutes became the home of organizations which women joined, such as the Women's Voluntary Service, War Savings Groups, Women's Institutes and the like. These organizations were all engaged in war work and the local authorities contributed to their endeavours by arranging lectures, discussions and practical demonstrations on food rationing and cooking and 'making do and mend' in the institutes.[23] By the end of 1944 about one-third of the institutes had either women members or provision for joint activities and a quarter had actual women's groups. These were usually branches of a national organization such as the Co-operative Women's Guild rather than independent institute 'ladies' sections', though these were evolving in districts like Nottinghamshire.[24] Nonetheless, independent observers

21. PRO POWE 1/35, July 1940. Four-fifths of the revenue raised by each district remained in their fund, so central funds were limited.
22. £37,970 per annum in 1939–45 compared to £320,173 per annum in 1921–39.
23. Miners' Welfare in War Time. Report of the Miners' Welfare Commission for 6½ years to 30 June 1946 (hereafter MWWT).
24. PRO POWE 1/38, September 1944 and National Miners' Welfare Joint Council (hereafter NMWJC) Ann. Rpt 1948. This was the National Coal Board–Miners' Welfare Commission joint body that acquired responsibility for planning and directing the welfare activities of mineworkers following the

continued to write that the most striking characteristic of leisure in mining communities remained 'the separation of sexes'.[25]

The drive begun in 1938 to raise all districts up to South Wales standards in the provision of youth clubs continued during the war and became an integral part of government policy on the recruitment of juvenile labour into the industry. The pre-war 'tendency for the occupation to be out of favour on social grounds' was continuing and the MWC argued that the expansion of the pit-head bath programme, combined with more comprehensive leisure and recreational provision, 'should assist miners in time to find a good social level and a "caste" consciousness as followers of an important and honourable calling of equal standing to any other'. More particularly, 'Boys' Clubs and Camps if suitably conducted might serve the purposes of attracting boys to the industry, holding their interest and helping to make them good citizens and good workmen.'[26] South Wales had been exceptional in having a very active Federation of Boys' Clubs, supported by district funds, whose size had grown to 150 clubs with 12,000 members by September 1942. Elsewhere progress was slow, with five districts (most prominently Warwickshire and Nottinghamshire) having only 32 clubs with 1,466 members between them, and further progress was hampered by the absence of quality leadership and facilities. Few districts could match Warwickshire which, for instance, organized a programme of events for its clubs during Easter week 1941 which included 1,300 participants in six-a-side football matches and relay races on Monday and a showing of Ministry of Information (MoI) films (*Coal Front*, *The Timber Front* and *Granton Trawler*) to 95 youths at Dordon on Thursday. The entertainments concluded with a visit by the senior boys to the Nuneaton Youth Centre. As the Youth Welfare Officer recorded, the programme consisted of performances of 'musical items, community singing, [a] talking film show and our drama group presented a short play called

(*note 24 continued*) nationalization of the coal industry in 1947. The purely social functions of the NMWJC became the responsibility of the Coal Industry Social Welfare Organization (CISWO) in 1952, at the abolition of the Miners' Welfare Commission.

25. F. Zweig, *Men in the Pits* (London, Gollancz, 1948) p. 104; M. Benny, *Charity Main. A Coalfield Chronicle* (London, Allen & Unwin, 1946), p. 24 also commented on 'the almost complete separation of the social life of the two sexes' in colliery villages in the Durham coalfield.

26. PRO POWE 1/36, November 1941.

Country Justice'. The visit concluded with an 'inspiring address' by the vicar of Nuneaton. Nottinghamshire did, however, organize flights of the Air Training Corps in the wake of the Battle of Britain.[27] By 1945 nine districts had youth schemes comprising 79 clubs, with a further 243 clubs (mainly in South Wales) grant-aided by district funds.[28] This only gradual progress in youth work reflected, in part, a widespread belief in the industry that it was 'undesirable to over emphasise the youth aspect. Adult status in the coalmining industry is quickly reached and the industry itself breeds self reliance at an early age. In consequence Youth Movements are held in some contempt by young miners.'[29]

The clubs tried hard to be attractive, however, and organized a wide range of outdoor activities which included football, cricket, swimming, hockey, tennis, rambling, cycling, camping and holiday visits. Indoor activities included not only physical training and games but 'more serious but no less absorbing activities' such as discussion groups, handicrafts, woodwork, music and drama. Most clubs also provided library and radio-listening facilities.[30] Two districts had their own ciné projectors and in others visits to local cinemas were arranged and the films discussed on a regular basis.[31] Following the recruitment of 'Bevin Boys' into the industry from December 1943 the Commission was expected to 'integrate the newcomers into the national mining communities ... instead of letting them seek their amusements as a class apart'.[32] This task proved more difficult than the official record suggests because many hostels were either too

27. PRO POWE 1/36, September 1942.
28. MWWT. There were 140 Youth Clubs in the colliery areas of South Wales, and they had access to the unique St Albans mining boys' camp, which provided a holiday for 28,276 of them in the period 1925–40. Ministry to Fuel and Power, *Regional Survey Report, South Wales Coalfield* (HMSO, 1946), pp. 152–3.
29. PRO POWE 1/38, September 1944. Certainly, districts like Leicestershire gave youth work a low priority and deferred a decision to appoint a youth leader at an annual salary of £250 for years. LRO DE 1177/33, 4 June 1942; 22 August 1944.
30. MWWT.
31. Mark Benny, in his role as district welfare officer, arranged for a ciné camera to be introduced at a youth club in a Durham miners' institute and showed films such as *Tyneside Story* (a Ministry of Information 'depression – better Britain' documentary, 1944) and Soviet 'social realism' feature, *The Road To Life* (1931). Benny, *Charity*, pp. 132–4.
32. MWWT.

Figure 12   Table games at a Miners' Welfare Boys' Club, c.1945

remote from existing facilities or had too many occupants to be satisfied by them, particularly since their sports fields and equipment had been neglected and they lacked opportunities for mixed social activity such as café-bars.[33] The adverse effects on the war effort were only too apparent. In Warwickshire, for instance, there was considerable concern 'over the prevalence of absenteeism in the miners' hostels' because of low morale, which was in large measure attributed to boredom induced by the lack of recreational facilities, particularly 'essential games equipment'. Similarly, Smallthorne Hostel, serving two pits in North Staffordshire, was noted in August 1944 for the 'absenteeism and low morale of the residents' who, in the absence of official ones, devised their own recreational pursuits, which included damaging the hostel, petty theft and secreting 'girls into the dormitories'.[34] Recruits from middle-class backgrounds had particular difficulty integrating: 'They are not great drinkers, but spend most of their time in the pictures ... loneliness is a great

33. PRO POWE 1/38, June 1944.
34. PRO LAB 26/83, Welfare Officer Monthly Reports, Midland Region, 14 July, 14 and 31 August 1944.

scourge that ravishes the ranks of Bevin boys, ... who sometimes develop strange habits in their isolation.'[35]

Indoor recreation and leisure were also encouraged and stimulated from other directions. Following the successful introduction of the Entertainments National Service Association (hereafter ENSA) entertainment at munitions factories, the organization proposed that concerts be given for miners. The MWC was not initially enthusiastic since district organizers had reported that there was no demand for them in mining communities because their offerings were of poor quality and much inferior to those of the Council for the Encouragement of Music and the Arts (CEMA). It was felt, however, that 'they might fill a need at institutes in isolated districts if good music, such as that provided by CEMA with a leavening of good humour were provided'. On being assured that the quality of ENSA's shows was improving, district and pit welfare managements were encouraged by headquarters to employ them at institutes 'on self-supporting terms'.[36] Since ENSA had no guarantee of recovering costs and was having some difficulty meeting demand for its services the initiative failed. By 1943, however, the Ministry of Fuel and Power, 'feeling that some ENSA entertainments would encourage miners and their families under the austerity of war conditions', persuaded the Treasury to subsidize its activities. According to the official account:

> From September 1943 onwards, E.N.S.A. parties toured in all the coalfields giving musicals, dramatic or variety entertainments in welfare halls, and even small miners' institutes and village halls in remote country districts, where sometimes the stage was inconvenient, the lighting poor and perhaps the piano indifferent. Notwithstanding all limitations, the entertainments were good and were greatly appreciated by the mining community.[37]

Moreover, although it was the Ministry of Labour's opinion that ENSA workplace entertainment 'at mid-shift times [was] not suitable at collieries', because it could obstruct the work of the canteen, disrupt transport arrangements or produce a loss of working time, by November 1942 colliery owners were pressing for it at the end of shifts in their canteens following a successful pioneering trial run

35. Zweig, *Men*, pp. 34–5.
36. PRO POWE 1/37, December 1941.
37. MWWT.

at Babbington colliery, Nottinghamshire.[38] Here ENSA entertainments of 'second rate comedians and singers' were organized at the end of the day shift and 'half of the day and afternoon shifts would be there sometime during the session' (there were about 1,400 miners employed on three shifts), with a hard-core audience of over 200, who were there for more than the subsidized, high-quality meals provided by the canteen. Popular songs and well-worn jokes were appreciated by the Babbington [39] audience but the special grant received from the Ministry of Labour to finance these efforts was resented by ENSA's principal competitor for the hearts and minds of the miners, CEMA, whose representatives were inclined to complain: 'To the great disappointment of the miners and their local representatives of the Miners' Welfare Commission, it would appear that we just leave them [canteen concerts] to ENSA through lack of similar funding.'[40] The MWC provided neither organization with financial support for these concerts since they 'may be regarded as being a temporary wartime measure with a production motive rather than a welfare motive'; and took an identical stance on the provision of radiograms and amplifiers in colliery canteens.[41]

CEMA was active in the coalfields from 1940, and the official record of its contribution to raising the morale of the mining community sounds impressive:

> CEMA has ... with the help of the Commission's staff, toured the mining districts with entertainments of an educational as well as recreational value ranging from full philharmonic orchestras and repertory companies to small concert parties of two or three performers. In the early days of the war the Old Vic. Theatre Company, including Dame Sybil Thorndike and Sir Lewis Casson, toured the mining towns of South Wales, Northumberland and Durham; and at collieries in Nottinghamshire and Cannock Chase a party, which included several famous artists, gave concerts underground. All through the war many excellent concerts were given by CEMA in miners' welfare halls in all Coal Districts at cheap prices, and their

38. PRO/LAB 26/85. Monthly Report, North Midlands Region, 20 November 1942, POWE 1/37, December 1942.
39. Interview with Alan Griffin, 26 May 1996, who worked at the colliery throughout the war and was trade union branch secretary from 1942.
40. PRO EL3/1, Report by Tom Harrison, Region 9 West Midlands, October 1944.
41. PRO POWE 1/37, December 1941.

success revealed a latent demand among mining people for good music and drama.[42]

This heroic account is somewhat at variance with the everyday reality of CEMA's work. A music touring party in the North Midlands in December 1940, for instance, found 'attendance rather disappointing ... probably due to bad publicity and partly to difficulty in getting the co-operation of the owners'.[43] It was not always the owners, however, who were an obstacle to a large, appreciative audience since CEMA area organizer, Eve Kisch, reported:

> Miners have a great reputation for their choirs and this was seriously given to me as a reason for their non-attendance at a CEMA concert in a Nottinghamshire mining town ('There's nobody makes such bad listeners as musicians, teachers and clergymen'). It was rather the same story when we sent a CEMA tour to Cumberland mining towns; one of the artists reported that the audiences seemed mainly composed of squawking children.[44]

The reception given to several CEMA tours in Staffordshire and Shropshire districts between 1941 and 1944 was very different, 'for these miners, as in Wales, are wonderful audiences', and 'during one tour there was such disappointment at one colliery because there was no canteen or suitable building (chapel or institute) the party gave a concert at the shaft bottom which was well received by the miners and the general public'.[45] An opera company led by Joan Cross toured the miners' welfare institutes in South Wales, Lancashire and Durham to great acclaim, aided, no doubt, by it lodging with miners and their families.[46] On the CEMA drama front a week's northern tour by the 'Market Theatre' Players to colliery villages in spring 1943 'was much appreciated', as was the six-week tour of South Wales by the 'Mary Newcombe' Players.[47]

The very success of CEMA's more higher-profile initiatives also generated its own problems. The sponsored north-eastern coalfield tour of the Old Vic Company in 1941 'left a deep impression in the

42. MWWT.
43. PRO LAB 26/81, Monthly Report, 21 December 1940.
44. PRO EL3/1, Report by E. Kisch, October 1944.
45. PRO EL3/1, Harrison Report.
46. A. Croft, 'Betrayed Spring: The Labour Government and British Literary Culture' in Fryth, *Labour's Promised Land?*, p. 200.
47. PRO POWE 1/37, June 1943.

area', but the failure to repeat it resulted in the district complaining in 1944 that 'CEMA has neglected it', as the staple diet of tours by small companies had 'given a good deal of pleasure' but had also whetted the appetite for prestigious tours by larger companies provided that they produced 'the right kind of play'.[48] Moreover, CEMA music performances in colliery canteens proved less digestible than their ENSA counterparts. At Babbington, for instance, 'string quartets, small orchestras, instrumentalists and singers accompanied by piano offered classical music that did not go down very well'.[49] The music offered was 'too serious' and that 'old fashioned outlook on the function of Artists in Society, resulting in a faulty attitude to workers' was probably not entirely absent on these occasions.[50]

Before the war dramatic and musical societies already existed in a number of institutes in certain districts, particularly in South Wales and the Midlands, and CEMA wartime performances, even if they appeared first in the West End lest the performers 'should not think that all their work was to be lost in the wilderness ... of Miners' Welfare Halls',[51] stimulated the formation of many new ones. By the end of the conflict almost every mining town and village in South Wales possessed both kinds of society and held a one-day eisteddfod in which they participated. Also, in 1945, 20 one-week drama festivals were held at different institutes in the coalfield. Choir and brass-band concerts were broadcast by the BBC from South Wales, Nottinghamshire and South Yorkshire and drama and music festivals were held in Nottinghamshire and Durham. Dramatic and music events were also becoming increasingly commonplace in mining

48. PRO EL3/1, Report by H. Munrow, Region 1, March 1944. *The Merchant of Venice* was 'excellently' received though the reaction to Medea was 'Oh yes, CEMA, what was that play called ... "Weary" ... "Dreary"?'.
49. Griffin interview, May 1996. See also A. R. Griffin, *Mining in the East Midlands 1550–1947* (London, Cass, 1971), p. 289.
50. Griffin interview and PRO EL3/1, Report on CEMA in Industry, 1944, by J. Jackson for a general criticism of artist presentation. She regarded 'A fresh, unpatronising approach' as essential, along with the avoidance of such presentational faults as 'bad announcing, general time-wasting on stage and misuse of the microphone'.
51. C. Landstone, *Off-Stage: A Personal Record of the First Twelve Years of State Sponsored Drama in Great Britain* (London, Elek, 1953) p. 54. The play of the pioneering tour in 1942 was O'Neill's *Days Without End* and, in Landstone's judgement, in spite of initial misgivings on the advisability of the whole enterprise, it was a great success.

communities in North Staffordshire, Warwickshire, North Wales, Cannock Chase and South Derbyshire.[52] In South Derbyshire, for instance, CEMA concerts stimulated the formation of the Swadlincote and District Committee for the Encouragement of Music under the auspices of the district welfare committee, whose opening celebrity concert of the 1941–42 season, held in the Majestic Cinema, featured 'three distinguished artistes', and Dame Myra Hess was booked to give a recital in December.[53]

The MWC had long encouraged non-vocational education in the institutes[54] and welcomed MoI-sponsored lecturers, such as Bernard Newman, who spoke 400 times in South Wales, often arriving in a colliery village 'to find 600 people packed inside the hall, out of a total population of perhaps 3,000'. He 'never had more intense or warmer audiences then these', and a similar reception greeted Eileen Bigland, for instance, when she lectured at Basford Hall Welfare Institute, Nottingham about the German siege of Moscow and her encounters with Stalin.[55]

According to Angus Calder, 'Post-war planning ... became a kind of universal craze with institutions great and small',[56] and the MWC's advanced planning for a better post-war Britain began in September 1942. A thorough review of pre-war achievements and an exploration of post-war possibilities eventually produced, in the wake of Churchill's four-year plan 'of general social advancement to be undertaken immediately after the war',[57] the Commission's plan for the shape of post-war activity, entitled *Miners Welfare Looks Forward* (*MWLF*), in February 1945. It proposed that all districts prepare both short-term and long-term plans and impressed upon them that planning was 'of greater importance than ever' and that there could be no repetition of the largely abortive 1934 planning initiative. Short-term plans should propose ways in which existing facilities could be improved or rehabilitated and their activities extended with

52. MWWT; Helen Munrow also claimed of the north-eastern coalfields: 'music making is an integral part of the life of the people ... comprising almost entirely of [sic] choirs', PRO EL3/1.
53. *Burton Daily Mail*, 15 September, 1941; MWWT.
54. MWWT.
55. It helped to make miners 'happier men by giving them fresh interests and a broader outlook on life'. *Departmental Committee*, 1931.
56. B. Newman, *British Journey* (London, Travel Book Club, 1946), p. 55; Griffin interview.
57. A. Calder, *The People's War* (London, Granada, 1971 edn), p. 630.

only minor alterations and additions. The implementation of long-term plans would be conditional upon the lifting of building restrictions, but districts should be ready to construct 'comprehensive community centres ... at suitable points and, around them, smaller schemes of the village hall type'. Much of the provision of the latter was already in place but there was a dearth of large centres 'for joint activities and large gatherings' in the districts. The Commission emphasized that short-term plans should include proposals for stimulating, in co-operation with local education authorities, 'cultural and health promoting activities' at institutes including the specific provision of activities for women of 'discussions and study of household subjects and current affairs, handicrafts, first-aid and home nursing, physical training and keep-fit classes'. Women, moreover, should be encouraged to take a more active role in the management of the centres. Activities particularly suitable for the 18–25 age group should be developed and youth clubs organized with other voluntary and statutory bodies for 14–18 year olds. The motto for all this endeavour was 'welfare as activity', though it was appreciated that the plans would be unrealizable without a new generation of professional, and more particularly, voluntary leadership, rather than simply the 'caretaker with the one arm or one leg' who had often served for past leadership in the institutes. This cohort could be developed and trained using local education authority expertise and by recruiting suitable personnel released from the armed forces.[58] Certainly the new community centres would provide a congenial working environment since the MWC's architects were also given a central role to play designing a new generation of buildings incorporating an ideal physical space, as shown in Figure 13.[59]

The MWC insisted that the Centre 'must fit closely into the cultural and social life of the community and reflect local circumstances',[60] yet there was no provision for that most popular of social venues: the licensed bar. The MWC had long considered them undesirable, not on moral grounds, but because they tended to preserve a masculine atmosphere; that the institutes were men's clubs devoted to drinking, billiards and table games and that at best the

58. PRO POWE 1/38, October 1944.
59. MWWT. By June 1944 £5,819,669 had been spent by the districts on 14,000 schemes equivalent to £2 a head 'of the mining population'. PRO POWE 1/38, June 1944.
60. PRO POWE 1/39, March 1946.

Hall	Craft and art rooms
Gymnasium	Rooms for discussion groups, dramatics rehearsals etc.
Library and reading rooms	
Games and billiard rooms	Café and kitchen
Boys' and girls' activity rooms	Office and staff room
Ladies' lounge and leisure room	

The halls should have modern stage and cinema equipment and the Centre should be surrounded by gardens, playing fields and facilities for outdoor recreation.

Figure 13   The Miners' Welfare Committee model community centre

presence of wives, sweethearts and offspring was a necessary evil rather than something to be positively encouraged. Supported by districts such as Leicestershire, the MWC continued to be unmoved by pressure from districts, such as Nottinghamshire, which insisted on adding a bar, at their own expense, in the belief that it was required to maximize male commitment to the institute and thereby guarantee its vitality.[61] Profits from bar sales also provided a substantial, steady income that could be spent on general needs such as subsidized holidays and trips for the retired. In Nottinghamshire alcohol was a social lubricant for both sexes, particularly at dances and celebrations, and architects were required to locate the bar and toilets accordingly. The MWC's contentious claim that 'It is beyond doubt that tone and welfare value are higher and membership is more comprehensive in community centres where there is no provision for the sale of intoxicants'[62] was simply ignored.

   MWLF was part of a wider endeavour to make coalmining a more attractive industry in which to work and mining communities more fulfilling and enjoyable places to live.[63] Nonetheless, the expansion plan raised two immediate concerns. Eighteen of the 25 districts

61. Ibid.
62. Leicestershire refused to join their neighbour's campaign to get sanctions against the provision of bars lifted. LRO De 11 77/33, 16 June 1937.
63. See also, for example, First Report on the Recruitment of Juveniles in the Coal-Mining Industry, 1942; H. Wilson, *New Deal For Coal* (London, Contact,

responded to the planning document and five of them 'interpreted the Commission's recommendations as an invasion of their territory and an attack upon their rights instead of an attempt to obtain their agreement to a broad conception of welfare aims and the way to obtain those aims'.[64] Leicestershire, for instance, thundered that 'the proposals have been designed to strengthen the hands of the administration at head quarters, the inevitable result being the delegation of the present limited control of the fund now exercised by the Industry to a body of civil servants'. A MWC delegation was told to their face that their general attitude towards the district 'was one of dictation' which Leicestershire would resist.[65] Nationalization of the industry soon made the squabble irrelevant.

There were also fears that future developments might be based on a single model of the needs of isolated mining communities located in remote rural areas when, in the Midlands, for instance, 'the vast majority of employees of collieries reside in towns and villages which are mixed communities providing in large measure the general activities and services of urban life'.[66] Even in South Wales, often considered the repository of archetypal homogeneous mining communities, the miners lived in three types of environment: isolated village, town and semi-urban/rural, and so the 'grand plan' was of doubtful validity even there.[67] There was further related concern that such a 'comprehensive welfare scheme' would result in 'the segregation of mine workers from the remainder of the population which is thought undesirable by many, both inside and outside the industry'.[68] This was a particularly sensitive issue, given that writers of travel books and autobiographical novels persisted in depicting miners and their families as 'a race apart' that was in no sense integrated into the national community even during a 'people's war'. For Bernard Newman, for instance:

> Miners are a tribe apart from the rest of the population ... . His parochial outlook tends to introspective brooding. Their community

(*note 63 continued*) 1945), pp. 153–6; NUM Annual Conference Report, 1946 discussion of the Miners Charter in the nationalized coal industry.

64. PRO POWE 1/39, March 1946.
65. LRO De 11 77/33, 20 June 1945.
66. Ministry of Fuel and Power, *Regional Survey Report, The Coalfields of the Midland Region* (HMSO), 1945.
67. Ibid., South Wales Coalfield.
68. Ibid., Bristol and Somerset Coalfield.

feels itself socially ostracised, a race apart. It develops that terrible malady, an 'inferiority complex,' for which the cure is long and painful. Here is to be found part of the answer to the question asked so frequently: why does the miner strike in war-time? After generations of life in a partly sealed community ... his outlook can scarcely be expected to expand at a moment's notice.[69]

Mark Benney told a similar story:

East Tanthope, this village that had lived by digging holes in the ground ... . The customs of the community, both underground and on the surface, were old and honoured for their age; the double isolation of craft and geography had turned these people in upon themselves, so that they took their standards from their forebears instead of from the strangers in the city.[70]

It was therefore decided that institutes and halls would be the 'focal point of community life in the mining area', whose facilities and activities 'should be shared not only by the miner, his wife and family, but also by the general public at large in the vicinity'.[71] 'The Welfare' was to become another project in the post-war integrated community schemes which built on the idealism of wartime experience. Similarly, the building of holiday camps exclusively for miners, which had been so encouraged before 1939, was questioned since it would deprive the miner and his family from the beneficial consequences 'of mixing with workers of different occupations and interests'.[72] The wartime local authority-organized 'holidays at home' programme had pointed one way forward for an integrated community leisure provision. In

69. Newman, *Journey*, p. 213.
70. Benny, *Charity*, p. 122.
71. It was envisaged that socially 'miners' community centres would strengthen the membership, break down social prejudice and afford opportunities for mine workers to meet people with fresh interests' and result in the organization of a wider range of leisure-time activities which could include 'art, music, drama, literature, discussion groups and handicrafts', MWWT; First Annual Report, NMWJC, 1948. For some brief, pertinent comments on this community building for a better planned tomorrow see **Hayes, 'An "English war"'** in this volume.
72. MWWT. The difficulties of fully achieving the objectives were not lost on Arthur Horner, general secretary of NUM and Commission member: 'The isolation of a large part of the mining community, and the necessity to develop a culture of its own was inescapable ... he did not believe in the segregation of mining communities, but one had to accept that pits were where pits were', CISWO Ann. Rpt 1952.

the coalfields the district miners' welfare officers had assisted in the organization and running of the programme by providing facilities at institutes at which 'Ingenuity and resource resulted in attractive programmes, including carnivals, children's sports, cycle events, gymkhanas, band competitions, baby shows and mining competitions for road-laying, rope splicing and capping, timbering, ambulance work etc.'[73] One such event was the annual 'Country Day and Gymkhana' organized at Chesterfield, Derbyshire which attracted an estimated 45,000 people in 1944.[74] The situation in Lancashire, where welfare recreational provision had always been considered largely irrelevant because the miner and his family enjoyed a ready access to the municipal and commercial leisure provision of the community at large, remained undisturbed, despite the MWC's reservations that 'the amount of first-class entertainment provided' encouraged 'spectator' rather than 'performer' recreational activity.[75]

Certainly the post-war community building was declared a great success as revamped and new 'welfare centres' became

> focal points of social welfare, meeting places for the community. Sporting grounds ... were provided in villages and towns which would not otherwise have possessed them. People with welfare enthusiasm in the mining areas were given the means and encouragement to organise or revitalise choirs and bands and drama groups, youth clubs and camps, sports days, competitions and festivals.[76]

The existence of the Miners' Welfare Fund coincided, however, with the parallel development of mass commercial leisure provision, and this raises the question of what was the relative importance of each to the miner and his family. Was welfare provision ever of more than marginal importance to the majority of mineworkers and their families and, more particularly for our present concerns, did the Second World War have any significant impact on participation in welfare-organized leisure?

73. MWWT.
74. PRO LAB 26/85, North Midland Region, 9 September 1944.
75. PRO POWE 1/38, June 1944.
76. CISWO Ann. Rpt 1952.

III

It is far easier to obtain evidence both on the buildings and facilities provided by the welfare fund and the official welfare philosophy which underpinned it, than to measure welfare 'activity'. Qualitative statements abound, but these are not usually supported by quantitative evidence and conflicting opinions are not unusual. A pre-war South Wales survey, for instance, offers both pessimistic and optimistic judgements on the impact of welfare provision on the mining community. The negative view first:

> The same pathetic little attempts of the welfare schemes to brighten village life ... it is not surprising that after a long and arduous day's work in the stifling atmosphere of a modern coalmine the miner finds repose in his arm chair more attractive and even more essential then the further exertion required by the playing of games ... there is very little [energy and vitality] left to fire them to seek knowledge and experience of the higher arts, the great majority only having the desire for easy and necessarily cheap entertainments, which fund outlets in such sports as whippet racing, rabbit coursing, quoit throwing ... miner sports provided by the village pub-darts, dominoes, card games ... we have the fellow whose sole recreation and literature is the Mid-Day Echo. A tanner flutter each way keeps things going. As a cinema fan nothing equals him ... unless it be his daughters ... The sale girls with painted faces, to hide their pale pallor underneath. With their slang phrases hot from the cinemas, Oh-yea, Baby; Its O.K. with me, I'll be right there, etc.[77]

A positive picture follows:

> With regard to recreation the welfare schemes appear to have functioned successfully and have ... supplied to a great extent what the workers have demanded ... . A typical institute comprises a reading room, library, lecture room, band room and a billiard room. Above is the cinema, or large hall, where the mass meetings and entertainment are held ... . The musical associations are many and varied, choral societies, symphony orchestras, brass bands. These three form the main interest, although dramatic societies have a strong footing

77. H. M. Watkins, *Coal and Men: An Economic and Social Study of the British and American Coalfields* (London, Allen & Unwin, 1934), pp. 396, 400, 411, 418.

in parts ... . The Welfare Movement, in bringing parks, with provision for tennis, bowls etc., is removing the sports blight.[78]

The MWC recognized in the late 1930s that 'some of the playing fields and institutes were not being used as well or fully as they might be by the mining population',[79] and the remedy, as we have seen, was the all-purpose, all-people community centre which had become enshrined in wartime thinking as 'more than an ideal, ... a target for the future'.[80] Increased participation in indoor activity certainly occurred during the war and provided an opportunity to build, for instance, on the advance of women and the work of CEMA and ENSA. In 1945 the MWC hoped that 'the time will come when all Miners' Welfare Centres have strong and active "Ladies Sections" which were not merely adjuncts to male activity'.[81] By 1948 there were eight sections or clubs in Nottinghamshire 'with music, drama, handicrafts and discussion groups' among their activities.[82] By 1962 that number was 28, with 1,700 members and still growing, while there were 20 in South Wales and a dozen in Scotland.[83] Nonetheless, in most coalfields 'institutes still had too much of the character of "men's clubs"', which only admitted women to the cinema or the Saturday night dances 'which attracted large crowds'.[84]

The MWC also continued to encourage the family holiday, an activity in which women and children participated as much as the mineworker. Despite initial wartime reservations the Skegness Holiday Centre reopened in 1947 and in its first year 14,000 miners and their families enjoyed a well-earned week's holiday there between Whitsun and the end of September.[85] Derbyshire soon added Rhyl holiday camp, and both were packed out for the whole season by 1952. The North-East also organized temporary centres for tenting enthusiasts on the Northumberland coast.[86] Other districts considered

78. Ibid., pp. 392–3, 418.
79. MWC Ann. Rpt 1938.
80. Miners' Welfare Commission, *Mining People* (HMSO, 1945). n.p.
81. MWWT.
82. NMWJC Ann. Rpt 1948.
83. CISWO Ann. Rpt 1952.
84. Zweig, *Men*, p. 108.
85. NMWJC Ann. Rpt 1948.
86. Both camps provided holidays for 20,000 miners and their families in 1952 and several hundred braved the more spartan facilities near Whitley Bay. CISWO Ann. Rpt 1953. The Derbyshire camp provided 'the two essentials –

following Derbyshire's example but, as in neighbouring Nottinghamshire, such initiatives were stillborn in the face of their mineworkers'
reluctance to agree to a colliery-closure rota system.[87] It was August
or bust for the majority of miners and it became increasingly common
for districts to encourage 'holidays away from home' to a wide range
of destinations through liaison with the British Travel and Holiday
Association.[88]

CEMA's replacement, the Arts Council, continued to work with
the MWC to bring music and drama to the coalfields. In 1947 a
joint initiative resulted in plays such as Priestley's *An Inspector Calls*
being shown at 118 miners' welfare centres in northern England
and South Wales. The plays certainly reached a large audience since
46,565 tickets were sold, 83 per cent of capacity. Following this
success 1948 saw such plays as Shaw's *Major Barbara* being performed
in 160 venues in four districts, 'with equally successful results'.[89] A
Welsh drama company of 'principally BBC artistes' toured South
Wales to great acclaim while in Scotland the Glasgow-based Unity
Theatre Company gave performances of plays such as *Men Should
Weep* at 16 institutes during the winter of 1947–48. The MWC
claimed that 'The work of the professional drama companies ... had
done much to stimulate interest in drama and to increase the number
of amateur dramatic societies.'[90] In Scotland, for instance, there were
21 societies in 1948 which grew to 60 by 1953, by which time the
annual Scottish Drama Festival was a firmly established event.[91]
Similarly, in the case of music, a joint venture saw the Covent
Garden opera chorus and four soloists touring South Wales in summer
1948 for three weeks, performing in Swansea, Cardiff, Treorchy,
Mountain Ash, Port Talbot and Llanelli. The venues for the semi-
staged operas, which ranged from *Carmen* to *Peter Grimes*, were

(*note 86 continued*) good food and good amusements', including professional
and amateur entertainers, and the family element was stressed in descriptions
of it 'children paddle, look for shells and make sand-castles. Women knit, sew,
read, or simply do nothing for a change. The men gather round talking,
laughing, singing' (or just sleeping), 'Skegness is so Bracing', *Coal* (August 1947).
87. CISWO, Nottinghamshire Area Sub-Committee, Ann. Conference Rpt 1953.
88. NMWJC, Ann. Rpt 1948: CISWO Ann. Rpt 1953.
89. NMWJC, Ann. Rpt 1948; PRO POWE 1/4, July 1947. During the 1948 tour
13,000 miners and their families saw plays by Priestley and Shaw in 33 mining
institutes in the North East. *Coal*, 2:1 (1948).
90. NMWJC, Ann Rpt 1948; PRO POWE 1/4, July 1947.
91. CISWO Ann. Rpt 1953.

packed.[92] In all coalfields choirs of all shapes and sizes and brass and silver bands were revived, enlarged and revitalized through welfare encouragement and expenditure. The high points were the bilingual Miners' Eisteddfod in South Wales which started as a one-day event in Porthcawl in 1948 and had grown to three days within two decades,[93] and the annual Yorkshire brass-band festival held in the City Hall, Sheffield to, typically, an audience of 2,400 listening to 33 competing bands in 1953.[94] All coalfields, however, held their choir and band festivals and competitions and institutes were alive with practising musicians on several nights of the week.[95] The recently formed National Coal Board also sought in 1947 to take a leaf out of the Arts Council's book by organizing, for instance, a display of miners' paintings and handicrafts. About 15,000 saw 300 works in London and a third of the collection was equally well received at leading municipal galleries during the exhibition's national tour.[96]

By the early 1950s, as a result of the encouragement given to female participation and music and drama, among other developments, CISWO could claim:

> There is a miners' welfare scheme in Warwickshire which is typical of many throughout the coalfields. It is situated six miles from the nearest town. It has a good hall, a band room, committee room and buffet bar. There is an excellent dance floor provision and for gymnastics and table tennis. There are adjacent cricket and football pitches and a bowling green being constructed.
>
> The institute is open every night from 7.00pm to 10.00pm. In the

92. *Coal*, **2**:2 (1948).
93. NMWJC Ann. Rpt 1948; Hywel Francis and David Smith, *The Fed. A History of the South Wales Miners in the Twentieth Century* (London, Lawrence & Wishart, 1980), p. 428.
94. CISWO Ann. Rpt 1953.
95. See, for instance, M. Pope, *Music All Powerful. A History of the Eastwood Collieries Male Voice Choir 1920–85* (Nottingham, privately published, 1995). There are dozens of such histories of colliery bands and choirs.
96. National Coal Board Ann. Rpt 1947. The Ashington Group, supported by the Northumberland district subcommittee, are the best known group of 'miner painters' but it is by no means unique. W. Weaver, *Pitmen Painters: The Ashington Group 1934–1984* (London, Constable, 1988) is the most detailed study of its work. See also Zweig, *Men*, p. 110, where he comments on the high standard of painting and model-making in Durham, South Wales, Northumberland, Yorkshire, Derbyshire and Nottinghamshire.

light refreshment buffet bar there will be groups playing dominoes, darts and draughts. In the committee room there may be a meeting of one of the sections; the fishing club or the ambulance corps. Or perhaps there is a meeting to discuss a proposal to form a youth club.

On one night the choral society will be rehearsing on another the junior or senior band. At another time there will be a dancing class with a member of the committee operating the radiogram. On Saturday night there is a dance, the ever-popular event of the week.

On one night in the year each section holds its own dinner and dance. Concerts are frequently held in aid of some good cause. The scheme is efficiently managed by a general committee representative of all the affiliated sections, and it is firmly established as the pride of every inhabitant in the mining village.[97]

A typical welfare institute on this account provided a balanced range of activities: indoor and outdoor and active and less active games and sports, 'serious' and more 'frivolous' leisure pursuits, provision for adults and youth of both sexes and the community event of the week, the Saturday rave-up. Nonetheless, to describe an impressive range of activity and assert that the institute is the 'pride' of the community still only provides a very impressionistic account of the contribution of the 'welfare' to recreational life. Moreover other non-official contemporary accounts offer a far less optimistic picture. Zweig, for instance, postulates that:

Nearly every mining village has its Welfare Institute, centre or club, or recreation hall ... [they] played a much greater part in the past than they do now. Where working men's clubs are widespread the whole life of the Welfare Institutes is falling ... because the clubs have their own [competing] facilities ... . Where the collieries are in close proximity to the towns the Welfare Institutes ... become lifeless, because cheap recreations of the same sort are provided in a large scale in the towns ... . Some welfare institutes have closed their reading and library rooms ... . The Welfare Institutes still have a vital part to play in remote and isolated villages, but in the villages with good communications they have become redundant ... . The miners now have sufficient money to get the recreation they want provided cheaply on a more or less commercial basis. ... But the same story was told nearly everywhere I went, and the same phrase was used: 'you don't need to do anything for yourself.' Even in South

97. CISWO Ann. Rpt 1952.

Wales, where traditions of cultural interests cultivated by the institution of the 'Eisteddfod' were very high, I was told that the choirs,
dramatic societies, poetry and musical clubs were not as popular as
they used to be. When I asked the reason, the answer was, 'the buses
have done that. You can more freely for a few pence and get any
amusement you want from outside the village'.[98]

The authors of that classic study of a South Yorkshire mining town,
Coal Is Our Life, similarly observe: 'In general, it can be said that
the Miners' Welfare Institute does not play a very important part in
the leisure time of the miner above the age of twenty ... at present
it provides little that is not provided elsewhere and it is chiefly
elsewhere that the miner in Ashton [Featherstone] spends his leisure
time'.[99] Nonetheless, Zweig admitted that there was a sizeable following for colliery football, cricket and rugby teams (particularly
football), that cinemas in welfare institutes in South Wales (open six
days a week) and Northumberland and Durham (open every day) in
particular were 'besieged the whole year round' and that everywhere
at weekends Institute dance halls were 'always very crowded' (usually
with the younger generation), the one at Featherstone being no
exception.[100] It would seem from this admittedly not entirely consistent evidence that the leisure provision of miners' institutes was
of relatively little importance except, perhaps, in the most isolated
communities. A unique survey undertaken for a whole coalfield in
1950 enables a firmer less impressionistic conclusion to be
drawn.[101]

98. Zweig, *Men*, pp. 110, 127–8.
99. N. Dennis, F. Henriques and C. Slaughter, *Coal Is Our Life. An Analysis of a
    Yorkshire Mining Community* (London, Tavistock; 1969 edn), p. 128. The
    Research was undertaken in the period 1952–54.
100. Zweig, *Men*, pp. 106–7. On this popularity of the cinema at welfare institutes
    see J. Davidson, *Northumberland Miners 1919–1939* (Newcastle-upon-Tyne,
    Co-operative Press, 1973) pp. 250–1; B. Hogenkamp, 'Miners' Cinemas in
    South Wales in the 1920's and 1930's', *Llafur*, 4:2 (1985), pp. 64–76. By
    popular demand, and despite efforts to show more 'educational and cultural'
    films, Hollywood movies and popular British cinema dominated the showings.
    There were no less than 44 miners' cinemas in South Wales in 1945: Coalfields
    Survey, South Wales, p. 152; Zweig, *Men*, p. 127; Dennis et al., *Coal*, pp.
    125–7.
101. National Miners' Welfare Joint Council. Nottingham Area Welfare Committee.
    *A Survey of Miners' Welfare Facilities and Activities in the Nottinghamshire
    Coalfield* (Nottingham, privately published, 1951).

There were 38,708 miners employed in Nottinghamshire in 1950, and although all were members of a welfare scheme by virtue of a deduction from their wages and welfare fund finances, the proportion of 'dead' membership which rarely, if ever, took part in the, multifarious organized 'club' activities was, at three-quarters, substantial though by no means overwhelming. Even less of their 'womenfolk' participated: 'only 10 per cent are connected with any Welfare Scheme. The reason for this is not far to seek. Women are less "Clubbable" than men and only attracted by a specific purpose and there is a paucity of opportunities for them in many schemes as yet.' [102] Nonetheless, the Survey revealed that no less than 39 active pursuits were organized in the Nottinghamshire institutes (see Table 2).[103]

Sport in all its guises was the most common pursuit, though gardening was the most popular single activity and there was a flourishing tradition of horticultural competitions. However, it was the Nottinghamshire chrysanthemum rather than the Durham leek that was especially prized. A quarter of its institutes organized a brass band or drama society (or both), while nearly half were the venue of competitive league indoor games, such as darts or dominoes. It was perhaps disappointing in the land of Robin Hood that there was only a single archery club as against seven devoted to golf. Activities more commonly associated, even more so than golf, with the middle class, such as photography, model engineering, the orchestra or dance band, also made an appearance. The district and institute committees clearly encouraged the widest variety of popular leisure activity which was enjoyed by a not inconspicuous minority of the mining population of both sexes, often in association with

102. Notts. Survey summary, p. 61. Women also continued to be 'tied a good deal more to the home than men are by household cares'. *Departmental Enquiry*, 1931, op. cit. Presumably a larger proportion of women attended the institutes' functions on a casual basis, such as dance night or for a celebration.

103. 42,481 miners and their dependants were members of the institutes so 21.8 per cent participated in their 'club' activities on the assumption that each member only undertook a single activity. There were also 2,837 participants from non-mining backgrounds, 23.4 per cent of total participants. The gender dimension is largely hidden, though women were to be found in considerable numbers in tennis clubs and dramatic societies and, more remarkably perhaps, a third of the 62-strong membership of the Clifton institute darts club were women.

Table 2: Activities in the 40 Nottinghamshire District Miners'
Welfare Institutes, 1950

Activity	Number of mining people participating	Number of institutes organizing the activities
Cricket	982	33
Football	749	30
Rugby	6	1
Hockey	40	1
Bowls	1,144	27
Tennis	682	21
Swimming	100	1
Cycling	10	1
Golf	49	7
Tug of War	15	1
Angling	113	4
Archery	7	1
Boxing	77	4
Physical Culture	120	5
Badminton	207	13
Indoor Organised Games	434	17
Rifle Club	112	2
Table Tennis	39	4
Ladies' Clubs	663	17
Girls' Clubs	210	5
Mixed Clubs	300	2
Boys' Clubs	765	15
Brass Bands	227	10
Dance Bands	12	2
Orchestra	5	1
Dramatic Society	188	9
Operatic Society	40	4
Male Voice Choir	96	1
Female Voice Choir	18	1
Debating Society	42	1

Activity	Number of mining people participating	Number of institutes organizing the activities
Model Engineering	40	1
Horticultural Society	60	1
Photographic Society	4	1
Fur and Feather Society	33	2
Gardening	1,221	11
Pig Club	260	3
Pigeon Club	39	2
Canine Society	85	2
Parent Teachers' Association	70	1
Total	9,279	

club members from non-mining backgrounds. These findings certainly that 'In pit villages, drinking and gambling in working men's clubs was the most common way workers enjoyed their spare time',[104] though it might be expected, on the basis of Zweig's conclusions, that the level of participation would vary according to the degree of geographical isolation of the institute. Nottinghamshire evidence suggests that the relationship is not quite so linear (see Table 3).[105]

A comparison of the experience of Basford Hall (Nottingham suburbia), Pinxton (Erewash Valley Coalfield; easy access to Nottingham), Bentinck (close to Mansfield and other mining towns in the Leen Valley Coalfield) and Bilsthorpe (an isolated mining community in the Dukeries coalfield) reveals that participation levels were conspicuously highest at Basford Hall than those of the other three. Basford Hall also had a relatively high number of participants from non-mining backgrounds. It was Basford Hall's reputation as 'perhaps the nearest approach to a community centre in the district' that explains its relative success in welfare ethos terms, and Bilsthorpe's comparative isolation doubtless explains the absence of non-mining participants though not, perhaps, its relatively low miner participation rate. Non-mining participants were most active in the cycling club at Bentinck and the Basford Hall and Bentinck tennis

104. Fielding et al., 'England Arise!', p. 156.
105. Notts. Survey, p. 14. Bilsthorpe was the only institute where the hall was used for film shows.

Table 3: Activity and participation in four Nottinghamshire
Miners' Welfare Institutes

		Institute			
		Basford Hall	*Pinxton*	*Bentinck*	*Bilsthorpe*
Miners		129	1,123	1,098	610
Mining Community		5,787	3,369	3,294	1,830
Outdoor Activities	(1)	248	276	64	108
	(2)	181	19	80	20
Indoor Activities	(1)	57	115	35	20
	(2)	46	12	23	10
Ladies' Section	(1)	24	40	90	40
	(2)	17	9	40	–
Youth Clubs	(1)	42	–	–	30
	(2)	52	–	–	–
Miners and dependants membership		1,800	3,000	1,700	1,530
% of active membership		20.6	14.4	11.1	12.5

Notes: 1 = Mining population   2 = Non-mining population

clubs. The dramatic societies at Pinxton and Bentinck drew on the talents of a wide section of the local population (there were 250 non-player members at Pinxton), as did the brass band at Basford Hall. All four institutes had a substantial ladies' section organizing leisure pursuits and events of their own, and doubtless acting as a ginger group to keep the men on their toes.

Though the Survey indicates that the majority of Nottinghamshire welfare institutes had a sufficient range of activities on offer so as not to belie the Warwickshire 'model',[106] the latter and the Survey,

106. Ibid. Harworth is an example of an institute 'in a self-contained village', nine miles equidistant from the towns of Worksop and Doncaster, comparable with the Warwickshire 'typical' institute. The facilities comprised: institute building with games room, three billiard tables, reading room, smoke room, hall with dance floor, licensed bar and stewards' quarters. Out of doors there were two crown bowling greens, one cricket pitch, two football pitches, one rugby pitch, three grass tennis courts, a children's playground and 'one very good pavilion'. Clubs and (membership) were: football, three teams (33), cricket, two teams

because of their concern to identify organized 'active' rather than spontaneous 'passive' pursuits, play down what was for the bulk of members one of the institute's central functions: a convenient drinking place with subsidized alcoholic beverages on offer. The 'dead' membership doubtless came miraculously alive at opening time, since only four institutes had no bar and only one institute with a bar did not also possess a hall where dances and other mass entertainment could be organized.[107] The bar was primarily a male preserve, though at Annesley, for instance, women were admitted 'in company with their men folk on certain evenings per week', including the Saturday dance night.[108] The Survey concluded that the miners' welfare organization had a greater impact on 'a greater number than any other voluntary organisation in the county', and this is without its contribution to the drinking habits of the miner being taken into account.

IV

By 1939 the achievements of the MWC in the field of recreational provision were considerable. Its initiatives had progressed beyond the experimental stage and it was encouraging the formulation, in the face of considerable apathy, of long-term plans with the idea of miners' institutes as focal points of social life in mining communities at the centre of them. There was pressure to break down the traditional masculine culture of the institutes and transform then into genuine centres of community leisure for the whole family. The opening of the first miners' holiday camp underlined this commitment. The war had both a negative and positive impact: it prevented the construction and remodelling of the institutes and outdoor sporting activities were severely curtailed. Sports grounds

(note 106 continued) (22), rugby (30), bowls (85), tennis (100), hockey (50), brass band (28), orchestra (10), operatic society (46), pigeon club (19) and angling (35). The cricket, football, rugby and bowls members played in league sport, though the colliery had its own knockout competitions in cricket and football in which 476 and 190 players respectively participated in 1950 out of a workforce approaching 2,000. The 450-seat hall was packed for concerts, productions, and dances.

107. Ibid. The facilities of each institute are fully described on pp. 13–36.

108. Ibid., p. 13.

became neglected or derelict to the detriment, in particular, of young people and the Bevin Boys who were being recruited into the industry. Existing indoor provision and activity did, however, become more a 'real family affair'.[109] Women, for instance, become more conspicuous. CEMA and ENSA 'artistes', also, were both performing and realizing their mission to encourage 'music-making and play-acting by the people themselves'.[110] The war also injected a new urgency into the planning process and fostered a determination among welfare enthusiasts not to miss the opportunities which would be afforded by peacetime to expand welfare on the basis of wartime experience and idealism. Were these aspirations realized? Zweig contended in 1948 that this endeavour was doomed to failure in the face of the onslaught of commercial leisure provision and that, moreover, 'The welfare Institutes played a much greater part in the past than they do now.'[111] Zweig, indeed, might be described as a premature member of what James Hinton has characterized as the 'Apathy School', who suggest that the war did nothing to arrest, and perhaps even encouraged, 'a turning away from choirs, dramatic societies and musical clubs' towards the vicarious pleasures of passive commercial leisure in mining communities.[112] The same could not be said of Hywel Francis, who proclaimed that most institutes in South Wales 'appear to blossom into a golden era', manured by the twin nutrients of welfare planning and a socialized coal industry, in the decade after 1945.[113] There is, perhaps, too much of the rhetorical in Francis's enthusiasm for post-war revivalism,[114] but it is closer to the reality than the Apathy School's gloom and doom, which is based on a concept of leisure which sees 'high' 'serious' (welfare) and 'popular' 'frivolous' (commercial) leisure activity as

109. *Mining People*, n.p.
110. Croft, 'Betrayed spring', p. 199.
111. Zweig, *Men*, p. 128. £906,000 (£130,000 per year) was spent on recreational provision in the period 1945–52 despite this warning of failure.
112. Fielding *et al.*, *'England Arise!'*, p. 156; J. Hinton, '1945 and the Apathy School', *History Workshop Journal*, 48 (1997), pp. 266–73.
113. H. Francis, 'The Origins of the South Wales Miners' Library', *History Workshop Journal*, 2 (1976), pp. 188–90. See also H. Francis and D. Smith, *The Fed.*, pp. 427–31.
114. It downplays the substantial pre-war achievement summarized in the *1945 Regional Survey* and is too dependent on the experience of the remarkable, and not entirely typical, community of Tredegar.

polar opposites locked in a mortal combat in which the winner is not in doubt.[115] The welfare enthusiasts responsible for building on the advantages envisaged in *Miners' Welfare Looks Forward* did not view leisure provision as being compartmentalized in this time-honoured tradition and sought to develop the institutes as centres of 'recreational, cultural and educational' pursuits; leisure for all 'where welfare activities are really communal, each sectional interest benefiting from the support of the others; and all combine to make well-being a live and vigorous reality'.[116] The evidence presented here indicates that, if the Nottinghamshire scene is any guide to the larger welfare canvas, in the immediate post-war years at least, the more idealistic notion of institutes as exemplars of national community was unrealistic, though not outrageously so, and that institutes as centres catering for the widest range of leisure pursuits, from drama to the bar discussion group,[117] approached the success claimed for it by the official record of the MWC. That both constituencies coalesced as performers and audience at an institute production of *The Merchant of Venice* or a musical comedy such as *The Country Girl*[118] is fitting testimony to wartime aspirations.[119] The oft-claimed trio of powerful commercial alternatives to voluntary leisure activity – the cinema, dance hall and bar – were incorporated, as the occasion demanded, into the leisure provision of the most successful institutes.[120] Whether they were

115. Compare W. L. Guttsman, *Workers' Culture in Weimar Germany* (Oxford, Berg, 1990), p. 132: 'It is tempting to see in the change in the pattern of entertainment and leisure the operation of a kind of Gresham's Law by which commercial culture, like debased coinage, draws out the sterling silver of High Culture.' Dennis *et al.*, *Coal*, p. 130, distinguish between 'frivolous' and 'improving' ways of spending leisure time.

116. *Mining People*, n.p.

117. Work and sport were the twin pillars of discussion in the bar. Dennis *et al.*, *Coal*, p. 144.

118. Ibid., p. 123; Notts. Survey, p. 63.

119. The strength of drama and musical activity in miners' institutes is at odds with Andy Croft's sweeping assertion that 'Within a few years the cultural forces unlocked by CEMA had been frustrated and the high hopes present at the formation of the Arts Council severely disappointed.' Croft, 'Betrayed Spring', p. 210.

120. Featherstone, lacking a bar, was not one of them and we must be wary, unlike the so-called Apathy School, of accepting Dennis *et al.*'s claim for the typicality of the Featherstone mining community. Dennis *et al.*, *Coal*, pp. 249–5.

subsequently successful in withstanding the post-1950 threat of television is another matter, but is a concern beyond the brief of this discussion of the consequences of the Second World War.[121]

121. A CISWO internal survey of 1955 concluded that 'Popular recreation, in the form of gardening and television now available at home' posed the greatest threat to welfare organized leisure provision. F. Henriques and F. Summers, CISWO Social Survey Extract.

'You and I – All of Us Ordinary People': Renegotiating 'Britishness' in Wartime

John Baxendale

Caroll Levis's film *Discoveries*, made in the summer of 1939 as a spin-off from his radio talent-show of the same name, while not destined to enter the canon of memorable British cinema, did contain one moment of cultural resonance. With war looming, the film rose to the occasion in a grand finale featuring Master Glyn Davies, the Welsh boy soprano, in midshipman's uniform, surrounded by a huge chorus of bell-bottomed sailors, and warbling a new song by Ross Parker and Hughie Charles called *There'll Always Be An England*.

The film was soon forgotten, but the song lived on: when war came it went straight to the top of the best-sellers list, and within two months 200,000 copies of the sheet music had been sold. It was the first great hit song of the war.[1] More than this, along with Parker and Charles's other big hit *We'll Meet Again*, it is one of the handful of wartime songs still remembered 50 years after the event. But while the longevity of *We'll Meet Again* owes a great deal to that of Dame Vera Lynn, *There'll Always Be An England* has lived on in a different cultural category: it is a national song – despite its Tin Pan Alley provenance, up there with *Land of Hope and Glory* and *Rule Britannia*, and deemed suitable to be taught to primary school children at the time of the Coronation in 1953, which is where the present author first encountered it.

With its marching rhythm and simple harmonies – no syncopation or other twentieth-century influences, and utterly uncroonable – *There'll Always Be An England* could have been written for the Boer

---

1. S. Seidenberg, M. Sellar and I. Jones, *You Must Remember This: Songs at the Heart of the War* (London, Boxtree, 1995), pp. 28–9.

War music hall: certainly, it bypasses everything that had happened musically since about 1910. The lyrics also aspire to a timeless and high-minded sense of nationhood: England (for which we may perhaps read 'Britain') will survive, and be free, as long as 'England means as much to you as England means to me.' But what *does* 'England mean to me'? The song is hardly explicit. The countryside is mentioned ('a cottage small'), but so is the town ('a city street'), the flag ('red, white and blue, what does it mean to you?' – but everyone has a flag), and finally the Empire; but it turns out that we are not fighting for the Empire – rather, the Empire is expected to fight for us: 'we can depend on you!' Later commentators have read the song variously as jingoistic, as ruralist, as 'understated and personal', or simply as 'vapid': it is, in fact, all these things.[2] Its subtext lies in its absence of specific content: it doesn't matter *what* England means, as long as it means *something*.

There'll Always Be An England's immediate successor at the top of the charts was rather different. *We're Gonna Hang Out The Washing On The Siegfried Line* achieves bravado through bathos, setting the comic domesticity of the music hall against Nazi militaristic pretensions, assisted by a satirical hint of the Germanic oompah band – any irony being entirely retrospective, post-May 1940. The war is assimilated to a familiar cheerful vulgarity which 'we' are confidently assumed already to share. As in the previous song, England/Britain (an elision which this essay will not explore) is not this image, or that national characteristic: it is simply 'us', and the familiar life we share, which can be as well evoked by a few shop-worn symbols and a bit of music-hall slapstick, as by any rhetorical evocation of national history or meditation on the national character.

I

We might have expected something more portentous, or at least more specific. Since 1945, it has been commonplace to regard the Second World War as a defining national moment, the time when

2. These contrasting views appear in, respectively, ibid., p. 29; M. J. Wiener, *English Culture and the Decline of the Industrial Spirit* (Cambridge, Cambridge UP, 1978), p. 41; A. Light, *Forever England* (London, Routledge, 1991), p. 154; and A. Calder, *The People's War* (London, Panther, 1971), p. 72.

at least we knew who we were.[3] Writing in 1955, one of the first historians of inter-war Britain, Charles Loch Mowat, saw September 1939 as a moment of national redemption and rebirth for the British people: 'As they awaited the Battle of Britain, they found themselves again, after twenty years of indecision. They turned away from past regrets and faced the future unafraid.'[4] Ten years later, for A. J. P. Taylor, 1945 was the critical, democratizing moment:

> Traditional values lost much of their force. Other values took their place. Imperial greatness was on its way out; the welfare state was on its way in. The British empire declined; the condition of the people improved. Few now sang 'Land of Hope and Glory'. Few even sang 'England Arise'. England had arisen all the same.[5]

The underlying narrative here was not just Dunkirk, the Blitz and D-Day, but the wartime coalition, Beveridge and finally the welfare state, forged in the crucible of 'the people's war', and triumphantly replacing the Empire as our defining national institution. Two or three decades on, the 'post-war' era was over, and the story had changed. The war still occupied a central position in the national narrative, but now the Right, and even some on the Left, identified it not as a radical but as a conservative moment. Margaret Thatcher revived Churchillian rhetoric to wage war on both Argentina and the welfare consensus, in the name of traditional British values which the post-war nation had somehow mislaid; while on the Left, Angus Calder reinterpreted 1940–41 as the origin, no longer of a leftward shift in national life, but of a new conservative national mythology, a moment when 'the Left would think ... it had captured History [while] in fact, it had been captured by it'.[6]

The mythology in question was 'the myth of the Blitz' – the 'finest hour', in which the British people were, supposedly, united and

---

3. See, among many others, A. Calder, *The Myth of the Blitz* (London, Jonathan Cape, 1991); A. Barnett, *Iron Britannia* (London, Allison & Busby, 1982); C. Barnett, *The Audit of War* (London, Macmillan, 1987); G. Hurd (ed.), *National Fictions: World War Two in British Films and Television* (London, BFI Publishing, 1984); T. Aldgate and J. Richards, *Britain Can Take It: the British Cinema in the Second World War* (Oxford, Blackwell, 1986).

4. C. L. Mowat, *Britain Between the Wars, 1918–1940* (London, Methuen, 1955), p. 657.

5. A. J. P. Taylor, *English History 1914–1945* (Oxford, Oxford UP, 1965), p. 600.

6. Calder, *Myth of the Blitz*, p. 15. See also R. Bromley, *Lost Narratives: Popular Fictions, Politics and Recent History* (London, Routledge, 1988), ch. 4.

heroic. Calder argues that it was essentially conservative because it reaffirmed what was already 'known' about England: 'not *discovery* but *rediscovery*, or *confirmation*. It is not, as "Armada" and "Glorious Revolution" once were, a myth for a rising nation. It is a myth for people "living in an old country".' The war effort was validated by, and in turn revalidated, the myths of 'Deep England' – timeless and pastoral, in no need of radical change. 'Believing that they were "making history" in harmony with the Absolute Spirit of "England" (or "Britain"), people tried to believe as that spirit seemed to dictate.' Hence, the overall effect of the war was to prop up 'an imperial power which was already in irreversible decline, and national institutions that had tottered into anachronism ... encapsulate a moment of retrenchment as a moment of rebirth ... [and] divert attention from the continuing need for radical change in British society'.[7]

Calder's analysis may reverse the received post-war view, but it still sees the war as a moment of strong consensus about national identity. In a similar vein, though from a rather different political perspective, Jeffrey Richards argues in his study of wartime films that, far from being transformed by the experience of war, the 'essential British national character', conservative in tone, and distinguished by humour, stoicism and tolerance, was reaffirmed, remaining 'in essence what it had been before the war', and indeed remaining much the same until the 1960s, when both it and all civilized values (according to Richards) crashed into ruins. So Richards, too, sees the war as a conservative moment, although for him this was evidently a good thing.[8]

That views of wartime national identity should change in this way is not surprising. Historical memory is not a copy of the real past, but a cultural construct, 'made and remade, investigated and analysed, fantasized and fought over, according to the changing needs and perceptions of succeeding generations', so that up to a point each era can construct the war which suits its purposes best.[9] The reversal in the war's reputation from radical reconstruction to conservative reaffirmation can be understood as a product of changing historical

7. Calder, *Myth of the Blitz*, pp. 7, 14–15.
8. J. Richards, *Films and English National Identity* (Manchester, Manchester UP, 1997), ch. 4.
9. J. Baxendale and C. Pawling, *Narrating the Thirties: A Decade in the Making* (London, Macmillan, 1996), p. 6.

circumstances: in particular, the collapse of the post-war order which the radical reading of the war had validated. It also reflects an intellectual shift, sometimes called the 'cultural turn' in the human sciences, in which the nation has come to be seen, not so much as a set of political institutions and policies, but as a cultural formation, constructed and sustained by cultural means.[10]

My own account of wartime national identity is no doubt equally shaped by the political and intellectual circumstances of our own time. However, it differs in certain respects from those discussed above. Calder and Richards, despite their political differences, seem to agree on two important propositions: first, that there was a single, 'dominant' ideology, narrative or myth of the nation; and second, that it is to be found in texts, such as political speeches, novels, journalism and films. Both of these premises seem questionable. Did national identity in wartime really have such clarity and coherence? I will argue instead that it was a discursive field crossed by many different and conflicting ideas, images and stories about the nation, representing different understandings of past and future, and replete with contradictions and unrealized possibilities which monolithically conservative constructions of 'Englishness' have tended to obscure. Does national identity exist primarily in textual form, as a discourse or a set of propositions about the nation? Words are its most accessible form, and words are what this essay analyses. But 'Englishness' and its textual forms have been so much discussed lately that we can easily forget that to have a national identity – to 'feel British' – you do not need to attribute any particular meaning to the nation at all. England doesn't have to mean *the same* to you as it does to me, simply *as much*.[11]

A light dose of theory may be appropriate here. Anthony Smith distinguishes between two senses of national 'identity', to which we may add a third. At the deepest level, 'national identity' is all about

10. A. D. Smith, *National Identity* (London, Penguin, 1991); Michael Billig, *Banal Nationalism* (London, Sage 1995); B. Anderson, *Imagined Communities. Reflections on the Origins and Spread of Nationalism* (London, Verso, 1995); E. Gellner, *Nations and Nationalism* (Oxford, Blackwell, 1983).
11. Recent discussions of 'Englishness' include R. Colls and P. Dodd (eds), *Englishness: Politics and Culture 1880–1920* (London, Croom Helm, 1986); Light, *Forever England*; P. Wright, *On Living in an Old Country* (London, Verso, 1985); R. Samuel (ed.), *Patriotism: the Making and Unmaking of British National Identity* (London, Routledge, 1989), 3 vols; Richards, *Films and English National Identity*.

a nation's 'peculiar genius, its own way of thinking, acting and communicating', which can be discovered in its history, language and culture, and which shapes its 'collective self' and path of national development. This is the idea of the nation first developed in the eighteenth century by writers such as Herder. It brings forth much rather lofty discourse about the true meaning, character and destiny of the nation, of which the war produced more than its share, in speeches and broadcasts, a torrent of books about national character and history, and innumerable magazine and newspaper articles, not to mention films, saying what the nation meant, and where it was (or ought to be) going. Before the war, such deep questions attracted little attention, and therefore wide agreement. In wartime, they were much discussed, and therefore became open to contestation and contradiction.[12]

But, as Smith points out, at a less profound level, identity also simply means 'sameness' – those things which members of a nation share with each other, and not with non-members, and which therefore sustain a sense of a common national life: dress, food, language, for example: the nationalism of the red pillar-box. 'Sameness' is evoked in innumerable wartime celebrations of familiar British things – a cup of tea or a radio catchphrase, Priestley's story of an artificial pie in a Bradford shop window, or a *Picture Post* photo-feature showing people going about their ordinary business amid wrecked buildings and snaking fire-hoses. But it mainly exists in the daily lives of the people, in their shared experience and familiar surroundings. In the destruction and disruption of war, the minutiae of ordinary life became all the more precious, a source of national pride, and just as much as democratic institutions, under Nazi threat. In 1942, H. V. Morton wrote the imaginary diary of a man living under a future German occupation, in which, even more than political persecution, the most oppressive aspect of Nazi ideology is its detailed intervention in symbolic aspects of everyday life, changing pub signs, pictures on the wall, popular music, the names of London stations, even Christmas.[13] These things represent what Michael Billig has called 'banal nationalism' – the everyday 'flagging' of the nation in thousands of different ways, from the 'B' in the BBC, or the symbols on the coinage, to national football leagues and weather fore-

12. Smith, *National Identity*, pp. 73–9.
13. H. V. Morton, *I, James Blunt* (London, Methuen, 1942).

casts.[14] Banal nationalism is about the arbitrary signs of nationhood: it attributes no particular meaning to the nation and makes no claims about its destiny. The point is not what the nation means, but that you belong to it.

At this point, we can also bring in Benedict Anderson's celebrated account of the nation as an 'imagined community' existing to a large extent in and through its continuous internal dialogue about itself.[15] Anderson's model is interesting because, although national identity is culturally constructed, it does not depend on everyone agreeing about what the nation is. It is the *process* of national culture which makes the nation, rather than the particular ideas or beliefs which the culture disseminates about it. Nationhood becomes possible when the cultural apparatus arrives ('print capitalism') which allows this internal dialogue to take place. By the late 1930s, with the advent of mass literacy, universal suffrage, the popular press, radio and cinema, this dialogue had expanded to include practically everyone, and listening to the BBC or reading a daily newspaper was part of banal, familiar everyday life. Indeed, one of the great issues at stake in wartime was the terms on which people were included in it: the 'tone' and content of the BBC, cinema and popular press.[16]

II

Undoubtedly, the war, especially after May 1940, was a time of particularly profound national self-absorption. Living in enforced isolation from the rest of the world, and imminently threatened with invasion, the British were acutely conscious of their own nationhood. News broadcasts, light entertainment, newspapers, films and political speeches – not to mention everyday conversation – dealt continually with the shared national predicament, allowing people not just to follow the progress of the war, but to identify themselves with far-off events and people as part of the same national story. Everyday life

14. M. Billig, *Banal Nationalism* (London, Sage, 1995), ch. 5.
15. Anderson, *Imagined Communities*, p. 6.
16. D. Cardiff and P. Scannell, 'Radio in World War II', Open University course U203, *Popular Culture*, unit 8 (Milton Keynes, Open UP, 1983); S. Nicholas, *The Echo of War: Home Front Propaganda and the Wartime BBC* (Manchester, Manchester UP, 1996); A. C. H. Smith, *Paper Voices: the Popular Press and Social Change, 1935–1965* (London, Chatto & Windus, 1975), ch. 3.

became pervaded with the bureaucratic mechanisms through which the national state was fighting the war – rationing, conscription, evacuation, the blackout. The impact of war on individuals' lives, bringing deprivation, dislocation and loss, was acknowledged and incorporated as part of a general national experience, something 'we' had to go through together.

Attempts were made to supplement this shared experience with some idea of 'what England means'. However, this proved easier said than done. There was little appetite in 1939 for heroic narratives of national destiny of the sort that had been widespread in 1914: as Clement Attlee observed during the 'phoney war', 'the majority of people in this country have now abandoned the old boastful imperialism'.[17] Recent historians – even those who argue for the continued importance of imperialist sentiment – tend to agree that the inter-war years saw a shift towards a more 'ordinary' and inward-looking idea of the nation: England as home and countryside rather than military glory and the Empire. This tendency was influenced, Alison Light argues, not only by disillusionment after the Great War, and Britain's declining world position, but also by long-term changes in the role of women, the shape of the family, and the middle-class suburban household. But was this 'feminized' nation in the right shape to fight a war?[18] The travel writer H. V. Morton was not alone in observing the lack of public demonstrativeness in 1939.

> There was no flag-waving, no bands, no appeals to patriotism, no pictures of the King and Queen; no one knew the names of any generals or admirals, and the attempt on the part of the press to give 'Tiger' Gort heroic status fell completely flat ... a nation waiting, almost pathetically, for something – anything – to happen.[19]

Morton blamed this apparent apathy on Chamberlain's 'tepid attitude' and lack of leadership, but even after May 1940, when the nation had supposedly woken up, the sense of nationhood seems to have remained low-key and undemonstrative. A Mass-Observation

17. C. Attlee, *War Comes to Britain* (London, Gollancz, 1940), p. 255 – broadcast of 3 February 1940.
18. Light, *Forever England*, esp. 'Introduction'; J. M. Mackenzie, *Propaganda and Empire: The Manipulation of British Public Opinion 1880–1960* (Manchester, Manchester UP, 1984), pp. 9–11.
19. H. V. Morton, *I Saw Two Englands* (London, Methuen, 1942), pp. 280–2.

survey compiled in September 1941 asked observers to write freely
on 'What does Britain Mean to You'.[20] As a guide to public feeling,
this survey is not necessarily reliable. Mass-Observers were not a
typical sample of the population, and their responses were filtered
through Tom Harrisson's judgement on what to include in the File
Report and his subsequent article in the *World Review*. Nevertheless,
for what it is worth, their images of Britain, however fervently
expressed, were predominantly small-scale and homely. At the top
of the list of associations came the countryside – evoked in 'long,
lyrical passages ... simple lists of place-names, catalogues of scenery
and landscapes' – followed by Politics, People and Home. None of
them at all seem to have picked out the Empire as a positive factor,
few cited public symbols such as the flag or the royal family; not
many more cited national literature or patriotic songs. Indeed, several
rejected the whole idea of Britain, which they associated with older
conceptions of nationhood – 'missionaries, gunboats and prestige',
'imperialism of the extreme and jingo type' – preferring instead to
write about England, 'her fields, her woods, her homes, her Words-
worth ... her soil and some of her cities ... her rain and her
sunshine ... England means home'. If England also meant freedom,
this was not an abstract principle, but 'a personal convenience', the
right to go, think and talk as one wishes, and 'the feeling that in
Britain *you need not be afraid*': 'easy tolerance and good humour',
and a tradition of improvised co-operation rather than central
direction, although along with this came 'muddle ... an irritating,
irrational, rather disorderly country', in which social problems were
neglected and institutions left unreformed.

Patriotism, Harrisson concluded, was motivated by 'tangible and
visible things they know and individual people whose characteristics
they have known and can trust and feel affection for' – the familiarity
of 'people who speak the same language, think in a familiar way,
accept most of the standards and beliefs in which one was brought
up'. 'People very seldom consider whether their land is better or
fairer or finer; this is the land you were brought up on, that is the
beginning and end of it.'[21]

20. The following quotes are from Mass-Observation File Reports 878, September
    1941, and 904, October 1941.
21. T. Harrisson, 'What Britain Means to Me', typescript in Mass-Observation
    File Report 904.

Nevertheless, the belief that something deeper was needed, a core national narrative which must be tapped in order to mobilize the 'home front', was firmly fixed in the official mind when war broke out. The job of uncovering and narrating this story fell first of all to the Ministry of Information (MoI), re-established at the start of the war partly to conduct home-front propaganda. The tragicomedy of the MoI's first year of life has been well documented, and it illustrates the difficulty of finding the right 'register' in which to address the nation, and the problems which divergent class outlooks and experience could cause, in a supposedly unified national community.[22] The MoI made it its business to counter what it feared was a lack of popular enthusiasm for the conflict by drawing on the resources of national history and culture to heighten the tone of national rhetoric. The longbowmen of Agincourt were proposed for an early poster campaign, symbolically combining two key national narratives – one of successful military engagement on the Continent, the other, because the bowmen supposedly came from the 'lower classes' (or, according to some versions, the sturdy independent yeomanry, which is not quite the same thing), a narrative of class collaboration in the national interest. With the Fall of France, the MoI continued to dig deep into the national past, urging the BBC to raise public morale, not with comedy or dance bands, but with folk music, both English and Celtic, which presumably was expected to stir the ancestral blood. Pamphlets were issued on the defeat of Napoleon, and the historical achievements of British naval power, and in the autumn of 1940, the MoI embarked on an 'Empire Crusade' campaign, but with little success; as Harold Nicolson observed, people 'do not want at present to be told about New Zealand'. But if they didn't want to know about the Empire, what were they fighting for? It was very perplexing.

One key to what was wrong lay in the social composition of the Ministry. As with most British cultural institutions, it was thought important to keep it in the right hands: it was therefore staffed by 'brilliant amateurs' of the proper social background, rather than professional communicators. 'Bloomsbury', as the *Documentary News Letter* tartly put it, was their temporal and spiritual home.[23]

22. I. McLaine, *Ministry of Morale: Home Front Morale and the Ministry of Information in World War Two* (London, George Allen & Unwin, 1979).
23. *Documentary News Letter*, September 1940.

It is significant that Hore-Belisha, Chamberlain's choice to succeed the failed Lord Macmillan at the MoI, was vetoed by Lord Halifax on the grounds that he was a Jew – acceptable at Defence or Trade, perhaps, but not in a post so closely concerned with national culture and identity.[24] The early MoI view of the nation reflected that of the class its leading lights came from, which regarded itself as the true exemplar of Englishness, and the mass of the people as, in Iain McLaine's words, 'an alien people ... rather dull ... somewhat bucolic', who could not be trusted to understand the nation's predicament, but were nonetheless deeply attached to folk culture, the Empire, and race memories of the Hundred Years War.[25] This people had to be virtually invented from scratch, since few MoI staff seemed to know much about the people who actually existed. Their idea of British national character seems to have been constructed by amalgamating what the historic moment required ('independence, toughness of fibre, sympathy with the underdog') with characteristics drawn from pre-war upper-class heroes, real and fictional. Scott of the Antarctic, Mr Chips, and Charters and Caldicott from Hitchcock's *The Lady Vanishes* were the exemplary figures singled out by Macmillan in his first memorandum on home propaganda. Although Jeffrey Richards presents this as a consensual view of national character in 1939, it was nothing of the sort: it was the British nation as seen from the playing-fields of Eton.[26]

By the time of Brendan Bracken's appointment to the MoI in 1941, the failure of exhortation had been acknowledged. Home Intelligence reports had revealed, not just the resilience of the people, but some resentment of class privilege, and a desire for post-war reform. The approach from now on was to play down the grandiose narratives of national character and destiny, and emphasize instead the immediate task at hand, and the prospect of change after it had been accomplished. But the MoI's early problems were symptomatic: however coherent the nation was at the level of everyday life, attempts to define its 'essential self' were fraught with problems and potentially divisive, because the national culture itself was fractured. The search for an underlying national narrative with the capacity to inspire everyone was, for the time being at least, an abject failure.

24. H. Pelling, *Britain and the Second World War* (London, Fontana, 1970), p. 60.
25. McLaine, *Ministry of Morale*, p. 22.
26. Richards, *Films and English National Identity*, p. 85.

The problem of finding an appropriate tone to address the nation in wartime continued to perplex some. The BBC underwent a minor revolution, moving away from Reithian paternalism towards more populist programming, based on audience demand.[27] Patriotic celebrations and images of the Empire were played down in favour of more prosaic and domestic portrayals of the nation, but for some the sticking-point was unmanly sentimentality in popular song, and the continued popularity with the troops of 'slushy' programmes, notably Vera Lynn's 'Sincerely Yours'. Surely, this kind of thing was un-British, and bad for morale. Could we not, asked the Director of Programmes in 1942, have more 'gay and patriotic musical numbers ... waltzes, marches and cheerful music of any kind', in place of these 'dreary jazz sophistications'? Could not the BBC get someone to write 'better and more virile lyrics'? A competition for rousing patriotic airs, and a 'man-to-man programme', full of 'marches and straight songs', were proposed. New rules were promulgated against 'crooning, sentimental numbers, drivelling words, slush, innuendoes', 'anaemic and debilitated vocal performances by male singers' and 'insincere, over-sentimental performances' by women. But Vera Lynn remained immensely popular with the troops, causing no obvious deterioration of morale.[28]

The cultural and sexual politics of this episode are interesting. Criticism of modern popular music as effeminate, and the attempt to stamp out 'crooning', were nothing new, but date back to the 1910s, when the new popular music was regarded as racially as well as sexually degenerate. Now the troops were being told yet again that the music they preferred was undermining their masculinity. But whose conception of masculinity was this? Presumably not that of the troops themselves. More likely, critics were drawing on a class-specific ideal of manhood associated with the public school, according to which the overt expression of emotion was regarded as unhealthy, to be counteracted by brisk marches, cold showers and the thought of duty – an ideal which, projected on to the nation as a whole, became an image of hearty unsentimentality and the stiff upper lip which, if Alison Light is correct, was as much at odds with the self-image of the majority as was Lord Macmillan's pantheon

27. Cardiff and Scannell, 'Radio in World War II'.
28. A. Briggs, *The War of Words* (Oxford, Oxford UP, 1970), pp. 569–78; Nicholas, *Echo of War*, pp. 238–9; V. Lynn, *Vocal Refrain: an Autobiography* (London, W. H. Allen, 1975), pp. 98–100.

of public-school heroes. 'As I saw it,' commented Vera Lynn in her memoirs, 'I was reminding the boys of what they were *really* fighting for, the precious personal things rather than the ideologies and theories.' A controversy over a style of singing thus tapped into deep conflicts about nation and gender, on which the classes were divided. In peacetime, for most working men, masculinity was tied up with providing for the home and family – 'the precious personal things': only a minority saw it primarily in terms of public duty. Which, then, was the more manly form of patriotism in wartime?

III

And yet, despite the new populism of radio and the press, the most celebrated wartime communicator and reinventor of the nation employed with great success a mode of address which could not have been more out of touch with the common speech of the people he was addressing. Winston Churchill's rhetoric, contrary to the conversational style of most twentieth-century politicians, was based on the principle that the speaker's linguistic register should be raised to match the significance of his subject. His best effects were achieved with a vivid touch of the archaic: as in his post-Alamein 'the bright gleam has caught the helmets of our soldiers'. But a device which proved stirring at historic turning-points could sound merely eccentric on more mundane occasions: his inability to refer to ordinary houses in any other way than as 'cottage homes' must have perplexed some of their occupants. Where successful, Churchill's rhetoric worked off both the familiarity and the special cultural status of seventeenth-century English: Shakespeare, the Authorized Version, the Anglican prayer-book, and its nineteenth-century reworking in the Protestant hymn-book and Victorian melodrama. For twentieth-century Britons, who knew they did not really live in cottages, this was the language of special occasions. Using it, Churchill could sound like a bishop, or a ham Shakespearean actor – the risk of bathos was considerable – but he always made events, and his listeners, sound important: 'This is indeed the grand heroic period of our history, and the light of glory shines on all' (broadcast, 27 April 1940).[29]

29. The Churchill quotes are drawn from W. Churchill, *Complete Speeches*, ed. R. R. James (New York, Chelsea House, 1974), Vols 6 and 7.

If the first effect of Churchill's rhetoric was to temporarily refocus the nation as a historic linguistic community, the second, closely tied in with the first, was to revive a heroic narrative of the nation, once familiar, but largely forgotten in the uncertain inter-war world. To some extent this narrative drew on past military glory – in the circumstances it was natural to mention the defeat of the Armada and Napoleon from time to time, and, since they were on our side, the Empire. But these were really no more than episodes in what was in essence the Whig narrative of national progress through the development of free institutions. 'Freedom', not patriotism, or militarism, was Churchill's key concept. It was Britain's historic mission to defend and promote freedom, and at this perilous moment Britain stood not just for her own freedom but for the freedom of all the world. At the heart of this historical narrative, at the heart of Churchill's nation – lay 'those Parliamentary institutions which have served us so well, ... which have proved themselves the most flexible instruments for securing ordered, unceasing change and progress ... and which, at this solemn moment in world history, are at once the proudest assertion of British freedom and the expression of an unconquerable national will' – this at the opening of Parliament on 21 November 1940. Parliament was more than the instrument and expression of national will, it was the expression of the cause for which the war was being fought, 'the cause of which, I will venture to say in no boastful way, the British Empire is the oldest custodian, namely, representative government based on the freedom and rights of the individual' (15 January 1942).

By contrast, despite Churchill's air of traditionalism, the Crown was sidelined as a national symbol. George VI was praised not for heroic leadership, but for playing his part in the war effort along with everybody else – and, in true Whig style, for his 'thorough comprehension of our Parliamentary and democratic Constitution' (15 May 1945). Although 'we are ranged beneath the crown of our ancient monarchy ... this is no war of chieftains or of princes ... it is a war of peoples and of causes' (14 July 1940). Such is the end-product of a history of progress: 'the wisdom of our ancestors has led us to an envied and enviable situation': a strong Parliament and a constitutional monarchy, 'which both rest solidly upon the will of the people expressed by free and fair election on the basis of universal suffrage' (15 May 1945).

These robust institutions expressed not just the will, but the character of the people and their way of life, which itself had been built up over centuries of progress: 'the spirit of the British nation ... the tough fibre of the Londoners, whose forebears played a leading part in the establishment of Parliamentary institutions and who have been bred to value freedom far above their lives' (1 September 1940). 'How complex, sensitive, resilient, is the society we have evolved over centuries, and how capable of withstanding the most unexpected strain!' (14 July 1941).

In short, the narrative which Churchill sought to revive was the same one through which 'Liberal England' had established itself in the nineteenth century: freeborn Englishmen led by rulers who respected their freedom. It also appealed to Americans, who drew on the same tradition. England stood not just for its own freedom, but for everyone else's as well. But this was a particular kind of freedom: it long pre-dated democracy – universal suffrage had existed for barely a decade in 1939. It could happily brush aside the problem of an Empire, most of whose inhabitants had no say in the running of their own affairs. It did not require equality, of wealth, power or opportunity – one of the rocks on which Liberal England had foundered – although, as Churchill acknowledged, 'progress' may lead in that direction. Such contradictions could be overlooked between 1939 and 1945, in the general anxiety to stress the opposition between efficient German totalitarianism and easy-going British freedom, appeal to 'neutral' Americans, and excuse our somewhat inglorious performance at the start of the war. Once again, 'freedom' and 'muddle' were close partners: 'in this peaceful country, governed by public opinion, democracy and parliament, we were not as thoroughly prepared at the outbreak as this Dictator State' (27 January 1940); however, 'if it is a case of the whole nation fighting and suffering together, that ought to suit us ... because we have been nurtured in freedom and individual responsibility and are the products, not of totalitarian uniformity, but of tolerance and variety' (20 August 1940); and 'the spirit and temperament bred under institutions of freedom will prove more enduring and resilient than anything that can be got out of the most efficiently enforced mechanical discipline' (5 September 1940).

The picture of the nation which emerges – historically free, democratically muddled and anti-militaristic, but dogged and formidable when roused – did not arise by coincidence out of 1,000 years of history, but was crafted to suit the moment. As a result, 'freedom' was applied by Churchill with a rhetorical broad brush, and when it was defined more closely, conflict could easily arise. Labour leaders, who certainly believed in progress, saw freedom not as the historical unfolding, through Parliament, of some eternal essential Britishness, but as something achieved and defended by popular struggle, against the resistance of those in power. For Clement Attlee, freedom of speech, thought and association, as well as the partial humanizing of the capitalist system, were victories which the workers had fought for, and which they must now defend, equally against the Nazi threat and against the remnants of the old order. In this struggle, elements of traditional 'Englishness' such as social inequality, lack of democracy and residual imperialist attitudes were potential sources of weakness which must be eliminated. Herbert Morrison, addressing Durham miners in 1941, gave national history a different spin:

> Your ancestors put paid to the French Napoleon. Their descendants in the 1820s and 1830s put paid to the industrial Napoleons of that day. The next generation fought the battles which built up the Trade Union movement as the bulwark of your industrial freedom and now you, as worthy sons of worthy sires, are called upon to wage a war for the preservation of freedom throughout Europe [and] a better and more rational social order after the war.

In this struggle, the upper class could not be trusted. 'This has always been a people's war. The people saw sooner than their government that Hitler and his gang were thugs who had to be stopped.'[30]

In many ways, the shape of Morrison's historical narrative is similar to Churchill's – Napoleon defeated, freedom advanced – but what emerges is not the Whig view of history seen from above, but its appropriation into the familiar story of 'the onward march of labour': a historical narrative which cast the working class as the champions of national progress, and Churchill's class as its opponents, and was to reach a kind of resolution in 1945.[31] In that year, Churchill's own grasp of the consensual value of 'freedom' slipped, when in his famous 'Gestapo' election broadcast he characterized the policies of his wartime coalition comrades as un-British, in almost exactly the same terms he had previously applied to Hitler's Germany: 'abhorrent to the British ideas of freedom' and antipathetic to Britain's

---

30. Attlee, *War Comes to Britain*, pp. 253–5; H. Morrison, *Looking Ahead: War-time Speeches* (London, Hodder & Stoughton, 1943), pp. 94, 96, 192.
31. F. Williams, *Fifty Years March* (London, Odhams Press, 1949).

role as the 'cradle and citadel of free democracy' (4 June 1945). The rhetoric of national character and history, it transpired, could be used to exclude as well as to embrace. This lesson the resolutely Churchillian Noel Coward had discovered as early as 1940. Telling Australians of the 'new comradeship' through which Britain had 'found dignity and greatness again', Coward was careful to exclude from this renewed national community the 'comfortable left-wing drawing-rooms' and 'the oddly pale hearts of young Oxford, in the pink parlours of Bloomsbury, where the rights of the workers were discussed with such flattering vehemence'; post-war Britain, he felt, would be better off without *that* sort of intellectual.[32]

On the Right, other variants of the national story appeared which did not quite fit Churchill's. Rebutting the 'Gestapo' broadcast, Attlee was to defend the Britishness of British socialism, and accuse his opponent of being in thrall to an Austrian professor, August von Hayek.[33] Hayek's free-market reasoning appealed to Churchill, but would certainly have made him a villain in Arthur Bryant's best-selling Tory history *English Saga 1840–1940*. Bryant's argument, in short, was that everything had been going downhill since 1840, when the free, tolerant old England of 'the yeoman and the ale house on the heath' was displaced by an England blinded by the theory of free trade and individualism. The starting-point of this narrative of decline and redemption could be found in England's former, and, presumably, natural state, Bryant's hopelessly idealized version of pre-industrial England, 'Christian, rural, half-democratic and half-authoritarian':

> A rough, simple, pastoral people, of great staying-power, invincible good humour, and delicate natural justice … . One loves to think of them in the taproom of the thatched ale house in the evening over their modest pint of mild when their day's work was done – the high settles in the chimney corner, the bacon rack on the oaken beam, the sanded floor, the old brightly-worn furniture gleaming in the flickering firelight.[34]

By nature and from conscious will, this was a nation 'of decent men and women, esteeming justice, honesty and freedom', their institutions moulded to that character, their society based on moral

32. N. Coward, *Australia Visited* (London, Heinemann, 1941), pp. 5, 28.
33. C. R. Attlee, *Purpose and Policy* (London, Hutchinson, 1946), p. 7.
34. A. Bryant, *English Saga 1840–1940* (London, Collins, 1940), p. 45.

responsibility. Through these virtues, the English became prosperous and powerful; but the temptations of that power and wealth led them to 'forget the historic purpose of their commonwealth' in the excesses of the industrial revolution, when this most pragmatic of peoples fell prey to an abstract theory: free trade, bringing in its train all the evils of urban, industrial life as the profit motive came to rule all. Elements of the old England still struggled beneath the surface: the jollity of the alehouse, the instinct of social responsibility, given expression by Disraeli and Chamberlain, and the Empire, in which migrants sought an idealized Englishness, and the nation a moral mission. But above all it was the strength of her institutions and the 'natural kindliness and good humour of her people' which saved England from the disasters which overtook others in the 1930s, and prepared her to fight 'a war of redemption not only for Europe but for her own soul', through which she might 'restate in a new form the ancient laws of her own moral purpose' and 'discover a common denominator for human reconstruction more glorious than anything in her long past'.[35]

Bryant's essential England was at odds with almost every aspect of modernity, embodied in a way of life which none now living (or dead, for that matter) had actually experienced, but which still in some mystical way survived in the character of the people. The popularity of this vision – Bryant's book went through no less than 12 impressions between its publication in 1940 and the end of 1945 – must be partly explained by a yearning for a more settled way of life at a time of anxiety and disruption, however sentimental – and, indeed, fictional – Bryant's vision was. But Bryant also addressed broader discontents of the time, the widespread feeling that the pre-war social and political system had failed disastrously, responsible for the Slump and the war itself, and that things must be different after the war. The idea that capitalism had failed united elements of Left and Right: *English Saga* opened with a quotation from J. B. Priestley, and posed 'the question now forming in millions of minds. *What is going to happen after the War?*' By contrast, Churchill evoked history not to criticize the present, but to show that it could be even more glorious than the past. His Whiggish narrative of progress could hardly encompass the idea that things had been going wrong for 100 years, and although he cautiously conceded the need

35. Ibid., pp. xii, 334 and passim.

for some social reform after the war, it was clear that he did not really believe there was anything fundamentally wrong with British society.

One further aspect of Bryant's story which undoubtedly appealed to its readership was its populism. The essential English virtues, which could save the world, were carried through history not by social elites (who would invariably let you down), but by the people themselves: 'decent men and women esteeming justice, honesty and freedom'. Indeed, during the war a seemingly limitless procession of celebrities queued up to tell the British people how wonderful they were – always with a few redeeming flaws to keep us human. The list of national virtues provided by the actor Leslie Howard in a broadcast to the USA in October 1940 was fairly typical, if longer than most: courage, devotion to duty, kindliness, humour, cool-headedness, balance, common sense, singleness of purpose, and idealism – virtues which the British do their best to conceal because they embarrass them (which I suppose adds modesty to the list).[36] Addressing Australians, Noel Coward cited humour, endurance, courage, justice, fair play and decency, although we were also prone to complacency and smugness, and to 'false snob values' which were now being swept aside.[37] Harold Nicolson found the British people 'by nature peaceful and kindly ... sensible and gentle ... sleepy, decent and most pacific, displaying a mixture of realism and idealism, if somewhat indolent by temperament'.[38] Writing for the British Council in 1941, W. A. Robson found in the British system of government evidence of the national temperament: 'kindliness and tolerance; an absence of hatred and vindictiveness; a consideration for the interests and feelings of minorities ... hatred of cruelty and persecution, a sense of decency and fair-play' and the avoidance of extremes, combined with a perhaps excessive tolerance for inequality.[39] Stanley Baldwin picked out considerateness, thoughtfulness for others, decency, tolerance, humour, individualism, love of independence, sentimentality and friendliness, moral fervour when roused, but a dislike of excessive enthusiasm and intellectual

36. Quoted in Aldgate and Richards, *Britain Can Take It*, pp. 70–1.
37. Coward, *Australia Visited*, pp. 5–7, 23, 47, 58 and passim.
38. H. Nicolson, *Why Britain is at War* (Harmondsworth, Penguin, 1940), p. 102.
39. W. A. Robson, 'The British System of Government', in The British Council, *British Life and Thought: An Illustrated Survey* (London, British Council, 1941), pp. 76–8.

theory, while conceding an inclination to grumble and a tendency to apathy.[40]

It might have been quicker to list the virtues the British did *not* possess, and this might also have given a clearer idea of what exactly the British people were supposed to be like. Nevertheless, scanning the most-repeated epithets we can easily see how they arose, not from any deep reading of national history or observation of national life, but out of the needs of the historical moment. The nature of the war required that the British people display qualities of courage, endurance and good humour. Germany and Britain must be defined in opposition to each other: freedom against tyranny; peace against aggression; the volunteer spirit against compulsion; friendliness and tolerance against brutality and persecution; muddle and improvisation against ruthless efficiency – and, as all Englishmen know, the Germans have no sense of humour. Our only faults, it seems, are sloth and muddle, the excusable obverse of our pacific virtues, going a long way towards explaining away appeasement and turning Dunkirk into a triumph. Of course, as historians have now shown, the myth of Nazi efficiency was indeed a myth, but it was essential to believe in it in order to maintain the polar opposition between the two sides. Equally, the British could hardly be allowed to be efficient, clever or warlike, no matter how often they displayed these virtues, or else the moral purpose of the war might be blurred and we might become like our enemy. Writers on 'Englishness' were anxious to get these things straight. But the evidence is that while the British people were quite happy to be told all these things about themselves, and to enjoy the paeans of praise to their own ordinariness – the lower-middle-class virtues of *This Happy Breed* – they were just as happy to cheer public-school heroes in *Ships with Wings*, the war as romance in *The Way to the Stars*, a Hollywood fantasy of Englishness in *Mrs Miniver*, or English fantasies of the past in the Gainsborough melodramas. It is futile to think that any of these discourses tell us what the British really thought of themselves, still less what the national character 'really' was. It is not to state a view of 'Englishness' that people go to the pictures.

The idea of national character was a source of sharp conflict as well as woolly consensus. While for many the public-school hero as

40. Lord Baldwin, 'The Englishman' in The British Council, *British Life*, pp. 439–62.

played by Leslie Howard, or the stiff upper lip of Noel Coward in
In Which We Serve stood for an essential England, to others such
elements of traditional 'Englishness' were irrelevant or positively
harmful. In his pamphlet *The English At War*, published in 1941,
William Connor, the popular *Daily Mirror* columnist Cassandra,
denounced the rigid class-bound traditionalism of the army in the
familiar 'anti-Blimp' manner of 1940–41. Officers were gentlemanly
amateurs, more familiar with polo ponies than tanks, while 'anyone
showing mechanical ability ... was apt to be dismissed as something
little better than a garage hand'. Promotion was determined by
'prejudice, friendship, snobbery and sheer luck', a decent public
school and a private income counting for more than military experience or technical qualifications. What is interesting about this polemic
is its reversal of the familiar terms of 'Englishness'. The muddle and
inefficiency which others found so endearingly and eccentrically
English is seen as both product and symptom of our traditional,
hierarchical society. It must be overthrown, not just in the interests
of democracy, but because otherwise we would risk losing the war.[41]

IV

The most celebrated radical wartime commentator was, of course,
J. B. Priestley. Already famous before the war as a best-selling novelist,
he was turned into a major national figure by his *Postscript* broadcasts
of 1940–41. Priestley, said Graham Greene, gave us an ideology.
Controversial for his left-wing views, and for 'premature' discussion
of post-war reconstruction, foreshadowing Beveridge and the welfare
state, and later on a mainstay of the 1942 Committee and the
Common Wealth movement which grew out of it to contest (and
win) wartime by-elections on a radical platform, for the post-war
Left, Priestley was a beacon who had lit the way to 1945. Post-'post-
war' commentators have not been so sure. Priestley talked about
England a great deal – he had even written a book about it – and
since all representations of Englishness were deemed to be reactionary, the hunt was on for retrogressive thinking in Priestley's works.
And, of course, in one so prolific, this was not difficult to find: the

41. W. Connor [Cassandra], *The English At War* (London, Searchlight Books,
    1941), pp. 61–87.

occasional rhapsody about the English countryside would serve (never mind that he was equally at home in the Arizona desert) – throw in a little selective quotation of 'anti-modern' sentiments, and a new Priestley emerges, no longer radical but reactionary and traditionalist, one who rejected modernity and believed the countryside was the essential England. None of this was true, but to find that out you would have to do a great deal of reading.[42]

There is no space here to refute these misconceptions in detail. Instead I shall offer a different view of Priestley, based upon his prolific wartime writings – in particular, his four novels, his broadcasts and some of his political writings – though he also produced five plays and innumerable newspaper and magazine articles. In this work we find a radical alternative to Churchill's Whiggery and Bryant's Toryism, which goes beyond support for particular policy measures into a critical, populist understanding of the nation as a whole, with its roots in the provincial radicalism of the nineteenth century. Priestley's was not a class-based socialist vision, though he recognized and deplored class divisions and probably regarded himself as a Socialist. Nor did he see the nation as the embodiment of an idea, a bearer of some transcendental meaning, but as a society containing many conflicting and co-operating forces, whose nature and direction were continually contested. At its heart was 'the people', and though that term could include anybody, it really meant the 'productive classes', workers or management, who represented both the creative energy and the moral values of the nation. 'What is Britain?', Priestley asked in his 1941 polemic *Out Of the People*, and he replied, 'Britain is the home of the British people ... before it is anything else, this country is their home.' The people are 'the true heroes and heroines of this war', he told his BBC audience, and 'it's among the byways and the humble folk who live in them, that you see and hear things that give you renewed hope and confidence in our species'. But since the Industrial Revolution, and before, the people had been robbed and put upon by a selfish and corrupt ruling class; now the future of the nation lay in their untapped energy and imagination. Democratization was not just fair play, it was essential to the post-war future.[43]

42. On Priestley's life and works, see J. Cook, *Priestley* (London, Bloomsbury, 1997); Baxendale and Pawling, *Narrating the Thirties*, pp. 46–78, 128–36.
43. J. B. Priestley, *Postscripts* (London, Heinemann, 1940), 1 September, 13 October; J. B. Priestley, *Out of the People* (London, Collins/Heinemann, 1941).

Priestley's first wartime novel, *Let The People Sing* (1939) – actually written just before the war, for Priestley to read on the BBC, but overshadowed by the 'anxious and darkening days of August' – puts forward this analysis in a clear allegory of English society at its moment of peril. The small town of Dunbury has fallen prey to two rival power-groups – the decadent gentry, led by the dowager Lady Foxfield, of cold, damp and decaying Dunbury Hall ('portraits and pieces of armour ... and shredding, moth-eaten lengths of tapestry'), and a soulless American-owned plastics factory, 'all white and glittering in its modernity'. Both want to get their hands on the Market Hall – the gentry to turn it into a museum, the plastics firm to use it as a showroom. The people of Dunbury want it for their town band, but are too cowed and apathetic to do anything about it, until roused by external forces in the improbable shape of an out-of-work music-hall comedian, a refugee East European professor, and an itinerant market trader and his energetic daughter. After an implausible sequence of events, punctuated with sub-Wodehousian comic set-pieces, the people (the 'collective unconscious Dunburyean') reawaken, and amid an explosion of popular radicalism (including strikes at the plastics factory and an outbreak of unprecedented impertinence towards upper-class residents), regain control of their Market Hall, their band, and, it is to be hoped, their historical destiny. The message about England – torn between decadent traditionalism and rapacious Americanization, to be rescued only if the people take matters in their own hands – is not easy to miss.[44]

The theme of national-popular awakening continued in Priestley's early wartime broadcasts.[45] The first, most celebrated 'Postscript' talk of 5 June, on Dunkirk, was also a masterpiece of extended metaphor, in which the 'little ships' became the nation, and the story of Dunkirk a projected narrative of the whole war. Just as the little pleasure-steamers which, according to myth, rescued the British troops, are called out of the 'ridiculous ... innocent, foolish ... almost old-fashioned' world of the Edwardian seaside, with its comedy props of bottled beer, pork pies and peppermint rock, to a rendezvous with destiny, so too, we infer, will the British people

44. J. B. Priestley, *Let the People Sing* (London, Heinemann, 1939).
45. Priestley, *Postscripts* (subsequent dates in the main text refer to the broadcasts as reprinted here).

– unsuited to martial glory, almost comical in their unheroic ordinariness, their muddle and blunder, make the 'excursion to hell', and come back glorious.

Those two great ideological markers of Englishness, the countryside and the national past, play little part in Priestley's rhetoric, and when they do appear are firmly yoked to the people as Priestley understands them. On 16 June 1940, he told listeners about his stint with the Local Defence Volunteers at his home on the Isle of Wight, and how this cross-section of rural society dealt with the extraordinary events of wartime by assimilating them to their own familiar lives as they have done for generations – not the end of the world, but just one more menace like blizzards or floods which countrymen must deal with. Priestley's national symbols insist on their ordinariness – ducks in the park, a Bradford pie-shop, a fat, roaring old woman on a stretcher, Sam Weller from the *Pickwick Papers*, a corny comedian in an ENSA factory show. When national leaders are praised it is for manifestations of ordinariness – a little dig in the ribs and a mischievous grin delivered by Winston Churchill to Ernest Bevin on the Treasury Bench (7 July).

Of course, all this is very sentimental, and rampantly idealistic. Priestley's people, like everybody else's, are a compendium of all the virtues: 'simple, kindly, humorous, brave', 'imaginative and romantic' (30 June), 'warmth of heart, and height of imagination' (11 August), 'patience, courage and good humour' (1 September), 'courage and resolution and cheerfulness' (15 September) – one could go on, *ad infinitum*, perhaps *ad nauseam*. But contrasted with these warm-hearted paragons we find not only the Nazi enemy, dehumanized and robotic ('thin-lipped, cold-eyed … a kind of overgrown species of warrior-ant', 9 June) – but also those sections of society traditionally idealized as 'typically English': the gentlemanly classes, in charge of property and the state. Far from being public-school heroes, the top people have become an obstacle. 'Sometimes I feel that you and I – all of us ordinary people – are on one side of a high fence, and on the other side … are the official and important personages: the pundits and mandarins', concerned only to order people about and keep them in the dark. As for the propertied classes, backbone of traditional England, they are a waste of space. They have fled the cities to the safety of country hotels, inconveniencing people travelling on war business (6 October) – or to North America, leaving behind country houses and estates which they expect the rest of us to defend for them (21 July) – and even when they have stayed at home, they refuse to make room for city evacuees (22 September).

It was the upper classes who had let the nation down in the 1920s and 1930s – 'the era of nightclub-haunting princes and gossip-writing peers ... an uneasy posturing plutocracy' – and would do so again if given the chance. The England beloved of sentimental Americans,

> the old Hall, the hunt breakfast, the hunt ball, the villagers touching their caps, all the old bag of tricks ... is not the England that is fighting this war. It could not last a couple of days. This is a war of machines and of the men who make and drive those machines ... . It is industrial England that is fighting this war. ... Most of the real work was being done by youngish technical men of the so-called middle-classes, men rarely given final authority, and men already feeling restless and dissatisfied because they were hampered by the incompetence, pedantry, lack of drive of the superior persons from whom they were often compelled to take orders. It was as if energy and virtue had been drained away from one strata to reappear, but waiting to be tapped, in another.[46]

Priestley's second wartime novel, the melodramatic spy thriller *Blackout in Gretley* (1942), takes up the theme. Gretley is a grim town, existing only to provide absentee employers with 'country mansions, grouse moors, deer forests, yachts and winters in Cannes and Monte Carlo' while they blustered on about 'our traditional way of life'. Its ordinary people are 'patient ... taking what was given them and asking for no more, except in their hearts'. Its spies, fifth-columnists, defeatists and black-marketeers are to be found entirely amongst its idle rich, notable among whom are the black-marketeer Mrs Jesmond, 'a handsome, luxurious, lecherous rat', and Colonel Tarlington, authoritarian local employer.[47]

In due course, Tarlington is unmasked as a spy, motivated by his desire to keep 'yourself and a few others securely on top, and the common people ... in their place for ever'. As for Mrs Jesmond, 'you're an exquisite, downy sort of creature, but just not worth your very expensive keep. You're one of the luxuries we can't afford.' As Perigo, the undercover Special Branch man, declares, the main obstacle to post-war national renewal will be 'about fifty thousand

46. Priestley, *Out of the People*, pp. 105, 31, 106–7.
47. J. B. Priestley, *Blackout in Gretley* (London, Heinemann, 1942), pp. 173, 158.

important, influential, gentlemanly persons', who will have to be told to 'shut up and do nothing'. Significantly, however, none of the villains and Nazi sympathizers is portrayed as unpatriotic: when they sing *Rule Britannia* and wrap themselves in the flag, they are being perfectly sincere. The division is not between patriots and traitors, but between those who, like Churchill, Roosevelt and Stalin, are on the side of the common man; and those who 'hate the democratic idea and despise ordinary decent folk'.[48]

In the third, and by far the best-realized of Priestley's wartime novels, *Daylight on Saturday* (1943), the national microcosm is an aircraft factory, at a low point of the war just before the first significant victory at Alamein. Production is down: is it because of divided management, bad workers, or just lack of good war news? The factory, and the post-war nation, are in the balance. The workers are uninspired and apathetic, a patchwork of disparate individuals: something has been lost since the heady, collective days of 1940. Forward-looking leadership is represented by Cheviot, the General Manager, upwardly mobile, classless in tone if a little paternalistic, who identifies with the workers and wants to take care of them. We also meet one of the 'youngish technical men' from the working class (Angleby), as well as an old-style 'rough diamond' works superintendent (Elrick), a languid, anti-industrial civil servant, a communist charge-hand, and a stuffed-shirt government minister (Lord Brixen), upwardly mobile from industry to the City. But also on the scene is a modernized authoritarian member of the upper class, in the shape of the gentlemanly but technically proficient Assistant Manager Blandford, arrogantly contemptuous of democracy and the ordinary workers: 'We English enjoy our social hierarchy. We wouldn't be without it.' The old ruling class has made a comeback and may yet seize back the reins of power.

For once, Priestley manages to combine a representative panorama of British society with convincing novelistic characters, each seen through the eyes of the others, so as to convey a complex sense of social relations and antagonisms. For once, too, he seems less than confident of the post-war outcome. The Elricks and Brixens have certainly had their day, but who will win through – Cheviot or Blandford? At the end of the novel, the issue is still unresolved. Cheviot pledges his future to the workers ('there could be for him

48. Ibid., pp. 207, 194–5, 82.

now no cosy settling down, no easy acceptance of bribe or pension
from the moneyed interests ... . He had to see them through'), but
Blandford too offers change and modernization, of an authoritarian
kind: 'Only machines and highly organized production can save us
from the Nazis and ... from a national decline after the war.' As
production picks up after the news of victory at Alamein, the future
of the nation is still in the balance.[49]

Much the same mood pervades Priestley's final war novel, *Three
Men in New Suits* (1945), in which three demobbed servicemen
resist the pressures and blandishments of their old lives, and the
apathetic and reactionary views of their families, and set off, in some
unspecified way, to save the world – under the leadership of upper-
class Alan, whom the war has taught the virtues of the common
people: 'an idea of fairness that goes deep, deep down ... kind,
patient, forgiving, never arrogant, not corrupted by power'.[50] But
as Priestley warned in his 1945 pamphlet, *Letter to a Returning
Serviceman*, if we cannot draw on the bottled-up energy of the
people, and rediscover the lost collective purpose of 1940, we may
find ourselves trapped, not in a cosy consensus, the pre-war 'sleepy
Tory Britain', but in the ruthless 'Lord Corporate-State Toryism' of
the Blandfords, little different in essence from Nazism.[51]

V

Churchill and Priestley both ended the war against Hitler accusing
their political opponents of harbouring visions of the national future
which were little better than Nazism. Whatever was to happen in
the coming years, this was hardly a picture of cosy consensus. It is
clear that at the level of public discourse, far from consolidating and
clarifying national identity, the war opened it up to keen, sometimes
bitter, debate. Blame for past mistakes – whether for appeasement
or for industrial capitalism itself – and the possibility of future change,
both raised fundamental questions about the nature of British society,
which were argued out from a range of different positions, with

49. J. B. Priestley, *Daylight on Saturday* (London, Heinemann, 1943), pp. 305–6,
    57–8.
50. J. B. Priestley, *Three Men in New Suits* (London, Heinemann, 1945), pp. 66–7.
51. J. B. Priestley, *Letter to a Returning Serviceman* (London, Home and Van Thal,
    1945), p. 15.

conflicting ideological roots, drawing on rival narratives of the nation. Churchill's Whiggery, Bryant's Toryism, Priestley's provincial industrial populism, and others, all sought to tell the British people who they were, where they had come from, and where they were going.

But were they listening? What did 'England mean' to them? Who knows: but perhaps the answer is, none of the above. The difficulty of communicating such lofty messages adequately to the people – even of knowing whether one had done so or not – was quickly recognized by wartime propagandists. Recent historians of the 'Apathy School' assert that contrary to myths of 'war radicalism', there was no great surge of political belief one way or another.[52] But even at moments of mass mobilization, politics is never at the centre of most people's lives. During the war, the 'banal nationalism' of shared experience and endurance, the desire not to have a familiar way of life destroyed by an alien political force, reinforced by the continuous national dialogue of press, radio and cinema, newly opened up to popular voices, gave people a stronger feeling of national identity – in the sense of 'sameness' or 'belonging' – than any narrative interpretation of what the nation meant. Any attempt to define things more closely, as we have seen, simply revealed the depth of historical class divisions and the difficulty of communicating across them. The dialectic between these divisions, reinforced by memories of the 1930s, and the strengthened collective identity of wartime, may have opened up the popular mind to the possibility of radical change in 1945, without necessarily converting everyone into theoretical Socialists. In the end, the 'we' who vainly resolved to hang out the washing on the Siegfried Line were simply, as Priestley optimistically put it, 'you and I – all of us ordinary people'.[53]

52. T. Mason and P. Thompson, '"Reflections on a Revolution"? The political mood in wartime Britain', in Nick Tiratsoo (ed.), *The Attlee Years* (Manchester, Manchester UP, 1995); S. Fielding, P. Thompson and N. Tiratsoo, *'England Arise!': The Labour Party and Popular Politics in 1940s Britain* (Manchester, Manchester UP, 1995).
53. Priestley, *Postscripts*, 30 June 1940.

Postscript:
A War Imagined

Jeff Hill

It is now something of a commonplace to remark, as E. H. Carr originally did, that history is 'an unending dialogue between the present and the past'.[1] But in this particular book we might be forgiven for repeating Carr's observation. Though there are ample academic reasons justifying a study of wartime cultural production, many of them alluded to by Nick Hayes in the Introduction, there is also a special British fascination with the war to be accounted for. More than 50 years after its conclusion, the war continues to engage the minds of British people. So much so that we might conceive of the impact of the war on late twentieth-century British life in terms comparable to that of the Revolution on the French in the nineteenth century: an event which shaped, perhaps even convulsed, the thoughts and actions of those who lived many years afterwards, whose lives were set in the shadow of the event and the ideas it generated. By contrast the French, and continental Europeans generally, have reacted differently to the Second World War. It has, overtly at least, been less of a national obsession, and its cultural legacy has been borne more lightly. For the British memories of the war occupy a key function in creating a sense of nation. The war has taken its place alongside the winning of the football World Cup in 1966 as the two most recent versions of 'their finest hour'.

This contrast in popular memories was neatly encapsulated in an episode of the BBC comedy programme *Fawlty Towers* in the 1970s. Following a particularly indelicate exchange with some German guests in his fictional Torquay hotel, the egregious Basil Fawlty warned his staff: 'don't mention the war; I did, but I think I got away with it'. What his guests were desperate to forget Fawlty was

1. E. H. Carr, *What Is History?* (London, Penguin, 1964), p. 30.

only too prone to recall. Many have shared Fawlty's inability to forget. Historians in particular have never been diffident about mentioning the Second World War. Indeed, it has provided many of them with a decent living (and to that extent they have perhaps 'got away with it'). Picking over the entrails of 'the people's war' has become something of a historians' growth industry which has itself contributed to the national fixation with the war, or at least what we imagine the war was like. It will continue to be remembered and imagined well into the twenty-first century. Though historians, including some in this volume, might successfully have demolished many of the interpretations previously associated with it, the events of 1939–45 continue to exercise a peculiar hold on the popular imagination. It has assumed a mythic status, the power of which will continue to influence people's thinking no matter how much historians might, to their own satisfaction, dispel what they see as the myths. The war has indeed become a myth, not in the sense of an untruth, misinterpretation or delusion to be exposed, but, as Roland Barthes once suggested, in the sense of an event which communicates meanings, a system of signification, a second-order language.[2] It has become a narrative of national identity. To use Clifford Geertz's celebrated phrase, it is 'a story we tell ourselves about ourselves'.[3] It has provided a reference point for how Britain should, or should not, be organized; and it has been a landmark for ideas about who and what the British people are: 'a defining national moment', as John Baxendale describes it.[4] Much of the war's power to influence derives from the assumed qualities which the war effort unleashed. The 'finest hour' was seen to have brought forth admirable British characteristics, all the more admired historically for their being absent in the present. Even when, eventually, a more sceptical view of the war developed in the 1980s, the events of 1939–45 still provided a touchstone for new (or old) ideas held to be more relevant for the condition of Britain in the late-twentieth century.

Ideas of the war have become especially embedded in popular culture. From being an event in which cultural production occupied

2. R. Barthes, *Mythologies* (Paris, Seuil, 1957).
3. C. Geertz, 'Deep Play: notes on the Balinese cockfight', *The Interpretation of Cultures: Selected Essays* (New York, Basic Books, 1973), p. 448.
4. J. Baxendale, 'You and I – All Of Us Ordinary People'.

a key role, for reasons of propaganda, the war has itself become a cultural product in the post-war world, capable of communicating meanings to people born many years after the event. The extraordinarily popular BBC situation comedy *Dad's Army* is a clear example of the war re-created in this way. Originally made in the late 1960s and early 1970s, at a time of disorientation when memories of wartime unity stimulated particularly nostalgic feelings, episodes are still being repeated on BBC television at the end of the 1990s. Though most of the actors who appeared in the show were by this time dead, their passing caused no apparent diminution in their appeal. Nor did the sometimes contrived and theatrical appearance of some of the early episodes, shot 'live' in the studio, seem to detract from the show's appeal. The continuing pleasure derived by television audiences from *Dad's Army* has, we may imagine, stemmed from the comforting ideas of England and English people (effectively English*men*) portrayed on the screen. To a degree the characters in the Home Guard platoon are made to represent the nation, though minimal use is made of regional 'types', apart from the mean Scotsman and the Cockney spiv. Essentially, what unfolds from the petty squabbling and jealousies of the Walmington-on-Sea platoon is an image of semi-rural southern England – 'Deep England' in Angus Calder's term,[5] specifically Kent – where status and hierarchy are sustained without any disturbance to the harmony in which the social classes coexist. Over and above the personal animosities and human frailties that drive the plot and provide the humour of the show is a prevailing sense of decency and unity, even if this is often imposed by the pompous, status-conscious platoon leader, Captain Mainwaring (pronounced, of course, 'Mannering'), with his frequent clichéd reminders that Britain is fighting for all that is good in the world. When 'the balloon goes up' Britain will be ready, and when the 'great referee blows no-side' British fair play will have won the day. The success of *Dad's Army* has much to do with the gentle, mocking tone its writers adopted towards 'the people's war', presented as it was in the deliberately unheroic form of aged shop-keepers in battledress. It could not have been farther removed from the left-wing idea of 'a people's army'. Dramatically it played upon conventions of amateurism and incompetence which, in English popular culture, are associated not with a radical critique of the

5. A. Calder, *The Myth of the Blitz* (London, Jonathan Cape, 1991), ch. 9.

established order so much as with all those notions of 'muddling through', determination and pluck which are summed up in the idea of the 'Dunkirk spirit' – a defeat paraded as a victory. In this sense it offered, in its original 1960s context, a conservative political counterpoint to Harold Wilson's modernizing 'white heat of technology', a concept always rather alien to the British cultural psyche. Above all *Dad's Army* perpetuated one of the most cherished, enduring and yet ambiguous of wartime images: the people together, pulling together.

Fifty years after the end of the war, and some 25 years after the first *Dad's Army*, it is noteworthy that the BBC could still employ some of these same themes as the formula for a new situation comedy. Between, on the one hand, a wartime community of pub and neighbourhood and, on the other, a de-centred Thatcherite present, Gary, the hero of *Goodnight Sweetheart*, implausibly time-travels. The programme, deemed sufficiently popular by the BBC to be continued through three series in the mid- to late 1990s, operates through a series of stark oppositions: community and individuality; innocence and sophistication; shortages and affluence; togetherness and loneliness. All of these serve to present the world of wartime London as somehow a 'better' place, which has not lost its roots and norms. Gary's frequent passages back to the war represent a reminder of a world we have lost. It possesses clear aims, if these are simply to see the war through to victory and to look forward to a future of peace and tranquillity. The 'postmodern' present, by contrast, seems devoid of purpose and satisfaction, symbolized in Gary's unhappy, childless marriage.

These are just two examples, drawn from one popular cultural form, of the way ideas of wartime Britain situate us ideologically in relation to our own present. There have been many more instances in television, radio and general literature that have constituted the popular culture of the past 30 or so years. Clearly, much of this reworking of wartime memories into popular culture acquires its meaning in moods of national uncertainty and change which occur at specific historical moments: the fracturing of 'consensus' in the late 1960s, for example; the unsettling phase of inflation and industrial conflict of the 1970s; fears of a 'big' Europe in the 1990s. In all of these circumstances the war was made to represent a moral certainty absent in the present. The war acted as a myth of origin which reminded the British people of their true nature and purpose.

But the war has not always been seen as the fixed star by which we set our course. Its meaning for the present has changed in relation to changing economic and political circumstances. Perhaps the most obvious instance of its intrusion into post-war life happened in the 1980s, and in politics rather than popular culture. This came about as a result of the systematic propaganda campaign conducted by a series of Conservative politicians against the quintessential legacy of the war: the 'social-democratic consensus'. Held to be the root cause of Britain's decline into dependency and a culture of welfare-ism, consensus politics were seen as having generated a host of folk devils. The vanguard of the host was usually seen to be composed of the state – in particular its benefits system – single parents, football hooligans and trade unions. Clearly, not all of these were to be attributed to the war, but voters were left in little doubt that the war had been responsible for the incubus of the big state, which in turn had allied itself to an over-mighty trade union movement, to which could be attributed that loss of individual responsibility which, the New Right averred, was at the heart of Britain's moral decline. Such ideas were communicated through the various channels of political discourse so effectively that they became almost 'common sense'. It was not unusual in the universities of the early 1990s, for example, to be presented with 'objective' contemporary history from some of the less perceptive undergraduates, which was based on a version of Conservative propaganda that they had imbibed in their political culture since childhood. There was, nevertheless, a contradiction in all this. The war carried equivocal meanings in Conservative thinking. First and foremost it was associated with a principal symbol of Conservatism – Winston Churchill. Margaret Thatcher, for all she despised the 'consensus' politics that the war was held to have spawned, was unable to distance herself from the Churchill myth simply because it communicated ideas of Britishness that were still essential to Toryism. She herself deployed some of them at the time of the Falklands/Malvinas war in 1982. To an extent, therefore, attention had to be shifted away from the war, in the same way that the New Right diverted attention away from many aspects of post-war liberal Toryism in favour of images of an older past of 'Victorian values' and Adam Smith free enterprise. Instead of the war as the source of all modern ills, the 1960s were chosen and re-presented in New Right propaganda as the devil's decade of social-democracy. The moral laxity attributed to this period combined with the perils of the Attlee welfare state to produce the root cause of what was wrong with Britain and what the New Right was going to rectify.[6]

In contrast to these apparently fixed ideological meanings of the war, academic history is able to offer few such certainties. The idea of a wartime Britain blessed by national unity and political consensus, forging ahead under the auspices of a powerful but benevolent state to create a planned future shorn of the excesses of commercialization – an idea which owes much to the seminal work of Richard Titmuss[7] – no longer wields the influence it once did on professional historians, though it continues to inform many popular portrayals of the war. Two of the most celebrated historians of the war have lent their support to a rather regretful, what-might-have-been perspective. Angus Calder's is an acerbic view of 'the people's war', a *révolution manquée* in which early opportunities for democratic reform were supplanted by a growing administrative conservatism: 'we see clearly enough that the effect of the war was not to sweep society onto a new course, but to hasten its progress along the old grooves'. Paul Addison, whose work as much as anyone's implanted the idea of 'consensus' as 'the natural order of British politics', has since withdrawn into a more circumscribed, less all-embracing vision of an 'elite' or 'Whitehall' consensus. Both accounts cast a jaundiced eye on the war as social unity.[8]

Heroic interpretations have now given way to what we might term a 'kaleidoscopic' view of wartime. 'Kaleidoscopic' in the sense that the war represents constantly varying patterns, difficult to pin down. Such a view is represented by the present volume, which charts what Jose Harris has described as 'the sheer diversity of

6. See the *No Turning Back* Group of Conservative MPs, *No Turning Back* and *Choice and Responsibility: the Enabling State* (London, Conservative Political Centre, 1985 and 1990).

7. See R. Titmuss, *Problems of Social Policy* (London, HMSO, 1950).

8. A. Calder, *The People's War: Britain 1939–45* (London, Panther edn, 1971), p. 20; P. Addison, *The Road to 1945: British Politics and the Second World War* (London, Pimlico revised edn, 1994), p. 278 and especially 'Epilogue: *The Road to 1945* Revisited'. 'The consensus described in this book was ... neither a social consensus, nor a consensus between party activists – many of whom, no doubt, wanted to nationalize the whole of industry, or to hold India down by force for twenty years – but a Whitehall consensus' (p. 281). Also, P. Addison, 'Consensus Revisited', *Twentieth Century British History*, 4 (1993), pp. 91–4.

wartime experience of different individuals, different localities, different organisations and different social groups'.[9] There are, in addition, different phases of the war, and a multitude of experiences and reactions to these phases. The essays in this volume underscore the point. There is no universal pattern, no grand design. Recognizing and studying this diversity is, as Harris has suggested, the way forward for historians. To be sure, certain recurring themes are evident in the varied contributions to the present volume: the intervention of the state; continuity and change in cultural life; the idea of 'the people'; and the quality of life and culture. But in all of these respects the historiography is now confusing and sometimes contradictory. The state, for example, appears in many guises of interventionism. As an instrument of some importance, for example, in the form of the Ministry of Information in the development of the wartime film industry; as a provider of public money to fund schemes such as the Entertainments National Service Association and the Council for the Encouragement of Music and the Arts; as a vague entity thought of as 'the war machine' for the writers discussed by Jo Alberti; and as something that had only a marginal role to play in the realm of sport and leisure.

In terms of the war as an agent of change similar cross-currents are apparent. Although is some areas – the mining communities discussed by Colin Griffin, for example – wartime experiences appear to have created interesting and quite progressive thinking, the field of cultural production generally provides ample illustration of conservatism. In so many areas 1945 emerges, not as the dawn of a new epoch, but as an opportunity to return to normality: in broadcasting, in sport, in the provision of voluntary and commercial leisure. The Labour Party, and intellectuals generally, exercised their minds far more in the 1950s over the problem of television and mass culture than ever they did on the issue of leisure during the war. In music and film, as Robert Mackay and James Chapman show in their essays, the wartime experience affirmed a conservative trend. Artistic production in these two areas revealed only ripples of innovation to set against a sea of continuing traditional forms. This was very evident in the insistence on 'English' music. In film

9. J. Harris, 'War and Social History: Britain and the Home Front during the Second World War', *Contemporary European History*, 1 (1992), pp. 17–35; p. 33.

the preference for realist drama, itself a conservative form, was tempered by a possibly greater emphasis than previously on 'serious' content, although pre-war British cinema had already promoted social-democratic consensus, notably in Victor Saville's *South Riding* of 1938. In terms of taste the experiment of CEMA confirmed only that classical music was not popular, while at the cinema most people continued to enjoy what they had enjoyed before the war, namely, American films.

If there was no clear trend towards cultural innovation during the war years, nor was there any marked 'improvement' in cultural taste. Though some critics – Priestley and Orwell were leading examples – sharpened their minds and pens on this issue, hoping that wartime opportunities would bring a more refined public approach to cultural matters (or, at least, forestall some of the grosser forms of Americanism), the reality was that cultural life could not be thus guided.[10] Most people resorted to what they enjoyed. The dilemma of the custodians of 'good' culture was typified by attitudes among the leaders of the BBC. As Siân Nicholas shows, broadcasting changed during the Second World War, though not in the ways that BBC chiefs would have wished. A pre-war 'cultural elitism' was replaced by an 'elevated classlessness' which, in the upper echelons of the Corporation, was seen as a retrograde step (no matter that the BBC's output probably became more popular). The end of hostilities presented an opportunity to return to 'proper' broadcasting, to restore standards and dignity to radio, concerns which were exemplified in the creation of the Third Programme.

The theme of cultural 'improvement' is touched on to a greater or lesser extent in many essays: in particular Bromley on the press, Hayes on CEMA and ENSA, Hill on the labour movement and Griffin on the miners' welfares. Most (Griffin's is the exception) are negative about qualitative improvement, in relation either to cultural provision or taste. This negativity results not so much from an inconclusiveness about the process but from a sense that cultural

---

10. Priestley in particular clung to a myth largely of his own making, namely that the war had created a thirst for artistic improvement. Looking back from the early 1960s – 'the most corrupting society that England has known in my lifetime' – he claimed to see in the Britain of 1945 a political and cultural atmosphere in which 'there was revolution in the air, a mild and very English revolution, with no heads about to roll, but bent on changing our society'. 'Fifty Years of the English', *New Statesman*, 19 April 1963, pp. 560–6.

'quality' cannot be seen in simple linear terms of 'improvement' or 'decline'; and that, perhaps, those who did see the issue in this light had really rather misunderstood the ways in which cultural relationships and experiences worked. To be sure, there were initiatives in wartime designed to lift the general level of cultural appreciation and understanding, though for every conversion to classical music through CEMA there were no doubt several new addictions to pulp fiction and cinematic costume drama. Though to some contemporaries, and some later historians, the Second World War was a 'good war' because it was thought to be improving standards,[11] the reality seems much less clear cut. In truth, the war was neither 'good' nor 'bad'. It was simply a phase of cultural development, not the epoch-making event it has sometimes been portrayed as.

What is often assumed about the war – and it strongly informs our own contemporary images in popular culture – is the notion of a social togetherness. It was a major element of wartime propaganda and the central theme of many propaganda ventures, of which the film *Millions Like Us* is a principal example. Some external contemporary observers also claimed to have found it. As Nick Hayes notes in his Introduction, the American Ralph Ingersoll made a big point of it in his 1941 study of wartime *mores*. The quality of common citizenship he affected to have found among the British at that time was doubtless designed to strike a chord with American readers. To them it would seem that, as a consequence of the Blitz and associated deprivations, the British were actually becoming like the Americans, or at least what the Americans imagined themselves to be. Reviewers like Tom Harrisson had a wry view of much of this, and Priestley observed the reverse of the coin in his visit to Bournemouth. But the notion of 'the people' served well in wartime, when this old and somewhat confusing concept underwent a new lease of life. It possessed, of course, radical overtones, coming as it did from the language of European revolutionaries of the late eighteeenth and nineteenth centuries. But in some ways this made it especially suited to the mood of reconstruction that developed from 1941 onwards. 'The people's war' – a phrase coined during the war itself, possibly by the ex-Communist Tom Wintringham – was a conflict in which

11. On the idea of a 'good war', and for an account which argues the case for cultural 'improvement', see P. Clarke, *Hope and Glory: Britain 1900–1990* (London, Penguin, 1996), ch. 6, esp. pp. 211–13.

all had a role to play, and all could look forward to a reward afterwards. '[T]his war will have been won by its people', declared the Labour Party's manifesto for the 1945 parliamentary election, 'not by any one man or set of men.'[12]

In this atmosphere politicians could talk about 'the people', or even the more elevated 'People', without too much apprehension of the subversive implications the term had once had. Formerly used to challenge the existing order, it was now being employed to give solidity and legitimacy to that very order. Its place in British political vocabulary had diminished considerably since its heyday in the early nineteenth century, when it was carried forward into Chartism from the ideological legacy of the French Revolution. In this context it was used, as Gareth Stedman Jones has shown, to counterpose an image of those who were worthy, useful and productive – 'the people' – against those who lived off the backs of others, the 'idle rich'.[13] 'The people' certainly had a revolutionary currency at that time, though without necessarily implying a social class; Chartists spoke of 'the people' without making the concept synonymous with workers. Labour's manifesto of 1945 consciously evoked some of these feelings. The use of the term during the Second World War also involved a resurrection of some of the old ideas of progress and social usefulness, their opposite recalled in Calder's use of the term 'old gang' to describe the British privileged elite. 'The people' might also, especially in the context of the alliance with the Soviet Union (which allowed even Stalin to be cast as an avuncular popular hero), have carried more revolutionary implications still, perhaps of the workers' control ideas that had flourished at the end of the previous war, or Wintringham's concept of a Spanish republican style of 'citizens' militia'.[14] But these meanings were probably checkmated by newer notions of togetherness and sociability engendered in, for example, the armed forces, air-raid shelters, British restaurants, the Navy, Army, and Air Force Institutes, the factory canteen or simply listening as part of the 'imagined nation' to the BBC's nine

12. The Labour Party, *Let Us Face The Future: a Declaration of Labour Policy for the Consideration of the Nation* (London, The Labour Party, 1945), p. 1.
13. G. Stedman Jones, 'Rethinking Chartism', in *Languages of Class: Studies in English Working Class History 1832–1982* (Cambridge, Cambridge UP, 1983), pp. 90–178.
14. See D. Fernbach, 'Tom Wintringham and Socialist Defense Strategy', *History Workshop: A Journal of Socialist and Feminist Historians*, **14** (1982), pp. 63–91.

o'clock news. There was thus a stock of images to be called upon in thousands of ways to depict the nation together. In these ways 'the people' were usually just ordinary folk, like the women workers of *Millions Like Us*, a feminine and rather earnest representation of the coming together of the classes and the regions into a British nation. Through the manipulation of images like these in a myriad of ways, the Second World War acquired a characteristic of collective endeavour that had never developed to the same extent in the First World War. This had much to do with the manner in which cultural productions such as *Millions Like Us* and *ITMA* presented, in the words of Wilfred Pickles's post-war radio show *Have A Go*, 'the people to the people'. It also had to do with the particular technology of the medium. There was an intimacy, a sensuousness even, about film and radio that older methods of communication did not have and which eased people into *feeling* part of a larger whole. Their messages also reinforced the view, which seems to have been universally accepted, that the war was a 'just' one which should be prosecuted to a definite conclusion.

But, as John Baxendale has suggested, the concept of togetherness is an ambiguous one.[15] We might wonder what all those representations of 'the people' meant to people themselves, especially perhaps to those who did not see themselves so clearly reflected back in the public images of 'the people': overseas immigrants, the Scots, Welsh and Irish, the elderly, the young, those who lived outside the Home Counties, and rural dwellers generally. There is some irony in the fact that, although much wartime propaganda was focused on the image of 'Deep England' – Frank Newbould's posters for the Army Bureau of Current Affairs are a fine example, with their reminder 'Your Britain – Fight For It Now' – subsequent research on the home front has been almost exclusively directed at urban Britain.[16] So many might have queried their visibility in the conventional depiction of 'the people'. Exceptionally, women were one traditionally excluded group whose presence was now recognized. *Millions Like Us* was, of course, a clear instance of this, novel in the way that it explicitly foregrounded the problems and relationships of a group of women workers. However, whether in or

15. Baxendale, 'You and I – All Of Us Ordinary People'.
16. See A. Howkins, 'A Country at War: Mass-Observation and Rural England, 1939–45', *Rural History*, 9 (1998), pp. 75–97.

out of the frame, 'the people', though in reality so frequently 'browned off', and with lives marked, as Mass-Observation claimed on one occasion, by 'aimlessness, irresponsibility and boredom',[17] were nevertheless presented to themselves as little short of heroic. Their endeavours were accorded a nobility and solidarity that were held to display the very best qualities of Britishness. We might surmise that contemporaries were more sceptical of this than later generations. It is perhaps not surprising that, faced with the didacticism which, for all its virtues, a film like *Millions Like Us* dealt in, cinema audiences should prefer something which preached to them a little less, and whose populism was not so transparently strained through the sieve of the British class system (even in such an apparently trivial form as the 'working man's' accent assumed by Eric Portman). And *Millions Like Us* was not the most blatant example of this. The American film fitted the bill better: more relaxed in its naturalism and technically superior as a product.[18]

Nontheless, messages of 'the people' possessed an enduring power. They remind us, for one thing, of the degree to which the wartime 'experience' was culturally constructed. Though many historians, following Marwick, have insisted on the idea of the Second World War as a 'total' war, there has tended to be an assumption that participation – a key feature of total war – created its own experiences. But how people knew, experienced and understood the war was only in part related to their individual understandings of it. What the war was 'all about' had to do with the many channels of communication – some of which are explored in this volume – and the meanings of war and its social relationships that were articulated through them. Later generations, quite as much as (if not more than) contemporaries, have also been influenced by them. If we are still obsessed with the war, if British, or English, national feeling derives much of its potency from memories of the war, still an essential part of what Michael Billig has called the 'constant flaggings of nationhood',[19] then all this has its origins in the cultural production of wartime itself and the images of 'the people' so generated. The

17. See Nick Hayes, 'An "English War", Wartime Culture and "Millions Like Us"'.
18. See R. McKibbin, *Classes and Cultures: England 1918–1951* (Oxford, Oxford UP, 1998), ch. XI, esp. p. 431.
19. M. Billig, *Banal Nationalism* (London, Sage, 1995), p. 174.

war that we imagine today is filtered ideologically through the images of the war that its participants themselves were asked to imagine over 50 years ago.

Index